A Process Algebraic Approach to Software Architecture Design

Alessandro Aldini · Marco Bernardo
Flavio Corradini

A Process Algebraic
Approach to Software
Architecture Design

Alessandro Aldini
Università di Urbino
Ist. di Scienze e Tecnologie dell'Informazione
Piazza della Repubblica 13
61029 Urbino
Italy
aldini@sti.uniurb.it

Flavio Corradini
Università di Camerino
Dip.to di Matematica e Informatica
Via Madonna delle Carceri 9
62032 Camerino
Italy
flavio.corradini@unicam.it

Marco Bernardo
Università di Urbino
Ist. di Scienze e Tecnologie dell'Informazione
Piazza della Repubblica 13
61029 Urbino
Italy
bernardo@sti.uniurb.it

ISBN 978-1-4471-5766-3   ISBN 978-1-84800-223-4 (eBook)
DOI 10.1007/978-1-84800-223-4
Springer London Dordrecht Heidelberg New York

British Library Cataloguing in Publication Data
A catalogue record for this book is available from the British Library

Cover design: KuenkelLopka GmbH

Printed on acid-free paper

Springer is part of Springer Science+Business Media (www.springer.com)

To Marilena and Emma

To Giuseppina and Andrea

To Monica, Alice, and Diego

Preface

In the field of formal methods in computer science, concurrency theory is receiving a constantly increasing interest. This is especially true for process algebra. Although it had been originally conceived as a means for reasoning about the semantics of concurrent programs, process algebraic formalisms like CCS, CSP, ACP, π-calculus, and their extensions (see, e.g., [154, 119, 112, 22, 155, 181, 30]) were soon used also for comprehending functional and nonfunctional aspects of the behavior of communicating concurrent systems.

The scientific impact of process calculi and behavioral equivalences at the base of process algebra is witnessed not only by a very rich literature. It is in fact worth mentioning the standardization procedure that led to the development of the process algebraic language LOTOS [49], as well as the implementation of several modeling and analysis tools based on process algebra, like CWB [70] and CADP [93], some of which have been used in industrial case studies. Furthermore, process calculi and behavioral equivalences are by now adopted in university-level courses to teach the foundations of concurrent programming as well as the model-driven design of concurrent, distributed, and mobile systems.

Nevertheless, after 30 years since its introduction, process algebra is rarely adopted in the practice of software development. On the one hand, its technicalities often obfuscate the way in which systems are modeled. As an example, if a process term comprises numerous occurrences of the parallel composition operator, it is hard to understand the communication scheme among the various subterms. On the other hand, process algebra is perceived as being difficult to learn and use by practitioners, as it is not close enough to the way they think of software systems. For instance, process algebra inherently supports compositionality and abstraction, but it does not support widespread paradigms like object orientation and component orientation. As a consequence, process algebra cannot compete with commonly accepted notations like UML, although it is more robust than them.

Some years ago, we thus began to address the following problem: *How to enhance the usability of process algebra?*

We think that an answer to this question should take the following three issues into account. Firstly, it is necessary to support a friendly component-oriented way of modeling systems with process algebra, so that the software designer can reason in terms of composable software units without having to worry about process algebra technicalities. Secondly, it is necessary to provide an efficient component-oriented way of analyzing functional and nonfunctional properties of systems modeled with process algebra, and to return component-oriented diagnostic information in the case that property violations are detected. Thirdly, it is necessary to integrate process algebra in the software development process, which amounts to single out the phases in which it can be usefully employed.

Starting from the last issue, we believe that a good choice is that of working at the software architecture level of design. In fact, a software architecture elucidates the elements constituting a system, their interactions, and the constraints on those elements and their interactions that provide a framework in which to satisfy the requirements and serve as a basis for the subsequent development phases [169,184]. Since the focus is not on algorithms and data structures, but on software components and connectors, as implicitly demonstrated in [18] this is the right abstraction level for a formal description technique like process algebra.

We also believe that using process algebra in the architectural design phase is beneficial for the development process. The architecture of a software system is typically represented as a document expressed in some graphical modeling notation or architectural description language. This document, which shows system structure and behavior at a high level of abstraction, should be shared by all the people who contribute to the various phases of the software development process. Thanks to its precise semantics and its verification techniques, process algebra can play a role in the formalization of this document. In particular, it opens the way to the possibility of analyzing behavioral properties in the early stages of software development [45], which has the advantage of avoiding delays and costs that may be incurred due to the late discovery of errors.

In view of such an architectural upgrade of process algebra, our original question can be refined as follows: *How to transform process algebra into an architectural description language? How to drive the whole software development process with the resulting process algebraic architectural description language?*

The second part of the book is devoted to answering these two questions. This is accomplished by constructing a process algebraic architectural description language and endowing it with a number of methods dealing with component-oriented functional verification, component-oriented performance evaluation, and the architecture-level integration of dependability and performance.

The second part comprises of four chapters. In Chap. 4, we provide a number of guidelines for transforming process algebra into a full-fledged architectural description language called PADL. In Chap. 5, we illustrate MISMDET, a topological reduction process for the detection of architecture-level mismatches, which relies on behavioral equivalences and exploits their congruence properties for efficiency reasons and their modal logic characterizations for diagnostic purposes. In Chap. 6, we present PERFSEL, a procedure for the performance-driven selection among alternative architectural designs, which is based on equipping process algebraic architectural descriptions with queueing network models allowing for the assessment of system-level and component-level performance measures. Finally, in Chap. 7 we discuss DEPPERF, a methodology for trading dependability features and performance indices in the architectural design phase, which builds on equivalence-checking-based noninterference analysis and standard numerical techniques.

The first part of the book instead provides background material on syntax and semantics for process calculi as well as on the bisimulation approach [168, 113], the testing approach [82, 111], and the trace approach [57] to the definition of behavioral equivalences. This is useful for a deeper understanding of the second part, as it reports on many concepts and results of process algebra theory in a quick and comparative way.

The first part comprises of three chapters. In Chap. 1, we introduce a process calculus in which no notion of time, probability, or priority is associated with actions. In order to represent real-time systems, in Chap. 2 we discuss two deterministically timed extensions of the original process calculus. The first one allows for delays between the execution of consecutive actions, whereas the second one assigns durations to actions, with both delays and durations being expressed through natural numbers. In order to represent shared-resource systems, in Chap. 3 we illustrate a stochastically timed extension of the original process calculus, in which actions are durational. Since durations are quantified through exponentially distributed random variables, the stochastic process governing the system evolution over time turns out to be a continuous-time Markov chain.

In Chaps. 1 and 3, we also show congruence properties, sound and complete axiomatizations, modal logic characterizations, and verification algorithms for nondeterministic and Markovian versions of bisimulation, testing, and trace equivalences. Moreover, following and extending [98], both in the nondeterministic case and in the Markovian case we compare the discriminating power of the considered behavioral equivalences and some of their variants. In contrast, in Chap. 2 we concentrate only on the properties of the bisimulation approach. Then, we examine different options related to the representation of time and time passing – durationless actions versus durational actions, relative time versus absolute time, global clock versus local clocks – as well as eager, lazy, and maximal progress interpretations of action execution, in order to study their expressiveness.

This book is intended for graduate students and software professionals. It covers different topics such as concurrency theory, software architecture, system modeling and verification, and dependability and performance evaluation. These topics may seem unrelated, but in reality they are deeply intertwined and should all be part of an integrated view in order to manage successfully the increasing complexity of recent software systems. Although it can be used in a course on formal methods in computer science, the book does not focus only on theoretical aspects. In fact, it also addresses methodological issues and contains application examples. Moreover, it gives the same importance to functional and nonfunctional aspects of systems, in an attempt to overcome the drawbacks arising from their separate consideration [88]. The book can thus be used also in a course on model-driven design of software architectures, in which case only its second part may be presented, with concepts of its first part being recalled whenever necessary.

We wish to thank our colleagues at the Universities of Urbino and Camerino, as well as our former colleagues at the Universities of Bologna, L'Aquila, and Torino, for many fruitful discussions over the years.

We are grateful to all the people with whom we have collaborated in the fields of process algebra and software architecture, in particular: Simonetta Balsamo, Antonia Bertolino, Edoardo Bontà, Mario Bravetti, Nadia Busi, Diletta Romana Cacciagrano, Paolo Ciancarini, Rance Cleaveland, Rocco De Nicola, Maria Rita Di Berardini, Alessandra Di Pierro, Lorenzo Donatiello, Francesco Franzè, Roberto Gorrieri, Paola Inverardi, Jeff Kramer, Jeff Magee, Henry Muccini, Marco Pistore, Marina Ribaudo, Marco Roccetti, Marta Simeoni, Angelo Troina, Walter Vogler, and Alex Wolf.

Many thanks also to Erik de Vink, Diego Latella, Michele Loreti, Mieke Massink, Henry Muccini, and Jeremy Sproston for their kind willingness to review early drafts of the book, and to Vittorio Cortellessa for having given on several occasions the opportunity to the second author of presenting the second part of the book as a lecture series at the University of L'Aquila.

Finally, we would like to thank our families for their patience and tolerance during the writing of this book.

Urbino, Italy   Alessandro Aldini
Urbino, Italy   Marco Bernardo
Camerino, Italy   Flavio Corradini

Contents

Part I
Process Calculi
and Behavioral Equivalences

Process algebra is a very rich theory developed over the last three decades, which underpins the semantics of concurrent programming and the understanding of concurrent, distributed, and mobile systems (see, e.g., [154, 119, 112, 22, 155, 181, 30]) as well as the tool-assisted modeling and analysis of the various functional and nonfunctional aspects of those systems (see, e.g., [49, 70, 93]).

Process calculi are action-based formalisms relying on a small set of powerful behavioral operators that support compositionality – i.e., the ability to build complex models by combining simpler models – and abstraction – i.e., the ability to neglect certain parts of a model. The meaning of each process term is formally defined through structural operational semantic rules, which construct the state transition graph corresponding to the process term. Both syntax-level and semantics-level manipulations are possible on process terms according to different behavioral equivalences, which capture different variants of the notion of same behavior possibly abstracting from unnecessary details.

The most studied approaches to the definition of behavioral equivalences are the bisimulation approach [168, 113], the testing approach [82, 111], and the trace approach [57]. In the first case, two processes are considered equivalent if they are able to mimic each other's behavior stepwise. In the second case, two processes are considered equivalent if no difference can be discovered when interacting with them by means of tests and comparing their reactions. In the third case, two processes are considered equivalent if they are able to execute the same sequences of actions.

In the first part of this book, we consider several process calculi sharing the same behavioral operators: action prefix, alternative composition, parallel composition, hiding, restriction, and relabeling. In Chap. 1, we introduce a process calculus in which no notion of time, probability, or priority is associated with actions. In order to represent real-time systems, in Chap. 2 we discuss two deterministically timed extensions of the original process calculus. The first one allows for delays between the execution of consecutive actions, whereas the second one assigns durations to actions, with both delays and durations being expressed through natural numbers. In order to represent shared-resource systems, in Chap. 3 we illustrate a stochastically timed extension of the original process calculus, in which actions are durational. Since durations are quantified through exponentially distributed random variables, the stochastic process governing the system evolution over time turns out to be a continuous-time Markov chain.

In Chaps. 1 and 3, we also show congruence properties, sound and complete axiomatizations, modal logic characterizations, and verification algorithms for nondeterministic and Markovian versions of bisimulation, testing, and trace equivalences. Moreover, following and extending [98], both in the nondeterministic case and in the Markovian case we compare the discriminating power of the considered behavioral equivalences and some of their variants. In contrast, in Chap. 2 we concentrate only on the properties of the bisimulation approach. Then, we examine different options related to the representation of time and time passing – durationless actions versus durational actions, relative time versus absolute time, global clock versus local clocks – as well as eager, lazy, and maximal progress interpretations of action execution, in order to study their expressiveness.

Chapter 1
Process Algebra

Abstract Process algebra is a formal tool for the specification and the verification of concurrent and distributed systems. It supports compositional modeling through a set of operators able to express concepts like sequential composition, alternative composition, and parallel composition of action-based descriptions. It also supports mathematical reasoning via a two-level semantics, which formalizes the behavior of a description by means of an abstract machine obtained from the application of structural operational rules and then introduces behavioral equivalences able to relate descriptions that are syntactically different. In this chapter, we present the typical behavioral operators and operational semantic rules for a process calculus in which no notion of time, probability, or priority is associated with actions. Then, we discuss the three most studied approaches to the definition of behavioral equivalences – bisimulation, testing, and trace – and we illustrate their congruence properties, sound and complete axiomatizations, modal logic characterizations, and verification algorithms. Finally, we show how these behavioral equivalences and some of their variants are related to each other on the basis of their discriminating power.

1.1 Concurrency, Communication, and Nondeterminism

A natural approach to the design of applications requiring a high degree of reactivity to external stimuli is that of structuring computing systems into a set of autonomous components that can evolve independently of each other and from time to time can communicate or simply synchronize. Due to the different speeds of the components, the interaction scheme among the components, and the scheduling policies that are adopted, the behavior of these communicating concurrent systems may exhibit interesting phenomena such as nondeterminism in the final result or in the computation itself. As a consequence, it is not appropriate to describe the behavior of these systems via a function from an input domain to an output domain as in the classic theory of computation [182].

A. Aldini et al., *A Process Algebraic Approach to Software Architecture Design*,
DOI 10.1007/978-1-84800-223-4_1, © Springer-Verlag London Limited 2010

For systems that cannot be viewed as input–output transformers, the key concern is that of capturing ongoing behavior and enabled interactions. While a sequential system executes only one step at a time, and hence can be characterized by a single current state, the various components of a communicating concurrent system can be in different current local states constituting the current global state. Moreover, intermediate states are as important as the initial state and the final state, because they determine the behavior of larger systems that may include the considered system as a component. The importance of taking into account intermediate states is even more evident when considering systems – like operating systems and embedded control systems – that are not designed to terminate, and hence to yield results, but to perform tasks endlessly as required by the external environment.

Communicating concurrent systems suffer from the state space explosion problem, because the number of states grows exponentially with the number of components rather than linearly in the number of steps as in sequential systems. This complexity can be managed only if formal techniques are employed in the modeling and verification process. This makes it possible to understand which combinations of local states can be reached and the consequences of the reached combinations, so that we can hopefully answer questions like: What are the computations that the system can exhibit? When can we replace a component with another one without affecting the whole behavior? How can we compose components and what is the result of their composition?

Several mathematical models have been proposed in the literature for describing and analyzing the behavior of communicating concurrent systems. One of the main differences among them is in the way concurrency is conceived. For instance, in truly concurrent models like the Petri net model [170] and the event structure model [192] two activities are concurrent if they are causally independent, in which case they may occur in either order or simultaneously.

In contrast, other models stress that communication and, hence, the ability or inability to interact with the external environment are the basic concepts in the study of communicating concurrent systems. Indeed, when composing two systems in parallel, it is their communication that determines the behavior of the composite system. These models treat independent activities as occurring in an arbitrary order but not simultaneously; hence, they are called interleaving models [28]. This yields a simpler and elegant theory, although it may not give a faithful picture of reality.

Two notable interleaving models are the trace model and the synchronization tree model. The trace model [119] associates with every system the set of sequences of actions that can be performed. This model is suitable for detecting all possible communications, but it is not satisfactory as it is not sensitive to deadlock. The synchronization tree model [153], instead, associates with every system a possibly infinite tree, whose nodes are the states of the system and whose branches are labeled with actions denoting possible communications with the external environment. Synchronization trees arise naturally when concurrency is reduced to nondeterministic interleaving, but they often discriminate too much; hence, they need to be factored by some equivalence in order to abstract from unwanted details.

In the modeling and verification of concurrent and distributed systems, the previously mentioned mathematical models need to be complemented by description notations that provide an adequate linguistic support. A typical description language having the same formal roots as those mathematical models is process algebra, where processes represent the behavior of systems. This notation is particularly appropriate as it supports compositional modeling through a restricted set of behavioral operators by means of which it is possible to express fundamental concepts like sequential composition, alternative composition, and parallel composition of action-based descriptions, as well as the capability of abstracting from certain aspects of the behavior. Among the proposals made in the literature we mention CCS [154], CSP [119], ACP [22], π-calculus [156], and the ISO standard LOTOS [49].

The various calculi that have been developed share the idea of combining actions by means of behavioral operators. Every action represents a system activity at a certain level of abstraction. Actions are classified into visible and invisible on the basis of their observability from an external viewpoint, where observability amounts to the possibility of being engaged in communications with the external environment. The communication among visible actions can be a pure synchronization or can support data exchange, in which case visible actions are further divided into input and output actions. Whenever actions are not equipped with quantitative information characterizing the duration, the probability, or the priority of their execution, the choice among several actions that are simultaneously enabled is nondeterministic.

On the other hand, the proposed calculi differ in the way their specific behavioral operators are conceived. As an example, the alternative composition operator can encode an external or internal choice mechanism depending on whether the selection can be influenced by the external environment or not. Another example is given by the parallel composition operator and its associated communication mechanism. For instance, communications can be synchronous or asynchronous depending on whether they require the simultaneous participation of all the involved parties or not. Moreover, there can be two-way communications, which are restricted to two actions only, and multiway communications, which are open to the participation of an arbitrary number of actions.

Process calculi support mathematical reasoning by means of a two-level semantics. The first level formalizes the behavior of a process term by means of an abstract machine described as a graph called labeled transition system. In this model, every vertex represents a state and corresponds to a process term into which the original process term can evolve, while every edge corresponds to a state transition and is labeled with the action that determines the corresponding state change. The labeled transition system is obtained by applying structural operational semantic rules [171], each associated with a specific behavioral operator, to the process term.

The transitional or step-by-step model produced in the first level is typically too concrete, because it is very close to the process syntax and hence includes all the details of the behavior described by the considered process term. For this reason, the second level introduces behavioral equivalences aimed at relating process terms that, although syntactically different, represent the same behavior in the sense that they are not distinguishable by an external observer.

In addition to their theoretical interest, behavioral equivalences are also useful from an application viewpoint whenever they are able to convey to the semantic level the compositionality and abstraction features that are made available by the syntax. In particular, they can be employed for establishing connections among process algebraic descriptions of the same system at different abstraction levels, thus supporting top-down modeling. Moreover, they can be exploited for manipulating process algebraic descriptions – e.g., for state space reduction purposes before analysis takes place – in a way that preserves certain properties.

Many different behavioral equivalences have been defined in the literature, giving rise to the so called linear-time/branching-time spectrum [98]. The reason for this heterogeneity is the large number of properties of communicating concurrent systems that can be interesting to analyze; hence, the large number of angles from which the behavior of such systems can be considered. The three most studied approaches to the definition of behavioral equivalences are the trace approach, the testing approach, and the bisimulation approach.

Taking inspiration from the theory of formal languages, in the trace approach [57] two process terms are considered equivalent if they are able to execute the same sequences of actions. This approach completely abstracts from any branching point possibly occurring in process term behavior. Therefore, it needs some adjustments in order to be adequate for communicating concurrent systems, as demonstrated by the fact that its basic version may relate a deadlock-free process term to a process term that can deadlock.

Such a drawback can also be remedied by distinguishing between sequences of actions that can be performed and sequences of actions that cannot be refused. This is the effect achieved by the testing approach [82, 111], in which two process terms are considered equivalent if no difference can be discovered when interacting with them by means of tests and comparing their reactions. Sensitivity to divergence is also naturally achieved, which is intended as the capability of detecting computations composed of invisible actions only. Unfortunately, this approach requires the analysis of process term behavior in response to all tests.

An effective proof technique is obtained in the bisimulation approach [168, 113], in which two process terms are considered equivalent if they are able to mimic each other's behavior after each single action execution. With this approach it is in fact sufficient to exhibit a relation that establishes a connection between any pair of corresponding states, without having to consider the execution of entire sequences of actions. However, this approach tends to be more discriminating than necessary, as it faithfully respects the branching structure of process terms.

Independent of the specific approach that has been followed for its definition and the consequent discriminating power, a behavioral equivalence should possess a number of properties. Firstly, it should be a congruence with respect to the behavioral operators. In this case compositional reasoning is supported because, given a process term, the replacement of any of its subterms with an equivalent subterm results in a modified process term that is equivalent to the original process term. Secondly, it should have a sound and complete axiomatization, which elucidates the fundamental equational laws of the equivalence with respect to the behavioral operators. These laws can be used as rewriting rules for syntactically manipulating process terms in a way that is consistent with the equivalence definition. Thirdly, it should have a modal logic characterization, which describes the behavioral properties that are preserved by the equivalence. The modal logic formulas can be used for explaining the reasons behind the inequivalence of two process terms. Fourthly, it should be able to abstract from invisible actions and be equipped with an efficient verification algorithm, in order for the equivalence to be of practical interest.

This chapter is organized as follows. In Sect. 1.2, we introduce a producer–consumer system that is used throughout the first part of the book as a running example in order to illustrate the definition of process syntax and semantics and the use of behavioral equivalences. In Sect. 1.3, we present the typical behavioral operators and operational semantic rules for a process calculus in which no notion of time, probability, or priority is associated with actions. This calculus includes visible and invisible actions with no support for data exchange, which are subject to a nondeterministic choice mechanism affectable by the external environment as well as a synchronous and multiway communication mechanism. In Sects. 1.4, 1.5, and 1.6, we define bisimulation equivalence, testing equivalence, and trace equivalence, respectively, and we illustrate their congruence properties, sound and complete axiomatizations, modal logic characterizations, and verification algorithms. Finally, in Sect. 1.7 we examine the linear-time/branching-time spectrum resulting from the three considered behavioral equivalences and some of their variants.

1.2 Running Example: Producer–Consumer System

The definition of the syntax and semantics of process terms and the application of behavioral equivalences is exemplified through various process algebraic descriptions of a producer–consumer system. In general, this system is composed of a producer, a finite-capacity buffer, and a consumer. The producer deposits items into the buffer as long as the buffer capacity is not exceeded. Stored items can then be withdrawn by the consumer according to some predefined discipline, like first come first served or last come first served.

For the sake of simplicity, we consider a scenario in which the buffer has only two positions. We also assume that the items are all identical, so that the specific discipline that has been adopted for withdrawals is not important from the point of view of an external observer.

1.3 PC: Process Calculus for Nondeterministic Processes

In this section, we present a process calculus inspired by [154, 119] that we call PC, in which no notion of time, probability, or priority is associated with actions. The calculus includes visible and invisible actions with no support for data exchange.

Actions are subject to a nondeterministic choice mechanism affectable by the external environment as well as a synchronous and multiway communication mechanism. The formal definition of the calculus is preceded by an informal discussion of the role of the actions and of the intended meaning of the behavioral operators.

1.3.1 Syntax: Actions and Behavioral Operators

In PC, action-based descriptions are combined by means of behavioral operators. Actions represent system activities at a certain abstraction level and are divided into visible and invisible. The set of visible action names of PC is denoted by $Name_v$. The special symbol τ is traditionally used for representing any invisible action. A single symbol is enough as there is no way for distinguishing among invisible actions from the point of view of an external observer. We then denote by $Name = Name_v \cup \{\tau\}$ the set of all action names of PC, which is ranged over by a, b.

Behavioral operators express fundamental concepts like sequential composition, alternative composition, and parallel composition of processes, which represent in turn the behavior of systems. More precisely, PC comprises the following behavioral operators, where P, Q are used as metavariables for the set of processes:

- Inactive process: $\underline{0}$ represents a terminated process.
- Action prefix operator: $a.P$ represents a process that can perform a and then behaves as P. This operator encodes an action-based sequential composition.
- Alternative composition operator: $P_1 + P_2$ represents a process that behaves as either P_1 or P_2 depending on which of them executes an action first. If several actions can be performed, the choice among them is solved nondeterministically due to the absence of quantitative information associated with them. The choice is completely internal if the actions that can be performed are all invisible, otherwise the choice can be influenced by the external environment.
- Parallel composition operator: $P_1 \|_S P_2$ represents a process that behaves as P_1 in parallel with P_2 under synchronization set $S \subseteq Name_v$. Actions whose name does not belong to S are executed autonomously by P_1 and P_2. In contrast, synchronization is forced between any action executed by P_1 and any action executed by P_2 that have the same name belonging to S, in which case the resulting action has the same name as the two original actions. When $S = \emptyset$, P_1 and P_2 can proceed independently of each other. When $S = Name_v$, P_1 and P_2 have to synchronize on every visible action name.
- Hiding operator: P/H represents a process that behaves as P in which every action whose name belongs to $H \subseteq Name_v$ is turned into τ. This operator encodes an abstraction mechanism with respect to certain actions and can be exploited for preventing a process from communicating with the external environment.
- Restriction operator: $P \backslash L$ represents a process that behaves as P in which every action whose name belongs to $L \subseteq Name_v$ is prevented from being executed. The effect of this operator is the same as the effect of a parallel composition with $\underline{0}$ in which L is used as synchronization set.

- Relabeling operator: $P[\varphi]$ represents a process that behaves as P in which every action is renamed according to a total relabeling function $\varphi : Name \rightarrow Name$ that preserves action visibility, i.e. $\varphi^{-1}(\tau) = \{\tau\}$. We denote by *Relab* the set of such relabeling functions. For convenience, a single relabeling can be written $a \mapsto b$ meaning that a is renamed b. The relabeling operator would subsume the hiding operator if relabeling functions were not obliged to preserve action visibility, and also the restriction operator if relabeling functions had not been total. This operator is useful for the concise representation of process algebraic descriptions that differ only for certain action names.
- Recursion: $recX : P$ represents a process that behaves as P in which every free occurrence of process variable X is replaced by $recX : P$. A process variable is said to occur free in a process term if it is not in the scope of a *rec* binder for that variable, otherwise it is said to be bound in that process term. A process term is said to be closed if all of its process variable occurrences are bound, otherwise it is said to be open. A process term is said to be guarded iff all of its occurrences of process variables are in the scope of action prefix operators. We denote by *Var* the set of process variables, which is ranged over by X, Y.

The process terms of PC arise from the combination of actions belonging to *Name* through the behavioral operators mentioned above. In order to avoid ambiguity, we assume that the unary operators take precedence over the alternative composition operator, which in turn takes precedence over the parallel composition operator. Moreover, we assume that the two binary operators are left associative.

Definition 1.1. The set of process terms of the process language $\mathscr{PL}$ is generated by the following syntax:

P ::=	$\underline{0}$	inactive process
|	$a.P$	action prefix
|	$P + P$	alternative composition
|	$P \|_S P$	parallel composition
|	P/H	hiding
|	$P \backslash L$	restriction
|	$P[\varphi]$	relabeling
|	X	process variable
|	$recX : P$	recursion

where $a \in Name$, $S, H, L \subseteq Name_v$, $\varphi \in Relab$, and $X \in Var$. We denote by $\mathbb{P}$ the set of closed and guarded process terms of $\mathscr{PL}$.

For modeling purposes, repetitive behaviors are more conveniently described by means of a set *Const* of process constants and their defining equations rather than through process variables and *rec* binders. A defining equation $B \stackrel{\Delta}{=} P$ establishes that process constant B behaves as process term P, with P possibly containing process constant invocations. In this case, closure amounts to the existence of a defining equation for every invoked process constant and guardedness amounts to every process constant invocation occurring inside the scope of an action prefix operator.

Example 1.1. Let us model with PC the producer–consumer system introduced in Sect. 1.2. We adopt the following conventions: action names are expressed through verbs composed of lower-case letters only, whereas process constant names are expressed through nouns starting with an upper-case letter.

Since the only observable activities are deposits and withdrawals, the producer–consumer system can be formalized through the following defining equations:

$$ProdCons_{0/2} \stackrel{\Delta}{=} deposit.ProdCons_{1/2}$$
$$ProdCons_{1/2} \stackrel{\Delta}{=} deposit.ProdCons_{2/2} + withdraw.ProdCons_{0/2}$$
$$ProdCons_{2/2} \stackrel{\Delta}{=} withdraw.ProdCons_{1/2}$$

where $ProdCons_{0/2}$ represents the initial state of the system (in which the buffer is empty), $ProdCons_{1/2}$ represents the state in which only one position of the buffer is occupied, and $ProdCons_{2/2}$ represents the state in which the buffer is full.

The structure-independent process algebraic description provided above can be viewed as a specification of the producer-consumer system with two positions to which every correct implementation should conform.

1.3.2 Semantics: Structural Operational Rules

The semantics for PC is formalized through a labeled transition system. This is a graph $(\mathbb{P}, Name, \longrightarrow)$ including all computations and branching points, where:

- $\mathbb{P}$ is the set of vertices, each denoting a state corresponding to a process term.
- *Name* is the set of edge labels, each corresponding to an action.
- $\longrightarrow \subseteq \mathbb{P} \times Name \times \mathbb{P}$ is the set of edges, forming a state transition relation.

Each labeled transition $(P, a, P') \in \longrightarrow$ is represented as $P \stackrel{a}{\longrightarrow} P'$ to emphasize its source and target states and the action that determines the corresponding state change. Given such a transition, we say that P' is an a-derivative of P.

The labeled transition system above is built by inferring one single transition at a time through the application of operational semantic rules to the source state of the transition itself, with the rules being defined by induction on the syntactical structure of process terms. More precisely, the transition relation $\longrightarrow$ is the smallest subset of $\mathbb{P} \times Name \times \mathbb{P}$ satisfying the operational semantic rules of Table 1.1. The labeled transition system for a specific process term $P \in \mathbb{P}$ is denoted by $[\![P]\!]$ and has P as initial state. It can be unwound into a synchronization tree in the obvious way.

The operational semantic rules of Table 1.1 are formed each by a premise (above the horizontal line) and a conclusion (below the horizontal line) and establish which actions can be performed and when they can be performed for the various behavioral operators. Since the inactive process cannot execute any action, there is no rule for it and hence $[\![0]\!]$ turns out to be a single state with no transitions.

The action prefix operator has a single rule with no premise, which means that the derivation of the transition shown in the conclusion is not subject to the satisfaction of any precondition. As a consequence, PRE is the basic rule for the entire process

Table 1.1 Operational semantic rules for PC

$$(\text{PRE}) \quad \frac{}{a.P \xrightarrow{\ a\ } P}$$

$$(\text{ALT}_1) \quad \frac{P_1 \xrightarrow{\ a\ } P_1'}{P_1 + P_2 \xrightarrow{\ a\ } P_1'} \qquad\qquad (\text{ALT}_2) \quad \frac{P_2 \xrightarrow{\ a\ } P_2'}{P_1 + P_2 \xrightarrow{\ a\ } P_2'}$$

$$(\text{PAR}_1) \quad \frac{P_1 \xrightarrow{\ a\ } P_1' \qquad a \notin S}{P_1 \parallel_S P_2 \xrightarrow{\ a\ } P_1' \parallel_S P_2} \qquad\qquad (\text{PAR}_2) \quad \frac{P_2 \xrightarrow{\ a\ } P_2' \qquad a \notin S}{P_1 \parallel_S P_2 \xrightarrow{\ a\ } P_1 \parallel_S P_2'}$$

$$(\text{SYN}) \quad \frac{P_1 \xrightarrow{\ a\ } P_1' \qquad P_2 \xrightarrow{\ a\ } P_2' \qquad a \in S}{P_1 \parallel_S P_2 \xrightarrow{\ a\ } P_1' \parallel_S P_2'}$$

$$(\text{HID}_1) \quad \frac{P \xrightarrow{\ a\ } P' \qquad a \in H}{P/H \xrightarrow{\ \tau\ } P'/H} \qquad\qquad (\text{HID}_2) \quad \frac{P \xrightarrow{\ a\ } P' \qquad a \notin H}{P/H \xrightarrow{\ a\ } P'/H}$$

$$(\text{RES}) \quad \frac{P \xrightarrow{\ a\ } P' \qquad a \notin L}{P \backslash L \xrightarrow{\ a\ } P' \backslash L}$$

$$(\text{REL}) \quad \frac{P \xrightarrow{\ a\ } P'}{P[\varphi] \xrightarrow{\ \varphi(a)\ } P'[\varphi]}$$

$$(\text{REC}) \quad \frac{P\{recX : P \hookrightarrow X\} \xrightarrow{\ a\ } P'}{recX : P \xrightarrow{\ a\ } P'}$$

of transition derivation. The alternative composition operator has two symmetric rules ALT_1 and ALT_2 expressing a nondeterministic choice, which can be external or internal depending on the visibility of the actions that can be performed. The action prefix operator and the alternative composition operator are called dynamic operators as the conclusions of their rules share the fact that the behavioral operator disappears when moving from the left-hand side to the right-hand side.

In contrast, the parallel composition operator, the hiding operator, the restriction operator, and the relabeling operator are called static operators as they occur on both sides of the conclusions of their rules. In particular, the parallel composition operator conveys information about the structure and the communication scheme inside a process. Its first two rules PAR_1 and PAR_2 express the autonomous execution of actions whose name does not belong to the synchronization set, while its third rule SYN formalizes a synchronous communication mechanism open to the participation of several actions having the same name.

The first two rules of the parallel composition operator encode the interleaving view of concurrency. As an example, take the following two process terms:

$$a.\underline{0} \parallel_\emptyset b.\underline{0}$$
$$a.b.\underline{0} + b.a.\underline{0}$$

The first one (concurrent term) executes a in parallel with b, while the second one (sequential term) executes either a followed by b, or b followed by a. These two syntactically and structurally different terms are behaviorally identical, as the application of semantic rules PAR_1, PAR_2, and PRE to the concurrent term and the application of semantic rules ALT_1, ALT_2, and PRE to the sequential term yield the same labeled transition system, which is shown below:

More precisely, the process terms associated with the various states of this labeled transition system are $a.\underline{0} \parallel_\emptyset b.\underline{0}, \underline{0} \parallel_\emptyset b.\underline{0}, a.\underline{0} \parallel_\emptyset \underline{0}, \underline{0} \parallel_\emptyset \underline{0}$ for the concurrent term and $a.b.\underline{0} + b.a.\underline{0}, b.\underline{0}, a.\underline{0}, \underline{0}$ for the sequential term. However, these differences are not important from the point of view of an external observer, as what matters is given by the actions that are executed and the order in which they are executed.

As far as the unary static operators are concerned, their rules tend to change the action labeling the transition when moving from the premise to the conclusion. In the case of the hiding operator, the first rule HID_1 transforms into τ every action whose name belongs to the hiding set, while the second rule HID_2 applies no transformation to actions whose name does not belong to the hiding set. The rule RES for the restriction operator filters only actions whose name does not belong to the restriction set. The rule REL for the relabeling operator transforms actions according to the relabeling function.

The rule REC for recursion unfolds the body of the *rec* binder by means of a syntactical substitution that replaces every free occurrence of the process variable with the recursive process term itself. In general, a syntactical substitution σ is a set of syntactical replacements each written $t \hookrightarrow x$ to indicate that term t substitutes for every free occurrence of variable x. The limitation to closed and guarded process terms guarantees that the unfolding process can take place and generates finitely many transitions out of any state; hence, the corresponding labeled transition systems are finitely branching. We also note that the labeled transition system for a specific process term is finite state, i.e., has finitely many states, as long as the body of each recursive definition occurring in the process term does not contain static operators. The rule equivalent to REC for process constants is as follows:

$$(\text{REC}') \quad \frac{B \overset{\Delta}{=} P \qquad P \overset{a}{\longrightarrow} P'}{B \overset{a}{\longrightarrow} P'}$$

Example 1.2. The labeled transition system $[\![ProdCons_{0/2}]\!]$ for the process algebraic description of Example 1.1 is depicted below, where also the process term associated with each state is shown:

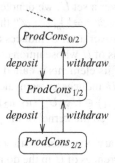

This labeled transition system has been obtained starting from $ProdCons_{0/2}$ by applying semantic rules REC′, ALT$_1$, ALT$_2$, and PRE.

1.4 Bisimulation Equivalence

Bisimulation equivalence relates two process terms whenever they are able to mimic each other's behavior stepwise. After recalling some basic notions about equivalence relations and preorders, in this section we provide the definition of bisimulation equivalence over $\mathbb{P}$ together with a necessary condition and a sufficient condition [168, 113, 154]. Then, we show that bisimulation equivalence is a congruence and we present its sound and complete axiomatization, its modal logic characterization, and its verification algorithm [113, 154, 128, 167]. Finally, we illustrate some variants that abstract from τ-actions [113, 154, 100, 128].

1.4.1 Equivalence Relations and Preorders

Here, we recall some basic notions about equivalence relations and preorders that are necessary for introducing behavioral equivalences and their properties.

Definition 1.2. A binary relation $\mathscr{R}$ over a set U, i.e. $\mathscr{R} \subseteq U \times U$, is said to be:

- Reflexive iff $(u, u) \in \mathscr{R}$ for all $u \in U$
- Symmetric iff $(u_1, u_2) \in \mathscr{R} \Longrightarrow (u_2, u_1) \in \mathscr{R}$ for all $u_1, u_2 \in U$
- Antisymmetric iff $(u_1, u_2) \in \mathscr{R} \wedge (u_2, u_1) \in \mathscr{R} \Longrightarrow u_1 = u_2$ for all $u_1, u_2 \in U$
- Transitive iff $(u_1, u_2) \in \mathscr{R} \wedge (u_2, u_3) \in \mathscr{R} \Longrightarrow (u_1, u_3) \in \mathscr{R}$ for all $u_1, u_2, u_3 \in U$
- Linear iff $(u_1, u_2) \in \mathscr{R} \vee (u_2, u_1) \in \mathscr{R}$ for all $u_1, u_2 \in U$

Definition 1.3. A binary relation $\mathscr{R}$ over a set U is said to be:

- An equivalence relation iff it is reflexive, symmetric, and transitive
- A preorder iff it is reflexive and transitive

- A partial order iff it is reflexive, antisymmetric, and transitive
- A total order iff it is reflexive, antisymmetric, transitive, and linear

Given a binary relation $\mathscr{R}$ over a set U, we denote by $\mathscr{R}^n$ the composition of $\mathscr{R}$ with itself $n \in \mathbb{N}_{>0}$ times and by $\mathscr{R}^+ = \bigcup_{n \in \mathbb{N}_{>0}} \mathscr{R}^n$ the transitive closure of $\mathscr{R}$.

Any equivalence relation $\mathscr{R}$ over a set U induces a partition of U; i.e., a family of nonempty and disjoint subsets of U whose union coincides with U. This partition is denoted by $U/\mathscr{R}$ and each of its elements is called an equivalence class.

Any preorder $\mathscr{R}$ over a set U induces an equivalence relation over U given by $\mathscr{R} \cap \mathscr{R}^{-1}$, where $\mathscr{R}^{-1} = \{(u_2, u_1) \in U \times U \mid (u_1, u_2) \in \mathscr{R}\}$ is the inverse relation of $\mathscr{R}$. Such an equivalence is called the kernel of the preorder.

Definition 1.4. Let op be an n-ary operation, with $n \in \mathbb{N}_{>0}$, over a set U, i.e. $op : U \times \cdots \times U \longrightarrow U$ with n occurrences of U in the domain. A binary relation $\mathscr{R}$ over U is said to be congruent with respect to op iff, whenever $(u_1, u_1'), \ldots, (u_n, u_n') \in \mathscr{R}$, then $(op(u_1, \ldots, u_n), op(u_1', \ldots, u_n')) \in \mathscr{R}$.

The elements of a set U composed through a family of operations $\mathcal{O}$ can be syntactically manipulated according to a binary relation $\mathscr{R}$ over U congruent with respect to $\mathcal{O}$ by means of a suitable deduction system. This includes inference rules corresponding to the properties of $\mathscr{R}$ – like reflexivity, symmetry, and transitivity in the case of an equivalence relation, plus substitutivity for congruence – as well as a set $\mathscr{X}$ of axioms expressing the basic equational laws of $\mathscr{R}$ with respect to $\mathcal{O}$.

The application of the deduction system based on $\mathscr{X}$, which is denoted by $Ded(\mathscr{X})$, induces a binary relation $\mathscr{R}_{\mathscr{X}}$ over U possessing the same properties as $\mathscr{R}$. The fact that in $Ded(\mathscr{X})$ it can be inferred that $u_1, u_2 \in U$ are related by $\mathscr{R}_{\mathscr{X}}$ is written $\mathscr{X} \vdash (u_1, u_2) \in \mathscr{R}_{\mathscr{X}}$. The two binary relations $\mathscr{R}$ and $\mathscr{R}_{\mathscr{X}}$ coincide iff $Ded(\mathscr{X})$ is sound and complete with respect to $\mathscr{R}$. The axiomatization is sound iff, whenever $\mathscr{X} \vdash (u_1, u_2) \in \mathscr{R}_{\mathscr{X}}$, then $(u_1, u_2) \in \mathscr{R}$. The axiomatization is complete iff, whenever $(u_1, u_2) \in \mathscr{R}$, then $\mathscr{X} \vdash (u_1, u_2) \in \mathscr{R}_{\mathscr{X}}$.

1.4.2 Definition of the Behavioral Equivalence

The basic idea behind bisimulation equivalence is that, whenever a process term can perform a certain action, then any process term equivalent to the given one has to be able to respond with the same action. Moreover, the derivative process terms into which all the previous process terms have evolved after executing that action must still be equivalent to each other, so that this game can go on endlessly.

Definition 1.5. A binary relation $\mathscr{B}$ over $\mathbb{P}$ is a bisimulation iff, whenever $(P_1, P_2) \in \mathscr{B}$, then for all actions $a \in Name$:

- Whenever $P_1 \xrightarrow{a} P_1'$, then $P_2 \xrightarrow{a} P_2'$ with $(P_1', P_2') \in \mathscr{B}$
- Whenever $P_2 \xrightarrow{a} P_2'$, then $P_1 \xrightarrow{a} P_1'$ with $(P_1', P_2') \in \mathscr{B}$

Since the union of all the bisimulations can be proved to be the largest bisimulation, the definition below follows.

Definition 1.6. Bisimulation equivalence (or bisimilarity), denoted $\sim_B$, is the union of all the bisimulations.

We observe that $\sim_B$ is indeed an equivalence relation and enjoys a very natural and appealing proof technique. In order to establish whether two process terms P_1 and P_2 are bisimilar, it is in fact sufficient to exhibit a bisimulation containing the pair (P_1, P_2).

Example 1.3. Let us model with PC a concurrent implementation of the producer-consumer system introduced in Sect. 1.2. In this case the two-position buffer is implemented as the parallel composition of two independent one-position buffers:

$$PC_{conc,2} \triangleq Prod \parallel_{\{deposit\}} (Buff \parallel_\emptyset Buff) \parallel_{\{withdraw\}} Cons$$
$$Prod \triangleq deposit.Prod$$
$$Buff \triangleq deposit.withdraw.Buff$$
$$Cons \triangleq withdraw.Cons$$

Is this a correct implementation of the specification provided in Example 1.1? In order to answer this question, we have to investigate the existence of some relation between $PC_{conc,2}$ and $ProdCons_{0/2}$. The first step consists of comparing $[\![PC_{conc,2}]\!]$ and $[\![ProdCons_{0/2}]\!]$, which are shown below:

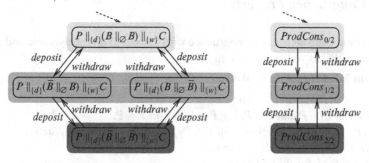

In the states of the labeled transition system on the left-hand side, every process constant and every action has been shortened with its initial. Moreover, $\bar{B}$ stands for *withdraw . Buff*.

What turns out is that $PC_{conc,2} \sim_B ProdCons_{0/2}$. The bisimulation proving this fact has been represented graphically by giving the same color to states in the same equivalence class and different colors to different equivalence classes. The depicted relation is a bisimulation because in both labeled transition systems:

- A light gray state can only reach a gray state by executing *deposit*
- A gray state can only reach a dark gray state by executing *deposit* or a light gray state by executing *withdraw*
- A dark gray state can only reach a gray state by executing *withdraw*

1.4.3 Conditions and Characterizations

A simple necessary condition for establishing whether two process terms are bisimilar is that they perform the same actions.

Proposition 1.1. *Let $P_1, P_2 \in \mathbb{P}$. Whenever $P_1 \sim_B P_2$, then for all $a \in Name$ it holds $P_1 \xrightarrow{a} P'_1$ iff $P_2 \xrightarrow{a} P'_2$ for some $P'_1, P'_2 \in \mathbb{P}$.*

We can also derive a sufficient condition based on the notion of bisimulation up to $\sim_B$. This is useful both for concentrating on the important pairs of process terms that form a bisimulation – thus ruling out redundant pairs – and for proving the congruence property of $\sim_B$ with respect to recursion.

Definition 1.7. A binary relation $\mathcal{B}$ over $\mathbb{P}$ is a bisimulation up to $\sim_B$ iff, whenever $(P_1, P_2) \in \mathcal{B}$, then for all actions $a \in Name$:

- Whenever $P_1 \xrightarrow{a} P'_1$, then $P_2 \xrightarrow{a} P'_2$ with $P'_1 \sim_B Q_1 \mathcal{B} Q_2 \sim_B P'_2$
- Whenever $P_2 \xrightarrow{a} P'_2$, then $P_1 \xrightarrow{a} P'_1$ with $P'_1 \sim_B Q_1 \mathcal{B} Q_2 \sim_B P'_2$

Proposition 1.2. *Let $\mathcal{B}$ be a binary relation over $\mathbb{P}$. Whenever $\mathcal{B}$ is a bisimulation up to $\sim_B$, then for all $P_1, P_2 \in \mathbb{P}$:*

$$(P_1, P_2) \in \mathcal{B} \implies P_1 \sim_B P_2$$

1.4.4 Congruence Property

Bisimulation equivalence is a congruence with respect to all the dynamic and static operators of PC as well as recursion.

Theorem 1.1. *Let $P_1, P_2 \in \mathbb{P}$. Whenever $P_1 \sim_B P_2$, then:*

1. $a . P_1 \sim_B a . P_2$ *for all $a \in Name$.*
2. $P_1 + P \sim_B P_2 + P$ *and $P + P_1 \sim_B P + P_2$ for all $P \in \mathbb{P}$.*
3. $P_1 \|_S P \sim_B P_2 \|_S P$ *and $P \|_S P_1 \sim_B P \|_S P_2$ for all $P \in \mathbb{P}$ and $S \subseteq Name_v$.*
4. $P_1 / H \sim_B P_2 / H$ *for all $H \subseteq Name_v$.*
5. $P_1 \backslash L \sim_B P_2 \backslash L$ *for all $L \subseteq Name_v$.*
6. $P_1 [\varphi] \sim_B P_2 [\varphi]$ *for all $\varphi \in Relab$.*

As far as recursion is concerned, we need to extend $\sim_B$ to open process terms by considering all possible syntactical substitutions replacing any free occurrence of a process variable with a closed process term.

Definition 1.8. *Let $P_1, P_2 \in \mathscr{PL}$ be guarded process terms containing free occurrences of $k \in \mathbb{N}$ process variables $X_1, \ldots, X_k \in Var$ at most. We define $P_1 \sim_B P_2$ iff $P_1 \{Q_i \hookrightarrow X_i \mid 1 \leq i \leq k\} \sim_B P_2 \{Q_i \hookrightarrow X_i \mid 1 \leq i \leq k\}$ for all $Q_1, \ldots, Q_k \in \mathbb{P}$.*

Theorem 1.2. *Let $P_1, P_2 \in \mathscr{PL}$ be guarded process terms containing free occurrences of $k \in \mathbb{N}$ process variables $X_1, \ldots, X_k \in Var$ at most. Whenever $P_1 \sim_B P_2$, then $recX : P_1 \sim_B recX : P_2$ for all $X \in Var$.*

1.4.5 Sound and Complete Axiomatization

Bisimulation equivalence has a sound and complete axiomatization over nonrecursive process terms, given by the set $\mathscr{X}_B$ of equational laws of Table 1.2.

Axioms $\mathscr{X}_{B,1}$, $\mathscr{X}_{B,2}$, and $\mathscr{X}_{B,3}$ establish that the alternative composition operator is commutative, associative, and has $\underline{0}$ as neutral element, respectively. Axiom $\mathscr{X}_{B,4}$, which states that the alternative composition operator is also idempotent, characterizes $\sim_B$ and distinguishes it from synchronization tree isomorphism.

The interleaving view of concurrency is expressed by axioms $\mathscr{X}_{B,5}$ to $\mathscr{X}_{B,8}$, where I and J are nonempty finite index sets and each summation on the right-hand side is taken to be $\underline{0}$ whenever its set of summands is empty. In particular, axiom $\mathscr{X}_{B,5}$ is called the expansion law, as it highlights how the parallel composition of $P \equiv \sum_{i \in I} a_i . P_i$ and $Q \equiv \sum_{j \in J} b_j . Q_j$ is rendered through all possible interleavings of the sequences of actions executable by P and Q. It is worth observing that the three summands on the right-hand side of the expansion law correspond to the three operational semantic rules for the parallel composition operator.

Table 1.2 Equational laws for $\sim_B$

$(\mathscr{X}_{B,1})$	$P_1 + P_2 = P_2 + P_1$	
$(\mathscr{X}_{B,2})$	$(P_1 + P_2) + P_3 = P_1 + (P_2 + P_3)$	
$(\mathscr{X}_{B,3})$	$P + \underline{0} = P$	
$(\mathscr{X}_{B,4})$	$P + P = P$	
$(\mathscr{X}_{B,5})$	$\displaystyle\sum_{i \in I} a_i . P_i \parallel_S \sum_{j \in J} b_j . Q_j = \sum_{k \in I, a_k \notin S} a_k . \left(P_k \parallel_S \sum_{j \in J} b_j . Q_j \right)$	
	$\displaystyle + \sum_{h \in J, b_h \notin S} b_h . \left(\sum_{i \in I} a_i . P_i \parallel_S Q_h \right)$	
	$\displaystyle + \sum_{k \in I, a_k \in S} \sum_{h \in J, b_h = a_k} a_k . (P_k \parallel_S Q_h)$	
$(\mathscr{X}_{B,6})$	$\displaystyle\sum_{i \in I} a_i . P_i \parallel_S \underline{0} = \sum_{k \in I, a_k \notin S} a_k . P_k$	
$(\mathscr{X}_{B,7})$	$\displaystyle\underline{0} \parallel_S \sum_{j \in J} b_j . Q_j = \sum_{h \in J, b_h \notin S} b_h . Q_h$	
$(\mathscr{X}_{B,8})$	$\underline{0} \parallel_S \underline{0} = \underline{0}$	
$(\mathscr{X}_{B,9})$	$\underline{0}/H = \underline{0}$	
$(\mathscr{X}_{B,10})$	$(a . P)/H = \tau . (P/H)$	if $a \in H$
$(\mathscr{X}_{B,11})$	$(a . P)/H = a . (P/H)$	if $a \notin H$
$(\mathscr{X}_{B,12})$	$(P_1 + P_2)/H = P_1/H + P_2/H$	
$(\mathscr{X}_{B,13})$	$\underline{0} \backslash L = \underline{0}$	
$(\mathscr{X}_{B,14})$	$(a . P) \backslash L = \underline{0}$	if $a \in L$
$(\mathscr{X}_{B,15})$	$(a . P) \backslash L = a . (P \backslash L)$	if $a \notin L$
$(\mathscr{X}_{B,16})$	$(P_1 + P_2) \backslash L = P_1 \backslash L + P_2 \backslash L$	
$(\mathscr{X}_{B,17})$	$\underline{0}[\varphi] = \underline{0}$	
$(\mathscr{X}_{B,18})$	$(a . P)[\varphi] = \varphi(a) . (P[\varphi])$	
$(\mathscr{X}_{B,19})$	$(P_1 + P_2)[\varphi] = P_1[\varphi] + P_2[\varphi]$	

The laws related to the unary static operators indicate that these operators are absorbed by $\underline{0}$ ($\mathcal{X}_{B,9}$, $\mathcal{X}_{B,13}$, $\mathcal{X}_{B,17}$), manifest their effect under the action prefix operator ($\mathcal{X}_{B,10}$, $\mathcal{X}_{B,11}$, $\mathcal{X}_{B,14}$, $\mathcal{X}_{B,15}$, $\mathcal{X}_{B,18}$), and distribute over the alternative composition operator ($\mathcal{X}_{B,12}$, $\mathcal{X}_{B,16}$, $\mathcal{X}_{B,19}$).

Theorem 1.3. *Let $P_1, P_2 \in \mathbb{P}$ be nonrecursive. Then:*

$$P_1 \sim_B P_2 \iff \mathcal{X}_B \vdash P_1 = P_2$$

1.4.6 Modal Logic Characterization

Bisimulation equivalence has a modal logic characterization based on the Hennessy–Milner logic (HML for short). In addition to basic truth values and propositional connectives, this logic includes an operator called diamond, which expresses the possibility of executing a certain action and subsequently behaving in a certain way.

Definition 1.9. The set of formulas of the modal language $\mathcal{ML}_B$ is generated by the following syntax:

$$\phi ::= \text{true} \mid \neg\phi \mid \phi \wedge \phi \mid \langle a \rangle \phi$$

where $a \in \textit{Name}$.

Definition 1.10. The satisfaction relation $\models_B$ of $\mathcal{ML}_B$ over $\mathbb{P}$ is defined by induction on the syntactical structure of formulas as follows:

$P \models_B$	true	
$P \models_B$	$\neg\phi$	if $P \not\models_B \phi$
$P \models_B$	$\phi_1 \wedge \phi_2$	if $P \models_B \phi_1$ and $P \models_B \phi_2$
$P \models_B$	$\langle a \rangle \phi$	if there exists $P' \in \mathbb{P}$ such that $P \xrightarrow{a} P'$ and $P' \models_B \phi$

where $\not\models_B$ denotes the complement of $\models_B$ with respect to $\mathbb{P} \times \mathcal{ML}_B$.

From the operators above we can derive other operators, among which the dual of the diamond operator. This modal operator, which expresses the necessity of behaving in a certain way after executing a certain action, is defined as follows:

$$[a]\phi \equiv \neg\langle a \rangle \neg\phi$$

with $P \models_B [a]\phi$ if for all $P' \in \mathbb{P}$, whenever $P \xrightarrow{a} P'$, then $P' \models_B \phi$.

The definition of HML comprises the modal language $\mathcal{ML}_B$ and its satisfaction relation $\models_B$ over process terms. This provides a modal logic characterization of $\sim_B$, in the sense that two process terms are bisimilar iff they satisfy the same set of formulas of HML.

Theorem 1.4. *Let $P_1, P_2 \in \mathbb{P}$. Then:*

$$P_1 \sim_B P_2 \iff (\forall \phi \in \mathcal{ML}_B . P_1 \models_B \phi \iff P_2 \models_B \phi)$$

1.4.7 Verification Algorithm

Bisimulation equivalence can be decided in polynomial time by means of a partition refinement algorithm that exploits the fact that $\sim_B$ can be characterized as the limit of a sequence of successively finer equivalence relations:

$$\sim_B = \bigcap_{i \in \mathbb{N}} \sim_{B,i}$$

Relation $\sim_{B,0}$ is $\mathbb{P} \times \mathbb{P}$ while $\sim_{B,i}$, $i \in \mathbb{N}_{\geq 1}$, is a binary relation over $\mathbb{P}$ defined as follows: whenever $P_1 \sim_{B,i} P_2$, then for all $a \in Name$:

- Whenever $P_1 \xrightarrow{\;a\;} P_1'$, then $P_2 \xrightarrow{\;a\;} P_2'$ with $P_1' \sim_{B,i-1} P_2'$
- Whenever $P_2 \xrightarrow{\;a\;} P_2'$, then $P_1 \xrightarrow{\;a\;} P_1'$ with $P_1' \sim_{B,i-1} P_2'$

Note that $\sim_{B,1}$ refines the partition $\{\mathbb{P}\}$ induced by $\sim_{B,0}$ by creating an equivalence class for each set of terms satisfying the necessary condition of Proposition 1.1.

Given $P_1, P_2 \in \mathbb{P}$ finite state and denoted by $Name_{P_1,P_2}$ the set of actions labeling the transitions of $[\![P_1]\!]$ or $[\![P_2]\!]$, the algorithm for checking whether $P_1 \sim_B P_2$ proceeds as follows:

1. Build an initial partition with a single class including all the states of $[\![P_1]\!]$ and all the states of $[\![P_2]\!]$.
2. Initialize a list of splitters with the above class as its only element.
3. While the list of splitters is not empty, select a splitter and remove it from the list after refining the current partition for each $a \in Name_{P_1,P_2}$:

   (a) Split each class of the current partition by comparing its states when performing actions of name a that lead to the selected splitter.
   (b) For each class split into a nonempty subclass of states reaching the selected splitter and a nonempty subclass of states not reaching the selected splitter, insert the smallest subclass into the list of splitters.

4. Return yes/no depending on whether the initial state of $[\![P_1]\!]$ and the initial state of $[\![P_2]\!]$ belong to the same class of the final partition or to different classes.

The time complexity is $O(m \cdot \log n)$, where n is the total number of states and m is the total number of transitions of $[\![P_1]\!]$ and $[\![P_2]\!]$. We mention that this algorithm can also be used for minimizing a labeled transition system with respect to $\sim_B$.

1.4.8 Abstracting from Invisible Actions

Bisimulation equivalence does not abstract from invisible actions, which limits its practical interest in spite of its good properties. Consider for instance process terms $a.b.\underline{0}$ and $a.\tau.b.\underline{0}$. From the point of view of an external observer, these two process terms are indistinguishable, as in both cases what can be observed is the execution of an a-action followed by the execution of a b-action. Unfortunately, the two process terms are not bisimilar, as the τ-action of the second process term cannot be matched by any action of the first process term.

We now define a weak variant of $\sim_B$ that is able to abstract from τ-actions. The idea is that of relaxing the notion of bisimulation in such a way that, whenever a process term can perform a certain action, then any process term equivalent to the given one has to be able to respond with the same action possibly preceded and followed by arbitrarily many τ-actions. In other words, the weak variant of $\sim_B$ should capture the ability of mimicking each other's visible behavior stepwise.

This is achieved by extending the transition relation $\longrightarrow$ to action sequences. Denoted by $Name^*$ the set of possibly empty sequences of finitely many actions, we use $\Longrightarrow$ to indicate the subset of $\mathbb{P} \times Name^* \times \mathbb{P}$ such that $P \xrightarrow{a_1 \ldots a_n} P'$ iff:

- Either $n = 0$ and P coincides with P', meaning that P stays idle
- Or $n \in \mathbb{N}_{\geq 1}$ and there exists $\{P_i \in \mathbb{P} \mid 0 \leq i \leq n\}$ such that P_0 coincides with P, $P_{i-1} \xrightarrow{a_i} P_i$ for all $1 \leq i \leq n$, and P_n coincides with P'

In particular, $\xLongrightarrow{\tau^*}$ represents the execution of a possibly empty sequence of finitely many τ-actions.

Definition 1.11. A binary relation $\mathscr{B}$ over $\mathbb{P}$ is a weak bisimulation iff, whenever $(P_1, P_2) \in \mathscr{B}$, then:

- Whenever $P_1 \xrightarrow{\tau} P_1'$, then $P_2 \xLongrightarrow{\tau^*} P_2'$ with $(P_1', P_2') \in \mathscr{B}$
- Whenever $P_2 \xrightarrow{\tau} P_2'$, then $P_1 \xLongrightarrow{\tau^*} P_1'$ with $(P_1', P_2') \in \mathscr{B}$

and for all visible actions $a \in Name_v$:

- Whenever $P_1 \xrightarrow{a} P_1'$, then $P_2 \xLongrightarrow{\tau^* a \tau^*} P_2'$ with $(P_1', P_2') \in \mathscr{B}$
- Whenever $P_2 \xrightarrow{a} P_2'$, then $P_1 \xLongrightarrow{\tau^* a \tau^*} P_1'$ with $(P_1', P_2') \in \mathscr{B}$

Since the union of all the weak bisimulations can be proved to be the largest weak bisimulation, the definition below follows.

Definition 1.12. Weak bisimulation equivalence (or weak bisimilarity), denoted $\approx_B$, is the union of all the weak bisimulations.

Weak bisimulation equivalence is again an equivalence relation and enjoys properties similar to those of $\sim_B$, except for congruence with respect to the alternative composition operator. In particular, the axiomatization of $\approx_B$ extends the axiomatization of $\sim_B$ shown in Table 1.2 by adding the axioms of Table 1.3. These further axioms are called τ-laws as they formalize the cases in which $\approx_B$ is able to abstract

Table 1.3 Equational laws characterizing $\approx_B$ (left) and $\approx_B^c$ (right)

$\tau . P = P$	
$a . \tau . P = a . P$	$a . \tau . P = a . P$
$P + \tau . P = \tau . P$	$P + \tau . P = \tau . P$
$a . (P_1 + \tau . P_2) + a . P_2 = a . (P_1 + \tau . P_2)$	$a . (P_1 + \tau . P_2) + a . P_2 = a . (P_1 + \tau . P_2)$

from τ-actions. The modal logic characterization of $\approx_B$ is given by a weak variant of HML in which $\langle a \rangle \phi$, $a \in Name$, is replaced by $\langle\langle \tau \rangle\rangle \phi$ and $\langle\langle a \rangle\rangle \phi$, $a \in Name_v$. In that case, $P \models_B \langle\langle \tau \rangle\rangle \phi$ if there exists $P' \in \mathbb{P}$ such that $P \overset{\tau^*}{\Longrightarrow} P'$ and $P' \models_B \phi$, while $P \models_B \langle\langle a \rangle\rangle \phi$ if there exists $P' \in \mathbb{P}$ such that $P \overset{\tau^* a \tau^*}{\Longrightarrow} P'$ and $P' \models_B \phi$. The verification algorithm for $\approx_B$ runs in $O(n^2 \cdot m \cdot \log n)$ time and is obtained by having the verification algorithm for $\sim_B$ preceded by the preprocessing step below:

0. Build the reflexive and transitive closure of $\overset{\tau}{\longrightarrow}$ in $[\![P_i]\!]$ for $i = 1, 2$:

   (a) Add a looping τ-transition to each state.
   (b) Add a τ-transition between the initial state and the final state of any sequence of at least two τ-transitions, if the two states are distinct and all the transitions in the sequence are distinct and nonlooping.
   (c) Add an a-transition, $a \in Name_v$, between the initial state and the final state of any sequence of at least two transitions in which one is labeled with a, if all the other transitions in the sequence are labeled with τ, distinct, and nonlooping.

The congruence problem of $\approx_B$ with respect to the alternative composition operator can be seen by considering process terms $a.\underline{0}$ and $\tau.a.\underline{0}$. These two process terms are weakly bisimilar, but they can be distinguished in the context of $\_ + b.\underline{0}$. In fact, $\tau.a.\underline{0} + b.\underline{0}$ can perform a τ-action that makes it evolve into $a.\underline{0}$, whereas $a.\underline{0} + b.\underline{0}$ cannot evolve into a process term weakly bisimilar to $a.\underline{0}$. This example shows that axiom $\tau.P = P$ cannot be freely used in all contexts when the process term on its right-hand side is stable; i.e., it cannot perform τ-actions. In fact, congruence with respect to the alternative composition operator can be restored by enforcing a matching on initial τ-actions in the equivalence definition.

Definition 1.13. Let $P_1, P_2 \in \mathbb{P}$. We say that P_1 is weakly bisimulation congruent to P_2, written $P_1 \approx_B^c P_2$, iff for all actions $a \in Name$:

- Whenever $P_1 \overset{a}{\longrightarrow} P_1'$, then $P_2 \overset{\tau^* a \tau^*}{\Longrightarrow} P_2'$ with $P_1' \approx_B P_2'$
- Whenever $P_2 \overset{a}{\longrightarrow} P_2'$, then $P_1 \overset{\tau^* a \tau^*}{\Longrightarrow} P_1'$ with $P_1' \approx_B P_2'$

Theorem 1.5. $\approx_B^c$ *is the largest congruence contained in* $\approx_B$.

From the equational standpoint, as shown in Table 1.3 axiom $\tau.P = P$ is no longer valid for $\approx_B^c$; hence, $\approx_B^c$ can abstract only from some intermediate τ-actions.

We also mention that $\approx_B$ does not fully retain the property possessed by $\sim_B$ of respecting the branching structure of process terms. Starting from $P_1 \approx_B P_2$, if $P_1 \overset{a}{\longrightarrow} P_1'$ then $P_2 \overset{\tau^*}{\Longrightarrow} Q \overset{a}{\longrightarrow} Q' \overset{\tau^*}{\Longrightarrow} P_2'$ with $P_1' \approx_B P_2'$, but we do not know whether any relation exists between P_1 and Q and between P_1' and Q'. The property can be restored by requiring that P_1 be equivalent to Q and that P_1' be equivalent to Q'. The resulting equivalence is called branching bisimulation equivalence, denoted $\approx_{B,b}$, and is characterized by a single τ-law stating that $a.(\tau.(P_1 + P_2) + P_1) = a.(P_1 + P_2)$. It turns out that $\approx_{B,b}$ coincides with $\approx_B$ on any pair of process terms with at most one of them reaching unstable process terms.

Example 1.4. Let us model with PC a pipeline implementation of the producer–consumer system introduced in Sect. 1.2. In this case, the two-position buffer is implemented as the parallel composition of two communicating one-position buffers:

$$PC_{\text{pipe},2} \overset{\Delta}{=} Prod \parallel_{\{deposit\}} (LBuff \parallel_{\{pass\}} RBuff) / \{pass\} \parallel_{\{withdraw\}} Cons$$
$$Prod \overset{\Delta}{=} deposit \, . \, Prod$$
$$LBuff \overset{\Delta}{=} deposit \, . \, pass \, . \, LBuff$$
$$RBuff \overset{\Delta}{=} pass \, . \, withdraw \, . \, RBuff$$
$$Cons \overset{\Delta}{=} withdraw \, . \, Cons$$

Note that action *pass* models the passage of one item from the left buffer to the right buffer and occurs both in the synchronization set and in the hiding set for *LBuff* and *RBuff*. We have decided to hide the execution of *pass* as it represents an implementation detail that should not be perceived by an external observer.

Is this a correct implementation of the specification provided in Example 1.1? Similar to the case of the concurrent implementation presented in Example 1.3, in order to answer this question we have to investigate the existence of some relation between $PC_{\text{pipe},2}$ and $ProdCons_{0/2}$. The first step consists of comparing $[\![PC_{\text{pipe},2}]\!]$ and $[\![ProdCons_{0/2}]\!]$, which are shown below:

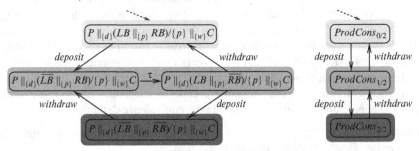

In addition to the same shorthands as before for process constants and action names on the left-hand side, we have $\overline{LB}$ for *pass . LBuff* and $\overline{RB}$ for *withdraw . RBuff*.

Since the labeled transition system on the left-hand side contains a τ-transition representing the passage of one item from the left buffer to the right buffer while the labeled transition system on the right-hand side does not contain any τ-transition, we cannot expect the two labeled transition systems to be related by a bisimulation, as happened with the concurrent implementation.

What turns out is that $PC_{\text{pipe},2} \approx_B ProdCons_{0/2}$ (and $PC_{\text{pipe},2} \approx_{B,b} ProdCons_{0/2}$ as only $[\![PC_{\text{pipe},2}]\!]$ has τ-transitions). Similar to Example 1.3, the weak bisimulation proving this fact has been represented graphically by giving the same color to equivalent states and different colors to different equivalence classes. The depicted relation is a weak bisimulation because in both labeled transition systems:

- A light gray state can only reach a gray state by executing *deposit*
- A gray state can only reach a dark gray state by executing *deposit* (possibly preceded by τ), a light gray state by executing *withdraw* (possibly preceded by τ), or a gray state by executing τ or staying idle
- A dark gray state can only reach a gray state by executing *withdraw*

1.5 Testing Equivalence

Testing equivalence relates two process terms whenever an external observer is not able to distinguish between them by interacting with them by means of tests and comparing their reactions. In this section, we provide the definition of testing equivalence over $\mathbb{P}$ based on the distinction between the possibility and the necessity of passing tests, together with two alternative characterizations [82]. Then, we show that testing equivalence is a congruence with respect to all operators except for alternative composition and we present its sound and complete axiomatization, its modal logic characterization, and its verification algorithm [82, 111, 69].

1.5.1 Definition of the Behavioral Equivalence

The basic idea behind testing equivalence is that of discovering differences in the behavior of process terms by experimenting on them through tests. The testing approach thus requires defining a set of tests, a procedure to perform tests, and a criterion for interpreting the execution of tests.

The simplest way to represent tests is through process terms. Experiments are conducted by making tests interact with process terms under test by means of a parallel composition operator that enforces synchronization on the set $Name_v$ of all visible action names. In order to establish whether a test has been passed or not, we include in the test syntax a success action ω. The meaning is that success is achieved whenever a point is reached in which ω can be performed. We denote by $\mathbb{T}$ the set of tests resulting from process terms of $\mathbb{P}$ possibly including occurrences of ω.

Testing equivalence is defined as the intersection of two behavioral equivalences, which are the kernels of two preorders related to the possibility and the necessity of passing tests, respectively. According to the first preorder, process term P_1 is less than or equal to process term P_2 iff, for every test, whenever P_1 is able to pass the test, then also P_2 is able to pass the test. In the case of the second preorder, P_1 is less than or equal to P_2 iff, for every test, whenever P_1 cannot fail the test, then also P_2 cannot fail the test. In addition to being natural, this distinction introduces sensitivity to divergence caused by the endless execution of τ-actions.

In order to formalize the possibility and the necessity of passing tests, we have to consider the computations obtained by putting a process term under test in parallel with a test. In general, by computation of a process term we mean a sequence of transitions that can be executed starting from the process term. We say that a computation is maximal iff the last state it traverses has no outgoing transitions. We denote by $\mathscr{C}_m(P)$ the set of maximal computations of $P \in \mathbb{P}$.

This terminology applies to any interaction system $P \|_{Name_v} T$ where $P \in \mathbb{P}$ and $T \in \mathbb{T}$. Each state of $[\![P\|_{Name_v} T]\!]$ is called a configuration, is formed by a process projection and a test projection, and is successful iff its test projection can perform ω. We say that a test-driven computation of P with respect to T – which is a computation of $P\|_{Name_v} T$ – is successful iff it traverses a successful configuration.

Definition 1.14. Let $P \in \mathbb{P}$ and $T \in \mathbb{T}$. We say that:

- P may pass T iff at least one computation in $\mathscr{C}_{\mathrm{m}}(P \|_{Name_v} T)$ is successful.
- P must pass T iff all computations in $\mathscr{C}_{\mathrm{m}}(P \|_{Name_v} T)$ are successful.

Definition 1.15. Let $P_1, P_2 \in \mathbb{P}$. We say that:

- P_1 is may-testing less than P_2, written $P_1 \precsim_{\mathrm{T,may}} P_2$, iff for all tests $T \in \mathbb{T}$, whenever P_1 may pass T, then P_2 may pass T.
- P_1 is must-testing less than P_2, written $P_1 \precsim_{\mathrm{T,must}} P_2$, iff for all tests $T \in \mathbb{T}$, whenever P_1 must pass T, then P_2 must pass T.

Definition 1.16. Let $P_1, P_2 \in \mathbb{P}$. We say that:

- P_1 is may-testing equivalent to P_2, written $P_1 \approx_{\mathrm{T,may}} P_2$, iff $P_1 \precsim_{\mathrm{T,may}} P_2$ and $P_2 \precsim_{\mathrm{T,may}} P_1$.
- P_1 is must-testing equivalent to P_2, written $P_1 \approx_{\mathrm{T,must}} P_2$, iff $P_1 \precsim_{\mathrm{T,must}} P_2$ and $P_2 \precsim_{\mathrm{T,must}} P_1$.
- P_1 is testing equivalent to P_2, written $P_1 \approx_{\mathrm{T}} P_2$, iff $P_1 \approx_{\mathrm{T,may}} P_2 \wedge P_1 \approx_{\mathrm{T,must}} P_2$.

1.5.2 Conditions and Characterizations

We now present an alternative characterization of $\precsim_{\mathrm{T,may}}$ and two alternative characterizations of $\precsim_{\mathrm{T,must}}$ (and hence of $\approx_{\mathrm{T}}$), which fully abstract from comparing process term behavior in response to tests. All of them are concerned with sequences of visible actions. Their linearity simplifies equivalence checking. In fact, while it is sufficient to find a suitable test in order to prove that two process terms are not testing equivalent, all tests have to be considered for demonstrating that two process terms are testing equivalent, with tests being arbitrarily branching.

The three characterizations are formalized by resorting to the extended transition relation $\Longrightarrow$. We start with the alternative characterization of $\precsim_{\mathrm{T,may}}$.

Theorem 1.6. Let $P_1, P_2 \in \mathbb{P}$. Then $P_1 \precsim_{\mathrm{T,may}} P_2$ iff, for all $a_1 \ldots a_n \in (Name_v)^*$ with $n \in \mathbb{N}_{>0}$, whenever $P_1 \overset{\tau^* a_1 \ldots \tau^* a_n}{=\!=\!=\!=\!=\!\Longrightarrow} P_1'$, then $P_2 \overset{\tau^* a_1 \ldots \tau^* a_n}{=\!=\!=\!=\!=\!\Longrightarrow} P_2'$ for some $P_1', P_2' \in \mathbb{P}$.

Unlike the operational definition based on tests, the two alternative characterizations of $\precsim_{\mathrm{T,must}}$ make sensitivity to divergence explicit.

Definition 1.17. Let $P \in \mathbb{P}$. We say that P diverges, written $P \Uparrow$, if P has an infinite computation of τ-transitions only, otherwise the convergence of P upon performing $\alpha \in (Name_v)^*$ is defined by induction on the syntactical structure of α as follows:

$P \Downarrow \varepsilon$	if $P \not\Uparrow$
$P \Downarrow a \circ \alpha'$	if $P \not\Uparrow$ and for all $P' \in \mathbb{P}$, whenever $P \overset{\tau^* a}{=\!=\!=\!\Longrightarrow} P'$, then $P' \Downarrow \alpha'$

where ε is the empty sequence of visible actions.

The first characterization of $\precsim_{\mathrm{T,must}}$ relies on the process terms reached after performing a sequence of visible actions and their capabilities with respect to enabling certain visible actions. In the following, we use $\_ \circ \_$ for sequence concatenation.

Definition 1.18. Let $P \in \mathbb{P}$ and $\alpha \in (Name_v)^*$. The set of process terms that P can reach after performing α is defined by induction on the syntactical structure of α as follows:

$$after(P, \alpha) = \begin{cases} \{P\} & \text{if } \alpha \equiv \varepsilon \\ \displaystyle\bigcup_{P \stackrel{\tau^* a}{\Longrightarrow} P'} after(P', \alpha') & \text{if } \alpha \equiv a \circ \alpha' \end{cases}$$

This is lifted to subsets of $\mathbb{P}$ by taking the union over their process terms.

Definition 1.19. Let $P \in \mathbb{P}$ and $\mathcal{E} \subseteq Name_v$ finite. We say that P must execute some action of $\mathcal{E}$ iff for all $P' \in \mathbb{P}$, whenever $P \stackrel{\tau^*}{\Longrightarrow} P'$, then there exist $a \in \mathcal{E}$ and $P'' \in \mathbb{P}$ such that $P' \stackrel{\tau^* a}{\Longrightarrow} P''$. We say that a subset of $\mathbb{P}$ must execute some action of $\mathcal{E}$ iff each of its process terms must execute some action of $\mathcal{E}$.

Theorem 1.7. Let $P_1, P_2 \in \mathbb{P}$. Then $P_1 \precsim_{\mathrm{T,must}} P_2$ iff for all $\alpha \in (Name_v)^*$, whenever $P_1 \Downarrow \alpha$, then:

- $P_2 \Downarrow \alpha$
- For all $\mathcal{E} \subseteq Name_v$ finite, if $after(P_1, \alpha)$ must execute some action of $\mathcal{E}$, then $after(P_2, \alpha)$ must execute some action of $\mathcal{E}$

Corollary 1.1. Let $P_1, P_2 \in \mathbb{P}$. Then $P_1 \approx_{\mathrm{T}} P_2$ iff for all $\alpha \in (Name_v)^*$:

- If $\alpha \equiv a_1 \ldots a_n$ with $n \in \mathbb{N}_{>0}$, then $P_1 \stackrel{\tau^* a_1 \ldots \tau^* a_n}{\Longrightarrow} P_1'$ iff $P_2 \stackrel{\tau^* a_1 \ldots \tau^* a_n}{\Longrightarrow} P_2'$ for some $P_1', P_2' \in \mathbb{P}$
- $P_1 \Downarrow \alpha$ iff $P_2 \Downarrow \alpha$ and, if both converge upon performing α, then for all $\mathcal{E} \subseteq Name_v$ finite it holds that $after(P_1, \alpha)$ must execute some action of $\mathcal{E}$ iff $after(P_2, \alpha)$ must execute some action of $\mathcal{E}$

A consequence of the alternative characterization of Corollary 1.1 is the identification of a set of canonical tests, i.e., a set of tests that are necessary and sufficient in order to establish whether two process terms are testing equivalent. Each of these canonical tests admits a main computation leading to a final state, which either denotes failure or reaches success in one step after executing any of its actions. The intermediate states and the final state are able to detect divergence through $\tau . \omega . \underline{0}$.

Definition 1.20. The set $\mathbb{T}_{c,may}$ of canonical may-tests is generated by the following syntax:

$$T ::= \omega . \underline{0} \mid a . T$$

where $a \in Name_v$. The set $\mathbb{T}_{c,must}$ of canonical must-tests is generated by the following syntax:

$$T ::= \underline{0} \mid \sum_{a \in \mathcal{E}} a . \omega . \underline{0} \mid b . T + \tau . \omega . \underline{0} \mid \tau . \omega . \underline{0}$$

where $\mathcal{E} \subseteq Name_v$ finite and $b \in Name_v$. We denote by $\mathbb{T}_c = \mathbb{T}_{c,may} \cup \mathbb{T}_{c,must}$ the set of canonical tests.

Corollary 1.2. *Let $P_1, P_2 \in \mathbb{P}$. Then:*

- $P_1 \precsim_{T,may} P_2$ *iff for all $T \in \mathbb{T}_{c,may}$, whenever P_1 may pass T, then P_2 may pass T.*
- $P_1 \precsim_{T,must} P_2$ *iff for all $T \in \mathbb{T}_{c,must}$, whenever P_1 must pass T, then P_2 must pass T.*
- $P_1 \approx_T P_2$ *iff for all $T \in \mathbb{T}_c$:*

  - *P_1 may pass T iff P_2 may pass T.*
  - *P_1 must pass T iff P_2 must pass T.*

The second characterization of $\precsim_{T,must}$ directly focuses on the family of sets of visible actions enabled by the stable process terms reached after performing a sequence of visible actions. Given $P \in \mathbb{P}$, we denote by *enabled*(P) the set of actions enabled by P, which is finite as P is finitely branching. In our setting, *enabled*(P) coincides with the set of actions that can be performed by P, but in general it may contain further actions present in P that are preempted by other actions of P.

Definition 1.21. Let $P \in \mathbb{P}$ and $\alpha \in (Name_v)^*$. The acceptance set of P after performing α is defined as follows:

$$AS(P,\alpha) = \begin{cases} \{enabled(P') \mid P \xrightarrow{\tau^*} P' \wedge P' \in \mathbb{P}_s\} & \text{if } \alpha \equiv \varepsilon \\ \{enabled(P') \mid P \xrightarrow{\tau^* a_1 \ldots \tau^* a_n \tau^*} P' \wedge P' \in \mathbb{P}_s\} & \text{if } \alpha \equiv a_1 \ldots a_n \end{cases}$$

where $\mathbb{P}_s$ is the set of stable process terms of $\mathbb{P}$ and $n \in \mathbb{N}_{>0}$. We call minimized version of $AS(P,\alpha)$, written $AS_{min}(P,\alpha)$, the acceptance set obtained from $AS(P,\alpha)$ by removing each of its elements that contains some of the other elements.

Definition 1.22. Let $AS_1, AS_2 \subseteq 2^{Name_v}$. We say that AS_1 is less nondeterministic than AS_2, written $AS_1 \subset\subset AS_2$, iff for each element of AS_1 there exists an element of AS_2 that is contained in the first element.

Theorem 1.8. *Let $P_1, P_2 \in \mathbb{P}$. Then $P_1 \precsim_{T,must} P_2$ iff for all $\alpha \in (Name_v)^*$, whenever $P_1 \Downarrow \alpha$, then $P_2 \Downarrow \alpha$ and $AS(P_2,\alpha) \subset\subset AS(P_1,\alpha)$.*

Corollary 1.3. *Let $P_1, P_2 \in \mathbb{P}$. Then $P_1 \approx_T P_2$ iff for all $\alpha \in (Name_v)^*$:*

- *If $\alpha \equiv a_1 \ldots a_n$ with $n \in \mathbb{N}_{>0}$, then $P_1 \xrightarrow{\tau^* a_1 \ldots \tau^* a_n} P_1'$ iff $P_2 \xrightarrow{\tau^* a_1 \ldots \tau^* a_n} P_2'$ for some $P_1', P_2' \in \mathbb{P}$*
- *$P_1 \Downarrow \alpha$ iff $P_2 \Downarrow \alpha$ and, if both converge upon performing α, then $AS_{min}(P_1,\alpha) = AS_{min}(P_2,\alpha)$*

Example 1.5. We exploit the alternative characterization of Corollary 1.3 in order to prove that $ProdCons_{0/2}$, $PC_{conc,2}$, and $PC_{pipe,2}$ – which are defined in Examples 1.1, 1.3, and 1.4, respectively – are testing equivalent.

Firstly, we note that they are may-testing equivalent. In fact, the only sequences of visible actions that all the three process constants can perform are the prefixes of the strings that comply with the following regular expression:

$$(deposit \circ (deposit \circ withdraw)^* \circ withdraw)^*$$

Secondly, observed that none of the states of $[\![ProdCons_{0/2}]\!]$, $[\![PC_{conc,2}]\!]$, and $[\![PC_{pipe,2}]\!]$ diverges, the three process constants turn out to be must-testing equivalent. In fact, we have that:

- After performing any sequence of visible actions corresponding to a string that complies with the above mentioned regular expression, the acceptance set is $\{\{deposit\}\}$ for all the reached stable states
- After performing one of the sequences of visible actions of the previous point followed by $deposit$, the acceptance set is $\{\{deposit, withdraw\}\}$ for all the reached stable states
- After performing one of the sequences of visible actions of the previous point followed by another $deposit$, the acceptance set is $\{\{withdraw\}\}$ for all the reached stable states

1.5.3 Congruence Property

Testing equivalence is a congruence with respect to the action prefix operator, all the static operators of PC, and recursion.

Theorem 1.9. Let $P_1, P_2 \in \mathbb{P}$. Whenever $P_1 \approx_T P_2$, then:

1. $a . P_1 \approx_T a . P_2$ for all $a \in Name$.
2. $P_1 \|_S P \approx_T P_2 \|_S P$ and $P \|_S P_1 \approx_T P \|_S P_2$ for all $P \in \mathbb{P}$ and $S \subseteq Name_v$.
3. $P_1/H \approx_T P_2/H$ for all $H \subseteq Name_v$.
4. $P_1 \backslash L \approx_T P_2 \backslash L$ for all $L \subseteq Name_v$.
5. $P_1[\varphi] \approx_T P_2[\varphi]$ for all $\varphi \in Relab$.

Definition 1.23. Let $P_1, P_2 \in \mathscr{PL}$ be guarded process terms containing free occurrences of $k \in \mathbb{N}$ process variables $X_1, \ldots, X_k \in Var$ at most. We define $P_1 \approx_T P_2$ iff $P_1\{Q_i \hookrightarrow X_i \mid 1 \le i \le k\} \approx_T P_2\{Q_i \hookrightarrow X_i \mid 1 \le i \le k\}$ for all $Q_1, \ldots, Q_k \in \mathbb{P}$.

Theorem 1.10. Let $P_1, P_2 \in \mathscr{PL}$ be guarded process terms containing free occurrences of $k \in \mathbb{N}$ process variables $X_1, \ldots, X_k \in Var$ at most. Whenever $P_1 \approx_T P_2$, then $recX : P_1 \approx_T recX : P_2$ for all $X \in Var$.

The congruence problem with respect to the alternative composition operator is similar to the one mentioned for $\approx_B$ and is caused by $\approx_{T,must}$. As an example, $a . \underline{0} \approx_{T,must} \tau . a . \underline{0}$, but these two process terms can be distinguished if placed in the context of $\_ + b . \underline{0}$. In fact, $a . \underline{0} + b . \underline{0}$ must pass $b . \omega . \underline{0}$ because their interaction system has a single maximal computation, which is formed by a b-transition and is successful. In contrast, $\tau . a . \underline{0} + b . \underline{0}$ can fail $b . \omega . \underline{0}$ because their interaction system has an unsuccessful maximal computation formed by a τ-transition. Also in this case, congruence with respect to the alternative composition operator can be restored by enforcing a matching on initial τ-actions, which has to be introduced in the definition of $\approx_{T,must}$.

Definition 1.24. Let $P_1, P_2 \in \mathbb{P}$. We say that:

- P_1 is must-testing congruent to P_2, written $P_1 \approx_{T,must}^c P_2$, iff $P_1 + P \approx_{T,must} P_2 + P$
  for all $P \in \mathbb{P}$.
- P_1 is testing congruent to P_2, written $P_1 \approx_T^c P_2$, iff $P_1 \approx_{T,may} P_2 \wedge P_1 \approx_{T,must}^c P_2$.

Theorem 1.11. Let $P_1, P_2 \in \mathbb{P}$. Then, $P_1 \approx_T^c P_2$ iff the following condition holds in addition to the two conditions of Corollary 1.1 or 1.3:

- $P_1 \not\Uparrow$ iff $P_2 \not\Uparrow$ and, if both do not diverge, then $P_1 \overset{\tau}{\longrightarrow} P_1'$ iff $P_2 \overset{\tau}{\longrightarrow} P_2'$ for some
  $P_1', P_2' \in \mathbb{P}$.

Theorem 1.12. $\approx_T^c$ (resp. $\approx_{T,must}^c$) is the largest congruence contained in $\approx_T$ (resp. $\approx_{T,must}$).

1.5.4 Sound and Complete Axiomatization

Testing congruence has a sound and complete axiomatization over nonrecursive (hence nondivergent) process terms, given by the set $\mathscr{X}_T^c$ of inequational laws of Table 1.4.

Due to the presence of inequalities, the corresponding deduction system is equipped with an additional rule for inferring $P_1 = P_2$ from $P_1 \sqsubseteq P_2$ and $P_2 \sqsubseteq P_1$. We also mention that a sound and complete axiomatization for $\approx_{T,must}^c$ can be obtained by adding axiom $\tau . P_1 + \tau . P_2 \sqsubseteq P_1$. On the other hand, a sound and complete axiomatization for $\approx_{T,may}$ can be obtained by adding axiom $P_1 \sqsubseteq \tau . P_1 + \tau . P_2$.

The only difference with respect to the equational laws for $\sim_B$ shown in Table 1.2 is given by the four additional axioms $\mathscr{X}_{T,5}^c$ to $\mathscr{X}_{T,8}^c$. They are related to τ-actions and imply the τ-laws for $\approx_B^c$ shown in Table 1.3. Moreover, they imply additional laws stating the extent to which the branching structure of process terms is respected by $\approx_T$. As an example, for $P \not\approx_B Q$ we have:

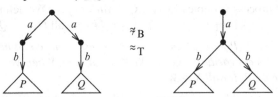

As can be noted, $\approx_B$ is highly sensitive to branching points, whereas $\approx_T$ allows choices to be deferred. This happens in the case of branches that start with the same action (see the two a-branches on the left-hand side) and are followed by the same set of actions (see $\{b\}$ after each of the two a-branches).

Theorem 1.13. Let $P_1, P_2 \in \mathbb{P}$ be nonrecursive. Then:

$$P_1 \approx_T^c P_2 \iff \mathscr{X}_T^c \vdash P_1 = P_2$$

Table 1.4 Inequational laws for $\approx_{\mathrm{T}}^{\mathrm{c}}$

$(\mathscr{X}_{\mathrm{T},1}^{\mathrm{c}})$	$P_1 + P_2 = P_2 + P_1$	
$(\mathscr{X}_{\mathrm{T},2}^{\mathrm{c}})$	$(P_1 + P_2) + P_3 = P_1 + (P_2 + P_3)$	
$(\mathscr{X}_{\mathrm{T},3}^{\mathrm{c}})$	$P + \underline{0} = P$	
$(\mathscr{X}_{\mathrm{T},4}^{\mathrm{c}})$	$P + P = P$	
$(\mathscr{X}_{\mathrm{T},5}^{\mathrm{c}})$	$a.P_1 + a.P_2 = a.(\tau.P_1 + \tau.P_2)$	
$(\mathscr{X}_{\mathrm{T},6}^{\mathrm{c}})$	$a.P_1 + \tau.(a.P_2 + P_3) = \tau.(a.P_1 + a.P_2 + P_3)$	
$(\mathscr{X}_{\mathrm{T},7}^{\mathrm{c}})$	$\tau.P \sqsubseteq P$	
$(\mathscr{X}_{\mathrm{T},8}^{\mathrm{c}})$	$P_1 + \tau.P_2 \sqsubseteq \tau.(P_1 + P_2)$	

$$(\mathscr{X}_{\mathrm{T},9}^{\mathrm{c}}) \quad \sum_{i \in I} a_i.P_i \parallel_S \sum_{j \in J} b_j.Q_j = \sum_{k \in I, a_k \notin S} a_k.\left(P_k \parallel_S \sum_{j \in J} b_j.Q_j\right)$$
$$+ \sum_{h \in J, b_h \notin S} b_h.\left(\sum_{i \in I} a_i.P_i \parallel_S Q_h\right)$$
$$+ \sum_{k \in I, a_k \in S} \sum_{h \in J, b_h = a_k} a_k.(P_k \parallel_S Q_h)$$

$$(\mathscr{X}_{\mathrm{T},10}^{\mathrm{c}}) \quad \sum_{i \in I} a_i.P_i \parallel_S \underline{0} = \sum_{k \in I, a_k \notin S} a_k.P_k$$

$$(\mathscr{X}_{\mathrm{T},11}^{\mathrm{c}}) \quad \underline{0} \parallel_S \sum_{j \in J} b_j.Q_j = \sum_{h \in J, b_h \notin S} b_h.Q_h$$

$$(\mathscr{X}_{\mathrm{T},12}^{\mathrm{c}}) \quad \underline{0} \parallel_S \underline{0} = \underline{0}$$

$(\mathscr{X}_{\mathrm{T},13}^{\mathrm{c}})$	$\underline{0}/H = \underline{0}$	
$(\mathscr{X}_{\mathrm{T},14}^{\mathrm{c}})$	$(a.P)/H = \tau.(P/H)$	if $a \in H$
$(\mathscr{X}_{\mathrm{T},15}^{\mathrm{c}})$	$(a.P)/H = a.(P/H)$	if $a \notin H$
$(\mathscr{X}_{\mathrm{T},16}^{\mathrm{c}})$	$(P_1 + P_2)/H = P_1/H + P_2/H$	
$(\mathscr{X}_{\mathrm{T},17}^{\mathrm{c}})$	$\underline{0} \backslash L = \underline{0}$	
$(\mathscr{X}_{\mathrm{T},18}^{\mathrm{c}})$	$(a.P) \backslash L = \underline{0}$	if $a \in L$
$(\mathscr{X}_{\mathrm{T},19}^{\mathrm{c}})$	$(a.P) \backslash L = a.(P \backslash L)$	if $a \notin L$
$(\mathscr{X}_{\mathrm{T},20}^{\mathrm{c}})$	$(P_1 + P_2) \backslash L = P_1 \backslash L + P_2 \backslash L$	
$(\mathscr{X}_{\mathrm{T},21}^{\mathrm{c}})$	$\underline{0}[\varphi] = \underline{0}$	
$(\mathscr{X}_{\mathrm{T},22}^{\mathrm{c}})$	$(a.P)[\varphi] = \varphi(a).(P[\varphi])$	
$(\mathscr{X}_{\mathrm{T},23}^{\mathrm{c}})$	$(P_1 + P_2)[\varphi] = P_1[\varphi] + P_2[\varphi]$	

1.5.5 Modal Logic Characterization

Testing equivalence has a modal logic characterization based on a modal language that, in accordance with the alternative characterization of Corollary 1.1, permits to check whether certain visible actions may be executed or cannot be refused after performing a given sequence of visible actions.

This modal language differs from HML because it has two kinds of formula and comprises a restricted set of logical operators, consistent with the decreased discriminating power with respect to $\sim_{\mathrm{B}}$ as regards branching points. In the top-level kind of formula, we have a modal operator on sequences of visible actions. In the bottom-level kind of formula, we have only true, disjunction, and diamond with no continuation for visible actions. In particular, note that negation is not included.

Definition 1.25. The set of formulas of the modal language $\mathscr{ML}_T$ is generated by the following syntax:

$$
\begin{aligned}
\phi &::= \lhd \alpha \rhd \psi \\
\psi &::= \text{true} \mid \psi \vee \psi \mid \langle\!\langle a \rangle\!\rangle
\end{aligned}
$$

where $\alpha \in (Name_v)^*$ and $a \in Name_v$.

Another important difference with respect to HML is the presence of two satisfaction relations instead of one. Consistent with the nature of $\approx_T$, these relations formalize the fact that a process term may satisfy or cannot refuse to satisfy, respectively, a bottom-level formula after executing a sequence of visible actions.

Definition 1.26. The may-satisfaction relation $\models_{T,may}$ and the must-satisfaction relation $\models_{T,must}$ of $\mathscr{ML}_T$ over $\mathbb{P}$ are defined by induction on the syntactical structure of formulas as follows:

P	$\models_{T,may}$	$\lhd a_1 \ldots a_n \rhd \psi$	if there exists $P' \in \mathbb{P}$ such that $P \xrightarrow{\tau^* a_1 \ldots \tau^* a_n} P'$ and $P' \models_{T,may} \psi$
P'	$\models_{T,may}$	true	
P'	$\models_{T,may}$	$\psi_1 \vee \psi_2$	if $P' \models_{T,may} \psi_1$ or $P' \models_{T,may} \psi_2$
P'	$\models_{T,may}$	$\langle\!\langle a \rangle\!\rangle$	if $P' \xrightarrow{\tau^* a} P''$ for some $P'' \in \mathbb{P}$
P	$\models_{T,must}$	$\lhd a_1 \ldots a_n \rhd \psi$	if $P \Downarrow a_1 \ldots a_n$ and for all $P' \in \mathbb{P}$, whenever $P \xrightarrow{\tau^* a_1 \ldots \tau^* a_n} P'$, then $P' \models_{T,must} \psi$
P'	$\models_{T,must}$	true	
P'	$\models_{T,must}$	$\psi_1 \vee \psi_2$	if $P' \models_{T,must} \psi_1$ or $P' \models_{T,must} \psi_2$
P'	$\models_{T,must}$	$\langle\!\langle a \rangle\!\rangle$	if for all $P'' \in \mathbb{P}$, whenever $P' \xrightarrow{\tau^*} P''$, then $P'' \xrightarrow{\tau^* a} P'''$ for some $P''' \in \mathbb{P}$

where $a_1 \ldots a_n \equiv \varepsilon$ and $P' \equiv P$ when $n = 0$.

Theorem 1.14. *Let $P_1, P_2 \in \mathbb{P}$. Then:*

$$
\begin{aligned}
P_1 \approx_T P_2 \iff (\forall \phi \in \mathscr{ML}_T . \, & P_1 \models_{T,may} \phi \iff P_2 \models_{T,may} \phi \\
\wedge \, & P_1 \models_{T,must} \phi \iff P_2 \models_{T,must} \phi)
\end{aligned}
$$

1.5.6 Verification Algorithm

The problem of deciding testing equivalence is PSPACE-complete and can be solved by exploiting the alternative characterization of Corollary 1.3 through the application of the verification algorithm for $\sim_B$ to suitable variants of labeled transition systems.

These are called acceptance graphs and are a particular class of deterministic labeled transition systems, so they have no τ-transitions and none of their states has multiple transitions labeled with the same action. Every state of an acceptance graph is labeled with two pieces of information, which are a Boolean and a family of sets of visible actions, respectively. The Boolean is true iff the family of sets of visible actions is not empty. Moreover, if the Boolean labeling a state is false, then the Booleans labeling the states reached by the transitions leaving the considered state are all false.

Given $P_1, P_2 \in \mathbb{P}$ finite state, the algorithm for checking whether $P_1 \approx_T P_2$ is obtained by having the verification algorithm for $\sim_B$ preceded by the preprocessing step below, where $closure_\tau(P) = \{P' \in \mathbb{P} \mid P \stackrel{\tau^*}{\Longrightarrow} P'\}$ for any $P \in \mathbb{P}$:

0. Build the acceptance graph associated with $[\![P_i]\!]$ for $i = 1, 2$:

    (a) The initial state of the acceptance graph is the pair $(closure_\tau(P_i), \text{true})$.
    (b) Initialize a list of states with the above initial state as its only element.
    (c) While the list of states is not empty, select a state $(closure_\tau(P), tv)$ and remove it from the list after constructing its labels and deriving its outgoing transitions:

    - Set the Boolean label bl of $(closure_\tau(P), tv)$ to the truth value tv if none of the states in $closure_\tau(P)$ diverges, false otherwise.
    - Change tv to bl.
    - If bl is true, then set the other label of $(closure_\tau(P), bl)$ to the minimized version of $\{enabled(P') \mid P' \in closure_\tau(P) \cap \mathbb{P}_s\}$, $\emptyset$ otherwise.
    - For each $a \in Name_v$ enabled in some state of $closure_\tau(P)$:
      - Build a transition labeled with a that goes from $(closure_\tau(P), bl)$ to $(closure_\tau(\{Q' \in \mathbb{P} \mid \exists Q \in closure_\tau(P). Q \stackrel{a}{\longrightarrow} Q'\}), bl)$.
      - Insert $(closure_\tau(\{Q' \in \mathbb{P} \mid \exists Q \in closure_\tau(P). Q \stackrel{a}{\longrightarrow} Q'\}), bl)$ into the list of states if it has not been encountered yet.

We also need to modify steps 1 and 2 of the verification algorithm for $\sim_B$ as follows:

1′. Build an initial partition with a single class for each set of states of the acceptance graphs associated with $[\![P_1]\!]$ and $[\![P_2]\!]$ that are labeled with the same family of sets of visible actions.
2′. Initialize a list of splitters with all the above classes as its only elements.

1.6 Trace Equivalence

Trace equivalence relates two process terms whenever they are able to perform the same computations. In this section, we provide the definition of trace equivalence over $\mathbb{P}$ [57]. Then, we show that trace equivalence is a congruence and we present its sound and complete axiomatization, its modal logic characterization, and its verification algorithm [57, 69].

1.6.1 Definition of the Behavioral Equivalence

The basic idea behind trace equivalence is to compare process terms on the basis of their traces, i.e., the sequences of visible actions that they can execute. In this way, the branching structure of process terms is completely overridden.

Definition 1.27. Let $P \in \mathbb{P}$. The trace set of P is defined as follows:

$$TS(P) = \{\varepsilon\} \cup \{a_1 \ldots a_n \in (Name_v)^* \mid n \in \mathbb{N}_{>0} \wedge \exists P' \in \mathbb{P}.P \xrightarrow{\tau^* a_1 \ldots \tau^* a_n} P'\}$$

where ε is the empty trace.

Definition 1.28. Let $P_1, P_2 \in \mathbb{P}$. We say that P_1 is trace equivalent to P_2, written $P_1 \approx_{Tr} P_2$, iff:

$$TS(P_1) = TS(P_2)$$

It is easy to see that $\approx_{Tr}$ coincides with language equivalence, provided that we assume that $Name_v$ is our alphabet and that all the states of the labeled transition systems underlying process terms are accepting. We also point out that $\approx_{Tr}$ does not preserve deadlock. For instance, the deadlock-free process term $rec X : a.X$ is trace equivalent to the process term $rec X : (a.X + a.\underline{0})$, which can instead deadlock.

Example 1.6. Let us consider again $ProdCons_{0/2}$, $PC_{conc,2}$, and $PC_{pipe,2}$, which are defined in Examples 1.1, 1.3, and 1.4, respectively. As already observed in Example 1.5, the only sequences of visible actions that all the three process constants can perform are the prefixes of the strings that comply with the following regular expression:

$$(deposit \circ (deposit \circ withdraw)^* \circ withdraw)^*$$

Hence, we can immediately conclude that $ProdCons_{0/2} \approx_{Tr} PC_{conc,2} \approx_{Tr} PC_{pipe,2}$.

1.6.2 Congruence Property

Trace equivalence is a congruence with respect to all the dynamic and static operators of PC as well as recursion.

Theorem 1.15. *Let $P_1, P_2 \in \mathbb{P}$. Whenever $P_1 \approx_{Tr} P_2$, then:*

1. $a.P_1 \approx_{Tr} a.P_2$ *for all $a \in Name$.*
2. $P_1 + P \approx_{Tr} P_2 + P$ *and $P + P_1 \approx_{Tr} P + P_2$ for all $P \in \mathbb{P}$.*
3. $P_1 \|_S P \approx_{Tr} P_2 \|_S P$ *and $P \|_S P_1 \approx_{Tr} P \|_S P_2$ for all $P \in \mathbb{P}$ and $S \subseteq Name_v$.*
4. $P_1/H \approx_{Tr} P_2/H$ *for all $H \subseteq Name_v$.*
5. $P_1 \backslash L \approx_{Tr} P_2 \backslash L$ *for all $L \subseteq Name_v$.*
6. $P_1[\varphi] \approx_{Tr} P_2[\varphi]$ *for all $\varphi \in Relab$.*

We observe that, although it abstracts from τ-actions, $\approx_{Tr}$ does not incur the congruence problem of $\approx_B$ with respect to the alternative composition operator. The reason is the insensitivity of $\approx_{Tr}$ to the branching structure of process terms.

Definition 1.29. Let $P_1, P_2 \in \mathscr{PL}$ be guarded process terms containing free occurrences of $k \in \mathbb{N}$ process variables $X_1, \ldots, X_k \in Var$ at most. We define $P_1 \approx_{Tr} P_2$ iff $P_1\{Q_i \hookrightarrow X_i \mid 1 \leq i \leq k\} \approx_{Tr} P_2\{Q_i \hookrightarrow X_i \mid 1 \leq i \leq k\}$ for all $Q_1, \ldots, Q_k \in \mathbb{P}$.

Theorem 1.16. Let $P_1, P_2 \in \mathscr{PL}$ be guarded process terms containing free occurrences of $k \in \mathbb{N}$ process variables $X_1, \ldots, X_k \in Var$ at most. Whenever $P_1 \approx_{Tr} P_2$, then $rec\,X : P_1 \approx_{Tr} rec\,X : P_2$ for all $X \in Var$.

1.6.3 Sound and Complete Axiomatization

Trace equivalence has a sound and complete axiomatization over nonrecursive process terms, given by the set $\mathscr{X}_{Tr}$ of equational laws of Table 1.5.

The axioms characterizing $\approx_{Tr}$ are $\mathscr{X}_{Tr,5}$ and $\mathscr{X}_{Tr,6}$, which are not included in the equational laws for $\sim_B$ shown in Table 1.2 and replace the inequational laws $\mathscr{X}_{T,5}^c$ to $\mathscr{X}_{T,8}^c$ for $\approx_T^c$ shown in Table 1.4.

While axiom $\mathscr{X}_{Tr,6}$ states that $\approx_{Tr}$ is able to abstract from any τ-action, axiom $\mathscr{X}_{Tr,5}$ states that $\approx_{Tr}$ does not respect at all the branching structure of process terms. As an example, for $b \neq d$ we have:

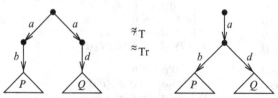

As can be noted, $\approx_{Tr}$ permits to postpone all choices whose branches start with the same action.

Theorem 1.17. Let $P_1, P_2 \in \mathbb{P}$ be nonrecursive. Then:

$$P_1 \approx_{Tr} P_2 \iff \mathscr{X}_{Tr} \vdash P_1 = P_2$$

1.6.4 Modal Logic Characterization

Trace equivalence has a modal logic characterization based on a variant of HML in which diamond is weakened as for $\approx_B$ and negation and conjunction are not present. Its satisfaction relation $\models_{Tr}$ is thus defined as $\models_B$ when restricted to its formulas.

Table 1.5 Equational laws for $\approx_{\mathrm{Tr}}$

$(\mathscr{X}_{\mathrm{Tr},1})$	$P_1 + P_2 = P_2 + P_1$	
$(\mathscr{X}_{\mathrm{Tr},2})$	$(P_1 + P_2) + P_3 = P_1 + (P_2 + P_3)$	
$(\mathscr{X}_{\mathrm{Tr},3})$	$P + \underline{0} = P$	
$(\mathscr{X}_{\mathrm{Tr},4})$	$P + P = P$	
$(\mathscr{X}_{\mathrm{Tr},5})$	$a.P_1 + a.P_2 = a.(P_1 + P_2)$	
$(\mathscr{X}_{\mathrm{Tr},6})$	$\tau.P = P$	

$$(\mathscr{X}_{\mathrm{Tr},7}) \quad \sum_{i \in I} a_i.P_i \parallel_S \sum_{j \in J} b_j.Q_j = \sum_{k \in I, a_k \notin S} a_k.\left(P_k \parallel_S \sum_{j \in J} b_j.Q_j\right)$$
$$+ \sum_{h \in J, b_h \notin S} b_h.\left(\sum_{i \in I} a_i.P_i \parallel_S Q_h\right)$$
$$+ \sum_{k \in I, a_k \in S} \sum_{h \in J, b_h = a_k} a_k.(P_k \parallel_S Q_h)$$

$$(\mathscr{X}_{\mathrm{Tr},8}) \quad \sum_{i \in I} a_i.P_i \parallel_S \underline{0} = \sum_{k \in I, a_k \notin S} a_k.P_k$$

$$(\mathscr{X}_{\mathrm{Tr},9}) \quad \underline{0} \parallel_S \sum_{j \in J} b_j.Q_j = \sum_{h \in J, b_h \notin S} b_h.Q_h$$

$(\mathscr{X}_{\mathrm{Tr},10})$	$\underline{0} \parallel_S \underline{0} = \underline{0}$	
$(\mathscr{X}_{\mathrm{Tr},11})$	$\underline{0}/H = \underline{0}$	
$(\mathscr{X}_{\mathrm{Tr},12})$	$(a.P)/H = \tau.(P/H)$	if $a \in H$
$(\mathscr{X}_{\mathrm{Tr},13})$	$(a.P)/H = a.(P/H)$	if $a \notin H$
$(\mathscr{X}_{\mathrm{Tr},14})$	$(P_1 + P_2)/H = P_1/H + P_2/H$	
$(\mathscr{X}_{\mathrm{Tr},15})$	$\underline{0} \backslash L = \underline{0}$	
$(\mathscr{X}_{\mathrm{Tr},16})$	$(a.P)\backslash L = \underline{0}$	if $a \in L$
$(\mathscr{X}_{\mathrm{Tr},17})$	$(a.P)\backslash L = a.(P\backslash L)$	if $a \notin L$
$(\mathscr{X}_{\mathrm{Tr},18})$	$(P_1 + P_2)\backslash L = P_1 \backslash L + P_2 \backslash L$	
$(\mathscr{X}_{\mathrm{Tr},19})$	$\underline{0}[\varphi] = \underline{0}$	
$(\mathscr{X}_{\mathrm{Tr},20})$	$(a.P)[\varphi] = \varphi(a).(P[\varphi])$	
$(\mathscr{X}_{\mathrm{Tr},21})$	$(P_1 + P_2)[\varphi] = P_1[\varphi] + P_2[\varphi]$	

Definition 1.30. The set of formulas of the modal language $\mathscr{ML}_{\mathrm{Tr}}$ is generated by the following syntax:

$$\phi ::= \mathrm{true} \mid \langle\!\langle \tau \rangle\!\rangle \phi \mid \langle\!\langle a \rangle\!\rangle \phi$$

where $a \in Name_{\mathrm{v}}$.

Theorem 1.18. *Let* $P_1, P_2 \in \mathbb{P}$. *Then:*

$$P_1 \approx_{\mathrm{Tr}} P_2 \iff (\forall \phi \in \mathscr{ML}_{\mathrm{Tr}}.P_1 \models_{\mathrm{Tr}} \phi \iff P_2 \models_{\mathrm{Tr}} \phi)$$

1.6.5 Verification Algorithm

The problem of deciding trace equivalence is PSPACE-complete and can be solved through the application of a slight variant of the verification algorithm for $\approx_{\mathrm{T}}$.

As regards the preprocessing step preceding the verification algorithm for $\sim_B$, each of the two acceptance graphs is built by assigning Boolean label false to every state constructed via τ-closure, so that the other label is the empty set. This simplification is motivated by the fact that $\approx_{Tr}$ is sensitive neither to divergence nor to the branching structure of process terms. Therefore, in this case the construction of an acceptance graph coincides with the usual method for building a deterministic automaton that is language equivalent to a given nondeterministic automaton.

Concerning the two initial steps of the verification algorithm for $\sim_B$, unlike the case of $\approx_T$ there is no need to modify them. The reason is that all the states have the same labels after executing the simplified preprocessing step described above.

1.7 The Linear-Time/Branching-Time Spectrum

In this section, we compare the discriminating power of the considered behavioral equivalences. Since $\approx_T$ is the only one sensitive to divergence, from their axiomatizations we can derive some relations if we restrict ourselves to strongly convergent process terms, i.e., process terms that cannot reach divergent process terms. We denote by $\mathbb{P}_{conv}$ the set of strongly convergent process terms of $\mathbb{P}$, and by $\mathbb{P}_{no\tau}$ the set of process terms of $\mathbb{P}_{conv}$ that cannot reach unstable process terms.

Proposition 1.3. *The following holds over* $\mathbb{P}_{conv}$*:*

$$\sim_B \subset \approx_{B,b} \subset \approx_B \subset \approx_T \subset \approx_{Tr}$$

Proposition 1.4. *The following holds over* $\mathbb{P}_{no\tau}$*:*

$$\sim_B = \approx_{B,b} = \approx_B \subset \approx_T \subset \approx_{Tr}$$

With regard to the testing approach, in general $\approx_{T,may}$ and $\approx_{T,must}$ are incomparable, but a relation can be established for strongly convergent process terms.

Proposition 1.5. *Let* $P_1, P_2 \in \mathbb{P}_{conv}$. *Then:*

$$P_1 \approx_{T,must} P_2 \implies P_1 \approx_{T,may} P_2$$

From the alternative characterizations provided in Sect. 1.5.2, it is straightforward to obtain the following result.

Proposition 1.6. *Let* $P_1, P_2 \in \mathbb{P}$. *Then:*

$$P_1 \approx_{T,may} P_2 \iff P_1 \approx_{Tr} P_2$$

In general, concurrency theory distinguishes between linear-time equivalences and branching-time equivalences. While in the former the behavior of process terms is determined by their possible computations, in the latter also the branching structure of process terms is taken into account. Having said this, it turns out that

$\approx_{Tr}$ is the standard example of a linear-time equivalence and $\sim_B$ is the standard example of a branching-time equivalence, whereas $\approx_T$ is somewhere in between.

Behavioral equivalences like $\approx_{Tr}$ and $\approx_T$ have the advantage of only distinguishing between process terms that can be told apart by some notion of observation or testing. In contrast, the mostly used argument for employing a behavioral equivalence like $\sim_B$ instead of $\approx_{Tr}$ (resp. $\approx_T$) is a proper treatment of deadlock (resp. the existence of a simpler proof technique). However, $\sim_B$ cannot be considered observational, in the sense that it makes distinctions between process terms that cannot be traced [48], unless the external observer is equipped with extraordinary tools such as the capability of global testing and a copying facility [153, 2].

Several variants of the considered behavioral equivalences have been defined in the literature. We now recall some of the most representative together with the linear-time/branching-time spectrum they constitute [98].

Let us start with a variant of $\sim_B$ called simulation equivalence [168], whose characterizing axiom is $a \cdot (P_1 + P_2) = a \cdot P_1 + a \cdot (P_1 + P_2)$ and whose corresponding modal language turns out to coincide with HML without negation [113].

Definition 1.31. A binary relation $\mathscr{S}$ over $\mathbb{P}$ is a simulation iff, whenever $(P_1, P_2) \in \mathscr{S}$, then for all actions $a \in Name$:

- Whenever $P_1 \xrightarrow{a} P_1'$, then $P_2 \xrightarrow{a} P_2'$ with $(P_1', P_2') \in \mathscr{S}$.

Definition 1.32. Simulation preorder, denoted $\preceq_S$, is the largest simulation.

Definition 1.33. Simulation equivalence, denoted $\sim_S$, is the kernel of simulation preorder, i.e., $\sim_S = \preceq_S \cap \preceq_S^{-1}$.

Another variant of $\sim_B$ is ready-simulation equivalence, which is the finest known behavioral equivalence whose distinctions can be traced by including reasonable operators in the process language [48]. Its characterizing axiom is the same as for $\sim_S$ provided that P_1 and P_2 can perform the same actions, and its corresponding modal language turns out to coincide with the one for $\sim_S$ plus a refusal predicate [136].

Definition 1.34. A binary relation $\mathscr{S}$ over $\mathbb{P}$ is a ready simulation iff, whenever $(P_1, P_2) \in \mathscr{S}$, then for all actions $a \in Name$:

- Whenever $P_1 \xrightarrow{a} P_1'$, then $P_2 \xrightarrow{a} P_2'$ with $(P_1', P_2') \in \mathscr{S}$
- Whenever P_1 cannot perform a, then P_2 cannot perform a either

Definition 1.35. Ready-simulation preorder, denoted $\preceq_{RS}$, is the largest ready simulation.

Definition 1.36. Ready-simulation equivalence, denoted $\sim_{RS}$, is the kernel of ready-simulation preorder, i.e., $\sim_{RS} = \preceq_{RS} \cap \preceq_{RS}^{-1}$.

Then, we introduce five variants of $\approx_{Tr}$, all of which restore deadlock sensitivity. The first one, called completed-trace equivalence, compares process terms also with respect to traces that lead to deadlock. Although more interesting than $\approx_{Tr}$, it has the disadvantage of being no longer a congruence with respect to the parallel composition operator. As an example, $a.b.\underline{0}+a.d.\underline{0}$ is equivalent to $a.(b.\underline{0}+d.\underline{0})$, but in the context $\_\|_{\{a,b,d\}} a.b.\underline{0}$ the former exhibits a trace leading to deadlock – resulting from a single transition labeled with a – which is not possessed by the latter. The next two behavioral equivalences, called failure equivalence [57] and ready equivalence [164], take into account the set of visible actions that can be refused or performed, respectively, after executing a trace. The last two behavioral equivalences, called failure-trace equivalence and ready-trace equivalence [21], also take into account the sets of visible actions that can be refused or performed, respectively, at each step during the execution of a trace.

Definition 1.37. Let $P \in \mathbb{P}$. The completed-trace set of P, denoted $CTS(P)$, is the set of traces of P such that the process terms reached at the end of their execution cannot perform any action.

Definition 1.38. Let $P_1, P_2 \in \mathbb{P}$. We say that P_1 is completed-trace equivalent to P_2, written $P_1 \approx_{Tr,c} P_2$, iff:

$$TS(P_1) = TS(P_2)$$
$$CTS(P_1) = CTS(P_2)$$

Definition 1.39. Let $P \in \mathbb{P}$. The failure-pair set of P, denoted $FS(P)$, is the set of failure pairs $(\alpha, F) \in (Name_v)^* \times 2^{Name_v}$ such that $\alpha \in TS(P)$ and the process terms reached at the end of the execution of α cannot perform any visible action in the failure set F.

Definition 1.40. Let $P_1, P_2 \in \mathbb{P}$. We say that P_1 is failure equivalent to P_2, written $P_1 \approx_F P_2$, iff:

$$FS(P_1) = FS(P_2)$$

Definition 1.41. Let $P \in \mathbb{P}$. The ready-pair set of P, denoted $RS(P)$, is the set of ready pairs $(\alpha, R) \in (Name_v)^* \times 2^{Name_v}$ such that $\alpha \in TS(P)$ and the set of visible actions that can be performed by the process terms reached at the end of the execution of α coincides with the ready set R.

Definition 1.42. Let $P_1, P_2 \in \mathbb{P}$. We say that P_1 is ready equivalent to P_2, written $P_1 \approx_R P_2$, iff:

$$RS(P_1) = RS(P_2)$$

Definition 1.43. Let $P \in \mathbb{P}$. The failure-trace set of P, denoted $FTS(P)$, is the set of failure traces $\zeta \in (Name_v \times 2^{Name_v})^*$ such that the trace projection α of ζ belongs to $TS(P)$ and each process term traversed during the execution of α cannot perform any visible action belonging to the corresponding failure set in the failure projection of ζ.

Definition 1.44. Let $P_1, P_2 \in \mathbb{P}$. We say that P_1 is failure-trace equivalent to P_2, written $P_1 \approx_{\text{FTr}} P_2$, iff:

$$FTS(P_1) = FTS(P_2)$$

Definition 1.45. Let $P \in \mathbb{P}$. The ready-trace set of P, denoted $RTS(P)$, is the set of ready traces $\eta \in (Name_v \times 2^{Name_v})^*$ such that the trace projection α of η belongs to $TS(P)$ and the set of visible actions that can be performed by each process term traversed during the execution of α coincides with the corresponding ready set in the ready projection of η.

Definition 1.46. Let $P_1, P_2 \in \mathbb{P}$. We say that P_1 is ready-trace equivalent to P_2, written $P_1 \approx_{\text{RTr}} P_2$, iff:

$$RTS(P_1) = RTS(P_2)$$

Theorem 1.19. *The linear-time/branching-time spectrum over* $\mathbb{P}_{\text{no}\tau}$ *is as follows:*

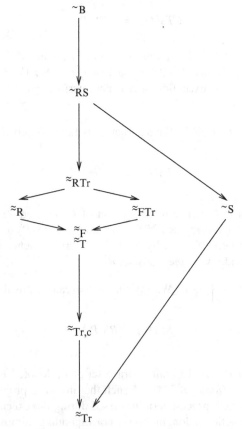

where arrows denote strict set inclusion.

We conclude by mentioning that all these behavioral equivalences coincide in the case of process terms whose underlying labeled transition systems are deterministic. This property has been exploited in Sects. 1.5.6 and 1.6.5 for reconducting the verification of $\approx_T$ and of $\approx_{Tr}$, respectively, to the verification of $\sim_B$.

Chapter 2
Deterministically Timed Process Algebra

Abstract Concurrent and distributed systems are characterized not only by their functional behavior, but also by their quantitative features. A prominent role is played by timing aspects, which express the temporal execution of system activities. There are several different options for introducing time and time passing in system descriptions: durationless actions or durational actions, relative time or absolute time, global clock or local clocks. In this chapter, we present two timed process calculi arising from certain combinations of the options mentioned above, which share a deterministic representation of time and time passing suitable for real-time systems. Then, we show the impact of eager, lazy, and maximal progress interpretations of action execution on the expressiveness of timed descriptions and their bisimulation semantics. This is accomplished through a number of semantics-preserving mappings, which demonstrate how some of the different choices are not irreconcilable by providing a better understanding of benefits and drawbacks of the various time-related options.

2.1 Concurrency, Communication, and Deterministic Time

The process calculus considered in Chap. 1 has no notion of time, probability, or priority associated with its actions; hence, it is purely nondeterministic. However, concurrent and distributed systems are characterized not only by their functional behavior, but also by their quantitative features. In particular, timing aspects play a fundamental role, as they describe the temporal execution of system activities. This is especially true for real-time systems, which are considered correct only if the execution of their activities satisfies certain temporal constraints.

When modeling these systems, time and time passing are represented deterministically through nonnegative numbers. In the following we refer to abstract time, in the sense that we use time as a parameter for expressing constraints about instants of occurrences of actions. Contrasted to physical time, abstract time permits simplifications that are convenient on the conceptual side and leads to tractable models.

A. Aldini et al., *A Process Algebraic Approach to Software Architecture Design*,
DOI 10.1007/978-1-84800-223-4_2, © Springer-Verlag London Limited 2010

Time instants can in general be taken from a dense or discrete time domain, which is a triple $(\mathscr{T}, +, \leq)$ where $+$ is an associative operation over $\mathscr{T}$ equipped with a neutral element and $\leq$ is a total order over $\mathscr{T}$ such that $t_1 \leq t_2$ iff there exists $t' \in \mathscr{T}$ such that $t_1 + t' = t_2$. For the sake of simplicity, we concentrate on a discrete time domain, and hence we can use natural numbers for modeling clock ticks.

Many deterministically timed process calculi have appeared in the literature. Among them we mention temporal CCS [157], timed CCS [199], timed CSP [174], real-time ACP [20], and urgent LOTOS [50], as well as CIPA [3], TPL [114], ATP [163], TIC [173], and PAFAS [78]. Due to the presence of several temporal properties of interest, as observed in [162, 74] these calculi differ on the basis of a number of time-related options, some of which are recalled below:

- Durationless actions versus durational actions. In the first case, actions are instantaneous events and time passes in between them; hence, functional behavior and time are orthogonal. In the second case, every action takes a fixed amount of time to be performed and time passes only due to action execution; hence, functional behavior and time are integrated.
- Relative time versus absolute time. Assuming that timestamps are associated with the events observed during system execution, in the first case each timestamp refers to the time instant of the previous observation, while in the second case all timestamps refer to the starting time of the system execution.
- Global clock versus local clocks. In the first case, there is a single clock that governs time passing. In the second case, there are several clocks associated with the various system parts, which elapse independent of each other although they define a unique notion of global time.

In this chapter, we present two different deterministically timed process calculi obtained by suitably combining the three time-related options mentioned above. More precisely, the first calculus is inspired by the two-phase functioning principle, according to which actions are durationless, time is relative, and there is a single global clock. In contrast, the second calculus is inspired by the one-phase functioning principle, according to which actions are durational, time is absolute, and several local clocks are present.

We then illustrate for these two deterministically timed process calculi different interpretations of action execution, in terms of whether and when it can be delayed. We consider the following three interpretations:

- Eagerness, which establishes that actions must be performed as soon as they become enabled without any delay, thereby implying that actions are urgent.
- Laziness, which establishes that actions can be delayed arbitrarily long before they are executed.
- Maximal progress, which establishes that actions can be delayed arbitrarily long unless they are involved in synchronizations, in which case they are urgent.

There are many reasons for presenting both calculi under the three different interpretations. Firstly, this should increase the familiarity with different approaches to modeling time and time passing. Secondly, it should provide a better understanding of the details of the different approaches, so as to emphasize their advantages and disadvantages. Thirdly, it shows that some of the various choices concerned with the time-related options are not irreconcilable by presenting a number of semantics-preserving mappings from one calculus to the other, thus permitting the interchange of concepts and analysis techniques. Fourthly, it demonstrates that the inessential differences among the two calculi are indeed inessential, while the important ones are really important.

The two deterministically timed process calculi have the same behavioral operators as the process calculus of Sect. 1.3. A variety of time-related behavioral operators such as timeouts and watchdogs have been proposed in the literature. Here, we do not take them into account because they do not have any impact on how abstract time is modeled, nor do they influence the time-related options discussed before.

Unlike Chap. 1, we do not deal with all the three approaches to the definition of behavioral equivalences, rather we focus on bisimulation equivalence only. The reason is that in this deterministically timed setting it is more interesting to compare the expressiveness of the two calculi under the three different interpretations of action execution by means of the semantics-preserving mappings mentioned above. As in Chap. 1, the two calculi and the related bisimulation equivalences are illustrated through the producer–consumer system running example.

This chapter is organized as follows. In Sect. 2.2, we define syntax and semantics for the two deterministically timed process calculi. In Sect. 2.3, we introduce a suitable bisimulation equivalence for each of the two calculi, then we show the properties of the two equivalences. In Sects. 2.4, 2.5, and 2.6, we discuss semantics-preserving mappings between the two calculi under eagerness, laziness, and maximal progress, respectively. Finally, in Sect. 2.7 we compare the expressiveness of eager, lazy, and maximal progress interpretations of action execution.

2.2 Deterministically Timed Process Calculi

In this section, we present two deterministically timed process calculi with urgent actions, which are obtained from the process calculus of Sect. 1.3. The timed process calculus TPC, which is inspired by [157], adheres to the two-phase functioning principle. In contrast, the durational process calculus DPC, which is inspired by [3, 77, 102, 74], complies with the one-phase functioning principle.

2.2.1 TPC: Timed Process Calculus with Durationless Actions

In TPC, actions are durationless, time is relative, and there is a single global clock. In this setting, actions are instantaneous and time passes in between them. As a consequence, in addition to the action prefix operator, TPC includes a time prefix operator for expressing processes like $(n).P$, which can evolve into process P after exactly $n \in \mathbb{N}_{>0}$ time units. Since there is a global clock, these n time units can elapse only if they can pass in all system parts.

TPC comprises the same behavioral operators as PC plus the time prefix operator mentioned above, whose delay is ranged over by n, m. We point out that in TPC the inactive process cannot proceed through time; hence, we denote it by $\overline{0}$ in order to distinguish it from $\underline{0}$. Moreover, TPC inherits from PC all of its syntactical categories for actions, relabeling functions, process variables, and process constants. Guardedness is extended in order to allow for the occurrence of process variables or constants in the scope of time prefix operators as well.

Definition 2.1. The set of process terms of the process language $\mathscr{PL}_{\mathrm{T}}$ is generated by the following syntax:

P ::=	$\overline{0}$	timed inactive process
	$a.P$	action prefix
	$(n).P$	time prefix
	$P+P$	alternative composition
	$P\|_S P$	parallel composition
	P/H	hiding
	$P\backslash L$	restriction
	$P[\varphi]$	relabeling
	X	process variable
	$recX : P$	recursion

where $a \in Name$, $n \in \mathbb{N}_{>0}$, $S, H, L \subseteq Name_{\mathrm{v}}$, $\varphi \in Relab$, and $X \in Var$. We denote by $\mathbb{P}_{\mathrm{T}}$ the set of closed and guarded process terms of $\mathscr{PL}_{\mathrm{T}}$.

Example 2.1. Let us model with TPC the producer–consumer system introduced in Sect. 1.2. Assuming that every deposit or withdrawal operation takes place n time units after the previous operation, it suffices to extend as follows the structure-independent process algebraic description provided in Example 1.1:

$$ProdCons^{\mathrm{T}}_{0/2} \triangleq deposit.(n).ProdCons^{\mathrm{T}}_{1/2}$$
$$ProdCons^{\mathrm{T}}_{1/2} \triangleq deposit.(n).ProdCons^{\mathrm{T}}_{2/2} + withdraw.(n).ProdCons^{\mathrm{T}}_{0/2}$$
$$ProdCons^{\mathrm{T}}_{2/2} \triangleq withdraw.(n).ProdCons^{\mathrm{T}}_{1/2}$$

The semantics for TPC is defined in the usual operational style through two distinct transition relations: one for action execution and one for time passing. The first transition relation coincides with the one for PC shown in Table 1.1. The second transition relation, denoted $\longrightarrow$, is the smallest subset of $\mathbb{P}_{\mathrm{T}} \times \mathbb{N}_{>0} \times \mathbb{P}_{\mathrm{T}}$ satisfying the operational semantic rules of Table 2.1. A transition of the form $P \overset{n}{\longrightarrow} P'$ means that P lets n time units pass, then becomes P'. Note that rules $\mathrm{DEC_T}$ and $\mathrm{SUM_T}$ allow the passage of time to be decomposed and summed, respectively, while rule $\mathrm{ALT_T}$ does not resolve the choice but lets the same amount of time pass in both alternatives. On the other hand, rule $\mathrm{SYN_T}$ encodes the global clock. The labeled transition system for a process term $P \in \mathbb{P}_{\mathrm{T}}$ is denoted by $[\![P]\!]_{\mathrm{T}}$.

Table 2.1 Time-related operational semantic rules for TPC

$$(\text{PRE}_T) \quad \frac{}{(n).P \overset{n}{\leadsto} P}$$

$$(\text{DEC}_T) \quad \frac{n = n_1 + n_2}{(n).P \overset{n_1}{\leadsto} (n_2).P} \qquad\qquad (\text{SUM}_T) \quad \frac{P \overset{n}{\leadsto} P'}{(m).P \overset{n+m}{\leadsto} P'}$$

$$(\text{ALT}_T) \quad \frac{P_1 \overset{n}{\leadsto} P_1' \qquad P_2 \overset{n}{\leadsto} P_2'}{P_1 + P_2 \overset{n}{\leadsto} P_1' + P_2'}$$

$$(\text{SYN}_T) \quad \frac{P_1 \overset{n}{\leadsto} P_1' \qquad P_2 \overset{n}{\leadsto} P_2'}{P_1 \parallel_S P_2 \overset{n}{\leadsto} P_1' \parallel_S P_2'}$$

$$(\text{HID}_T) \quad \frac{P \overset{n}{\leadsto} P'}{P/H \overset{n}{\leadsto} P'/H}$$

$$(\text{RES}_T) \quad \frac{P \overset{n}{\leadsto} P'}{P \backslash L \overset{n}{\leadsto} P' \backslash L}$$

$$(\text{REL}_T) \quad \frac{P \overset{n}{\leadsto} P'}{P[\varphi] \overset{n}{\leadsto} P'[\varphi]}$$

$$(\text{REC}_T) \quad \frac{P\{recX : P \hookrightarrow X\} \overset{n}{\leadsto} P'}{recX : P \overset{n}{\leadsto} P'}$$

The transition relation $\leadsto$ meets time continuity; i.e., it holds $P \overset{n_1+n_2}{\leadsto} P'$ iff $P \overset{n_1}{\leadsto} Q$ and $Q \overset{n_2}{\leadsto} P'$ for some $Q \in \mathbb{P}_T$. As a consequence, we have $P \overset{n}{\leadsto} P'$ iff there exist $P_0, P_1, \ldots, P_n \in \mathbb{P}_T$ such that $P_0 \equiv P$, $P_{i-1} \overset{1}{\leadsto} P_i$ for $1 \leq i \leq n$, and $P_n \equiv P'$. We also note that $\overline{0}$ and action prefix do not let time progress as there are no time-related operational semantic rules for them, which in particular implies that actions are urgent. In contrast, $recX : (1).X$ is the simplest process term that can let any amount of time pass as $recX : (1).X \overset{n}{\leadsto} recX : (1).X$ for every $n \in \mathbb{N}_{>0}$.

Example 2.2. The labeled transition system $[\![ProdCons^T_{0/2}]\!]_T$ for the process algebraic description of Example 2.1 is depicted below, where the two different kinds of transition are represented by means of two different kinds of edge:

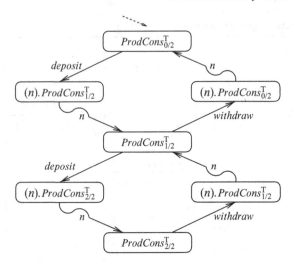

For the sake of simplicity, the time transitions shown above are only the ones allowing the entire specified delays to elapse. By virtue of time continuity, for each such time transition there exists a number of alternative sequences of time transitions, such that the source state of the first time transition in each sequence and the target state of the last time transition in each sequence correspond to the source state and to the target state, respectively, of the considered time transition.

2.2.2 DPC: Timed Process Calculus with Durational Actions

In DPC, actions are durational, time is absolute, and there are several local clocks associated with the various system parts. In this setting, we assume maximal parallelism; i.e., whenever a system part is activated, there is always some computational resource available for it, thus avoiding the need of serializing the parallel execution of the various parts.

In DPC, a timed action is represented as a pair $<a,n>$, where $a \in Name$ is the name of the action and $n \in \mathbb{N}_{>0}$ is the duration of the action. Since the duration of any action is greater than zero, DPC does not admit Zeno processes; i.e., processes capable of performing infinitely many actions in a finite amount of time.

The synchronization discipline adopted in DPC is restricted to actions of the same name that have the same duration and start at the same time. The reason for this limitation is that synchronizing actions starting at different time instants contradicts the existence of a unique notion of global time. Moreover, it would be unclear how to define the duration of the synchronization of actions with different durations.

DPC comprises the same behavioral operators and syntactical categories as PC, plus the set of actions $Act_D = Name \times \mathbb{N}_{>0}$ where durations are ranged over by n, m. A process like $<a,n>.P$ lets exactly $n \in \mathbb{N}_{>0}$ time units pass and then evolves into process P. Similar to the case of TPC, in which the global clock is implicit, also in DPC local clocks are implicit as they are not part of the process term syntax.

Definition 2.2. The set of process terms of the process language $\mathscr{PL}_D$ is generated by the following syntax:

$$
\begin{array}{lll}
P ::= & \underline{0} & \text{inactive process} \\
| & <a,n>.P & \text{timed action prefix} \\
| & P+P & \text{alternative composition} \\
| & P\|_S P & \text{parallel composition} \\
| & P/H & \text{hiding} \\
| & P\backslash L & \text{restriction} \\
| & P[\varphi] & \text{relabeling} \\
| & X & \text{process variable} \\
| & recX : P & \text{recursion}
\end{array}
$$

where $a \in Name$, $n \in \mathbb{N}_{>0}$, $S,H,L \subseteq Name_v$, $\varphi \in Relab$, and $X \in Var$. We denote by $\mathbb{P}_D$ the set of closed and guarded process terms of $\mathscr{PL}_D$.

Example 2.3. Let us model with DPC the producer–consumer system introduced in Sect. 1.2. Assuming that both *deposit* and *withdraw* have duration n so as to be somehow consistent with Example 2.1, it suffices to extend as follows the structure-independent process algebraic description provided in Example 1.1:

$$
\begin{aligned}
ProdCons^D_{0/2} &\triangleq <deposit,n>.ProdCons^D_{1/2} \\
ProdCons^D_{1/2} &\triangleq <deposit,n>.ProdCons^D_{2/2} + <withdraw,n>.ProdCons^D_{0/2} \\
ProdCons^D_{2/2} &\triangleq <withdraw,n>.ProdCons^D_{1/2}
\end{aligned}
$$

The semantics for DPC is defined in the usual operational style, with states formalized as process terms preceded by local clocks each holding a value $t \in \mathbb{N}$. These local clocks keep track of the time elapsed in the sequential parts of a process term.

Definition 2.3. The set of process terms with local clocks of the process language $\mathscr{KL}_D$ is generated by the following syntax:

$$
\begin{array}{ll}
K ::= & t \Rightarrow \underline{0} \\
| & t \Rightarrow <a,n>.P \\
| & K+K \\
| & K\|_S K \\
| & K/H \\
| & K\backslash L \\
| & K[\varphi] \\
| & t \Rightarrow recX : P
\end{array}
$$

where $t \in \mathbb{N}$, $a \in Name$, $n \in \mathbb{N}_{>0}$, $P \in \mathscr{PL}_D$, $S,H,L \subseteq Name_v$, $\varphi \in Relab$, and $X \in Var$. We denote by $\mathbb{K}_D$ the set of closed and guarded process terms of $\mathscr{KL}_D$.

In order to simplify the definition of the operational semantics for DPC, when using the shorthand $t \Rightarrow P$ it is understood that t distributes over all behavioral operators till the inactive process, a timed action prefix, or recursion is encountered. This is formalized through the following clock distribution equations:

$$
\begin{array}{rcl}
t \Rightarrow (P_1 + P_2) &=& (t \Rightarrow P_1) + (t \Rightarrow P_2) \\
t \Rightarrow (P_1 \|_S P_2) &=& (t \Rightarrow P_1) \|_S (t \Rightarrow P_2) \\
t \Rightarrow (P/H) &=& (t \Rightarrow P)/H \\
t \Rightarrow (P \backslash L) &=& (t \Rightarrow P) \backslash L \\
t \Rightarrow (P[\varphi]) &=& (t \Rightarrow P)[\varphi]
\end{array}
$$

The transition relation $\longrightarrow_D$ is the smallest subset of $\mathbb{K}_D \times Act_D \times \mathbb{N} \times \mathbb{K}_D$ satisfying the operational semantic rules of Table 2.2. A transition of the form $K \xrightarrow[t]{a,n}_D K'$ means that K performs an action of name a and duration n at time t, then becomes K'. We note that rule $\mathrm{PRE_D}$ takes care of updating the local clock on the basis of the action duration. Rules $\mathrm{ALT_{D,1}}$, $\mathrm{ALT_{D,2}}$, $\mathrm{PAR_{D,1}}$, and $\mathrm{PAR_{D,2}}$ have a negative premise establishing that one of the two subterms of an alternative or parallel composition can evolve by performing some action at a certain time only if the other subterm cannot evolve earlier, which ensures action urgency. Rule $\mathrm{SYN_D}$ permits synchronizations only among actions of the same name and duration that are executed at the same time, which guarantees a unique global time in spite of the presence of several local clocks. Due to the time constraints on action synchronization, no negative premise is needed in $\mathrm{SYN_D}$. The labeled transition system for a process term $P \in \mathbb{P}_D$ is denoted by $[\![P]\!]_D$ and its initial state is $0 \Rightarrow P$.

The transition relation $\longrightarrow_D$ meets well timedness; i.e., $K \xrightarrow[t']{a',n'}_D K'$ and $K' \xrightarrow[t'']{a'',n''}_D K''$ imply $t' \leq t''$, meaning that time does not decrease as the execution proceeds. This is a consequence of the negative premises in rules $\mathrm{ALT_{D,1}}$, $\mathrm{ALT_{D,2}}$, $\mathrm{PAR_{D,1}}$, and $\mathrm{PAR_{D,2}}$ as they eliminate the ill-timed phenomenon; i.e., the presence of computations that do not respect the order given by time. Consider, for instance, $<a,2>.<b,1>.\underline{0} \|_\emptyset <d,3>.\underline{0}$. Under maximal parallelism, an external observer can see the execution of the a-action from time 0 to time 2, the execution of the b-action from time 2 to time 3, and the execution of the d-action from time 0 to time 3. In the absence of the negative premises above, after observing the starting of the a-action at time 0 and then the starting of the b-action at time 2, it is possible to observe the starting of the d-action at time 0. This is correct from a causality viewpoint, but it is as if time went back, which does not happen if the starting of the d-action at time 0 is observed before the starting of the b-action at time 2. The negative premises in Table 2.2 enforce computations that are both well caused and well timed, without introducing any inconsistency when applying the operational semantic rules.

A consequence of the adoption of absolute time and of the fact that time does not decrease is that the labeled transition systems underlying process terms of $\mathbb{P}_D$ typically have infinitely many states. However, a finite representation of $[\![P]\!]_D$ is possible for all process terms $P \in \mathbb{P}_D$ such that $[\![P]\!]$ has finitely many states, where

Table 2.2 Time-integrated operational semantic rules for DPC

$$(\text{PRE}_D) \quad \frac{}{t \Rightarrow <a,n>.P \xrightarrow[t]{a,n}_D (t+n) \Rightarrow P}$$

$$(\text{ALT}_{D,1}) \quad \frac{K_1 \xrightarrow[t]{a,n}_D K_1' \qquad \neg(K_2 \xrightarrow[t']{d',n'}_D K_2' \wedge t' < t)}{K_1 + K_2 \xrightarrow[t]{a,n}_D K_1'}$$

$$(\text{ALT}_{D,2}) \quad \frac{K_2 \xrightarrow[t]{a,n}_D K_2' \qquad \neg(K_1 \xrightarrow[t']{d',n'}_D K_1' \wedge t' < t)}{K_1 + K_2 \xrightarrow[t]{a,n}_D K_2'}$$

$$(\text{PAR}_{D,1}) \quad \frac{K_1 \xrightarrow[t]{a,n}_D K_1' \qquad \neg(K_2 \xrightarrow[t']{d',n'}_D K_2' \wedge t' < t) \qquad a \notin S}{K_1 \|_S K_2 \xrightarrow[t]{a,n}_D K_1' \|_S K_2}$$

$$(\text{PAR}_{D,2}) \quad \frac{K_2 \xrightarrow[t]{a,n}_D K_2' \qquad \neg(K_1 \xrightarrow[t']{d',n'}_D K_1' \wedge t' < t) \qquad a \notin S}{K_1 \|_S K_2 \xrightarrow[t]{a,n}_D K_1 \|_S K_2'}$$

$$(\text{SYN}_D) \quad \frac{K_1 \xrightarrow[t]{a,n}_D K_1' \qquad K_2 \xrightarrow[t]{a,n}_D K_2' \qquad a \in S}{K_1 \|_S K_2 \xrightarrow[t]{a,n}_D K_1' \|_S K_2'}$$

$$(\text{HID}_{D,1}) \quad \frac{K \xrightarrow[t]{a,n}_D K' \qquad a \in H}{K/H \xrightarrow[t]{\tau,n}_D K'/H}$$

$$(\text{HID}_{D,2}) \quad \frac{K \xrightarrow[t]{a,n}_D K' \qquad a \notin H}{K/H \xrightarrow[t]{a,n}_D K'/H}$$

$$(\text{RES}_D) \quad \frac{K \xrightarrow[t]{a,n}_D K' \qquad a \notin L}{K \backslash L \xrightarrow[t]{a,n}_D K' \backslash L}$$

$$(\text{REL}_D) \quad \frac{K \xrightarrow[t]{a,n}_D K'}{K[\varphi] \xrightarrow[t]{\varphi(a),n}_D K'[\varphi]}$$

$$(\text{REC}_D) \quad \frac{t \Rightarrow P\{recX : P \hookrightarrow X\} \xrightarrow[t]{a,n}_D K'}{t \Rightarrow recX : P \xrightarrow[t]{a,n}_D K'}$$

the latter labeled transition system is the one obtained by applying the operational semantic rules for PC shown in Table 1.1 when ignoring action durations.

We also point out that in this timed setting with durational actions the interleaving view of concurrency is not fully respected. As an example, take the following two process terms:

$$<a,n>.\underline{0} \parallel_\emptyset <b,m>.\underline{0}$$
$$<a,n>.<b,m>.\underline{0} + <b,m>.<a,n>.\underline{0}$$

The first one (concurrent term) executes a having duration n in parallel with b having duration m, while the second one (sequential term) executes either a having duration n followed by b having duration m, or b having duration m followed by a having duration n. Different from the nondeterministic case, as shown below the labeled transition systems for the two process terms are not isomorphic:

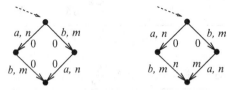

The reason is that in the concurrent term all actions start their execution at time 0, whereas this is not the case in the sequential term.

Example 2.4. The labeled transition system $[\![ProdCons_{0/2}^D]\!]_D$ for the process algebraic description of Example 2.3 is depicted below through its finite representation:

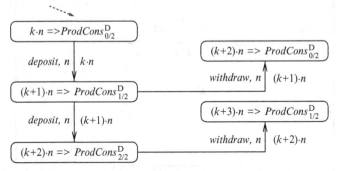

where k ranges over $\mathbb{N}$.

2.3 Deterministically Timed Behavioral Equivalences

Among the various approaches to the definition of behavioral equivalences, in the deterministically timed setting we focus on bisimulation equivalence, which relates two process terms whenever they are able to mimic each other's functional and time behavior stepwise. In this section, we provide the definition of timed bisimulation equivalence over $\mathbb{P}_T$, we show that it is a congruence, and we present its sound and complete axiomatization, its modal logic characterization, and its verification algorithm [157]. Then, we provide the definition of durational bisimulation equivalence over $\mathbb{P}_D$ and we mention that it is a congruence and has a modal logic characterization [3, 77, 102, 73].

2.3.1 Definition of Timed Bisimulation Equivalence

In the case of durationless actions, the timed extension of bisimulation equivalence must coincide with $\sim_B$ as long as action execution is concerned. With regard to time passing, whenever a process term can let a certain amount of time elapse, then any process term equivalent to the given one has to be able to let the same amount of time elapse, with the derivative process terms into which all the previous process terms have evolved being still equivalent to each other.

Definition 2.4. A binary relation $\mathscr{B}$ over $\mathbb{P}_T$ is a timed bisimulation iff, whenever $(P_1, P_2) \in \mathscr{B}$, then for all actions $a \in Name$ and delays $n \in \mathbb{N}_{>0}$:

- Whenever $P_1 \xrightarrow{a} P_1'$, then $P_2 \xrightarrow{a} P_2'$ with $(P_1', P_2') \in \mathscr{B}$
- Whenever $P_1 \overset{n}{\rightsquigarrow} P_1'$, then $P_2 \overset{n}{\rightsquigarrow} P_2'$ with $(P_1', P_2') \in \mathscr{B}$
- Whenever $P_2 \xrightarrow{a} P_2'$, then $P_1 \xrightarrow{a} P_1'$ with $(P_1', P_2') \in \mathscr{B}$
- Whenever $P_2 \overset{n}{\rightsquigarrow} P_2'$, then $P_1 \overset{n}{\rightsquigarrow} P_1'$ with $(P_1', P_2') \in \mathscr{B}$

Since the union of all the timed bisimulations can be proved to be the largest timed bisimulation, the definition below follows.

Definition 2.5. Timed bisimulation equivalence (or timed bisimilarity), denoted $\sim_{TB}$, is the union of all the timed bisimulations.

Example 2.5. Let us model with TPC the concurrent implementation considered in Example 1.3 of the producer–consumer system introduced in Sect. 1.2. The process algebraic description extended with delays consistent with those of Example 2.1 is as follows:

$$PC_{conc,2}^T \triangleq Prod^T \parallel_{\{deposit\}} (Buff^T \parallel_\emptyset Buff^T) \parallel_{\{withdraw\}} Cons^T$$
$$Prod^T \triangleq deposit.(n).Prod^T$$
$$Buff^T \triangleq deposit.(n).withdraw.(n).Buff^T$$
$$Cons^T \triangleq withdraw.(n).Cons^T$$

It turns out that $PC_{conc,2}^T \nsim_{TB} ProdCons_{0/2}^T$ because $PC_{conc,2}^T$ reaches a deadlock state after the deposit of the first item. In fact:

$$PC_{conc,2}^T \xrightarrow{deposit}$$
$$(n).Prod^T \parallel_{\{deposit\}} ((n).withdraw.(n).Buff^T \parallel_\emptyset Buff^T) \parallel_{\{withdraw\}} Cons^T$$

but the target state cannot let time pass – because $Cons^T$ enables action *withdraw* – nor can it perform actions – as no synchronization on *withdraw* can take place. In contrast, $ProdCons^T_{0/2}$ can perform action *deposit* and then can also let time pass:

$$ProdCons^T_{0/2} \xrightarrow{deposit} (n).ProdCons^T_{1/2} \xrightarrow{n} ProdCons^T_{1/2}$$

The problem with the concurrent implementation of the timed producer–consumer system is that the other one-position buffer is ready to receive items immediately, while the producer can deliver items only every n time units. Similarly, the consumer is ready to withdraw items immediately, while items can be in the buffer only every n time units. In order to overcome this synchronization problem, we may delay the other one-position buffer and the consumer, thereby revising the process algebraic description above as follows:

$$PC'^T_{conc,2} \stackrel{\Delta}{=} Prod^T \parallel_{\{deposit\}} (Buff^T \parallel_\emptyset (n).Buff^T) \parallel_{\{withdraw\}} (n).Cons^T$$

After performing action *deposit*, the following state is reached:

$$(n).Prod^T \parallel_{\{deposit\}} ((n).withdraw.(n).Buff^T \parallel_\emptyset (n).Buff^T) \parallel_{\{withdraw\}} (n).Cons^T$$

then n time units pass and the following state is reached:

$$Prod^T \parallel_{\{deposit\}} (withdraw.(n).Buff^T \parallel_\emptyset Buff^T) \parallel_{\{withdraw\}} Cons^T$$

Afterwards, this state can perform action *withdraw* thus reaching:

$$Prod^T \parallel_{\{deposit\}} ((n).Buff^T \parallel_\emptyset Buff^T) \parallel_{\{withdraw\}} (n).Cons^T$$

which then performs action *deposit* and reaches:

$$(n).Prod^T \parallel_{\{deposit\}} ((n).Buff^T \parallel_\emptyset (n).withdraw.(n).Buff^T) \parallel_{\{withdraw\}} (n).Cons^T$$

In other words, $PC'^T_{conc,2}$ does not deadlock, but at certain points it is able to perform both *deposit* and *withdraw* at the same time, which is not possible in $ProdCons^T_{0/2}$ where the two actions are separated by a delay or are alternative to each other.

2.3.2 Congruence Property

Timed bisimulation equivalence is a congruence with respect to all the dynamic and static operators of TPC as well as recursion.

Theorem 2.1. *Let $P_1, P_2 \in \mathbb{P}_T$. Whenever $P_1 \sim_{TB} P_2$, then:*

1. $a.P_1 \sim_{TB} a.P_2$ *for all $a \in Name$.*
2. $(n).P_1 \sim_{TB} (n).P_2$ *for all $n \in \mathbb{N}_{>0}$.*
3. $P_1 + P \sim_{TB} P_2 + P$ *and $P + P_1 \sim_{TB} P + P_2$ for all $P \in \mathbb{P}_T$.*

4. $P_1 \|_S P \sim_{\mathrm{TB}} P_2 \|_S P$ and $P \|_S P_1 \sim_{\mathrm{TB}} P \|_S P_2$ for all $P \in \mathbb{P}_\mathrm{T}$ and $S \subseteq Name_\mathrm{v}$.
5. $P_1/H \sim_{\mathrm{TB}} P_2/H$ for all $H \subseteq Name_\mathrm{v}$.
6. $P_1 \backslash L \sim_{\mathrm{TB}} P_2 \backslash L$ for all $L \subseteq Name_\mathrm{v}$.
7. $P_1[\varphi] \sim_{\mathrm{TB}} P_2[\varphi]$ for all $\varphi \in Relab$.

Definition 2.6. Let $P_1, P_2 \in \mathscr{PL}_\mathrm{T}$ be guarded process terms containing free occurrences of $k \in \mathbb{N}$ process variables $X_1, \ldots, X_k \in Var$ at most. We define $P_1 \sim_{\mathrm{TB}} P_2$ iff $P_1\{Q_i \hookrightarrow X_i \mid 1 \le i \le k\} \sim_{\mathrm{TB}} P_2\{Q_i \hookrightarrow X_i \mid 1 \le i \le k\}$ for all $Q_1, \ldots, Q_k \in \mathbb{P}_\mathrm{T}$.

Theorem 2.2. *Let $P_1, P_2 \in \mathscr{PL}_\mathrm{T}$ be guarded process terms containing free occurrences of $k \in \mathbb{N}$ process variables $X_1, \ldots, X_k \in Var$ at most. Whenever $P_1 \sim_{\mathrm{TB}} P_2$, then $recX : P_1 \sim_{\mathrm{TB}} recX : P_2$ for all $X \in Var$.*

2.3.3 Sound and Complete Axiomatization

Timed bisimulation equivalence has a sound and complete axiomatization over non-recursive process terms, given by the set $\mathscr{X}_\mathrm{TB}$ of equational laws of Table 2.3.

Apart from the fact that the alternative composition operator is still commutative, associative, and idempotent and the fact that the parallel composition operator obeys the usual expansion law for action execution up to a suitable treatment of $\overline{0}$, there are many differences with respect to the axiomatization of $\sim_\mathrm{B}$ shown in Table 1.2. First of all, an axiom like $P + \overline{0} = P$ is not valid as $\overline{0}$ does not let time pass.

Concerning the alternative composition operator, axioms $\mathscr{X}_{\mathrm{TB},4}$ and $\mathscr{X}_{\mathrm{TB},5}$ establish that $\overline{0}$ behaves as a neutral element in the case of action prefix and as an absorbing element in the case of time prefix, respectively. Then, axiom $\mathscr{X}_{\mathrm{TB},6}$ emphasizes action urgency, while axioms $\mathscr{X}_{\mathrm{TB},7}$ and $\mathscr{X}_{\mathrm{TB},8}$ show how to decompose and factor delays.

As regards the parallel composition operator, axioms $\mathscr{X}_{\mathrm{TB},13}$ to $\mathscr{X}_{\mathrm{TB},17}$ are a reformulation of the axioms preceding them when considering time prefix. We note that having a single time prefix summand without any alternative action or time prefix summands is enough due to axioms $\mathscr{X}_{\mathrm{TB},6}$ and $\mathscr{X}_{\mathrm{TB},8}$.

Finally, for the unary static operators we have the same equational laws as Table 1.2 plus axioms $\mathscr{X}_{\mathrm{TB},21}$, $\mathscr{X}_{\mathrm{TB},26}$, and $\mathscr{X}_{\mathrm{TB},30}$ related to time prefix.

Theorem 2.3. *Let $P_1, P_2 \in \mathbb{P}_\mathrm{T}$ be nonrecursive. Then:*

$$P_1 \sim_{\mathrm{TB}} P_2 \iff \mathscr{X}_\mathrm{TB} \vdash P_1 = P_2$$

2.3.4 Modal Logic Characterization

Timed bisimulation equivalence has a modal logic characterization based on a variant of HML – the modal logic introduced in Sect. 1.4.6 – which includes a diamond operator for delays too.

Table 2.3 Equational laws for $\sim_{\mathrm{TB}}$

$(\mathscr{X}_{\mathrm{TB},1})$	$P_1 + P_2 = P_2 + P_1$	
$(\mathscr{X}_{\mathrm{TB},2})$	$(P_1 + P_2) + P_3 = P_1 + (P_2 + P_3)$	
$(\mathscr{X}_{\mathrm{TB},3})$	$P + P = P$	
$(\mathscr{X}_{\mathrm{TB},4})$	$a.P + \overline{0} = a.P$	
$(\mathscr{X}_{\mathrm{TB},5})$	$(n).P + \overline{0} = \overline{0}$	
$(\mathscr{X}_{\mathrm{TB},6})$	$a.P + (n).Q = a.P$	
$(\mathscr{X}_{\mathrm{TB},7})$	$(n_1 + n_2).P = (n_1).(n_2).P$	
$(\mathscr{X}_{\mathrm{TB},8})$	$(n).P_1 + (n).P_2 = (n).(P_1 + P_2)$	

$$(\mathscr{X}_{\mathrm{TB},9})\quad \sum_{i \in I} a_i.P_i \parallel_S \sum_{j \in J} b_j.Q_j = \sum_{k \in I, a_k \notin S} a_k.\left(P_k \parallel_S \sum_{j \in J} b_j.Q_j\right)$$
$$+ \sum_{h \in J, b_h \notin S} b_h.\left(\sum_{i \in I} a_i.P_i \parallel_S Q_h\right)$$
$$+ \sum_{k \in I, a_k \in S}\ \sum_{h \in J, b_h = a_k} a_k.(P_k \parallel_S Q_h)$$

$$(\mathscr{X}_{\mathrm{TB},10})\quad \sum_{i \in I} a_i.P_i \parallel_S \overline{0} = \sum_{k \in I, a_k \notin S} a_k.(P_k \parallel_S \overline{0})$$

$$(\mathscr{X}_{\mathrm{TB},11})\quad \overline{0} \parallel_S \sum_{j \in J} b_j.Q_j = \sum_{h \in J, b_h \notin S} b_h.(\overline{0} \parallel_S Q_h)$$

$$(\mathscr{X}_{\mathrm{TB},12})\quad \overline{0} \parallel_S \overline{0} = \overline{0}$$

$$(\mathscr{X}_{\mathrm{TB},13})\quad \sum_{i \in I} a_i.P_i \parallel_S (m).Q = \sum_{k \in I, a_k \notin S} a_k.(P_k \parallel_S (m).Q)$$

$$(\mathscr{X}_{\mathrm{TB},14})\quad (n).P \parallel_S \sum_{j \in J} b_j.Q_j = \sum_{h \in J, b_h \notin S} b_h.((n).P \parallel_S Q_h)$$

$(\mathscr{X}_{\mathrm{TB},15})$	$(n).P \parallel_S (n).Q = (n).(P \parallel_S Q)$	
$(\mathscr{X}_{\mathrm{TB},16})$	$(n).P \parallel_S \overline{0} = \overline{0}$	
$(\mathscr{X}_{\mathrm{TB},17})$	$\overline{0} \parallel_S (m).Q = \overline{0}$	
$(\mathscr{X}_{\mathrm{TB},18})$	$\overline{0}/H = \overline{0}$	
$(\mathscr{X}_{\mathrm{TB},19})$	$(a.P)/H = \tau.(P/H)$	if $a \in H$
$(\mathscr{X}_{\mathrm{TB},20})$	$(a.P)/H = a.(P/H)$	if $a \notin H$
$(\mathscr{X}_{\mathrm{TB},21})$	$((n).P)/H = (n).(P/H)$	
$(\mathscr{X}_{\mathrm{TB},22})$	$(P_1 + P_2)/H = P_1/H + P_2/H$	
$(\mathscr{X}_{\mathrm{TB},23})$	$\overline{0} \backslash L = \overline{0}$	
$(\mathscr{X}_{\mathrm{TB},24})$	$(a.P)\backslash L = \overline{0}$	if $a \in L$
$(\mathscr{X}_{\mathrm{TB},25})$	$(a.P)\backslash L = a.(P\backslash L)$	if $a \notin L$
$(\mathscr{X}_{\mathrm{TB},26})$	$((n).P)\backslash L = (n).(P\backslash L)$	
$(\mathscr{X}_{\mathrm{TB},27})$	$(P_1 + P_2)\backslash L = P_1\backslash L + P_2\backslash L$	
$(\mathscr{X}_{\mathrm{TB},28})$	$\overline{0}[\varphi] = \overline{0}$	
$(\mathscr{X}_{\mathrm{TB},29})$	$(a.P)[\varphi] = \varphi(a).(P[\varphi])$	
$(\mathscr{X}_{\mathrm{TB},30})$	$((n).P)[\varphi] = (n).(P[\varphi])$	
$(\mathscr{X}_{\mathrm{TB},31})$	$(P_1 + P_2)[\varphi] = P_1[\varphi] + P_2[\varphi]$	

Definition 2.7. The set of formulas of the modal language $\mathcal{ML}_{TB}$ is generated by the following syntax:

$$\phi ::= \text{true} \mid \neg\phi \mid \phi \wedge \phi \mid \langle a \rangle \varphi \mid \langle\langle n \rangle\rangle \varphi$$

where $a \in Name$ and $n \in \mathbb{N}_{>0}$.

Definition 2.8. The satisfaction relation $\models_{TB}$ of $\mathcal{ML}_{TB}$ over $\mathbb{P}_T$ is defined by induction on the syntactical structure of formulas as follows:

$P \models_{TB} \text{true}$		
$P \models_{TB} \neg\phi$	if $P \not\models_{TB} \phi$	
$P \models_{TB} \phi_1 \wedge \phi_2$	if $P \models_{TB} \phi_1$ and $P \models_{TB} \phi_2$	
$P \models_{TB} \langle a \rangle \phi$	if there exists $P' \in \mathbb{P}_T$ such that $P \overset{a}{\longrightarrow} P'$ and $P' \models_{TB} \phi$	
$P \models_{TB} \langle\langle n \rangle\rangle \phi$	if there exists $P' \in \mathbb{P}_T$ such that $P \overset{n}{\longrightarrow} P'$ and $P' \models_{TB} \phi$	

where $\not\models_{TB}$ denotes the complement of $\models_{TB}$ with respect to $\mathbb{P}_T \times \mathcal{ML}_{TB}$.

Theorem 2.4. *Let* $P_1, P_2 \in \mathbb{P}_T$. *Then:*
$$P_1 \sim_{TB} P_2 \iff (\forall \phi \in \mathcal{ML}_{TB}.\, P_1 \models_{TB} \phi \iff P_2 \models_{TB} \phi)$$

2.3.5 Verification Algorithm

Timed bisimulation equivalence can be decided in polynomial time by means of the partition refinement algorithm for $\sim_B$ presented in Sect. 1.4.7, provided that the splitting operation is performed also with respect to every delay n labeling the time transitions of the two process terms under consideration.

2.3.6 Durational Bisimulation Equivalence and its Properties

In the case of durational actions, the timed extension of bisimulation equivalence must take into account durations and starting times too. Whenever a process term can perform an action with a certain name and a certain duration starting at a certain time, then any process term equivalent to the given one has to be able to respond with an action having the same name and the same duration starting at the same time. Moreover, the derivative process terms into which all the previous process terms have evolved after executing that action must still be equivalent to each other.

Definition 2.9. A binary relation $\mathscr{B}$ over $\mathbb{K}_D$ is a durational bisimulation iff, whenever $(K_1, K_2) \in \mathscr{B}$, then for all action names $a \in Name$, action durations $n \in \mathbb{N}_{>0}$, and time instants $t \in \mathbb{N}$:

- Whenever $K_1 \xrightarrow[t]{a,n}_D K_1'$, then $K_2 \xrightarrow[t]{a,n}_D K_2'$ with $(K_1', K_2') \in \mathscr{B}$
- Whenever $K_2 \xrightarrow[t]{a,n}_D K_2'$, then $K_1 \xrightarrow[t]{a,n}_D K_1'$ with $(K_1', K_2') \in \mathscr{B}$

Since the union of all the durational bisimulations can be proved to be the largest durational bisimulation, the definition below follows.

Definition 2.10. Durational bisimulation equivalence (or durational bisimilarity), denoted $\sim_{DB}$, is the union of all the durational bisimulations.

Definition 2.11. Let $P_1, P_2 \in \mathbb{P}_D$. We say that P_1 is durational bisimulation equivalent to P_2, still written $P_1 \sim_{DB} P_2$, iff $0 \Rightarrow P_1 \sim_{DB} 0 \Rightarrow P_2$.

The investigation of the properties of durational bisimulation equivalence is made complicated by the fact that the underlying operational semantics is not fully interleaving. However, it can be shown that $\sim_{DB}$ is a congruence with respect to all the dynamic and static operators of DPC as well as recursion, and that it has a modal logic characterization based on a variant of HML in which the diamond operator embodies action names, durations, and starting times.

Example 2.6. Let us model with DPC the concurrent implementation considered in Example 1.3 of the producer–consumer system introduced in Sect. 1.2. The process algebraic description extended with action durations consistent with those of Example 2.3 is as follows:

$$PC^D_{conc,2} \triangleq Prod^D \parallel_{\{deposit\}} (Buff^D \parallel_\emptyset Buff^D) \parallel_{\{withdraw\}} Cons^D$$
$$Prod^D \triangleq <deposit,n>.Prod^D$$
$$Buff^D \triangleq <deposit,n>.<withdraw,n>.Buff^D$$
$$Cons^D \triangleq <withdraw,n>.Cons^D$$

It turns out that $PC^D_{conc,2} \not\sim_{DB} ProdCons^D_{0/2}$ because, similar to Example 2.5, $PC^D_{conc,2}$ reaches a deadlock state after the deposit of the first item. In fact:

$$0 \Rightarrow PC^D_{conc,2} \xrightarrow[0]{deposit,n}_D$$
$$n \Rightarrow <deposit,n>.Prod^D \parallel_{\{deposit\}}$$
$$(n \Rightarrow <withdraw,n>.Buff^D \parallel_\emptyset 0 \Rightarrow <deposit,n>.<withdraw,n>.Buff^D)$$
$$\parallel_{\{withdraw\}} 0 \Rightarrow <withdraw,n>.Cons^D$$

but the target state cannot perform any action because synchronizations on *deposit* or *withdraw* are not permitted due to the different values of the local clocks of the involved subterms. In contrast, $ProdCons^D_{0/2}$ cannot deadlock.

Analogous to Example 2.5, the synchronization problem may be solved by introducing suitable $<\tau,n>$ actions for implementing delays, thereby revising the process algebraic description as follows:

$$PC'^{D}_{conc,2} \triangleq Prod^{D} \|_{\{deposit\}} (Buff^{D} \|_{\emptyset} <\tau,n>.Buff^{D}) \|_{\{withdraw\}} <\tau,n>.Cons^{D}$$

but these actions can never be matched by $ProdCons^{D}_{0/2}$.

2.4 Semantics-Preserving Mapping for Eagerness

In this section, we present a formal comparison between TPC and DPC; i.e., between the two-phase functioning principle and the one-phase functioning principle under eager action execution. We first discuss some conceptual differences between the two deterministically timed process calculi, then we define a semantics-preserving mapping inspired by [74] showing that the different design decisions at the base of the two calculi are not irreconcilable.

2.4.1 Differences Between TPC and DPC

We start by contrasting the main operators used to extend the untimed process calculus PC into the deterministically timed process calculi TPC and DPC. There is a substantial difference between the TPC term $(n).P$ and the DPC term $<\tau,n>.P$. This is because $<\tau,n>.P$ is just a timed version of the PC term $\tau.P$ and, in fact, $<\tau,n>.P$ can be seen as an abbreviation for $(<a,n>.\underline{0}\|_{\{a\}}<a,n>.\underline{0})/\{a\}$. This immediately leads to distinguish a choice followed by a wait from a wait followed by a choice. In particular, $<\tau,n>.P_1 + <\tau,n>.P_2$ is not durational bisimilar to $<\tau,n>.(P_1 + P_2)$, thus representing a timed version of the distinction between $\tau.P_1 + \tau.P_2$ and $\tau.(P_1 + P_2)$. On the other hand, TPC does not allow the passage of time to decide a choice and, in fact, we have that $(n).P_1 + (n).P_2$ is timed bisimilar to $(n).(P_1 + P_2)$, because any initial passage of time must be permitted by both $(n).P_1$ and $(n).P_2$.

Another substantial difference between TPC and DPC is related to their inactive processes. The one of DPC, which is denoted by $\underline{0}$, behaves as the neutral element for the alternative composition operator and (to some extent) for the parallel composition operator. In contrast, the one of TPC, denoted by $\overline{0}$, behaves as an absorbing element for the alternative composition operator and for the parallel composition operator when one of the two subterms starts with a time prefix. The reason is that $\overline{0}$ does not let time pass. Consider, for instance, the DPC term $\underline{0}\|_{\emptyset}<a,n>.<b,m>.\underline{0}$. When starting execution at time 0, this process term can perform an action of name a and duration n at time 0 followed by an action of name b and duration m at time n. On a different side, the TPC term $\overline{0}\|_{\emptyset}a.(n).b.(m).\overline{0}$ can perform only an a-action and then reaches the deadlock state described by process term $\overline{0}\|_{\emptyset}(n).b.(m).\overline{0}$, which is timed bisimilar to $\overline{0}$. In order to find a TPC term that behaves like the DPC inactive process $\underline{0}$, we need to avoid the execution of actions while letting any amount of time pass. An example of such a term is $recX:(1).X$.

The example above illustrates a phenomenon due to the behavior of $\overline{0}$ called timestop, which arises when a stop of the time passing causes a stop of the system behavior as a whole. A more dynamic example of timestop can be seen by considering the TPC term $a.d.\overline{0}\|_{\{a,d\}}a.(n).b.(m).\overline{0}$. It can perform only an a-action and then reaches the deadlock state described by process term $d.\overline{0}\|_{\{a,d\}}(n).b.(m).\overline{0}$. Again, this is because the leftmost subterm cannot let time pass, nor can it execute any action due to the synchronization constraint on d. A similar example based on the restriction operator is given by the TPC term $(d.\overline{0})\backslash\{d\}\|_{\emptyset}a.(n).b.(m).\overline{0}$.

2.4.2 From DPC to TPC Under Eagerness

When synchronizations and restrictions are left out, it turns out that TPC and DPC are strictly related despite their differences. To see this, we first define a mapping $\Pi[\![\_]\!]:\mathbb{P}_{D,srf}\to\mathbb{P}_{T,srf}$ as the smallest relation satisfying the rules shown in the upper part of Table 2.4, where $\mathbb{P}_{D,srf}$ and $\mathbb{P}_{T,srf}$ are the sets of synchronization- and restriction-free process terms of $\mathbb{P}_D$ and $\mathbb{P}_T$, respectively. The basic idea is to split a durational action $<a,n>$ into an a-action prefix followed by an n-time prefix.

Then, we observe that the mapping is semantics preserving; i.e., two process terms of $\mathbb{P}_{D,srf}$ are durational bisimilar iff their corresponding process terms of $\mathbb{P}_{T,srf}$ are timed bisimilar. Since $\sim_{DB}$ is defined over $\mathbb{K}_D$, we need to introduce an

Table 2.4 Rules for mapping DPC into TPC under eagerness

$$
\begin{aligned}
\Pi[\![\underline{0}]\!] &= recX:(1).X \\
\Pi[\![<a,n>.P]\!] &= a.(n).\Pi[\![P]\!] \\
\Pi[\![P_1+P_2]\!] &= \Pi[\![P_1]\!]+\Pi[\![P_2]\!] \\
\Pi[\![P_1\|_\emptyset P_2]\!] &= \Pi[\![P_1]\!]\|_\emptyset \Pi_e[\![P_2]\!] \\
\Pi[\![P/H]\!] &= \Pi[\![P]\!]/H \\
\Pi[\![P\backslash\emptyset]\!] &= \Pi[\![P]\!]\backslash\emptyset \\
\Pi[\![P[\varphi]]\!] &= \Pi[\![P]\!][\varphi] \\
\Pi[\![X]\!] &= X \\
\Pi[\![recX:P]\!] &= recX:\Pi[\![P]\!]
\end{aligned}
$$

$$
\begin{aligned}
\Delta[\![0\Rightarrow\underline{0}]\!] &= \Pi[\![\underline{0}]\!] \\
\Delta[\![t\Rightarrow\underline{0}]\!] &= (t).\Pi[\![\underline{0}]\!] & \text{if } t>0 \\
\Delta[\![0\Rightarrow<a,n>.P]\!] &= \Pi[\![<a,n>.P]\!] \\
\Delta[\![t\Rightarrow<a,n>.P]\!] &= (t).\Pi[\![<a,n>.P]\!] & \text{if } t>0 \\
\Delta[\![K_1+K_2]\!] &= \Delta[\![K_1]\!]+\Delta[\![K_2]\!] \\
\Delta[\![K_1\|_\emptyset K_2]\!] &= \Delta[\![K_1]\!]\|_\emptyset \Delta[\![K_2]\!] \\
\Delta[\![K/H]\!] &= \Delta[\![K]\!]/H \\
\Delta[\![K\backslash\emptyset]\!] &= \Delta[\![K]\!]\backslash\emptyset \\
\Delta[\![K[\varphi]]\!] &= \Delta[\![K]\!][\varphi] \\
\Delta[\![0\Rightarrow recX:P]\!] &= \Pi[\![recX:P]\!] \\
\Delta[\![t\Rightarrow recX:P]\!] &= (t).\Pi[\![recX:P]\!] & \text{if } t>0
\end{aligned}
$$

auxiliary mapping $\Delta[\![\_]\!] : \mathbb{K}_{D,srf} \to \mathbb{P}_{T,srf}$, which is formalized as the smallest relation satisfying the rules in the lower part of Table 2.4.

Theorem 2.5. *Let* $P_1, P_2 \in \mathbb{P}_{D,srf}$. *Then:*

$$P_1 \sim_{DB} P_2 \iff \Pi[\![P_1]\!] \sim_{TB} \Pi[\![P_2]\!]$$

2.5 Semantics-Preserving Mapping for Laziness

So far, we have considered deterministically timed process calculi with urgent actions–i.e., actions that must be performed as soon as they become enabled–in which synchronizations can take place only if the participating actions are executed at the same time. In this context, we have seen that synchronizations and restrictions may cause the deadlock of a single system part, which in turn may cause the deadlock of the entire system because of the timestop phenomenon.

In this section, we reconsider TPC and DPC under lazy action execution; i.e., we now assume that actions can be delayed arbitrarily long before their are executed. After revising the semantics for the two calculi in accordance with [158,76], following [74] we show that under laziness it is possible to define a semantics-preserving mapping that includes synchronizations and restrictions too.

2.5.1 Lazy TPC

The lazy variant of TPC has the same syntax as TPC; hence, we still use $\mathbb{P}_T$ to denote the set of its closed and guarded process terms.

As far as the operational semantics is concerned, the action transition relation is unchanged, whereas the time transition relation $\longrightarrow_l$ is the smallest subset of $\mathbb{P}_T \times \mathbb{N}_{>0} \times \mathbb{P}_T$ satisfying the operational semantic rules shown in Table 2.1 as well as the semantic rules of Table 2.5 added in order to introduce laziness. Rules $\text{NIL}_{T,l}$ and $\text{PRE}_{T,l}$ establish that the timed inactive process and every action prefix can let any amount of time pass, so that each process term can let any amount of time pass as well, and hence the problems discussed in Sect. 2.4.1 no longer arise. In the lazy case, we denote by $[\![P]\!]_{T,l}$ the labeled transition system for a process term $P \in \mathbb{P}_T$.

Table 2.5 Additional time-related operational semantic rules for lazy TPC

$$(\text{NIL}_{T,l}) \quad \frac{}{\underline{0} \xrightarrow{n}_l \underline{0}}$$

$$(\text{PRE}_{T,l}) \quad \frac{}{a.P \xrightarrow{n}_l a.P}$$

The notion of lazy timed bisimulation equivalence (or lazy timed bisimilarity), denoted $\sim_{\text{TB},\text{l}}$, is defined in the same way as $\sim_{\text{TB}}$ and enjoys similar properties.

Example 2.7. Let us reconsider $ProdCons^{\text{T}}_{0/2}$ and $PC^{\text{T}}_{\text{conc},2}$ in the lazy setting. Although their descriptions are unchanged, their underlying labeled transition systems are different with respect to the eager case due to the two additional semantic rules.

It turns out that $PC^{\text{T}}_{\text{conc},2} \not\sim_{\text{TB},\text{l}} ProdCons^{\text{T}}_{0/2}$. In fact, $PC^{\text{T}}_{\text{conc},2}$ has no longer the synchronization problem observed in Example 2.5, because the state reached after the deposit of the first item can now let time pass, thereby enabling after n time units a further deposit or withdrawal operation through synchronizations between suitable subterms. However, at certain points $PC^{\text{T}}_{\text{conc},2}$ can still perform both *deposit* and *withdraw* at the same time, which is not possible in $ProdCons^{\text{T}}_{0/2}$ where in any case the two actions are separated by a delay or are alternative to each other.

2.5.2 Lazy DPC

The lazy variant of DPC has the same syntax as DPC; hence, we still use $\mathbb{P}_{\text{D}}$ to denote the set of its closed and guarded process terms.

As far as the operational semantics is concerned, transitions have a starting time that can now be greater than the value of any local clock because of laziness. Moreover, the syntax of process terms with local clocks that represent states must be extended in order to record the value of the global clock. This is not necessary in an eager setting because actions are urgent and hence the local clocks automatically define a unique notion of global time, whereas in a lazy setting ambiguities may arise. In order to avoid them, the value of the global clock is assumed to coincide with the value of the minimum local clock.

A process term with local clocks and global clock is of the form $K \rhd gt$ where $K \in \mathcal{K}\mathcal{L}_{\text{D}}$ and $gt \in \mathbb{N}$. We denote by $\mathbb{K}'_{\text{D}}$ the set of closed and guarded process terms with local clocks and global clock. The transition relation $\longrightarrow_{\text{D},\text{l}}$ is the smallest subset of $\mathbb{K}'_{\text{D}} \times Act_{\text{D}} \times \mathbb{N} \times \mathbb{K}'_{\text{D}}$ satisfying the operational semantic rules of Table 2.6. Rule $\text{PRE}_{\text{D},\text{l}}$ states that the execution of an action can start at any time greater than the global clock and the local clock of the process term enabling the action, then updates the local clock by taking into account the global clock value. Since actions are no longer urgent, the rules for the alternative and parallel composition operators no longer include the negative premises contained in the corresponding rules shown in Table 2.2. The labeled transition system for a process term $P \in \mathbb{P}_{\text{D}}$ is denoted by $[\![P]\!]_{\text{D},\text{l}}$ in the lazy case and its initial state is $(0 \Rightarrow P) \rhd 0$.

The notion of lazy durational bisimulation equivalence (or lazy durational bisimilarity), denoted $\sim_{\text{DB},\text{l}}$, is defined in a way similar to $\sim_{\text{DB}}$ and has similar properties. The additional constraint to meet is that equivalent process terms with local clocks and global clock must have the same global clock value.

Table 2.6 Time-integrated operational semantic rules for lazy DPC

$$(\text{PRE}_{D,l}) \quad \frac{gt' \geq \max(gt,t)}{(t \Rightarrow <a,n>.P) \triangleright gt \xrightarrow[gt']{a,n}_{D,l} ((gt'+n) \Rightarrow P) \triangleright gt'}$$

$$(\text{ALT}_{D,l,1}) \quad \frac{K_1 \triangleright gt \xrightarrow[gt']{a,n}_{D,l} K_1' \triangleright gt'}{(K_1 + K_2) \triangleright gt \xrightarrow[gt']{a,n}_{D,l} K_1' \triangleright gt'}$$

$$(\text{ALT}_{D,l,2}) \quad \frac{K_2 \triangleright gt \xrightarrow[gt']{a,n}_{D,l} K_2' \triangleright gt'}{(K_1 + K_2) \triangleright gt \xrightarrow[gt']{a,n}_{D,l} K_2' \triangleright gt'}$$

$$(\text{PAR}_{D,l,1}) \quad \frac{K_1 \triangleright gt \xrightarrow[gt']{a,n}_{D,l} K_1' \triangleright gt' \qquad a \notin S}{(K_1 \|_S K_2) \triangleright gt \xrightarrow[gt']{a,n}_{D,l} (K_1' \|_S K_2) \triangleright gt'}$$

$$(\text{PAR}_{D,l,2}) \quad \frac{K_2 \triangleright gt \xrightarrow[gt']{a,n}_{D,l} K_2' \triangleright gt' \qquad a \notin S}{(K_1 \|_S K_2) \triangleright gt \xrightarrow[gt']{a,n}_{D,l} (K_1 \|_S K_2') \triangleright gt'}$$

$$(\text{SYN}_{D,l}) \quad \frac{K_1 \triangleright gt \xrightarrow[gt']{a,n}_{D,l} K_1' \triangleright gt' \qquad K_2 \triangleright gt \xrightarrow[gt']{a,n}_{D,l} K_2' \triangleright gt' \qquad a \in S}{(K_1 \|_S K_2) \triangleright gt \xrightarrow[gt']{a,n}_{D,l} (K_1' \|_S K_2') \triangleright gt'}$$

$$(\text{HID}_{D,l,1}) \quad \frac{K \triangleright gt \xrightarrow[gt']{a,n}_{D,l} K' \triangleright gt' \qquad a \in H}{(K/H) \triangleright gt \xrightarrow[gt']{\tau,n}_{D,l} (K'/H) \triangleright gt'}$$

$$(\text{HID}_{D,l,2}) \quad \frac{K \triangleright gt \xrightarrow[gt']{a,n}_{D,l} K' \triangleright gt' \qquad a \notin H}{(K/H) \triangleright gt \xrightarrow[gt']{a,n}_{D,l} (K'/H) \triangleright gt'}$$

$$(\text{RES}_{D,l}) \quad \frac{K \triangleright gt \xrightarrow[gt']{a,n}_{D,l} K' \triangleright gt' \qquad a \notin L}{(K \backslash L) \triangleright gt \xrightarrow[gt']{a,n}_{D,l} (K' \backslash L) \triangleright gt'}$$

$$(\text{REL}_{D,l}) \quad \frac{K \triangleright gt \xrightarrow[gt']{a,n}_{D,l} K' \triangleright gt'}{(K[\varphi]) \triangleright gt \xrightarrow[gt']{\varphi(a),n}_{D,l} (K'[\varphi]) \triangleright gt'}$$

$$(\text{REC}_{D,l}) \quad \frac{(t \Rightarrow P\{recX : P \hookrightarrow X\}) \triangleright gt \xrightarrow[gt']{a,n}_{D,l} K' \triangleright gt'}{(t \Rightarrow recX : P) \triangleright gt \xrightarrow[gt']{a,n}_{D,l} K' \triangleright gt'}$$

Example 2.8. Let us reconsider $ProdCons_{0/2}^D$ and $PC_{conc,2}^D$ in the lazy setting. Although their descriptions are unchanged, their underlying labeled transition systems are different with respect to the eager case because the semantic rules are different.

It turns out that $PC_{conc,2}^D \not\sim_{DB,1} ProdCons_{0/2}^D$. In fact, $PC_{conc,2}^D$ has no longer the synchronization problem observed in Example 2.6, because the state reached after the deposit of the first item can now permit a further deposit or withdrawal operation through lazy synchronizations between suitable subterms. However, $PC_{conc,2}^D$ may exploit its concurrent structure for starting several actions at the same time, which is not possible in $ProdCons_{0/2}^D$. For instance:

$$(0 \Rightarrow PC_{conc,2}^D) \triangleright 0$$

$$\xrightarrow[\quad 0 \quad]{\substack{deposit,n \\ \text{D,1}}}$$

$$(n \Rightarrow <deposit,n>.Prod^D \parallel_{\{deposit\}}$$
$$(n \Rightarrow <withdraw,n>.Buff^D \parallel_{\emptyset} 0 \Rightarrow Buff^D)$$
$$\parallel_{\{withdraw\}} 0 \Rightarrow <withdraw,n>.Cons^D) \triangleright 0$$

$$\xrightarrow[\quad n \quad]{\substack{deposit,n \\ \text{D,1}}}$$

$$(2 \cdot n \Rightarrow <deposit,n>.Prod^D \parallel_{\{deposit\}}$$
$$(n \Rightarrow <withdraw,n>.Buff^D \parallel_{\emptyset} 2 \cdot n \Rightarrow <withdraw,n>.Buff^D)$$
$$\parallel_{\{withdraw\}} 0 \Rightarrow <withdraw,n>.Cons^D) \triangleright n$$

$$\xrightarrow[\quad n \quad]{\substack{withdraw,n \\ \text{D,1}}}$$

$$(2 \cdot n \Rightarrow <deposit,n>.Prod^D \parallel_{\{deposit\}}$$
$$(2 \cdot n \Rightarrow Buff^D \parallel_{\emptyset} 2 \cdot n \Rightarrow <withdraw,n>.Buff^D)$$
$$\parallel_{\{withdraw\}} 2 \cdot n \Rightarrow <withdraw,n>.Cons^D) \triangleright n$$

whereas:

$$(0 \Rightarrow ProdCons_{0/2}^D) \triangleright 0$$

$$\xrightarrow[\quad 0 \quad]{\substack{deposit,n \\ \text{D,1}}}$$

$$(n \Rightarrow ProdCons_{1/2}^D) \triangleright 0$$

$$\xrightarrow[\quad n \quad]{\substack{deposit,n \\ \text{D,1}}}$$

$$(2 \cdot n \Rightarrow ProdCons_{2/2}^D) \triangleright n$$

$$\xrightarrow[\quad 2 \cdot n \quad]{\substack{withdraw,n \\ \text{D,1}}}$$

$$(3 \cdot n \Rightarrow ProdCons_{1/2}^D) \triangleright 2 \cdot n$$

with the two withdrawals being started at different time instants in the two systems and the last two states having different global clock values.

Table 2.7 Rules for mapping DPC into TPC under laziness and maximal progress

$$
\begin{aligned}
\Pi'[\![\underline{0}]\!] &= \overline{0} \\
\Pi'[\![<a,n>.P]\!] &= a.(n).\Pi'[\![P]\!] \\
\Pi'[\![P_1 + P_2]\!] &= \Pi'[\![P_1]\!] + \Pi'[\![P_2]\!] \\
\Pi'[\![P_1 \|_S P_2]\!] &= \Pi'[\![P_1]\!] \|_S \Pi'[\![P_2]\!] \\
\Pi'[\![P/H]\!] &= \Pi'[\![P]\!]/H \\
\Pi'[\![P\backslash L]\!] &= \Pi'[\![P]\!]\backslash L \\
\Pi'[\![P[\varphi]]\!] &= \Pi'[\![P]\!][\varphi] \\
\Pi'[\![X]\!] &= X \\
\Pi'[\![recX:P]\!] &= recX:\Pi'[\![P]\!]
\end{aligned}
$$

$$
\begin{aligned}
\Delta'[\![(0 \Rightarrow \underline{0}) \triangleright gt]\!] &= \Pi'[\![\underline{0}]\!] \\
\Delta'[\![(t \Rightarrow \underline{0}) \triangleright gt]\!] &= (t).\Pi'[\![\underline{0}]\!] && \text{if } t > 0 \\
\Delta'[\![(0 \Rightarrow <a,n>.P) \triangleright gt]\!] &= \Pi'[\![<a,n>.P]\!] \\
\Delta'[\![(t \Rightarrow <a,n>.P) \triangleright gt]\!] &= (t).\Pi'[\![<a,n>.P]\!] && \text{if } t > 0 \\
\Delta'[\![(K_1 + K_2) \triangleright gt]\!] &= \Delta'[\![K_1 \triangleright gt]\!] + \Delta'[\![K_2 \triangleright gt]\!] \\
\Delta'[\![(K_1 \|_S K_2) \triangleright gt]\!] &= \Delta'[\![K_1 \triangleright gt]\!] \|_S \Delta'[\![K_2 \triangleright gt]\!] \\
\Delta'[\![(K/H) \triangleright gt]\!] &= \Delta'[\![K \triangleright gt]\!]/H \\
\Delta'[\![(K\backslash L) \triangleright gt]\!] &= \Delta'[\![K \triangleright gt]\!]\backslash L \\
\Delta'[\![(K[\varphi]) \triangleright gt]\!] &= \Delta'[\![K \triangleright gt]\!][\varphi] \\
\Delta'[\![(0 \Rightarrow recX:P) \triangleright gt]\!] &= \Pi'[\![recX:P]\!] \\
\Delta'[\![(t \Rightarrow recX:P) \triangleright gt]\!] &= (t).\Pi'[\![recX:P]\!] && \text{if } t > 0
\end{aligned}
$$

2.5.3 From DPC to TPC Under Laziness

We relate lazy TPC and lazy DPC by defining a mapping $\Pi'[\![\_]\!] : \mathbb{P}_D \to \mathbb{P}_T$ as the smallest relation satisfying the rules shown in the upper part of Table 2.7, together with an auxiliary mapping $\Delta'[\![\_]\!] : \mathbb{K}'_D \to \mathbb{P}_T$ formalized as the smallest relation satisfying the rules in the lower part of Table 2.7.

The basic idea is still that of splitting a durational action $<a,n>$ into an a-action prefix followed by an n-time prefix. Moreover, by virtue of laziness, it is now possible to translate $\underline{0}$ into $\overline{0}$ and to include synchronizations and restrictions. Also this mapping is semantics preserving, thus showing that TPC and DPC are in some sense compatible under laziness as well.

Theorem 2.6. Let $P_1, P_2 \in \mathbb{P}_D$. Then:

$$P_1 \sim_{DB,l} P_2 \iff \Pi'[\![P_1]\!] \sim_{TB,l} \Pi'[\![P_2]\!]$$

2.6 Semantics-Preserving Mapping for Maximal Progress

Maximal progress establishes that actions can be delayed arbitrarily long like in the lazy case, unless they are involved in synchronizations, in which case they are urgent. In other words, a system part is lazy as long as it does not interact with other parts, but no delay is admitted if other parts are willing to communicate with it.

Technically speaking, this amounts to considering visible actions as being lazy and invisible actions as being urgent, as each τ-action can be thought of as deriving from the complete synchronization of several actions, like in $(a \cdot P_1 \parallel_{\{a\}} a \cdot P_2)/\{a\}$. By complete synchronization we mean that all the system parts that are expected to synchronize actually do, and hence it is not necessary to wait for further parts to be involved in the synchronization.

In this section, we reconsider TPC and DPC under maximal progress. After revising the semantics for the two calculi in accordance with [199, 114, 78], following [74] we show that also in the case of maximal progress it is possible to define a semantics-preserving mapping.

2.6.1 Maximal Progress TPC

The maximal progress variant of TPC has the same syntax as TPC; hence, we still use $\mathbb{P}_T$ to denote the set of its closed and guarded process terms.

As far as the operational semantics is concerned, the action transition relation is unchanged, whereas the time transition relation $\overset{}{\longrightarrow}_{mp}$ is the smallest subset of $\mathbb{P}_T \times \mathbb{N}_{>0} \times \mathbb{P}_T$ satisfying the operational semantic rules of Table 2.8. Note that rule $\text{PRE}_{T,mp,2}$ establishes that only visible actions can be delayed. Moreover, the negative premise of rule $\text{HID}_{T,mp}$ ensures that visible actions to be hidden are not delayed, unless they are preceded by a time prefix. In order for this rule to work, we assume by convention that $P \overset{0}{\longrightarrow}_{mp} P$ for all $P \in \mathbb{P}_T$. In the maximal progress case, we denote by $[\![P]\!]_{T,mp}$ the labeled transition system for a process term $P \in \mathbb{P}_T$.

The notion of maximal progress timed bisimulation equivalence (or maximal progress timed bisimilarity), denoted $\sim_{TB,mp}$, is defined in the same way as $\sim_{TB}$ and enjoys similar properties.

Example 2.9. If we reconsider $ProdCons_{0/2}^T$ and $PC_{conc,2}^T$ in the maximal progress setting, their underlying labeled transition systems are unchanged with respect to the lazy case because they contain no τ-transitions. As a consequence, it turns out that $PC_{conc,2}^T \nsim_{TB,mp} ProdCons_{0/2}^T$ for the same reason explained in Example 2.7.

2.6.2 Maximal Progress DPC

The maximal progress variant of DPC has the same syntax as DPC; hence, we still use $\mathbb{P}_D$ to denote the set of its closed and guarded process terms.

As far as the operational semantics is concerned, similar to the lazy case states contain the global clock in addition to local clocks. The transition relation $\overset{}{\longrightarrow}_{D,mp}$ is the smallest subset of $\mathbb{K}'_D \times Act_D \times \mathbb{N} \times \mathbb{K}'_D$ satisfying the operational semantic rules of Table 2.9. Note that rule $\text{PRE}_{D,mp}$ establishes that only visible actions can be delayed. Moreover, the negative premises of rules $\text{ALT}_{D,mp,1}$,

Table 2.8 Time-related operational semantic rules for maximal progress TPC

$$(\text{NIL}_{\text{T,mp}}) \quad \frac{}{\overline{0} \xrightarrow{\;n\;}_{\text{mp}} \overline{0}}$$

$$(\text{PRE}_{\text{T,mp,1}}) \quad \frac{}{(n).P \xrightarrow{\;n\;}_{\text{mp}} P}$$

$$(\text{PRE}_{\text{T,mp,2}}) \quad \frac{a \in Name_{\text{v}}}{a.P \xrightarrow{\;n\;}_{\text{mp}} a.P}$$

$$(\text{DEC}_{\text{T,mp}}) \quad \frac{n = n_1 + n_2}{(n).P \xrightarrow{\;n_1\;}_{\text{mp}} (n_2).P} \qquad (\text{SUM}_{\text{T,mp}}) \quad \frac{P \xrightarrow{\;n\;}_{\text{mp}} P'}{(m).P \xrightarrow{\;n+m\;}_{\text{mp}} P'}$$

$$(\text{ALT}_{\text{T,mp}}) \quad \frac{P_1 \xrightarrow{\;n\;}_{\text{mp}} P_1' \qquad P_2 \xrightarrow{\;n\;}_{\text{mp}} P_2'}{P_1 + P_2 \xrightarrow{\;n\;}_{\text{mp}} P_1' + P_2'}$$

$$(\text{SYN}_{\text{T,mp}}) \quad \frac{P_1 \xrightarrow{\;n\;}_{\text{mp}} P_1' \qquad P_2 \xrightarrow{\;n\;}_{\text{mp}} P_2'}{P_1 \parallel_S P_2 \xrightarrow{\;n\;}_{\text{mp}} P_1' \parallel_S P_2'}$$

$$(\text{HID}_{\text{T,mp}}) \quad \frac{P \xrightarrow{\;n\;}_{\text{mp}} P' \qquad \neg(P \xrightarrow{\;m\;}_{\text{mp}} Q \wedge m < n \wedge Q \xrightarrow{\;a\;} Q' \wedge a \in H)}{P/H \xrightarrow{\;n\;}_{\text{mp}} P'/H}$$

$$(\text{RES}_{\text{T,mp}}) \quad \frac{P \xrightarrow{\;n\;}_{\text{mp}} P'}{P \backslash L \xrightarrow{\;n\;}_{\text{mp}} P' \backslash L}$$

$$(\text{REL}_{\text{T,mp}}) \quad \frac{P \xrightarrow{\;n\;}_{\text{mp}} P'}{P[\varphi] \xrightarrow{\;n\;}_{\text{mp}} P'[\varphi]}$$

$$(\text{REC}_{\text{T,mp}}) \quad \frac{P\{rec\,X : P \hookrightarrow X\} \xrightarrow{\;n\;}_{\text{mp}} P'}{rec\,X : P \xrightarrow{\;n\;}_{\text{mp}} P'}$$

$\text{ALT}_{\text{D,mp,2}}$, $\text{PRE}_{\text{D,mp,1}}$, $\text{PRE}_{\text{D,mp,2}}$, $\text{HID}_{\text{D,mp,1}}$, and $\text{HID}_{\text{D,mp,2}}$ ensure that invisible actions or visible actions to be hidden take precedence over actions whose execution starts later. In the maximal progress case, we denote by $[\![P]\!]_{\text{D,mp}}$ the labeled transition system for a process term $P \in \mathbb{P}_{\text{D}}$.

The notion of maximal progress durational bisimulation equivalence (or maximal progress durational bisimilarity), denoted $\sim_{\text{DB,mp}}$, is defined in a way similar to $\sim_{\text{DB,l}}$ and has similar properties.

Table 2.9 Time-integrated operational semantic rules for maximal progress DPC

$$(\text{PRE}_{D,mp}) \quad \frac{(a \in Name_v \wedge gt' \geq \max(gt,t)) \vee (a = \tau \wedge gt' = t \geq gt)}{(t \Rightarrow <a,n>.P) \rhd gt \xrightarrow[gt']{a,n}_{D,mp} ((gt'+n) \Rightarrow P) \rhd gt'}$$

$$(\text{ALT}_{D,mp,1}) \quad \frac{K_1 \rhd gt \xrightarrow[gt']{a,n}_{D,mp} K_1' \rhd gt' \qquad \neg(K_2 \rhd gt \xrightarrow[gt'']{\tau,n'}_{D,mp} K_2' \rhd gt'' \wedge gt'' < gt')}{(K_1 + K_2) \rhd gt \xrightarrow[gt']{a,n}_{D,mp} K_1' \rhd gt'}$$

$$(\text{ALT}_{D,mp,2}) \quad \frac{K_2 \rhd gt \xrightarrow[gt']{a,n}_{D,mp} K_2' \rhd gt' \qquad \neg(K_1 \rhd gt \xrightarrow[gt'']{\tau,n'}_{D,mp} K_1' \rhd gt'' \wedge gt'' < gt')}{(K_1 + K_2) \rhd gt \xrightarrow[gt']{a,n}_{D,mp} K_2' \rhd gt'}$$

$$(\text{PAR}_{D,mp,1}) \quad \frac{K_1 \rhd gt \xrightarrow[gt']{a,n}_{D,mp} K_1' \rhd gt' \qquad \neg(K_2 \rhd gt \xrightarrow[gt'']{\tau,n'}_{D,mp} K_2' \rhd gt'' \wedge gt'' < gt') \qquad a \notin S}{(K_1 \parallel_S K_2) \rhd gt \xrightarrow[gt']{a,n}_{D,mp} (K_1' \parallel_S K_2) \rhd gt'}$$

$$(\text{PAR}_{D,mp,2}) \quad \frac{K_2 \rhd gt \xrightarrow[gt']{a,n}_{D,mp} K_2' \rhd gt' \qquad \neg(K_1 \rhd gt \xrightarrow[gt'']{\tau,n'}_{D,mp} K_1' \rhd gt'' \wedge gt'' < gt') \qquad a \notin S}{(K_1 \parallel_S K_2) \rhd gt \xrightarrow[gt']{a,n}_{D,mp} (K_1 \parallel_S K_2') \rhd gt'}$$

$$(\text{SYN}_{D,mp}) \quad \frac{K_1 \rhd gt \xrightarrow[gt']{a,n}_{D,mp} K_1' \rhd gt' \qquad K_2 \rhd gt \xrightarrow[gt']{a,n}_{D,mp} K_2' \rhd gt' \qquad a \in S}{(K_1 \parallel_S K_2) \rhd gt \xrightarrow[gt']{a,n}_{D,mp} (K_1' \parallel_S K_2') \rhd gt'}$$

$$(\text{HID}_{D,mp,1}) \quad \frac{K \rhd gt \xrightarrow[gt']{a,n}_{D,mp} K' \rhd gt' \qquad \neg(K \rhd gt \xrightarrow[gt'']{b,n'}_{D,mp} K' \rhd gt'' \wedge gt'' < gt' \wedge b \in H) \qquad a \in H}{(K/H) \rhd gt \xrightarrow[gt']{\tau,n}_{D,mp} (K'/H) \rhd gt'}$$

$$(\text{HID}_{D,mp,2}) \quad \frac{K \rhd gt \xrightarrow[gt']{a,n}_{D,mp} K' \rhd gt' \qquad \neg(K \rhd gt \xrightarrow[gt'']{b,n'}_{D,mp} K' \rhd gt'' \wedge gt'' < gt' \wedge b \in H) \qquad a \notin H}{(K/H) \rhd gt \xrightarrow[gt']{a,n}_{D,mp} (K'/H) \rhd gt'}$$

$$(\text{RES}_{D,mp}) \quad \frac{K \rhd gt \xrightarrow[gt']{a,n}_{D,mp} K' \rhd gt' \qquad a \notin L}{(K \backslash L) \rhd gt \xrightarrow[gt']{a,n}_{D,mp} (K' \backslash L) \rhd gt'}$$

$$(\text{REL}_{D,mp}) \quad \frac{K \rhd gt \xrightarrow[gt']{a,n}_{D,mp} K' \rhd gt'}{(K[\varphi]) \rhd gt \xrightarrow[gt']{\varphi(a),n}_{D,mp} (K'[\varphi]) \rhd gt'}$$

$$(\text{REC}_{D,mp}) \quad \frac{(t \Rightarrow P\{recX : P \hookrightarrow X\}) \rhd gt \xrightarrow[gt']{a,n}_{D,mp} K' \rhd gt'}{(t \Rightarrow recX : P) \rhd gt \xrightarrow[gt']{a,n}_{D,mp} K' \rhd gt'}$$

Example 2.10. If we reconsider $ProdCons_{0/2}^{D}$ and $PC_{conc,2}^{D}$ in the maximal progress setting, their underlying labeled transition systems are unchanged with respect to the lazy case because they contain no τ-transitions. As a consequence, it turns out that $PC_{conc,2}^{D} \not\sim_{DB,mp} ProdCons_{0/2}^{D}$ for the same reason explained in Example 2.8.

2.6.3 From DPC to TPC Under Maximal Progress

Maximal progress TPC and maximal progress DPC can be related by means of the mapping for the lazy versions of the two calculi shown in Table 2.7. Therefore, TPC and DPC turn out to be somehow compatible under maximal progress too.

Theorem 2.7. *Let* $P_1, P_2 \in \mathbb{P}_D$. *Then:*

$$P_1 \sim_{DB,mp} P_2 \iff \Pi'[\![P_1]\!] \sim_{TB,mp} \Pi'[\![P_2]\!]$$

2.7 Expressiveness of Eagerness, Laziness, Maximal Progress

In the last three sections, we have contrasted by means of semantics-preserving mappings the two deterministically timed process calculi based on the two-phase functioning principle and on the one-phase functioning principle, respectively. In this section, we study instead the semantic relationships among the different interpretations of action execution. Following [75], we concentrate on the expressiveness of eagerness, laziness, and maximal progress in the context of DPC in order to compare the discriminating power of $\sim_{DB}$, $\sim_{DB,l}$, and $\sim_{DB,mp}$.

The study is conducted by focusing on different variants of DPC that are significant from the point of view of action urgency or patience. In particular, we consider the following linguistic features related to synchronization of actions, choice among actions, and number of actions that can be executed in a finite amount of time:

- The language admits only independent executions of actions or also action synchronizations.
- The language admits choices only at the same time or also at different times. The former case refers to timed alternative compositions (e.g., having a snack or lunch now), where choices involve only system functionality. In contrast, the latter case refers to alternative timed compositions (e.g., having a snack now or lunch at noon), where choices involve timing as well.
- The language admits processes that can perform only finitely many actions in a finite amount of time or also infinitely many actions.

The outcome of the comparison is that $\sim_{DB}$, $\sim_{DB,l}$, and $\sim_{DB,mp}$ turn out to coincide only in the case of sequential processes; i.e., systems with a single local clock.

This demonstrates that eagerness, laziness, and maximal progress are primitive concepts in deterministically timed process calculi, in the sense that in general they are not able to simulate each other.

2.7.1 Synchronization Issues

Considering different synchronization capabilities shows that $\sim_{DB}$, $\sim_{DB,l}$, and $\sim_{DB,mp}$ are in general incomparable.

Proposition 2.1. *There exist* $P, Q \in \mathbb{P}_D$ *such that* $P \sim_{DB} Q$ *but neither* $P \sim_{DB,l} Q$ *nor* $P \sim_{DB,mp} Q$.

Take for example the following two process terms:

$$P \equiv <a,1>.\underline{0}$$
$$Q \equiv <a,1>.<b,1>.\underline{0}\|_{\{b\}} <b,1>.<d,1>.\underline{0}$$

They are durational bisimilar, but they are neither lazy nor maximal progress durational bisimilar. Indeed, in the eager case, the following transition:

$$0 \Rightarrow <a,1>.\underline{0} \xrightarrow[0]{a,1}_D 1 \Rightarrow \underline{0}$$

can be matched by the following transition:

$$0 \Rightarrow <a,1>.<b,1>.\underline{0}\|_{\{b\}} 0 \Rightarrow <b,1>.<d,1>.\underline{0} \xrightarrow[0]{a,1}_D$$
$$1 \Rightarrow <b,1>.\underline{0}\|_{\{b\}} 0 \Rightarrow <b,1>.<d,1>.\underline{0}$$

The state reached by the second transition cannot perform any further action because the two parallel subterms are not able to synchronize on b at the same time, as required by rule SYN_D of Table 2.2. In contrast, the synchronization is possible according to the operational semantic rules of Tables 2.6 and 2.9 for the lazy case and the maximal progress case, respectively, as they allow the right-hand side subterm to delay the execution of its b-action.

Proposition 2.2. *There exist* $P, Q \in \mathbb{P}_D$ *such that* $P \sim_{DB,l} Q$ *and* $P \sim_{DB,mp} Q$ *but not* $P \sim_{DB} Q$.

Take, for example, the following two process terms:

$$P \equiv <a,1>.(<b,1>.\underline{0}\|_{\{b\}} <b,1>.<d,1>.\underline{0})$$
$$Q \equiv <a,1>.<b,1>.\underline{0}\|_{\{b\}} <b,1>.<d,1>.\underline{0}$$

They are lazy and maximal progress durational bisimilar, but not durational bisimilar. Indeed, in the lazy (and maximal progress) case, the following transition:

$$(0 \Rightarrow <a,1>.(<b,1>.\underline{0}\,\|_{\{b\}}<b,1>.<d,1>.\underline{0}))\triangleright 0 \xrightarrow[0]{a,1} {}_{\mathrm{D,l}}$$

$$(1 \Rightarrow <b,1>\underline{0}\,\|_{\{b\}}\,1 \Rightarrow <b,1>.<d,1>.\underline{0})\triangleright 0$$

can be matched by the following transition:

$$(0 \Rightarrow <a,1>.<b,1>.\underline{0}\,\|_{\{b\}}\,0 \Rightarrow <b,1>.<d,1>.\underline{0})\triangleright 0 \xrightarrow[0]{a,1} {}_{\mathrm{D,l}}$$

$$(1 \Rightarrow <b,1>.\underline{0}\,\|_{\{b\}}\,0 \Rightarrow <b,1>.<d,1>.\underline{0})\triangleright 0$$

where the two reached states are lazy durational bisimilar as they both permit a synchronization on b. In contrast, this synchronization is not possible in the eager case for the second reached state because its two local clocks are different.

Proposition 2.3. *There exist* $P, Q \in \mathbb{P}_D$ *such that* $P \sim_{\mathrm{DB,mp}} Q$ *but not* $P \sim_{\mathrm{DB,l}} Q$.

Take, for example, the following two process terms:

$$P \equiv <\tau,3>.<a,1>.<b,1>.\underline{0}\,\|_{\{a\}}<\tau,1>.(<\tau,1>.\underline{0}+<a,1>.\underline{0})$$
$$Q \equiv <\tau,3>.\underline{0}\,\|_{\emptyset}<\tau,1>.<\tau,1>.\underline{0}$$

They are maximal progress durational bisimilar, but not lazy durational bisimilar. Indeed, in the maximal progress case P has the following sequence of transitions:

$$(0 \Rightarrow <\tau,3>.<a,1>.<b,1>.\underline{0}\,\|_{\{a\}}\,0 \Rightarrow <\tau,1>.(<\tau,1>.\underline{0}+<a,1>.\underline{0}))\triangleright 0$$

$$\xrightarrow[0]{\tau,3} {}_{\mathrm{D,mp}}$$

$$(3 \Rightarrow <a,1>.<b,1>.\underline{0}\,\|_{\{a\}}\,0 \Rightarrow <\tau,1>.(<\tau,1>.\underline{0}+<a,1>.\underline{0}))\triangleright 0$$

$$\xrightarrow[0]{\tau,1} {}_{\mathrm{D,mp}}$$

$$(3 \Rightarrow <a,1>.<b,1>.\underline{0}\,\|_{\{a\}}\,1 \Rightarrow <\tau,1>.\underline{0}+<a,1>.\underline{0})\triangleright 0$$

where a synchronization on a is not possible since the a-action in the right-hand side subterm cannot be delayed till time 3 due to the presence of an alternative τ-action whose execution starts at time 1. In contrast, in the lazy case P has the following sequence of transitions at the end of which a synchronization on a is possible:

$$(0 \Rightarrow <\tau,3>.<a,1>.<b,1>.\underline{0}\,\|_{\{a\}}\,0 \Rightarrow <\tau,1>.(<\tau,1>.\underline{0}+<a,1>.\underline{0}))\triangleright 0$$

$$\xrightarrow[0]{\tau,3} {}_{\mathrm{D,l}}$$

$$(3 \Rightarrow <a,1>.<b,1>.\underline{0}\,\|_{\{a\}}\,0 \Rightarrow <\tau,1>.(<\tau,1>.\underline{0}+<a,1>.\underline{0}))\triangleright 0$$

$$\xrightarrow[2]{\tau,1} {}_{\mathrm{D,l}}$$

$$(3 \Rightarrow <a,1>.<b,1>.\underline{0}\,\|_{\{a\}}\,3 \Rightarrow <\tau,1>.\underline{0}+<a,1>.\underline{0})\triangleright 2$$

We now mention a positive result, which establishes that $\sim_{\mathrm{DB,l}}$ is strictly finer than $\sim_{\mathrm{DB,mp}}$.

Proposition 2.4. *Let $P_1, P_2 \in \mathbb{P}_D$. Then:*

$$P_1 \sim_{DB,1} P_2 \implies P_1 \sim_{DB,mp} P_2$$

Unless stated otherwise, in the following we consider only visible actions, hence τ-actions are not permitted and the hiding operator reduces to $\_/\emptyset$. Under this limitation, $\sim_{DB,mp}$ turns out to coincide with $\sim_{DB,1}$. Furthermore, we consider only independent executions of actions. As a consequence, in order to avoid synchronizations and all kinds of restriction, the parallel composition operator reduces to $\_\|_\emptyset\_$ and the restriction operator reduces to $\_\backslash\emptyset$. We denote by $\mathbb{P}'_D$ the corresponding set of process terms of $\mathbb{P}_D$.

2.7.2 Choosing at Different Times

Systems that allow different alternatives to be chosen at different times are not expressible in DPC. However, they can be included by adding the time prefix operator of TPC together with the following three operational semantic rules for the eager case, the lazy case, and the maximal progress case, respectively:

$$
(\text{DEL}_D) \quad \frac{t+n \Rightarrow P \xrightarrow[t']{a,n'}_D K'}{t \Rightarrow (n).P \xrightarrow[t']{a,n'}_D K'}
$$

$$
(\text{DEL}_{D,1}) \quad \frac{((t+n) \Rightarrow P) \rhd gt \xrightarrow[gt']{a,n'}_{D,1} K \rhd gt'}{(t \Rightarrow (n).P) \rhd gt \xrightarrow[gt']{a,n'}_{D,1} K \rhd gt'}
$$

$$
(\text{DEL}_{D,mp}) \quad \frac{((t+n) \Rightarrow P) \rhd gt \xrightarrow[gt']{a,n'}_{D,mp} K \rhd gt'}{(t \Rightarrow (n).P) \rhd gt \xrightarrow[gt']{a,n'}_{D,mp} K \rhd gt'}
$$

With this operator we can now express both alternative timed compositions of the form $(n_1).P_1 + (n_2).P_2$, where $n_1 \neq n_2$ and P_1 and P_2 do not contain time prefixes at the top level, and timed alternative compositions of the form $(n).(P_1 + P_2)$. These two choices are conceptually different, because the latter involves only system functionality, whereas the former involves timing aspects as well.

In this durational setting extended with the time prefix operator, it turns out that $\sim_{DB,1}$ is strictly finer than $\sim_{DB}$.

Proposition 2.5. *Let P_1 and P_2 be obtained from process terms of $\mathbb{P}'_D$ by possibly including occurrences of the time prefix operator. Then:*

$$P_1 \sim_{DB,l} P_2 \implies P_1 \sim_{DB} P_2$$

To see why the inclusion is strict, consider the following two process terms:

$$P \equiv (<a,1>.\underline{0}\|_\emptyset(1).<b,1>.\underline{0}) + <a,1>.<b,1>.\underline{0}$$
$$Q \equiv <a,1>.\underline{0}\|_\emptyset(1).<b,1>.\underline{0}$$

They are durational bisimilar because the delay preceding two of the b-actions is equal to the duration of the a-actions. However, they are not lazy durational bisimilar. Indeed, in the lazy case, when P does the following transition:

$$((0 \Rightarrow <a,1>.\underline{0}\|_\emptyset 0 \Rightarrow (1).<b,1>.\underline{0}) + 0 \Rightarrow <a,1>.<b,1>.\underline{0}) \triangleright 0$$

$$\xrightarrow[1]{\quad a,1 \quad}_{D,l}$$

$$(2 \Rightarrow <b,1>.\underline{0}) \triangleright 1$$

then Q responds with the following transition:

$$(0 \Rightarrow <a,1>.\underline{0}\|_\emptyset 0 \Rightarrow (1).<b,1>.\underline{0}) \triangleright 0$$

$$\xrightarrow[1]{\quad a,1 \quad}_{D,l}$$

$$(2 \Rightarrow \underline{0}\|_\emptyset 0 \Rightarrow (1).<b,1>.\underline{0}) \triangleright 1$$

At this point, the minimum time at which the state reached by Q can perform a b-transition is 1, whereas the minimum time at which the state reached by P can perform a b-transition is 2.

In order to try to reduce the discriminating power of $\sim_{DB,l}$, in the following we consider only choices taking place at the same time, as is the case with $\mathbb{P}'_D$.

2.7.3 Performing Infinitely Many Actions at the Same Time

We now focus on the number of actions that can be performed in a finite amount of time. Let us consider the following two process terms:

$$P \equiv \prod_{i \in \mathbb{N}} <a,1>.\underline{0} \quad \text{and} \quad Q \equiv \sum_{i \in \mathbb{N}} \underbrace{<a,1>.\underline{0}\|_\emptyset \dots \|_\emptyset <a,1>.\underline{0}}_{i \text{ times}}$$

On the one hand, P can perform an infinite sequence of a-actions all starting at time 0, as it is the parallel composition of infinitely many subterms each of which can perform only an a-action. The same effect can be achieved by means of an unguarded process term like $recX : (X \|_\emptyset <a,1>.\underline{0})$. On the other hand, Q can perform infinitely many finite sequences of a-actions, as it is the alternative composition of infinitely many subterms each constituting a finite approximation of P.

Even if we allow for infinite parallel composition and unguarded recursion, it turns out that $\sim_{DB,l}$ is strictly finer than $\sim_{DB}$.

Proposition 2.6. *Let P_1 and P_2 be obtained from process terms of $\mathbb{P}'_D$ by admitting infinite parallel composition and unguarded recursion. Then:*

$$P_1 \sim_{DB,l} P_2 \implies P_1 \sim_{DB} P_2$$

To see why the inclusion is strict, consider the following two process terms:

$$P \equiv <b,2>.<f,1>.\underline{0}\|_\emptyset <d,1>.P_\infty$$
$$Q \equiv <b,2>.\underline{0}\|_\emptyset <d,1>.P_\infty$$

where P_∞ denotes any process term that can perform infinitely many a-actions all starting at time 0. The two process terms are durational bisimilar, but not lazy durational bisimilar. Indeed, in the eager case, they must both perform a b-action and a d-action at time 0, after which they reach states $2 \Rightarrow <f,1>.\underline{0}\|_\emptyset 1 \Rightarrow P_\infty$ and $2 \Rightarrow \underline{0}\|_\emptyset 1 \Rightarrow P_\infty$, respectively. Since actions are urgent and P_∞ can immediately perform infinitely many actions, the first reached state cannot execute the f-action, and hence the two reached states are equivalent. The f-action can instead be executed in the lazy case; hence, in that case the two reached states are not equivalent.

2.7.4 Performing Finitely Many Actions at the Same Time

Not even the exclusion of infinite parallel composition and unguarded recursion reduces the discriminating power of $\sim_{DB,l}$.

Proposition 2.7. *Let $P_1, P_2 \in \mathbb{P}'_D$. Then:*

$$P_1 \sim_{DB,l} P_2 \implies P_1 \sim_{DB} P_2$$

To see why the inclusion is strict, consider the following two process terms:

$$P \equiv <a,1>.<d,1>.\underline{0}\|_\emptyset <b,1>.\underline{0}$$
$$Q \equiv <a,1>.\underline{0}\|_\emptyset <b,1>.<d,1>.\underline{0}$$

They are durational bisimilar, but not lazy durational bisimilar. Indeed, in the eager case, they must both perform an a-action and a b-action at time 0, after which they reach states $1 \Rightarrow <d,1>.\underline{0}\|_\emptyset 1 \Rightarrow \underline{0}$ and $1 \Rightarrow \underline{0}\|_\emptyset 1 \Rightarrow <d,1>.\underline{0}$, respectively. These two states are clearly equivalent. However, in the lazy case, when P does the following transition:

$$(0 \Rightarrow P)\triangleright 0 \xrightarrow[\;0\;]{a,1} {}_{D,l} (1 \Rightarrow <d,1>.\underline{0}\|_\emptyset 0 \Rightarrow <b,1>.\underline{0})\triangleright 0$$

then Q responds with the following transition:

$$(0 \Rightarrow Q) \triangleright 0 \xrightarrow[0]{a,1} {}_{\text{D,l}} (1 \Rightarrow \underline{0} \|_\emptyset 0 \Rightarrow <b,1>.<d,1>.\underline{0}) \triangleright 0$$

The two reached states are not lazy durational bisimilar because the former can perform a d-action while the latter cannot.

2.7.5 Coincidence Result for Sequential Processes

All the previous examples demonstrate that, in order to reduce the discriminating power of $\sim_{\text{DB,l}}$, we need to remove the parallel composition operator. In fact, if we restrict ourselves to sequential processes, it turns out that the three considered behavioral equivalences coincide, as in the presence of a single local clock the power of laziness and maximal progress is not observable. We denote by $\mathbb{P}_\text{D}''$ the set of process terms of $\mathbb{P}_\text{D}'$ containing no occurrence of the parallel composition operator.

Theorem 2.8. Let $P_1, P_2 \in \mathbb{P}_\text{D}''$. Then:

$$P_1 \sim_{\text{DB}} P_2 \iff P_1 \sim_{\text{DB,l}} P_2 \iff P_1 \sim_{\text{DB,mp}} P_2$$

Chapter 3
Stochastically Timed Process Algebra

Abstract Timing aspects of concurrent and distributed systems can be expressed not only deterministically, but also probabilistically, which is particularly appropriate for shared-resource systems. When these aspects are modeled by using only exponentially distributed random variables, the stochastic process governing the system evolution over time turns out to be a Markov chain. From a process algebraic perspective, this limitation results in a simpler mathematical treatment both on the semantic side and on the stochastic side without sacrificing expressiveness. In this chapter, we introduce a Markovian process calculus with durational actions, then we discuss congruence properties, sound and complete axiomatizations, modal logic characterizations, and verification algorithms for Markovian versions of bisimulation equivalence, testing equivalence, and trace equivalence. We also examine a further property called exactness, which is related to Markov-chain-level aggregations induced by Markovian behavioral equivalences. Finally, we show how the linear-time/branching-time spectrum collapses in the Markovian case.

3.1 Concurrency, Communication, and Stochastic Time

In Chap. 2, we have seen how to represent time and time passing in a process algebraic context. This has been accomplished through nonnegative numbers, which express action durations or delays between the execution of consecutive actions. This enables the modeling of real-time systems and the verification of temporal constraints. However, it is not the only way of describing timing aspects, nor are real-time systems the only systems where time plays a fundamental role.

An important alternative way is to make use of nonnegative random variables. This is particularly appropriate when the time taken for executing an action is not known in advance, but fluctuates according to some probability distribution. For instance, this is the case with shared-resource systems, in which there is a variable number of demands competing for the same resources, which cause mutual interference, delays due to contention, and service quality varying over time. In this setting,

A. Aldini et al., *A Process Algebraic Approach to Software Architecture Design*,
DOI 10.1007/978-1-84800-223-4_3, © Springer-Verlag London Limited 2010

relevant properties are, e.g., average performance measures like system throughput and resource utilization as well as the probability of satisfying temporal constraints.

Although there are many probability distributions that can be used for modeling timing aspects, most of the work appeared in the literature in the field of stochastically timed process algebra has concentrated on exponential distributions. Since in this case the underlying stochastic process governing the system evolution over time turns out to be a Markov chain [188], the resulting languages are called Markovian process calculi. Among them we mention TIPP [104, 116], PEPA [118], MPA [59], $EMPA_{gr}$ [44, 40], $S\pi$ [172], IMC [115], and PIOA [187].

The reason for using only exponential distributions is that they yield a simpler mathematical treatment both on the semantic side and on the stochastic side:

- A Markov chain can be represented as a labeled transition system
- Its memoryless property fits well with the interleaving view of concurrency
- State sojourn times and transition probabilities can be easily computed

without sacrificing expressiveness:

- Exponential distributions are adequate for modeling the timing of many real-life phenomena like arrival processes, failure events, and chemical reactions
- An exponential distribution is the most appropriate stochastic approximation in the case in which only the average duration of an activity is known [79]
- Proper combinations of exponential distributions, called phase-type distributions [161], can approximate most of general distributions arbitrarily closely

The direct handling of arbitrary distributions requires adopting semantic models richer than labeled transition systems [80] or abandoning the interleaving semantics framework [54]. Since this results in a much more complicated theory without bringing a significant advantage in terms of expressiveness, we address stochastically timed process algebra where timing aspects are quantified only through exponentially distributed random variables. Each such variable is concisely represented as a positive real number called a rate, which uniquely identifies the probability distribution of the values of the variable.

Markovian process calculi differ for the action representation and the synchronization discipline. Like in the case of deterministically timed process algebra, we have two options for action representation. The first option, called orthogonal time, is to consider actions as being instantaneous; hence, their execution is separated from time passing and the choice among several enabled actions is nondeterministic. The second option, called integrated time, is to consider actions as being durational, so that time passing is embedded into action execution and the choice among several enabled exponentially timed actions is solved probabilistically.

While in the orthogonal time case action synchronization is governed as in the absence of timing information, in the integrated time case action synchronization can be handled in different ways. Thanks to the memoryless property of exponential distributions, unlike deterministically timed process algebra with durational actions it is not necessary to require that synchronizing actions start at the same time. Moreover, they can have different durations, in which case a natural choice for deciding the duration of their synchronization is to take the maximum of their exponentially distributed durations, but unfortunately it is not exponentially distributed.

In order to restrict ourselves to exponentially distributed random variables in the integrated time case, there are two possibilities. The first possibility, called symmetric synchronization, consists of assuming that the duration of a synchronization is exponentially distributed. In this case, the rate at which the synchronization takes place is defined through an associative and commutative operator applied to the rates of the participating exponentially timed actions. The second possibility, called asymmetric synchronization, is to introduce actions whose duration is undefined, called passive actions, and impose that an exponentially timed action can synchronize only with those actions, thus determining the overall duration.

Regardless of the specific synchronization discipline, in the integrated time case an important issue is that the rate at which an action is carried out should not increase when synchronizing that action with other actions possibly alternative to each other. This conservative law, called the bounded capacity assumption [117], guarantees a safe handling of synchronization rates and is naturally respected in asymmetric synchronizations, whereas it requires the application of suitable operators on rates in symmetric synchronizations.

In this chapter, we focus on a Markovian extension of the process calculus introduced in Sect. 1.3, in which we adopt integrated time and an asymmetric synchronization discipline obeying the bounded capacity assumption. In this stochastic setting, the choice of integrated time cuts off nondeterminism in favor of a more natural modeling style in which actions are durational. On the other hand, the choice of an asymmetric synchronization discipline restores some nondeterminism via passive actions and is dictated by its frequent use in the modeling practice.

The resulting Markovian process calculus is the basis for introducing Markovian versions of bisimulation equivalence, testing equivalence, and trace equivalence [118, 31, 194]. As in Chap. 1, for each such Markovian behavioral equivalence we present its congruence property, its sound and complete axiomatization, its modal logic characterization, and its verification algorithm. Moreover, both the calculus and the three equivalences are illustrated through the producer–consumer system running example.

In addition, we discuss one more property called exactness. This property refers to aggregations induced at the Markov chain level by Markovian behavioral equivalences. It is desirable that such aggregations be exact, which means that the transient/stationary probability of being in a macrostate of an aggregated Markov chain is the sum of the transient/stationary probabilities of being in one of the constituent microstates of the original Markov chain. Exactness guarantees the preservation of performance characteristics when going from the original Markov chain to the aggregated one induced by a Markovian behavioral equivalence.

We also highlight how the linear-time/branching-time spectrum changes in the Markovian setting. Unlike the scenario examined in Sect. 1.7, where bisimulation equivalence, testing equivalence, trace equivalence, and some of their variants constitute a lattice-like structure for nondeterministic processes, the spectrum for the Markovian versions of the same behavioral equivalences collapses into a line.

This chapter is organized as follows. In Sect. 3.2, we recall some basic notions from Markov chain theory, then we define syntax and semantics for a Markovian process calculus with durational actions that adopts an asymmetric synchronization discipline respecting the bounded capacity assumption. In Sects. 3.3, 3.4, and 3.5, we introduce Markovian bisimulation equivalence, Markovian testing equivalence, and Markovian trace equivalence, respectively, and we illustrate their congruence properties, sound and complete axiomatizations, modal logic characterizations, and verification algorithms. In Sect. 3.6, we discuss the exactness of the three Markovian behavioral equivalences. Finally, in Sect. 3.7 we show the collapse of the linear-time/branching-time spectrum in the Markovian setting.

3.2 MPC: Markovian Process Calculus with Durational Actions

In this section, we present a Markovian process calculus inspired by [40] that we call MPC, which is obtained from the process calculus of Sect. 1.3 by associating with each action a rate that uniquely identifies its exponentially distributed duration. We also add passive actions for enforcing an asymmetric synchronization discipline consistent with the bounded capacity assumption. The formal definition of the calculus is preceded by some notions about Markov chains [188].

3.2.1 Markov Chains

A stochastic process describes the evolution of some random phenomenon over time. Formally, it is a set of random variables, one for each time instant. A special case of stochastic process is a Markov process, which is characterized by a state space and the memoryless property. The state space is the set of values that the random variables constituting the process can take on. The memoryless property establishes that the probability of moving from one state to another does not depend on the particular path that has been followed in the past to reach the current state. In other words, the past history is completely summarized by the current state.

In a process algebraic framework the state space is discrete; hence, we are concerned with discrete-state Markov processes. These stochastic processes are commonly termed Markov chains.

Definition 3.1. A discrete-state stochastic process $\{RV(t) \mid t \in \mathbb{R}_{\geq 0}\}$ is a Markov chain iff for all $n \in \mathbb{N}$, time instants $t_0 < t_1 < \cdots < t_n < t_{n+1}$, and states $s_0, s_1, \ldots, s_n, s_{n+1} \in S$:

$$\boxed{\begin{aligned} \Pr\{RV(t_{n+1}) = s_{n+1} \mid RV(t_0) = s_0 \wedge RV(t_1) = s_1 \wedge \ldots \wedge RV(t_n) = s_n\} \\ = \Pr\{RV(t_{n+1}) = s_{n+1} \mid RV(t_n) = s_n\} \end{aligned}}$$

where s_n is the current state and s_{n+1} is the next state.

A Markov chain can be represented as a labeled transition system or as a state-indexed matrix. In the first case, each transition is labeled with some probabilistic information describing the evolution from the source state to the target state. In the second case, the same information is stored into the entry of the matrix corresponding to the two states. The value of this probabilistic information is a function that depends on the time at which the state change takes place. For the sake of simplicity, we restrict ourselves to time-homogeneous Markov chains, so that the considered information is simply a number.

The solution of a time-homogeneous Markov chain is the probability distribution $\pi()$ of being in the various states of the Markov chain at a certain time instant. State probabilities form the basis for deriving typical performance measures as weighted sums, where weights highlight those states contributing to the measures and the extent to which they contribute. The way $\pi()$ is computed depends on whether the Markov chain is a discrete-time Markov chain (DTMC) or a continuous-time Markov chain (CTMC).

The names DTMC and CTMC have historical reasons. A more precise terminology would call time-abstract a Markov chain of the former type, as time does not come into play, and time-aware a Markov chain of the latter type, due to the explicit reference to time. A discrete-time interpretation is appropriate only in settings where all state changes occur at equidistant time points.

In the case of a time-homogeneous DTMC, state transitions are described by a probability matrix P whose entry $p_{i,j} \in \mathbb{R}_{[0,1]}$ represents the probability of going from state s_i to state s_j through a single transition, hence all rows sum up to 1. The sojourn time in any state is geometrically distributed: if $p \in \mathbb{R}_{]0,1[}$ is the sum of the probabilities of the transitions that depart from s and do not return to s, then the probability of leaving s after executing $k \in \mathbb{N}_{>0}$ transitions is given by $(1-p)^{k-1} \cdot p$. For a time-homogeneous DTMC we have that:

- Given $\pi(0)$, the transient solution $\pi(n)$ after the execution of $n \in \mathbb{N}_{>0}$ transitions is computed in the following way:

$$\boxed{\pi(n) = \pi(0) \cdot P^n}$$

- The stationary solution $\pi = \lim_{n \to \infty} \pi(n)$ is obtained (if any) by solving:

$$\boxed{\begin{aligned} \pi &= \pi \cdot P \\ \sum_{s \in S} \pi[s] &= 1 \end{aligned}}$$

In the case of a time-homogeneous CTMC, state transitions are described by a rate matrix Q whose entry $q_{i,j} \in \mathbb{R}_{\geq 0}$, $i \neq j$, represents the speed at which it is possible to go from state s_i to state s_j through a single transition, while $q_{i,i}$ is set to $-\sum_{j \neq i} q_{i,j}$, thus causing all rows to sum up to 0. The sojourn time in any state is exponentially distributed: if $q \in \mathbb{R}_{>0}$ is the sum of the rates of the transitions that depart from s and do not return to s, then the probability of leaving s within time $t \in \mathbb{R}_{>0}$ is given by $1 - e^{-q \cdot t}$. For a time-homogeneous CTMC we have that:

- Given $\pi(0)$, the transient solution $\pi(t)$ at time $t \in \mathbb{R}_{>0}$ is obtained by solving:

$$\boxed{\pi(t) \cdot Q = \frac{d\pi(t)}{dt}}$$

- The stationary solution $\pi = \lim_{t \to \infty} \pi(t)$ is obtained (if any) by solving:

$$\boxed{\begin{aligned} \pi \cdot Q &= 0 \\ \sum_{s \in S} \pi[s] &= 1 \end{aligned}}$$

We observe that every CTMC has an embedded DTMC, whose probability matrix is obtained from the rate matrix of the CTMC by dividing the rate of each transition by the sum of the rates of the transitions that depart from the source state. We also point out that the family of geometrically (resp. exponentially) distributed random variables is the only family of discrete (resp. continuous) random variables satisfying the memoryless property:

$$\boxed{\Pr\{RV \le v + v' \mid RV > v'\} = \Pr\{RV \le v\}}$$

3.2.2 Syntax and Semantics

In MPC, an exponentially timed action is represented as a pair $<a, \lambda>$, where $a \in Name$ is the name of the action and $\lambda \in \mathbb{R}_{>0}$ is the rate of the exponentially distributed random variable Exp quantifying the duration of the action, i.e., $\Pr\{Exp \le t\} = 1 - e^{-\lambda \cdot t}$ for $t \in \mathbb{R}_{>0}$. The average duration of the action is equal to the reciprocal of its rate, i.e., $1/\lambda$. When several exponentially timed actions are enabled, the race policy is adopted: the action that is executed is the fastest one.

The sojourn time associated with a process term P is thus the minimum of the random variables quantifying the durations of the exponentially timed actions enabled by P. Since the minimum of several exponentially distributed random variables is exponentially distributed and its rate is the sum of the rates of the original variables, the sojourn time associated with P is exponentially distributed with rate equal to the sum of the rates of the actions enabled by P. Therefore, the average sojourn time associated with P is the reciprocal of the sum of the rates of the actions it enables. The probability of executing one of those actions is given by the action rate divided by the sum of the rates of all the considered actions.

Passive actions of the form $<a, *_w>$ are also included in MPC, where $w \in \mathbb{R}_{>0}$ is the weight of the action. The duration of a passive action is undefined. When several passive actions are enabled, the reactive preselection policy is adopted. This means that, within every set of enabled passive actions having the same name, each such action is given an execution probability equal to the action weight divided by the sum of the weights of all the actions in the set. Instead, the choice among passive actions having different names is nondeterministic. Likewise, the choice between a passive action and an exponentially timed action is nondeterministic.

MPC relies on an asymmetric synchronization discipline, according to which an exponentially timed action can synchronize only with a passive action having the same name. In other words, the synchronization between two exponentially timed actions is forbidden. Following the terminology of [99], the adopted synchronization discipline mixes generative and reactive probabilistic aspects. Firstly, among all the enabled exponentially timed actions, the proposal of an action name is generated through a selection based on the rates of those actions. Secondly, the enabled passive actions that have the same name as the proposed one react by means of a selection based on their weights. Thirdly, the exponentially timed action winning the generative selection and the passive action winning the reactive selection synchronize with each other. The rate of the synchronization complies with the bounded capacity assumption as it is given by the rate of the selected exponentially timed action multiplied by the execution probability of the selected passive action. Multiway synchronizations are allowed provided that they involve at most one exponentially timed action, with all the other actions being passive.

Similar to DPC, MPC comprises the same behavioral operators and syntactical categories as PC, plus the set of actions $Act_M = Name \times Rate$ where $Rate = \mathbb{R}_{>0} \cup \{*_w \mid w \in \mathbb{R}_{>0}\}$ is the set of action rates, which is ranged over by $\tilde{\lambda}, \tilde{\mu}$.

Definition 3.2. The set of process terms of the process language $\mathscr{PL}_M$ is generated by the following syntax:

$P ::=$	$\underline{0}$	inactive process
	$<a, \lambda>.P$	exponentially timed action prefix
	$<a, *_w>.P$	passive action prefix
	$P + P$	alternative composition
	$P \parallel_S P$	parallel composition
	P/H	hiding
	$P \backslash L$	restriction
	$P[\varphi]$	relabeling
	X	process variable
	$recX : P$	recursion

where $a \in Name$, $\lambda, w \in \mathbb{R}_{>0}$, $S, H, L \subseteq Name_v$, $\varphi \in Relab$, and $X \in Var$. We denote by $\mathbb{P}_M$ the set of closed and guarded process terms of $\mathscr{PL}_M$.

Example 3.1. Let us model with MPC the producer–consumer system introduced in Sect. 1.2. Assuming that items are produced at rate λ and consumed at rate μ, thanks to the memoryless property of exponential distributions it suffices to extend as follows the structure-independent process algebraic description provided in Example 1.1:

$$ProdCons_{0/2}^M \overset{\Delta}{=} <deposit, \lambda>.ProdCons_{1/2}^M$$
$$ProdCons_{1/2}^M \overset{\Delta}{=} <deposit, \lambda>.ProdCons_{2/2}^M + <withdraw, \mu>.ProdCons_{0/2}^M$$
$$ProdCons_{2/2}^M \overset{\Delta}{=} <withdraw, \mu>.ProdCons_{1/2}^M$$

We point out that λ is the speed of the producer in isolation and μ is the speed of the consumer in isolation. The actual number of items deposited per unit of time is less than λ and the actual number of items withdrawn per unit of time is less than μ. The reason is that the finite capacity of the buffer may sometimes block the producer, which is more likely to happen if $\lambda > \mu$. Similarly, the consumer is blocked when the buffer is empty, which is more likely to happen if $\mu > \lambda$.

The semantics for MPC is defined in the usual operational style by taking into account that the alternative composition operator is not idempotent. For instance, process term $<a,\lambda>.\underline{0} + <a,\lambda>.\underline{0}$ is not the same as $<a,\lambda>.\underline{0}$, because the average sojourn time associated with the latter, i.e., $1/\lambda$, is twice the average sojourn time associated with the former, i.e., $1/(\lambda + \lambda)$. In order to assign distinct semantic models to process terms like the two considered above, it is sufficient to keep track of the multiplicity of each transition, intended as the number of different proofs for the transition derivation. Therefore, we define the multitransition relation $\longrightarrow_M$ as the smallest multiset of elements of $\mathbb{P}_M \times Act_M \times \mathbb{P}_M$ satisfying the operational semantic rules of Table 3.1, in which $\{|$ and $|\}$ denote multiset parentheses. Thanks to the memoryless property of exponential distributions, unlike DPC it is not necessary to label transitions with their starting time. The labeled multitransition system for a process term $P \in \mathbb{P}_M$ is denoted by $[\![P]\!]_M$.

In addition to the presence of rates in the transition labels, the operational semantic rules in Table 3.1 have two characteristics. The first one is that there are two rules for the action prefix operator: one for exponentially timed actions, $PRE_{M,1}$, and one for passive actions, $PRE_{M,2}$. The second one is that there are three rules for synchronization: $SYN_{M,1}$ and $SYN_{M,2}$ formalize generative–reactive synchronizations between an exponentially timed action and a passive action, while $SYN_{M,3}$ formalizes reactive–reactive synchronizations between two passive actions.

As far as parallel composition is concerned, we observe that exponential distributions fit well with the interleaving view of concurrency. In fact, due to their memoryless property, the execution of an exponentially timed action can be thought of as being started in the last state in which the action is enabled. Moreover, due to their infinite support, the probability that two concurrent exponentially timed actions terminate simultaneously is zero. As an example, take the following two process terms:

$$<a,\lambda>.\underline{0} \parallel_\emptyset <b,\mu>.\underline{0}$$
$$<a,\lambda>.<b,\mu>.\underline{0} + <b,\mu>.<a,\lambda>.\underline{0}$$

The first one (concurrent term) executes a at rate λ in parallel with b at rate μ, while the second one (sequential term) executes either a at rate λ followed by b at rate μ, or b at rate μ followed by a at rate λ. These two syntactically and structurally different terms are behaviorally identical, as they are represented by the same labeled multitransition system, which is shown below:

Table 3.1 Time-integrated operational semantic rules for MPC

$$(\text{PRE}_{M,1}) \quad \frac{}{<a,\lambda>.P \xrightarrow{a,\lambda}_M P} \qquad\qquad (\text{PRE}_{M,2}) \quad \frac{}{<a,*_w>.P \xrightarrow{a,*_w}_M P}$$

$$(\text{ALT}_{M,1}) \quad \frac{P_1 \xrightarrow{a,\tilde{\lambda}}_M P_1'}{P_1 + P_2 \xrightarrow{a,\tilde{\lambda}}_M P_1'} \qquad\qquad (\text{ALT}_{M,2}) \quad \frac{P_2 \xrightarrow{a,\tilde{\lambda}}_M P_2'}{P_1 + P_2 \xrightarrow{a,\tilde{\lambda}}_M P_2'}$$

$$(\text{PAR}_{M,1}) \quad \frac{P_1 \xrightarrow{a,\tilde{\lambda}}_M P_1' \quad a \notin S}{P_1 \|_S P_2 \xrightarrow{a,\tilde{\lambda}}_M P_1' \|_S P_2} \qquad (\text{PAR}_{M,2}) \quad \frac{P_2 \xrightarrow{a,\tilde{\lambda}}_M P_2' \quad a \notin S}{P_1 \|_S P_2 \xrightarrow{a,\tilde{\lambda}}_M P_1 \|_S P_2'}$$

$$(\text{SYN}_{M,1}) \quad \frac{P_1 \xrightarrow{a,\lambda}_M P_1' \quad P_2 \xrightarrow{a,*_w}_M P_2' \quad a \in S}{P_1 \|_S P_2 \xrightarrow{a,\lambda \cdot \frac{w}{weight(P_2,a)}}_M P_1' \|_S P_2'}$$

$$(\text{SYN}_{M,2}) \quad \frac{P_1 \xrightarrow{a,*_w}_M P_1' \quad P_2 \xrightarrow{a,\lambda}_M P_2' \quad a \in S}{P_1 \|_S P_2 \xrightarrow{a,\lambda \cdot \frac{w}{weight(P_1,a)}}_M P_1' \|_S P_2'}$$

$$(\text{SYN}_{M,3}) \quad \frac{P_1 \xrightarrow{a,*_{w_1}}_M P_1' \quad P_2 \xrightarrow{a,*_{w_2}}_M P_2' \quad a \in S}{P_1 \|_S P_2 \xrightarrow{a,*_{norm(w_1,w_2,a,P_1,P_2)}}_M P_1' \|_S P_2'}$$

$$(\text{HID}_{M,1}) \quad \frac{P \xrightarrow{a,\tilde{\lambda}}_M P' \quad a \in H}{P/H \xrightarrow{\tau,\tilde{\lambda}}_M P'/H} \qquad (\text{HID}_{M,2}) \quad \frac{P \xrightarrow{a,\tilde{\lambda}}_M P' \quad a \notin H}{P/H \xrightarrow{a,\tilde{\lambda}}_M P'/H}$$

$$(\text{RES}_M) \quad \frac{P \xrightarrow{a,\tilde{\lambda}}_M P' \quad a \notin L}{P\backslash L \xrightarrow{a,\tilde{\lambda}}_M P'\backslash L}$$

$$(\text{REL}_M) \quad \frac{P \xrightarrow{a,\tilde{\lambda}}_M P'}{P[\varphi] \xrightarrow{\varphi(a),\tilde{\lambda}}_M P'[\varphi]}$$

$$(\text{REC}_M) \quad \frac{P\{rec\,X : P \hookrightarrow X\} \xrightarrow{a,\tilde{\lambda}}_M P'}{rec\,X : P \xrightarrow{a,\tilde{\lambda}}_M P'}$$

$$weight(P,a) = \Sigma\{|\, w \in \mathbb{R}_{>0} \mid \exists P' \in \mathbb{P}_M . P \xrightarrow{a,*_w}_M P' \,|\}$$

$$norm(w_1,w_2,a,P_1,P_2) = \frac{w_1}{weight(P_1,a)} \cdot \frac{w_2}{weight(P_2,a)} \cdot (weight(P_1,a) + weight(P_2,a))$$

In the initial state, both actions are enabled, hence the average sojourn time is $1/(\lambda + \mu)$. Then, $<a,\lambda>$ can be executed with probability $\lambda/(\lambda + \mu)$, while $<b,\mu>$ can be executed with probability $\mu/(\lambda + \mu)$. Note that there is no transition going directly from the initial state to the final one as, in the case of the concurrent term, $<a,\lambda>$ and $<b,\mu>$ cannot terminate simultaneously. Suppose that $<a,\lambda>$ terminates first. Then, a state is reached – the leftmost in the figure – in which only $<b,\mu>$ is enabled. The question arises as to what rate should label the b-transition departing from that state, given that in the concurrent term $<b,\mu>$ started executing in the initial state and some time has elapsed on the way from the initial state to the current one. Thanks to the memoryless property, we can forget about the time elapsed before reaching the current state, and hence the rate labeling the considered transition is simply μ. Therefore, concurrent exponentially timed actions can freely interleave without the need of adjusting the rates of the corresponding transitions.

The time-homogeneous CTMC underlying a process term $P \in \mathbb{P}_M$ can be easily derived from $[\![P]\!]_M$ by (1) discarding action names from transition labels and (2) collapsing all the transitions between any two states into a single transition whose rate is the sum of the rates of the original transitions. However, this procedure can be applied only to performance-closed process terms; i.e., process terms whose semantic model has no passive transitions. We denote by $\mathbb{P}_{M,pc}$ the set of performance-closed process terms of $\mathbb{P}_M$.

Example 3.2. The labeled multitransition system $[\![ProdCons^M_{0/2}]\!]_M$ for the process algebraic description of Example 3.1 is depicted below:

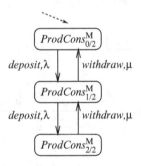

The corresponding time-homogeneous CTMC is simply obtained by eliminating action names *deposit* and *withdraw* from all transition labels.

3.3 Markovian Bisimulation Equivalence

Markovian bisimulation equivalence relates two process terms whenever they are able to mimic each other's functional and performance behavior stepwise. In this section, we provide the definition of Markovian bisimulation equivalence over $\mathbb{P}_M$ based on process term exit rates, together with a necessary condition, a sufficient condition, and an alternative characterization [118, 40, 56, 24]. Then, we show that

Markovian bisimulation equivalence is a congruence and we present its sound and complete axiomatization, its modal logic characterization, and its verification algorithm [118,116,40,56,65,84]. Finally, we illustrate a variant that abstracts from τ-actions with zero duration [115,176,35].

3.3.1 Exit Rates and Exit Probabilities

The exit rate of a process term $P \in \mathbb{P}_M$ is the rate at which P can execute actions of a certain name that lead to a certain set of terms and is given by the sum of the rates of those actions due to the race policy. We consider a two-level definition of exit rate, where level 0 corresponds to exponentially timed actions and level -1 corresponds to passive actions.

Definition 3.3. Let $P \in \mathbb{P}_M$, $a \in Name$, $l \in \{0,-1\}$, and $D \subseteq \mathbb{P}_M$. The exit rate at which P executes actions of name a and level l that lead to destination D is defined through the following nonnegative real function:

$$rate_e(P,a,l,D) = \begin{cases} \sum\{\!\mid \lambda \in \mathbb{R}_{>0} \mid \exists P' \in D. P \xrightarrow{a,\lambda}_M P' \mid\!\} & \text{if } l = 0 \\ \sum\{\!\mid w \in \mathbb{R}_{>0} \mid \exists P' \in D. P \xrightarrow{a,*_w}_M P' \mid\!\} & \text{if } l = -1 \end{cases}$$

where each summation is taken to be zero whenever its multiset is empty.

By summing up the rates of all the actions of a certain level that a process term P can execute, we obtain the total exit rate of P at the considered level.

Definition 3.4. Let $P \in \mathbb{P}_M$ and $l \in \{0,-1\}$. The total exit rate of P at level l is defined as follows:

$$rate_t(P,l) = \sum_{a \in Name} rate_o(P,a,l)$$

where:

$$rate_o(P,a,l) = rate_e(P,a,l,\mathbb{P}_M)$$

is the overall exit rate of P with respect to a at level l. We also denote by $rate_o(P,N,l)$ the sum of the overall exit rates of P with respect to all $a \in N \subseteq Name$ at level l.

If P is performance closed, then $rate_t(P,0)$ coincides with the reciprocal of the average sojourn time associated with P. Instead, $rate_o(P,a,-1)$ coincides with $weight(P,a)$.

Similarly, we can define the exit probability of a process term P as the probability with which P can execute actions of a certain name and level that lead to a certain set of terms. Following the terminology of [99], in the case of exponentially timed actions we have a generative probability, whereas in the case of passive actions we have a reactive probability.

Definition 3.5. Let $P \in \mathbb{P}_M$, $a \in Name$, $l \in \{0, -1\}$, and $D \subseteq \mathbb{P}_M$. The exit probability with which P executes actions of name a and level l that lead to destination D is defined through the following $\mathbb{R}_{[0,1]}$-valued function:

$$prob_e(P,a,l,D) = \begin{cases} rate_e(P,a,l,D) \,/\, rate_t(P,l) & \text{if } l = 0 \\ rate_e(P,a,l,D) \,/\, rate_o(P,a,l) & \text{if } l = -1 \end{cases}$$

where each division is taken to be zero whenever its divisor is zero.

3.3.2 Definition of the Behavioral Equivalence

The basic idea behind Markovian bisimulation equivalence is that, whenever a process term can perform actions with a certain name that reach a certain set of terms at a certain speed, then any process term equivalent to the given one has to be able to respond with actions with the same name that reach an equivalent set of terms at the same speed. This can be easily formalized through the comparison of the process term exit rates when executing actions of the same name and level that lead to the same set of equivalent terms, rather than in terms of individual transitions as it has been done for $\sim_B$ in Sect. 1.4.2.

Definition 3.6. An equivalence relation $\mathcal{B}$ over $\mathbb{P}_M$ is a Markovian bisimulation iff, whenever $(P_1, P_2) \in \mathcal{B}$, then for all action names $a \in Name$, levels $l \in \{0, -1\}$, and equivalence classes $D \in \mathbb{P}_M / \mathcal{B}$:

$$rate_e(P_1, a, l, D) = rate_e(P_2, a, l, D)$$

Since the union of all the Markovian bisimulations can be proved to be the largest Markovian bisimulation, the definition below follows.

Definition 3.7. Markovian bisimulation equivalence (or Markovian bisimilarity), denoted $\sim_{MB}$, is the union of all the Markovian bisimulations.

It turns out that $\sim_{MB}$ is strictly finer than $\sim_B$. Take, for instance, the following two process terms:

$$<a, \lambda>.P + <b, \mu>.Q$$
$$<a, \mu>.P + <b, \lambda>.Q$$

where $a \neq b$ and $\lambda \neq \mu$. Then, the two process terms are bisimilar – as rates do not come into play – but they are not Markovian bisimilar. The reason is that the a-action and the b-action are different from each other and have different rates in the two terms. Therefore, if we perform the comparison of the exit rates with respect to a (resp. b) at level 0 towards the equivalence class containing P (resp. Q), then we end up with different values, and hence the check for exit rate equality fails.

Likewise, it turns out that $\sim_{MB}$ is strictly finer than probabilistic bisimulation equivalence [136]. Take, for instance, the following two process terms:

$$<a, \lambda>.P + <b, \mu>.Q$$
$$<a, 2 \cdot \lambda>.P + <b, 2 \cdot \mu>.Q$$

Then, the two process terms are probabilistic bisimilar – as they have the same exit probabilities $\lambda/(\lambda + \mu)$ towards the class containing P and $\mu/(\lambda + \mu)$ towards the class containing Q – but they are not Markovian bisimilar. Here the reason is that the average sojourn time $1/(\lambda + \mu)$ in the first process term is twice the average sojourn time $1/(2 \cdot \lambda + 2 \cdot \mu)$ in the second process term; hence, the check for exit rate equality fails since the second term is twice faster than the first one.

Example 3.3. Let us model with MPC the concurrent implementation considered in Example 1.3 of the producer–consumer system introduced in Sect. 1.2. The process algebraic description extended with action rates consistent with those of Example 3.1 is as follows:

$$PC^{\mathrm{M}}_{\mathrm{conc},2} \triangleq Prod^{\mathrm{M}} \|_{\{deposit\}} (Buff^{\mathrm{M}} \|_{\emptyset} Buff^{\mathrm{M}}) \|_{\{withdraw\}} Cons^{\mathrm{M}}$$
$$Prod^{\mathrm{M}} \triangleq <deposit, \lambda>.Prod^{\mathrm{M}}$$
$$Buff^{\mathrm{M}} \triangleq <deposit, *_1>.<withdraw, *_1>.Buff^{\mathrm{M}}$$
$$Cons^{\mathrm{M}} \triangleq <withdraw, \mu>.Cons^{\mathrm{M}}$$

All the actions occurring in the buffer are passive, consistent with the fact that the buffer is a passive entity in the context of the producer–consumer system, in the sense that it can only wait for items to be deposited or withdrawn.

The labeled multitransition systems $[\![PC^{\mathrm{M}}_{\mathrm{conc},2}]\!]_{\mathrm{M}}$ and $[\![ProdCons^{\mathrm{M}}_{0/2}]\!]_{\mathrm{M}}$ are shown below, where the usual shorthands for process constants and action names have been used on the left-hand side:

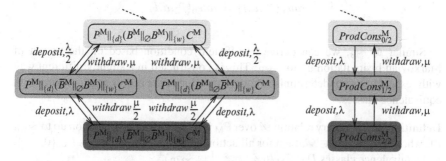

We observe that the initial state (resp. bottom state) of the labeled multitransition system on the left-hand side has both outgoing transitions labeled with $\lambda/2$, not λ (resp. $\mu/2$, not μ). The reason is that the exponentially timed action $<deposit, \lambda>$ of the producer (resp. $<withdraw, \mu>$ of the consumer) can synchronize either with the passive action $<deposit, *_1>$ (resp. $<withdraw, *_1>$) of the first one-position buffer or with the passive action $<deposit, *_1>$ (resp. $<withdraw, *_1>$) of the second one-position buffer. Since each such passive action has execution probability $1/2$ in the initial state (resp. bottom state), the two transitions resulting from the two synchronizations are labeled with $\lambda/2$ (resp. $\mu/2$). This is a consequence of the bounded capacity assumption, according to which the average sojourn time in the initial state (resp. bottom state) must be $1/\lambda$ (resp. $1/\mu$) as in that state there is only one enabled exponentially timed action and its rate is λ (resp. μ).

What turns out is that $PC^{M}_{conc,2} \sim_{MB} ProdCons^{M}_{0/2}$. Like in Example 1.3, we have used state coloring for graphically representing the equivalence classes of the Markovian bisimulation proving this fact. The depicted relation is a Markovian bisimulation because in both labeled multitransition systems:

- A light gray state can only reach the class of gray states by executing exponentially timed actions of name *deposit* at total rate λ
- A gray state can only reach the class of dark gray states by executing exponentially timed actions of name *deposit* at total rate λ or the class of light gray states by executing exponentially timed actions of name *withdraw* at total rate μ
- A dark gray state can only reach the class of gray states by executing exponentially timed actions of name *withdraw* at total rate μ

3.3.3 Conditions and Characterizations

A simple necessary condition for establishing whether two process terms are Markovian bisimilar is that they have the same overall exit rates with respect to all action names and levels.

Proposition 3.1. *Let* $P_1, P_2 \in \mathbb{P}_M$. *Whenever* $P_1 \sim_{MB} P_2$, *then for all* $a \in Name$ *and* $l \in \{0, -1\}$:

$$rate_o(P_1, a, l) = rate_o(P_2, a, l)$$

Similar to $\sim_B$, we can derive a sufficient condition based on the notion of Markovian bisimulation up to $\sim_{MB}$. This is constructed in a slightly different way with respect to its nondeterministic counterpart due to the necessity of working with equivalence classes.

Definition 3.8. A binary relation $\mathscr{B}$ over $\mathbb{P}_M$ is a Markovian bisimulation up to $\sim_{MB}$ iff, whenever $(P_1, P_2) \in \mathscr{B}$, then for all action names $a \in Name$, levels $l \in \{0, -1\}$, and equivalence classes $D \in \mathbb{P}_M/(\mathscr{B} \cup \mathscr{B}^{-1} \cup \sim_{MB})^+$:

$$rate_e(P_1, a, l, D) = rate_e(P_2, a, l, D)$$

Proposition 3.2. *Let* $\mathscr{B}$ *be a binary relation over* $\mathbb{P}_M$. *Whenever* $\mathscr{B}$ *is a Markovian bisimulation up to* $\sim_{MB}$, *then for all* $P_1, P_2 \in \mathbb{P}_M$:

$$(P_1, P_2) \in \mathscr{B} \implies P_1 \sim_{MB} P_2$$

We conclude by presenting an alternative characterization of $\sim_{MB}$ in which time and probability – usually subsumed by rates – are kept separate. The alternative characterization makes use of exit probabilities; hence, it relies on probabilistic bisimulation equivalence [136] over embedded DTMCs.

Definition 3.9. An equivalence relation $\mathscr{B}$ over $\mathbb{P}_M$ is a separate Markovian bisimulation iff, whenever $(P_1, P_2) \in \mathscr{B}$, then for all action names $a \in Name$ and levels $l \in \{0, -1\}$:

$$rate_o(P_1, a, l) = rate_o(P_2, a, l)$$

and for all equivalence classes $D \in \mathbb{P}_M / \mathscr{B}$:

$$prob_e(P_1, a, l, D) = prob_e(P_2, a, l, D)$$

Since the union of all the separate Markovian bisimulations can be proved to be the largest separate Markovian bisimulation, the definition below follows.

Definition 3.10. Separate Markovian bisimulation equivalence (or separate Markovian bisimilarity), denoted $\sim_{MB,s}$, is the union of all the separate Markovian bisimulations.

Proposition 3.3. Let $P_1, P_2 \in \mathbb{P}_M$. Then:

$$P_1 \sim_{MB,s} P_2 \iff P_1 \sim_{MB} P_2$$

3.3.4 Congruence Property

Markovian bisimulation equivalence is a congruence with respect to all the dynamic and static operators of MPC as well as recursion.

Theorem 3.1. Let $P_1, P_2 \in \mathbb{P}_M$. Whenever $P_1 \sim_{MB} P_2$, then:

1. $<a, \tilde{\lambda}>.P_1 \sim_{MB} <a, \tilde{\lambda}>.P_2$ for all $<a, \tilde{\lambda}> \in Act_M$.
2. $P_1 + P \sim_{MB} P_2 + P$ and $P + P_1 \sim_{MB} P + P_2$ for all $P \in \mathbb{P}_M$.
3. $P_1 \|_S P \sim_{MB} P_2 \|_S P$ and $P \|_S P_1 \sim_{MB} P \|_S P_2$ for all $P \in \mathbb{P}_M$ and $S \subseteq Name_v$.
4. $P_1 / H \sim_{MB} P_2 / H$ for all $H \subseteq Name_v$.
5. $P_1 \backslash L \sim_{MB} P_2 \backslash L$ for all $L \subseteq Name_v$.
6. $P_1[\varphi] \sim_{MB} P_2[\varphi]$ for all $\varphi \in Relab$.

Definition 3.11. Let $P_1, P_2 \in \mathscr{PL}_M$ be guarded process terms containing free occurrences of $k \in \mathbb{N}$ process variables $X_1, \ldots, X_k \in Var$ at most. We define $P_1 \sim_{MB} P_2$ iff $P_1\{Q_i \hookrightarrow X_i \mid 1 \leq i \leq k\} \sim_{MB} P_2\{Q_i \hookrightarrow X_i \mid 1 \leq i \leq k\}$ for all $Q_1, \ldots, Q_k \in \mathbb{P}_M$.

Theorem 3.2. Let $P_1, P_2 \in \mathscr{PL}_M$ be guarded process terms containing free occurrences of $k \in \mathbb{N}$ process variables $X_1, \ldots, X_k \in Var$ at most. Whenever $P_1 \sim_{MB} P_2$, then $rec X : P_1 \sim_{MB} rec X : P_2$ for all $X \in Var$.

3.3.5 Sound and Complete Axiomatization

Markovian bisimulation equivalence has a sound and complete axiomatization over nonrecursive process terms, given by the set $\mathscr{X}_{MB}$ of equational laws of Table 3.2.

Noted that the alternative composition operator is commutative, associative, and has $\underline{0}$ as neutral element like in the nondeterministic case, axioms $\mathscr{X}_{MB,4}$ and $\mathscr{X}_{MB,5}$ represent the race policy and the reactive preselection policy, respectively. They

Table 3.2 Equational laws for $\sim_{MB}$

$$(\mathscr{X}_{MB,1}) \qquad P_1 + P_2 = P_2 + P_1$$
$$(\mathscr{X}_{MB,2}) \qquad (P_1 + P_2) + P_3 = P_1 + (P_2 + P_3)$$
$$(\mathscr{X}_{MB,3}) \qquad P + \underline{0} = P$$

$$(\mathscr{X}_{MB,4}) \qquad <a, \lambda_1>.P + <a, \lambda_2>.P = <a, \lambda_1 + \lambda_2>.P$$
$$(\mathscr{X}_{MB,5}) \qquad <a, *_{w_1}>.P + <a, *_{w_2}>.P = <a, *_{w_1 + w_2}>.P$$

$$(\mathscr{X}_{MB,6}) \quad \sum_{i \in I} <a_i, \tilde{\lambda}_i>.P_i \parallel_S \sum_{j \in J} <b_j, \tilde{\mu}_j>.Q_j$$

$$= \sum_{k \in I, a_k \notin S} <a_k, \tilde{\lambda}_k>. \left(P_k \parallel_S \sum_{j \in J} <b_j, \tilde{\mu}_j>.Q_j \right)$$

$$+ \sum_{h \in J, b_h \notin S} <b_h, \tilde{\mu}_h>. \left(\sum_{i \in I} <a_i, \tilde{\lambda}_i>.P_i \parallel_S Q_h \right)$$

$$+ \sum_{k \in I, a_k \in S, \tilde{\lambda}_k \in \mathbb{R}_{>0}} \sum_{h \in J, b_h = a_k, \tilde{\mu}_h = *_{w_h}} <a_k, \tilde{\lambda}_k \cdot \frac{w_h}{weight(Q, b_h)}>.(P_k \parallel_S Q_h)$$

$$+ \sum_{h \in J, b_h \in S, \tilde{\mu}_h \in \mathbb{R}_{>0}} \sum_{k \in I, a_k = b_h, \tilde{\lambda}_k = *_{v_k}} <b_h, \tilde{\mu}_h \cdot \frac{v_k}{weight(P, a_k)}>.(P_k \parallel_S Q_h)$$

$$+ \sum_{k \in I, a_k \in S, \tilde{\lambda}_k = *_{v_k}} \sum_{h \in J, b_h = a_k, \tilde{\mu}_h = *_{w_h}} <a_k, *_{norm(v_k, w_h, a_k, P, Q)}>.(P_k \parallel_S Q_h)$$

$$(\mathscr{X}_{MB,7}) \qquad \sum_{i \in I} <a_i, \tilde{\lambda}_i>.P_i \parallel_S \underline{0} = \sum_{k \in I, a_k \notin S} <a_k, \tilde{\lambda}_k>.P_k$$

$$(\mathscr{X}_{MB,8}) \qquad \underline{0} \parallel_S \sum_{j \in J} <b_j, \tilde{\mu}_j>.Q_j = \sum_{h \in J, b_h \notin S} <b_h, \tilde{\mu}_h>.Q_h$$

$$(\mathscr{X}_{MB,9}) \qquad \underline{0} \parallel_S \underline{0} = \underline{0}$$

$$(\mathscr{X}_{MB,10}) \qquad \underline{0}/H = \underline{0}$$
$$(\mathscr{X}_{MB,11}) \qquad (<a, \tilde{\lambda}>.P)/H = <\tau, \tilde{\lambda}>.(P/H) \quad \text{if } a \in H$$
$$(\mathscr{X}_{MB,12}) \qquad (<a, \tilde{\lambda}>.P)/H = <a, \tilde{\lambda}>.(P/H) \quad \text{if } a \notin H$$
$$(\mathscr{X}_{MB,13}) \qquad (P_1 + P_2)/H = P_1/H + P_2/H$$

$$(\mathscr{X}_{MB,14}) \qquad \underline{0} \backslash L = \underline{0}$$
$$(\mathscr{X}_{MB,15}) \qquad (<a, \tilde{\lambda}>.P) \backslash L = \underline{0} \quad \text{if } a \in L$$
$$(\mathscr{X}_{MB,16}) \qquad (<a, \tilde{\lambda}>.P) \backslash L = <a, \tilde{\lambda}>.(P \backslash L) \quad \text{if } a \notin L$$
$$(\mathscr{X}_{MB,17}) \qquad (P_1 + P_2) \backslash L = P_1 \backslash L + P_2 \backslash L$$

$$(\mathscr{X}_{MB,18}) \qquad \underline{0}[\varphi] = \underline{0}$$
$$(\mathscr{X}_{MB,19}) \qquad (<a, \tilde{\lambda}>.P)[\varphi] = <\varphi(a), \tilde{\lambda}>.(P[\varphi])$$
$$(\mathscr{X}_{MB,20}) \qquad (P_1 + P_2)[\varphi] = P_1[\varphi] + P_2[\varphi]$$

constitute the most important difference with respect to the axiomatization of $\sim_{\text{B}}$ shown in Table 1.2, where axiom $\mathscr{X}_{\text{B},4}$ states instead the idempotency of the alternative composition operator.

The interleaving view of concurrency supported by the memoryless property of exponential distributions is expressed by axioms $\mathscr{X}_{\text{MB},6}$ to $\mathscr{X}_{\text{MB},9}$, where I and J are nonempty finite index sets and each summation on the right-hand side is taken to be $\underline{0}$ whenever its set of summands is empty. In particular, axiom $\mathscr{X}_{\text{MB},6}$ is the expansion law for the parallel composition of $P \equiv \sum_{i \in I} <a_i, \tilde{\lambda}_i>.P_i$ and $Q \equiv \sum_{j \in J} <b_j, \tilde{\mu}_j>.Q_j$ when enforcing generative–reactive and reactive–reactive synchronizations.

Finally, for the unary static operators we have the same equational laws as Table 1.2 up to the presence of action rates.

Theorem 3.3. *Let* $P_1, P_2 \in \mathbb{P}_{\text{M}}$ *be nonrecursive. Then:*

$$P_1 \sim_{\text{MB}} P_2 \iff \mathscr{X}_{\text{MB}} \vdash P_1 = P_2$$

3.3.6 Modal Logic Characterization

Markovian bisimulation equivalence has a modal logic characterization based on a Markovian variant of HML, the modal logic introduced in Sect 1.4.6.

The diamond operator of the new modal language is decorated with a lower bound on the rate (resp. weight) with which exponentially timed (resp. passive) actions with a certain name should be executed. Enriching individual action-based modal operators with quantitative information is consistent with the fact that $\sim_{\text{MB}}$ captures step-by-step behavior mimicking.

Definition 3.12. The set of formulas of the modal language $\mathscr{ML}_{\text{MB}}$ is generated by the following syntax:

$$\phi ::= \text{true} \mid \neg\phi \mid \phi \wedge \phi \mid \langle a \rangle_\lambda \phi \mid \langle a \rangle_{*_w} \phi$$

where $a \in \textit{Name}$ and $\lambda, w \in \mathbb{R}_{>0}$.

Definition 3.13. The satisfaction relation $\models_{\text{MB}}$ of $\mathscr{ML}_{\text{MB}}$ over $\mathbb{P}_{\text{M}}$ is defined by induction on the syntactical structure of formulas as follows:

$$
\begin{array}{lll}
P \models_{\text{MB}} \text{true} & & \\
P \models_{\text{MB}} \neg\phi & \text{if } P \not\models_{\text{MB}} \phi & \\
P \models_{\text{MB}} \phi_1 \wedge \phi_2 & \text{if } P \models_{\text{MB}} \phi_1 \text{ and } P \models_{\text{MB}} \phi_2 & \\
P \models_{\text{MB}} \langle a \rangle_\lambda \phi & \text{if } \textit{rate}_{\text{e}}(P, a, 0, sat(\phi)) \geq \lambda & \\
P \models_{\text{MB}} \langle a \rangle_{*_w} \phi & \text{if } \textit{rate}_{\text{e}}(P, a, -1, sat(\phi)) \geq w &
\end{array}
$$

where $sat(\phi) = \{P' \in \mathbb{P}_{\text{M}} \mid P' \models_{\text{MB}} \phi\}$.

Theorem 3.4. *Let $P_1, P_2 \in \mathbb{P}_M$. Then:*

$$P_1 \sim_{MB} P_2 \iff (\forall \phi \in \mathcal{ML}_{MB}.P_1 \models_{MB} \phi \iff P_2 \models_{MB} \phi)$$

3.3.7 Verification Algorithm

Markovian bisimulation equivalence can be decided in polynomial time by means of a variant of the partition refinement algorithm for $\sim_B$ presented in Sect. 1.4.7, which exploits – as in the nondeterministic case – the fact that $\sim_{MB}$ can be characterized as the limit of a sequence of successively finer equivalence relations:

$$\sim_{MB} = \bigcap_{i \in \mathbb{N}} \sim_{MB,i}$$

Relation $\sim_{MB,0}$ is $\mathbb{P}_M \times \mathbb{P}_M$ while $\sim_{MB,i}$, $i \in \mathbb{N}_{\geq 1}$, is an equivalence relation over $\mathbb{P}_M$ defined as follows: whenever $P_1 \sim_{MB,i} P_2$, then for all $a \in Name$, $l \in \{0, -1\}$, and $D \in \mathbb{P}_M/\sim_{MB,i-1}$:

$$rate_e(P_1, a, l, D) = rate_e(P_2, a, l, D)$$

Note that $\sim_{MB,1}$ refines the partition $\{\mathbb{P}_M\}$ induced by $\sim_{MB,0}$ by creating an equivalence class for each set of terms satisfying the necessary condition of Proposition 3.1.

Given $P_1, P_2 \in \mathbb{P}_M$ finite state and denoted by $Name_{P_1,P_2}$ the set of action names labeling the transitions of $[\![P_1]\!]_M$ or $[\![P_2]\!]_M$, the algorithm for checking whether $P_1 \sim_{MB} P_2$ proceeds as follows:

1. Build an initial partition with a single class including all the states of $[\![P_1]\!]_M$ and all the states of $[\![P_2]\!]_M$.
2. Initialize a list of splitters with the above class as its only element.
3. While the list of splitters is not empty, select a splitter and remove it from the list after refining the current partition for each $a \in Name_{P_1,P_2}$ and $l \in \{0, -1\}$:

   (a) Split each class of the current partition by comparing the exit rates of its states when performing actions of name a and level l that lead to the selected splitter.
   (b) For each class that has been split, insert into the list of splitters all the resulting subclasses except for the largest one.

4. Return yes/no depending on whether the initial state of $[\![P_1]\!]_M$ and the initial state of $[\![P_2]\!]_M$ belong to the same class of the final partition or to different classes.

The time complexity is still $O(m \cdot \log n)$, where n is the total number of states and m is the total number of transitions of $[\![P_1]\!]_M$ and $[\![P_2]\!]_M$, provided that a splay tree is used for storing the subclasses arising from the splitting of a class. This necessity is due to the fact that, unlike the nondeterministic case, such subclasses can be more than two. We mention that this algorithm can also be used for minimizing a labeled multitransition system with respect to $\sim_{MB}$.

3.3.8 Abstracting from Invisible Actions with Zero Duration

Markovian bisimulation equivalence has no abstraction capability as τ-actions are durational in MPC. These actions would be completely unobservable if they had duration zero. Unfortunately, this cannot be the case. Although combinations of exponential distributions can approximate many arbitrary distributions, some useful distributions like the one representing a zero duration are left out.

However, it is advisable to support zero durations for several reasons. From a theoretical point of view, the possibility of expressing zero durations constitutes the performance counterpart of the functional abstraction mechanism given by the invisible action name τ. This mechanism is appropriate to handle systems encompassing activities that are several orders of magnitude faster than the activities that are important for the evaluation of certain performance measures. From a modeling standpoint, there are situations in which using zero durations is unavoidable. This is the case with choices among logical events – like, e.g., the reception of a message vs. its loss – as no timing can be associated with them.

We now extend MPC with actions having zero duration, which are called immediate actions, and then we define a weak variant of $\sim_{MB}$ that is able to abstract from immediate τ-actions in several cases. In this framework, immediate actions are inspired by immediate transitions of generalized stochastic Petri nets [5], and hence allow for prioritized/probabilistic choices too.

An immediate action is of the form $<a, \infty_{l,w}>$, where $l \in \mathbb{N}_{>0}$ is the priority level of the action and $w \in \mathbb{R}_{>0}$ is the weight of the action. An immediate action has duration zero, as expressed by its infinite rate, and takes precedence over exponentially timed actions. Whenever several immediate actions are enabled, the generative preselection policy is adopted. This means that the lower priority immediate actions are discarded, whereas each of the highest priority immediate actions is given an execution probability equal to the action weight divided by the sum of the weights of all the highest priority immediate actions. Consistent with the adopted asymmetric synchronization discipline, an immediate action can synchronize only with a passive action having the same name. The rate of the resulting action is given by the rate of the immediate action, whose weight is multiplied by the execution probability of the passive action.

In the calculus resulting from the introduction of immediate actions, we also associate priority constraints $l' \in \mathbb{N}$ with passive actions. These actions thus become of the form $<a, *_{l',w}>$ and are subject to a reactive preselection policy that takes priority constraints into account besides action names. Passive actions with $l' = 0$ can synchronize only with exponentially timed actions having the same name. Passive actions with $l' \geq 1$ can instead synchronize only with immediate actions having the same name and priority level equal to l'. Priority constraints are useful to achieve congruence for weak variants of $\sim_{MB}$, as they locally convey information about the global priority structure.

In the extended calculus MPC_x, we denote by $Act_{M,x} = Name \times Rate_x$ the set of actions, where $Rate_x = \mathbb{R}_{>0} \cup \{\infty_{l,w} \mid l \in \mathbb{N}_{>0} \wedge w \in \mathbb{R}_{>0}\} \cup \{*_{l',w} \mid l' \in \mathbb{N} \wedge w \in \mathbb{R}_{>0}\}$ is the set of action rates. We then denote by $\mathscr{PL}_{M,x}$ the set of process terms and by $\mathbb{P}_{M,x}$ the set of closed and guarded process terms. The multitransition relation $\longrightarrow_{M,x}$, and hence the labeled multitransition system $[\![P]\!]_{M,x}$ for a process term $P \in \mathbb{P}_{M,x}$, are defined on the basis of a variant of the operational semantic rules for MPC shown in Table 3.1 in which passive actions are extended with priority constraints and functions *weight* and *norm* are given a further parameter related to priority constraints, plus the following additional rules:

$$(\text{PREM},3) \quad \frac{}{<a,\infty_{l,w}>.P \xrightarrow{a,\infty_{l,w}}_{M,x} P}$$

$$(\text{SYN}_{M,4}) \quad \frac{P_1 \xrightarrow{a,\infty_{l,w}}_{M,x} P_1' \qquad P_2 \xrightarrow{a,*_{l,v}}_{M,x} P_2' \qquad a \in S}{P_1 \|_S P_2 \xrightarrow{a,\infty_{l,w \cdot \frac{v}{weight(P_2,a,l)}}}_{M,x} P_1' \|_S P_2'}$$

$$(\text{SYN}_{M,5}) \quad \frac{P_1 \xrightarrow{a,*_{l,v}}_{M,x} P_1' \qquad P_2 \xrightarrow{a,\infty_{l,w}}_{M,x} P_2' \qquad a \in S}{P_1 \|_S P_2 \xrightarrow{a,\infty_{l,w \cdot \frac{v}{weight(P_1,a,l)}}}_{M,x} P_1' \|_S P_2'}$$

Denoted by $\mathbb{P}_{M,x,pc}$ the set of performance-closed process terms of $\mathbb{P}_{M,x}$, we observe that the stochastic process underlying a process term $P \in \mathbb{P}_{M,x,pc}$ is a time-homogeneous CTMC possibly extended with immediate transitions. States having outgoing immediate transitions are called vanishing as the sojourn time in these states is zero. In order to retrieve a pure CTMC stochastically equivalent to an extended CTMC, we need to eliminate all vanishing states. This is accomplished by making as many copies of every transition entering a vanishing state as there are highest priority immediate transitions departing from the vanishing state. Then, each copy is directly connected to the destination state of one of the highest priority immediate transitions leaving the vanishing state. The rate of each copy is given by the rate of the original incoming transition multiplied by the execution probability of the highest priority immediate transition corresponding to the copy.

On the basis of the extended calculus MPC_x, we can define a weak variant of $\sim_{MB}$ that abstracts from immediate τ-actions.

The first step consists of extending the notion of exit rate to immediate actions. Since these actions may have different priorities and passive actions may have different constraints, we need a multilevel definition of exit rate. The level of an action is encoded through a number in $\mathbb{Z}$, which is 0 if the action is exponentially timed, l if the action rate is $\infty_{l,w}$, $-l'-1$ if the action rate is $*_{l',w}$. Given $P \in \mathbb{P}_{M,x}$, $a \in Name$, $l \in \mathbb{Z}$, and $D \subseteq \mathbb{P}_{M,x}$, we let:

$$rate_e(P,a,l,D) = \begin{cases} \sum\{\!| \lambda \in \mathbb{R}_{>0} \mid \exists P' \in D.P \xrightarrow{a,\lambda}_{M,x} P' |\!\} & \text{if } l = 0 \\ \sum\{\!| w \in \mathbb{R}_{>0} \mid \exists P' \in D.P \xrightarrow{a,\infty_{l,w}}_{M,x} P' |\!\} & \text{if } l > 0 \\ \sum\{\!| w \in \mathbb{R}_{>0} \mid \exists P' \in D.P \xrightarrow{a,*_{-l-1,w}}_{M,x} P' |\!\} & \text{if } l < 0 \end{cases}$$

When comparing process term exit rates, we have to take into account that immediate actions take precedence over exponentially timed actions. If the name of an immediate action is not τ, then that action may be prevented from being executed in a parallel composition or restriction context; thus, we cannot neglect the exit rate comparison for lower priority actions. If instead its name is τ, then executing that action may be hampered only by an alternative immediate action having an equal or higher priority. Therefore, the exit rate comparison should be conducted only in the absence of higher priority immediate τ-actions, as they preempt all the lower priority actions. We denote by $pri_\infty^\tau(P)$ the priority level of the highest priority immediate τ-action enabled by a process term $P \in \mathbb{P}_{M,x}$, and we set $pri_\infty^\tau(P) = 0$ if P does not enable any immediate τ-action. Moreover, given $l \in \mathbb{Z}$, we use $no\text{-}pre(l,P)$ to denote that no action of level l can be preempted in P. Formally, this is the case whenever $l \geq pri_\infty^\tau(P)$ or $-l - 1 \geq pri_\infty^\tau(P)$.

The second step consists of weakening the notion of exit rate. The idea is that, if a given class of process terms is not reached directly after executing an action of a certain name and level, then we have to explore the possibility of reaching that class by performing a finite-length sequence of immediate τ-actions starting from the term reached after executing the considered action. If this is possible, the probability of executing those action sequences has to be taken into account too.

Definition 3.14. Let $P \in \mathbb{P}_{M,x}$ and $l \in \mathbb{N}_{>0}$. We say that P is l-unobservable iff $pri_\infty^\tau(P) = l$ and P does not enable any immediate visible action with priority level $l' \geq l$, nor any passive action with priority constraint $l' \geq l$.

Definition 3.15. Let $n \in \mathbb{N}_{>0}$ and $P_1, \ldots, P_{n+1} \in \mathbb{P}_{M,x}$. A computation c of length n:

$$P_1 \xrightarrow{\tau,\infty l_1,w_1}_{M,x} P_2 \xrightarrow{\tau,\infty l_2,w_2}_{M,x} \cdots \xrightarrow{\tau,\infty l_n,w_n}_{M,x} P_{n+1}$$

is unobservable iff for all $i = 1, \ldots, n$ process term P_i is l_i-unobservable. In that case:

$$prob(c) = \prod_{i=1}^{n} \frac{w_i}{rate_0(P_i, \tau, l_i)}$$

Definition 3.16. Let $P \in \mathbb{P}_{M,x}$, $a \in Name$, $l \in \mathbb{Z}$, and $D \subseteq \mathbb{P}_{M,x}$. The weak exit rate at which P executes actions of name a and level l that lead to destination D is defined through the following nonnegative real function:

$$rate_{e,w}(P, a, l, D) = \sum_{P' \in D_w} rate_e(P, a, l, \{P'\}) \cdot prob_w(P', D)$$

where D_w is the weak backward closure of D:

$D_w = D \cup \{Q \in \mathbb{P}_{M,x} - D \mid Q$ can reach D via unobservable computations$\}$ and $prob_w$ is a $\mathbb{R}_{[0,1]}$-valued function representing the sum of the probabilities of all the unobservable computations from a process term in D_w to D:

$$prob_w(P', D) = \begin{cases} 1 & \text{if } P' \in D \\ \sum\{|prob(c)| \mid c \text{ unobs. comp. from } P' \text{ to } D|\} & \text{if } P' \in D_w - D \end{cases}$$

When comparing process term weak exit rates, besides taking preemption into account, we also have to skip the comparison for classes that contain certain unobservable process terms. More precisely, we distinguish among observable, initially unobservable, and fully unobservable process terms:

- An observable process term is a term that enables a visible action that cannot be preempted by any enabled immediate τ-action.
- An initially unobservable process term is a term in which all the enabled visible actions are preempted by some enabled immediate τ-action, but at least one of the computations starting at this term with one of the higher priority enabled immediate τ-actions reaches an observable process term.
- A fully unobservable process term is a term in which all the enabled visible actions are preempted by some enabled immediate τ-action, and all the computations starting at this term with one of the higher priority enabled immediate τ-actions are unobservable.

The weak exit rate comparison with respect to observable and fully unobservable classes must obviously be performed. In order to maximize the abstraction power in the presence of quantitative information attached to immediate τ-actions, the comparison should be conducted with respect to all fully unobservable classes together; i.e., the whole set $\mathbb{P}_{M,x,fu}$ of fully unobservable process terms of $\mathbb{P}_{M,x}$ should be considered. In contrast, the comparison with respect to initially unobservable classes should be skipped, otherwise process terms like the following would not be weakly Markovian bisimilar to each other:

$$<a,\lambda>.<\tau,\infty_{l_1,w_1}>.<b,\mu>.\underline{0}$$
$$<a,\lambda>.<\tau,\infty_{l_2,w_2}>.<b,\mu>.\underline{0}$$
$$<a,\lambda>.<b,\mu>.\underline{0}$$

In fact, the initially unobservable process term $<\tau,\infty_{l_1,w_1}>.<b,\mu>.\underline{0}$ reached by the first one is not weakly Markovian bisimilar to the initially unobservable process term $<\tau,\infty_{l_2,w_2}>.<b,\mu>.\underline{0}$ reached by the second one if $l_1 \neq l_2$ or $w_1 \neq w_2$, with neither of those initially unobservable process terms being reached by the third one.

Definition 3.17. An equivalence relation $\mathscr{B}$ over $\mathbb{P}_{M,x}$ is a weak Markovian bisimulation iff, whenever $(P_1, P_2) \in \mathscr{B}$, then for all action names $a \in$ *Name* and levels $l \in \mathbb{Z}$ such that *no-pre*(l, P_1) and *no-pre*(l, P_2):

$$rate_{e,w}(P_1, a, l, D) = rate_{e,w}(P_2, a, l, D) \qquad \text{for all obs. } D \in \mathbb{P}_{M,x}/\mathscr{B}$$
$$rate_{e,w}(P_1, a, l, \mathbb{P}_{M,x,fu}) = rate_{e,w}(P_2, a, l, \mathbb{P}_{M,x,fu})$$

Definition 3.18. Weak Markovian bisimulation equivalence (or weak Markovian bisimilarity), denoted $\approx_{MB}$, is the union of all the weak Markovian bisimulations.

Weak Markovian bisimulation equivalence enjoys properties similar to those of $\sim_{MB}$, except for congruence with respect to the parallel composition operator. In order to restore compositionality, we have to restrict ourselves to a well-prioritized subset of $\mathbb{P}_{M,x,nd}$, the set of nondivergent process terms of $\mathbb{P}_{M,x}$.

The problem with divergence, intended as the capability of reaching a point at which only an infinite unobservable computation can be executed, has to do with different interactions with time passing that are possible within the set of fully unobservable process terms. While some of them can terminate (like $<\tau,\infty_{l,w}>.\underline{0}$), others keep performing immediate τ-actions forever (like $recX : <\tau,\infty_{l,w}>.X$). These two families of fully unobservable terms can be considered equivalent in an untimed framework, but can always be distinguished in a timed setting by placing them in parallel with process terms that can perform actions whose duration is greater than zero. In fact, terms of the first family allow sooner or later the considered actions to be executed – and hence time to advance – whereas this is not the case with terms of the second family – as endless preemption prevents time from passing.

The problem with priorities is that, when composing each of two weak Markovian bisimilar process terms in parallel with a third process term, the degree of observability of the states underlying the two terms as well as the preemption scheme for their transitions may change differently in the two terms. This may expose parts of the behavior of the two terms that have not been considered when applying the weak exit rate comparison to the two terms; hence, those parts may not be equivalent to each other. A set of terms of $\mathbb{P}_{M,x}$ is well prioritized if, taken two arbitrary terms P_1 and P_2 in the set, any immediate/passive transition of each of $[\![P_1]\!]_{M,x}$ and $[\![P_2]\!]_{M,x}$ has priority level/constraint less than the priority level of any highest priority immediate τ-transition departing from an unobservable state of the other one.

We conclude with the axiomatization of $\approx_{MB}$ over a well-prioritized subset of $\mathbb{P}_{M,x,nd}$, which extends the axiomatization of $\sim_{MB}$ shown in Table 3.2 by replacing axioms $\mathcal{X}_{MB,4}$ and $\mathcal{X}_{MB,5}$ with those of Table 3.3. The first three laws represent the race policy, the generative preselection policy, and the reactive preselection policy, respectively. The next three laws express the preemption exercised by higher priority immediate τ-actions over lower priority actions. The last three laws (where I is a nonempty finite index set) describe the capability of abstracting from immediate τ-actions and encode the procedure for removing vanishing states. Note that, as a

Table 3.3 Equational laws characterizing $\approx_{MB}$

$$
\begin{aligned}
<a,\lambda_1>.P + <a,\lambda_2>.P &= <a,\lambda_1+\lambda_2>.P \\
<a,\infty_{l,w_1}>.P + <a,\infty_{l,w_2}>.P &= <a,\infty_{l,w_1+w_2}>.P \\
<a,*_{l,w_1}>.P + <a,*_{l,w_2}>.P &= <a,*_{l,w_1+w_2}>.P \\
\\
<\tau,\infty_{l,w}>.P + <a,\lambda>.Q &= <\tau,\infty_{l,w}>.P \\
<\tau,\infty_{l,w}>.P + <a,\infty_{l',w'}>.Q &= <\tau,\infty_{l,w}>.P \qquad \text{if } l > l' \\
<\tau,\infty_{l,w}>.P + <a,*_{l',w'}>.Q &= <\tau,\infty_{l,w}>.P \qquad \text{if } l > l' \\
\\
<a,\lambda>.\sum_{i\in I}<\tau,\infty_{l,w_i}>.P_i &= \sum_{i\in I}<a,\lambda\cdot w_i/\sum_{k\in I}w_k>.P_i \\
<a,\infty_{l',w'}>.\sum_{i\in I}<\tau,\infty_{l,w_i}>.P_i &= \sum_{i\in I}<a,\infty_{l',w'\cdot w_i/\sum_{k\in I}w_k}>.P_i \\
<a,*_{l',w'}>.\sum_{i\in I}<\tau,\infty_{l,w_i}>.P_i &= \sum_{i\in I}<a,*_{l',w'\cdot w_i/\sum_{k\in I}w_k}>.P_i
\end{aligned}
$$

consequence of the fact that Definition 3.16 requires the execution of at least one action, $\approx_{MB}$ does not permit to abstract from initial immediate τ-actions; hence, it does not incur the congruence problem with respect to the alternative composition operator discussed in Sect. 1.4.8 for $\approx_B$.

Example 3.4. Let us model with MPC the pipeline implementation considered in Example 1.4 of the producer–consumer system introduced in Sect. 1.2. The process algebraic description extended with action rates consistent with those of Example 3.1 is as follows:

$$PC_{\text{pipe},2}^M \triangleq Prod^M \|_{\{deposit\}} (LBuff^M \|_{\{pass\}} RBuff^M) / \{pass\} \|_{\{withdraw\}} Cons^M$$
$$Prod^M \triangleq <deposit, \lambda>.Prod^M$$
$$LBuff^M \triangleq <deposit, *_{0,1}>.<pass, \infty_{1,1}>.LBuff^M$$
$$RBuff^M \triangleq <pass, *_{1,1}>.<withdraw, *_{0,1}>.RBuff^M$$
$$Cons^M \triangleq <withdraw, \mu>.Cons^M$$

Note that action *pass* is immediate in the left buffer, as it has been assumed that its execution takes a negligible amount of time compared to deposits and withdrawals.

The labeled multitransition systems $[\![PC_{\text{pipe},2}^M]\!]_{M,x}$ and $[\![ProdCons_{0/2}^M]\!]_{M,x}$ are shown below, where the usual shorthands for process constants and action names have been used on the left-hand side:

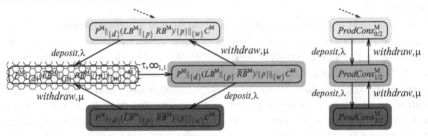

Note that all the states are observable except for the leftmost state of the labeled multitransition system on the left-hand side, which is initially unobservable.

Since the labeled multitransition system on the left-hand side contains an immediate τ-transition representing the passage of one item from the left buffer to the right buffer while the labeled multitransition system on the right-hand side does not contain any immediate τ-transition, similar to Example 1.4 we cannot expect the two labeled multitransition systems to be related by a Markovian bisimulation, as happened with the concurrent implementation.

What turns out is that $PC_{\text{pipe},2}^M \approx_{MB} ProdCons_{0/2}^M$. Like in Example 1.4, we have used state coloring for graphically representing the observable equivalence classes of the weak Markovian bisimulation proving this fact. The depicted relation is a weak Markovian bisimulation because in both labeled multitransition systems:

- A light gray state can only reach the class of observable gray states by executing exponentially timed actions of name *deposit* at total rate λ (possibly followed by $<\tau, \infty_{1,1}>$)

- An observable gray state can only reach the class of dark gray states by executing exponentially timed actions of name *deposit* at total rate λ or the class of light gray states by executing exponentially timed actions of name *withdraw* at total rate μ
- A dark gray state can only reach the class of observable gray states by executing exponentially timed actions of name *withdraw* at total rate μ (possibly followed by $<\tau, \infty_{1,1}>$)

3.4 Markovian Testing Equivalence

Markovian testing equivalence relates two process terms whenever an external observer is not able to distinguish between them from a functional or performance viewpoint by interacting with them by means of tests and comparing their reactions. In this section, we provide the definition of Markovian testing equivalence over $\mathbb{P}_{M,pc}$ based on quantitative information associated with test-driven computations of process terms, together with a necessary condition and four alternative characterizations [31, 42, 34]. Then, we show that Markovian testing equivalence is a congruence and we present its sound and complete axiomatization, its modal logic characterization, and its verification algorithm [31, 33, 34].

3.4.1 Probability and Duration of Computations

We recall that a computation of a process term is a sequence of transitions that can be executed starting from the process term. The length of a computation is given by the number of transitions occurring in it. We denote by $\mathscr{C}_f(P)$ the multiset of finite-length computations of $P \in \mathbb{P}_M$. We say that two distinct computations are independent of each other iff neither is a proper prefix of the other one. In the following, we focus on finite multisets of independent, finite-length computations.

Below we define the concrete trace, the probability, and the duration of an element of $\mathscr{C}_f(P)$, using $\_ \circ \_$ for sequence concatenation and $|\_|$ for sequence length.

Definition 3.19. Let $P \in \mathbb{P}_M$ and $c \in \mathscr{C}_f(P)$. The concrete trace associated with c is the sequence of action names labeling the transitions of c, which is defined by induction on the length of c through the following *Name**-valued function:

$$trace_c(c) = \begin{cases} \varepsilon & \text{if } |c| = 0 \\ a \circ trace_c(c') & \text{if } c \equiv P \xrightarrow{a,\tilde{\lambda}}_M c' \end{cases}$$

where ε is the empty trace. We denote by $trace(c)$ the visible part of $trace_c(c)$, i.e., the subsequence of $trace_c(c)$ obtained by removing all the occurrences of τ.

Definition 3.20. Let $P \in \mathbb{P}_{M,pc}$ and $c \in \mathscr{C}_f(P)$. The probability of executing c is the product of the execution probabilities of the transitions of c, which is defined by induction on the length of c through the following $\mathbb{R}_{[0,1]}$-valued function:

$$prob(c) = \begin{cases} 1 & \text{if } |c| = 0 \\ \dfrac{\lambda}{rate_t(P,0)} \cdot prob(c') & \text{if } c \equiv P \xrightarrow{\ a,\lambda\ }_M c' \end{cases}$$

We also define the probability of executing a computation in $C \subseteq \mathscr{C}_f(P)$ as:

$$prob(C) = \sum_{c \in C} prob(c)$$

whenever C is finite and all of its computations are independent of each other.

Definition 3.21. Let $P \in \mathbb{P}_{M,pc}$ and $c \in \mathscr{C}_f(P)$. The stepwise average duration of c is the sequence of average sojourn times in the states traversed by c, which is defined by induction on the length of c through the following $(\mathbb{R}_{>0})^*$-valued function:

$$time_a(c) = \begin{cases} \varepsilon & \text{if } |c| = 0 \\ \dfrac{1}{rate_t(P,0)} \circ time_a(c') & \text{if } c \equiv P \xrightarrow{\ a,\lambda\ }_M c' \end{cases}$$

where ε is the empty stepwise average duration. We also define the multiset of computations in $C \subseteq \mathscr{C}_f(P)$ whose stepwise average duration is not greater than $\theta \in (\mathbb{R}_{>0})^*$ as:

$$C_{\leq\theta} = \{|c \in C \mid |c| \leq |\theta| \wedge \forall i = 1,\ldots,|c|.time_a(c)[i] \leq \theta[i] \, |\}$$

Moreover, we denote by C^l the multiset of computations in $C \subseteq \mathscr{C}_f(P)$ whose length is equal to $l \in \mathbb{N}$.

Definition 3.22. Let $P \in \mathbb{P}_{M,pc}$ and $c \in \mathscr{C}_f(P)$. The stepwise duration of c is the sequence of random variables quantifying the sojourn times in the states traversed by c, which is defined by induction on the length of c through the following random-variable-sequence-valued function:

$$time_d(c) = \begin{cases} \varepsilon & \text{if } |c| = 0 \\ Exp_{rate_t(P,0)} \circ time_d(c') & \text{if } c \equiv P \xrightarrow{\ a,\lambda\ }_M c' \end{cases}$$

where ε is the empty stepwise duration while $Exp_{rate_t(P,0)}$ is the exponentially distributed random variable with rate $rate_t(P,0) \in \mathbb{R}_{>0}$. We also define the probability distribution of executing a computation in $C \subseteq \mathscr{C}_f(P)$ within a sequence $\theta \in (\mathbb{R}_{>0})^*$ of time units as:

$$prob_d(C,\theta) = \sum_{c \in C}^{|c| \leq |\theta|} prob(c) \cdot \prod_{i=1}^{|c|} \Pr\{time_d(c)[i] \leq \theta[i]\}$$

whenever C is finite and all of its computations are independent of each other, where $\Pr\{time_{\mathrm{d}}(c)[i] \leq \theta[i]\} = 1 - \mathrm{e}^{-\theta[i]/time_{\mathrm{a}}(c)[i]}$ is the cumulative distribution function of the exponentially distributed random variable $time_{\mathrm{d}}(c)[i]$, whose expected value is $time_{\mathrm{a}}(c)[i]$.

We conclude by observing that the average duration (resp. the duration) of a finite-length computation has been defined as the sequence of average sojourn times (resp. of random variables expressing the sojourn times) in the states traversed by the computation. The same quantity could have been defined as the sum of the same basic ingredients, but this would not have been appropriate. Consider, for instance, the following two process terms:

$$<g,\gamma>.<a,\lambda>.<b,\mu>.\underline{0} + <g,\gamma>.<a,\mu>.<d,\lambda>.\underline{0}$$
$$<g,\gamma>.<a,\lambda>.<d,\mu>.\underline{0} + <g,\gamma>.<a,\mu>.<b,\lambda>.\underline{0}$$

where $\lambda \neq \mu$ and $b \neq d$. Observed that the two process terms have identical non-maximal computations, we further notice that the first process term has the following two maximal computations each with probability $1/2$:

$$c_{1,1} \equiv . \xrightarrow{g,\gamma} \mathrm{M} . \xrightarrow{a,\lambda} \mathrm{M} . \xrightarrow{b,\mu} \mathrm{M} .$$
$$c_{1,2} \equiv . \xrightarrow{g,\gamma} \mathrm{M} . \xrightarrow{a,\mu} \mathrm{M} . \xrightarrow{d,\lambda} \mathrm{M} .$$

while the second process term has the following two maximal computations each with probability $1/2$:

$$c_{2,1} \equiv . \xrightarrow{g,\gamma} \mathrm{M} . \xrightarrow{a,\lambda} \mathrm{M} . \xrightarrow{d,\mu} \mathrm{M} .$$
$$c_{2,2} \equiv . \xrightarrow{g,\gamma} \mathrm{M} . \xrightarrow{a,\mu} \mathrm{M} . \xrightarrow{b,\lambda} \mathrm{M} .$$

If the average duration were defined as the sum of the average sojourn times, then $c_{1,1}$ and $c_{2,2}$ would have the same concrete trace $g \circ a \circ b$ and the same average duration $\frac{1}{2\cdot\gamma} + \frac{1}{\lambda} + \frac{1}{\mu}$, and similarly $c_{1,2}$ and $c_{2,1}$ would have the same concrete trace $g \circ a \circ d$ and the same average duration $\frac{1}{2\cdot\gamma} + \frac{1}{\mu} + \frac{1}{\lambda}$. This would lead to conclude that the two process terms are equivalent. However, an external observer equipped with a button-pushing machine displaying the names of the actions that are performed and the instants at which they are performed would be able to distinguish between the two process terms [194]. Hence, the necessity of considering the sequence of average sojourn times rather than their sum.

3.4.2 Definition of the Behavioral Equivalence

The basic idea behind the testing approach is to infer information about the behavior of process terms by interacting with them by means of tests and comparing their reactions. In a Markovian setting, we are not only interested in verifying whether tests are passed or not, but also in measuring the probability with which they are passed and the time taken to pass them, hence the restriction to $\mathbb{P}_{\mathrm{M,pc}}$.

As in the nondeterministic setting, the most convenient way to represent a test is through a process term, which interacts with any process term under test by means of a parallel composition operator that enforces synchronization on the set $Name_v$ of all visible action names. Due to the adoption of an asymmetric synchronization discipline, a test can comprise only passive visible actions, so that the composite term inherits performance closure from the process term under test.

From a testing viewpoint, in any of its states a process term under test generates the proposal of an action to be executed by means of a race among the exponentially timed actions enabled in that state. If the name of the proposed action is τ, then the process term advances by itself. Otherwise, the test either reacts by participating in the interaction with the process term through a passive action having the same name as the proposed exponentially timed action, or blocks the interaction if it has no passive actions with the proposed name.

Markovian testing equivalence relies on comparing the process term probabilities of performing successful test-driven computations within arbitrary sequences of average amounts of time. Due to the presence of these average time upper bounds, for the test representation we can restrict ourselves to nonrecursive process terms. In other words, the expressiveness provided by finite-state labeled multitransition systems with an acyclic structure is enough for tests.

In order not to interfere with the quantitative aspects of the behavior of process terms under test, we avoid the introduction of a success action ω. The successful completion of a test is formalized in the text syntax by replacing $\underline{0}$ with a zeroary operator s denoting a success state. Ambiguous tests including several summands among which at least one equal to s are avoided through a two-level syntax.

Definition 3.23. The set $\mathbb{T}_R$ of reactive tests is generated by the following syntax:

$$
\begin{array}{ll}
T & ::= \ \mathsf{s} \mid T' \\
T' & ::= \ <a,*_w>.T \mid T' + T'
\end{array}
$$

where $a \in Name_v$ and $w \in \mathbb{R}_{>0}$.

Given $P \in \mathbb{P}_{M,pc}$ and $T \in \mathbb{T}_R$, the interaction system of P and T is process term $P \|_{Name_v} T \in \mathbb{P}_{M,pc}$. We remind that each state of $[\![P \|_{Name_v} T]\!]_M$ is called a configuration and is formed by a process projection and a test projection, whereas its transitions constitute the test-driven computations of P with respect to T. We say that a configuration is successful iff its test projection is s and that a test-driven computation is successful iff it traverses a successful configuration. We denote by $\mathscr{SC}(P,T)$ the multiset of successful computations of $P \|_{Name_v} T$.

If a process term $P \in \mathbb{P}_{M,pc}$ under test has no exponentially timed τ-actions, then for all reactive tests $T \in \mathbb{T}_R$ it turns out that: (1) all the computations in $\mathscr{SC}(P,T)$ have a finite length due to the restrictions imposed on the test syntax; (2) all the computations in $\mathscr{SC}(P,T)$ are independent of each other because of their maximality; (3) the multiset $\mathscr{SC}(P,T)$ is finite because P and T are finitely branching. Thus, all definitions of Sect. 3.4.1 are applicable to $\mathscr{SC}(P,T)$ and also to $\mathscr{SC}_{\leq\theta}(P,T)$ for any sequence $\theta \in (\mathbb{R}_{>0})^*$ of average amounts of time.

In order to cope with the possible presence of exponentially timed τ-actions within P in such a way that all the properties above hold – especially independence – we have to consider subsets of $\mathscr{SC}_{\leq\theta}(P,T)$ including all successful test-driven computations of the same length. This is also necessary to distinguish among process terms comprising only exponentially timed τ-actions – like $<\tau,\lambda>.\underline{0}$ and $<\tau,\mu>.\underline{0}$ with $\lambda \neq \mu$ – as there is a single test, s, that those process terms can pass. The only option is to compare them after executing the same number of τ-actions.

Since no element of $\mathscr{SC}_{\leq\theta}(P,T)$ can be longer than $|\theta|$, we should consider every possible subset $\mathscr{SC}^l_{\leq\theta}(P,T)$ for $0 \leq l \leq |\theta|$. However, it is enough to consider $\mathscr{SC}^{|\theta|}_{\leq\theta}(P,T)$, as shorter successful test-driven computations can be taken into account when imposing prefixes of θ as average time upper bounds.

Definition 3.24. Let $P_1, P_2 \in \mathbb{P}_{M,pc}$. We say that P_1 is Markovian testing equivalent to P_2, written $P_1 \sim_{MT} P_2$, iff for all reactive tests $T \in \mathbb{T}_R$ and sequences $\theta \in (\mathbb{R}_{>0})^*$ of average amounts of time:

$$prob(\mathscr{SC}^{|\theta|}_{\leq\theta}(P_1,T)) = prob(\mathscr{SC}^{|\theta|}_{\leq\theta}(P_2,T))$$

Note that we have not defined a may equivalence and a must equivalence as in Sect. 1.5.1. The reason is that in this Markovian framework the possibility and the necessity of passing a test are not sufficient to discriminate among process terms, as they are qualitative concepts. What we have considered here is a single quantitative notion given by the probability of passing a test (within an average time upper bound); hence, the definition of a single equivalence. This quantitative notion subsumes both the possibility of passing a test – which can be encoded as the probability of passing the test being greater than zero – and the necessity of passing a test – which can be encoded as the probability of passing the test being equal to one.

Although we could have defined Markovian testing equivalence as the kernel of a Markovian testing preorder, this has not been done. The reason is that such a preorder would have boiled down to an equivalence relation, because for each reactive test passed by P_1 within θ with a probability less than the probability with which P_2 passes the same test within θ, in general it is possible to find a dual reactive test for which the relation between the two probabilities is inverted.

Another important difference with respect to $\approx_T$ is that the presence of average time upper bounds makes it possible to decide whether a test is passed or not even if the process term under test can execute infinitely many exponentially timed τ-actions. In other words, divergence does not need to be taken into account.

Using the same examples as Sect. 3.3.2, it is easy to see that $\sim_{MT}$ is strictly finer than $\approx_T$ and probabilistic testing equivalence [64, 68].

3.4.3 Conditions and Characterizations

A necessary condition for establishing whether two process terms are Markovian testing equivalent is that for each computation of any of the two terms there exists a computation of the other term with the same concrete trace and the same stepwise average duration, such that any pair of corresponding states traversed by the two computations have the same overall exit rates with respect to all action names.

Proposition 3.4. *Let* $P_1, P_2 \in \mathbb{P}_{M,pc}$. *Whenever* $P_1 \sim_{MT} P_2$, *then for all* $c_k \in \mathscr{C}_f(P_k)$ *with* $k \in \{1,2\}$ *there exists* $c_h \in \mathscr{C}_f(P_h)$ *with* $h \in \{1,2\} - \{k\}$ *such that:*

$$trace_c(c_k) = trace_c(c_h)$$
$$time_a(c_k) = time_a(c_h)$$

and for all $a \in Name$ *and* $i \in \{0, \ldots, |c_k|\}$:

$$rate_o(P_k^i, a, 0) = rate_o(P_h^i, a, 0)$$

with P_k^i *(resp.* P_h^i) *being the ith state traversed by* c_k *(resp.* c_h).

We now present four alternative characterizations of $\sim_{MT}$. The first three provide further justifications for the way in which $\sim_{MT}$ has been defined. The first one establishes that the discriminating power does not change if we consider a set $\mathbb{T}_{R,lib}$ of tests with the following more liberal syntax:

$$T ::= s \mid <a, *_w>.T \mid T + T$$

provided that in this setting by successful configuration we mean a configuration whose test projection includes s as top-level summand. Let us denote by $\sim_{MT,lib}$ the resulting variant of $\sim_{MT}$.

Proposition 3.5. *Let* $P_1, P_2 \in \mathbb{P}_{M,pc}$. *Then:*

$$P_1 \sim_{MT,lib} P_2 \iff P_1 \sim_{MT} P_2$$

The second characterization establishes that the discriminating power does not change if we consider a set $\mathbb{T}_{R,\tau}$ of tests capable of moving autonomously by executing exponentially timed τ-actions:

$$T ::= s \mid T'$$
$$T' ::= <a, *_w>.T \mid <\tau, \lambda>.T \mid T' + T'$$

Let us denote by $\sim_{MT,\tau}$ the resulting variant of $\sim_{MT}$.

Proposition 3.6. *Let* $P_1, P_2 \in \mathbb{P}_{M,pc}$. *Then:*

$$P_1 \sim_{MT,\tau} P_2 \iff P_1 \sim_{MT} P_2$$

While the previous two characterizations justify the restrictions imposed on the test structure, the third characterization justifies the use of expected values instead of random variables when considering the step-by-step duration of successful test-driven computations. In fact, the third characterization establishes that the discriminating power does not change if we consider the probability distribution of passing tests within arbitrary sequences of amounts of time, rather than the probability of passing tests within arbitrary sequences of average amounts of time. In other words, considering the (more accurate) stepwise durations of test-driven computations leads to the same equivalence as considering the (easier to work with) stepwise average durations.

Definition 3.25. Let $P_1, P_2 \in \mathbb{P}_{M,pc}$. We say that P_1 is Markovian distribution-testing equivalent to P_2, written $P_1 \sim_{MT,d} P_2$, iff for all reactive tests $T \in \mathbb{T}_R$ and sequences $\theta \in (\mathbb{R}_{>0})^*$ of amounts of time:

$$prob_d(\mathscr{SC}^{|\theta|}(P_1, T), \theta) = prob_d(\mathscr{SC}^{|\theta|}(P_2, T), \theta)$$

Proposition 3.7. *Let* $P_1, P_2 \in \mathbb{P}_{M,pc}$. *Then:*

$$P_1 \sim_{MT,d} P_2 \iff P_1 \sim_{MT} P_2$$

The fourth characterization of $\sim_{MT}$ fully abstracts from comparing process term behavior in response to tests. It is based on traces that are extended at each step with the set of visible action names permitted by the environment at that step.

Definition 3.26. An element ξ of $(Name_v \times 2^{Name_v})^*$ is an extended trace iff:

- Either ξ is the empty sequence ε
- Or $\xi \equiv (a_1, \mathscr{E}_1) \circ (a_2, \mathscr{E}_2) \circ \cdots \circ (a_n, \mathscr{E}_n)$ for some $n \in \mathbb{N}_{>0}$ with $a_i \in \mathscr{E}_i$ and $\mathscr{E}_i$ finite for each $i = 1, \ldots, n$.

We denote by $\mathscr{ET}$ the set of extended traces.

Definition 3.27. Let $\xi \in \mathscr{ET}$. The trace associated with ξ is defined by induction on the length of ξ through the following $(Name_v)^*$-valued function:

$$trace_{et}(\xi) = \begin{cases} \varepsilon & \text{if } |\xi| = 0 \\ a \circ trace_{et}(\xi') & \text{if } \xi \equiv (a, \mathscr{E}) \circ \xi' \end{cases}$$

where ε is the empty trace.

Definition 3.28. Let $P \in \mathbb{P}_{M,pc}$, $c \in \mathscr{C}_f(P)$, and $\xi \in \mathscr{ET}$. We say that c is compatible with ξ iff:

$$trace(c) = trace_{et}(\xi)$$

We denote by $\mathscr{CC}(P, \xi)$ the multiset of computations in $\mathscr{C}_f(P)$ that are compatible with ξ.

For any computation compatible with $\xi \in \mathscr{ET}$, its probability and its duration have to be calculated by considering only the action names permitted at each step by ξ.

Definition 3.29. Let $P \in \mathbb{P}_{M,pc}$, $\xi \in \mathscr{E}\mathscr{T}$, and $c \in \mathscr{C}\mathscr{C}(P,\xi)$. The probability of executing c with respect to ξ is defined by induction on the length of c through the following $\mathbb{R}_{]0,1]}$-valued function:

$$prob_\xi(c) = \begin{cases} 1 & \text{if } |c| = 0 \\[2mm] \dfrac{\lambda}{rate_o(P,\mathscr{E}\cup\{\tau\},0)} \cdot prob_{\xi'}(c') & \text{if } c \equiv P \xrightarrow{a,\lambda}_M c' \\ & \text{with } \xi \equiv (a,\mathscr{E}) \circ \xi' \\[2mm] \dfrac{\lambda}{rate_o(P,\mathscr{E}\cup\{\tau\},0)} \cdot prob_\xi(c') & \text{if } c \equiv P \xrightarrow{\tau,\lambda}_M c' \\ & \text{with } \xi \equiv (a,\mathscr{E}) \circ \xi' \\[2mm] \dfrac{\lambda}{rate_o(P,\tau,0)} \cdot prob_\xi(c') & \text{if } c \equiv P \xrightarrow{\tau,\lambda}_M c' \wedge \xi \equiv \varepsilon \end{cases}$$

We also define the probability of executing a computation in $C \subseteq \mathscr{C}\mathscr{C}(P,\xi)$ with respect to ξ as:

$$prob_\xi(C) = \sum_{c \in C} prob_\xi(c)$$

whenever C is finite and all of its computations are independent of each other.

Definition 3.30. Let $P \in \mathbb{P}_{M,pc}$, $\xi \in \mathscr{E}\mathscr{T}$, and $c \in \mathscr{C}\mathscr{C}(P,\xi)$. The stepwise average duration of c with respect to ξ is defined by induction on the length of c through the following $(\mathbb{R}_{>0})^*$-valued function:

$$time_{a,\xi}(c) = \begin{cases} \varepsilon & \text{if } |c| = 0 \\[2mm] \dfrac{1}{rate_o(P,\mathscr{E}\cup\{\tau\},0)} \circ time_{a,\xi'}(c') & \text{if } c \equiv P \xrightarrow{a,\lambda}_M c' \\ & \text{with } \xi \equiv (a,\mathscr{E}) \circ \xi' \\[2mm] \dfrac{1}{rate_o(P,\mathscr{E}\cup\{\tau\},0)} \circ time_{a,\xi}(c') & \text{if } c \equiv P \xrightarrow{\tau,\lambda}_M c' \\ & \text{with } \xi \equiv (a,\mathscr{E}) \circ \xi' \\[2mm] \dfrac{1}{rate_o(P,\tau,0)} \circ time_{a,\xi}(c') & \text{if } c \equiv P \xrightarrow{\tau,\lambda}_M c' \wedge \xi \equiv \varepsilon \end{cases}$$

where ε is the empty stepwise average duration. We also define the multiset of computations in $C \subseteq \mathscr{C}\mathscr{C}(P,\xi)$ whose stepwise average duration with respect to ξ is not greater than $\theta \in (\mathbb{R}_{>0})^*$ as:

$$C_{\le\theta,\xi} = \{|\, c \in C \mid |c| \le |\theta| \wedge \forall i = 1,\dots,|c|.\, time_{a,\xi}(c)[i] \le \theta[i] \,|\}$$

Moreover, as before we denote by C^l the multiset of computations in $C \subseteq \mathscr{C}\mathscr{C}(P,\xi)$ whose length is equal to $l \in \mathbb{N}$.

Definition 3.31. Let $P_1, P_2 \in \mathbb{P}_{M,pc}$. We say that P_1 is Markovian extended-trace equivalent to P_2, written $P_1 \sim_{MTr,e} P_2$, iff for all extended traces $\xi \in \mathscr{E}\mathscr{T}$ and sequences $\theta \in (\mathbb{R}_{>0})^*$ of average amounts of time:

$$prob_\xi(\mathscr{C}\mathscr{C}^{|\theta|}_{\le\theta,\xi}(P_1,\xi)) = prob_\xi(\mathscr{C}\mathscr{C}^{|\theta|}_{\le\theta,\xi}(P_2,\xi))$$

Theorem 3.5. *Let $P_1, P_2 \in \mathbb{P}_{M,pc}$. Then:*

$$P_1 \sim_{\text{MTr,e}} P_2 \iff P_1 \sim_{\text{MT}} P_2$$

A consequence of the structure of extended traces is the identification of a set of canonical reactive tests; i.e., a set of reactive tests that are necessary and sufficient in order to establish whether two process terms are Markovian testing equivalent. Similar to the case of probabilistic testing equivalence [64, 68], each of these canonical reactive tests admits a main computation leading to success, whose intermediate states can have additional computations each leading to failure in one step. In order to represent failure, we assume that $Name_v$ includes an action name z that can occur within canonical reactive tests but not within process terms under test. We point out that canonical reactive tests are name deterministic, in the sense that the names of the passive actions occurring in any of their branches are all distinct.

Definition 3.32. The set $\mathbb{T}_{R,c}$ of canonical reactive tests is generated by the following syntax:

$$\boxed{T ::= \text{s} \mid <a, *_1>.T + \sum_{b \in \mathscr{E} - \{a\}} <b, *_1>.<z, *_1>.\text{s}}$$

where $a \in \mathscr{E}$, $\mathscr{E} \subseteq Name_v$ finite, and the summation is absent whenever $\mathscr{E} = \{a\}$.

Corollary 3.1. *Let $P_1, P_2 \in \mathbb{P}_{M,pc}$. Then $P_1 \sim_{\text{MT}} P_2$ iff for all $T \in \mathbb{T}_{R,c}$ and $\theta \in (\mathbb{R}_{>0})^*$:*

$$prob(\mathscr{SC}_{\leq \theta}^{|\theta|}(P_1, T)) = prob(\mathscr{SC}_{\leq \theta}^{|\theta|}(P_2, T))$$

Example 3.5. We exploit the alternative characterization of Theorem 3.5 in order to prove that $ProdCons_{0/2}^M$ and $PC_{\text{conc},2}^M$ – which are defined in Examples 3.1 and 3.3, respectively – are Markovian testing equivalent.

Similar to Example 1.5, we observe first of all that the only sequences of visible actions that the two process constants can perform are the prefixes of the strings that comply with the following regular expression:

$$(deposit \circ (deposit \circ withdraw)^* \circ withdraw)^*$$

As a consequence, the only significant extended traces to be considered in this scenario are those whose associated traces coincide with the previously mentioned prefixes. Note that their nonempty finite sets of visible actions permitted at the various steps necessarily contain at least one between *deposit* and *withdraw*.

If we take one such extended trace, say ξ, it is easy to see that any two computations of $ProdCons_{0/2}^M$ and $PC_{\text{conc},2}^M$, respectively, that are compatible with ξ traverse states that pairwise enable sets of actions with the same names and total rates. Therefore, the stepwise average durations with respect to ξ of the considered computations are identical.

As far as the execution probabilities with respect to ξ of $\mathscr{CC}(ProdCons_{0/2}^M, \xi)$ and $\mathscr{CC}(PC_{\text{conc},2}^M, \xi)$ are concerned, observed that all these computations have the same length as none of them includes exponentially timed τ-transitions, we have four basic cases corresponding to the four shortest nontrivial prefixes of the strings complying with the regular expression above:

- If $\xi \equiv (deposit, \mathscr{E})$, then for both sets of computations the execution probability is 1
- If $\xi \equiv (deposit, \mathscr{E}_1) \circ (withdraw, \mathscr{E}_2)$, then for both sets of computations the execution probability is 1 if $\mathscr{E}_2$ does not contain $deposit$, $\frac{\mu}{\lambda+\mu}$ otherwise
- If $\xi \equiv (deposit, \mathscr{E}_1) \circ (deposit, \mathscr{E}_2)$, then for both sets of computations the execution probability is 1 if $\mathscr{E}_2$ does not contain $withdraw$, $\frac{\lambda}{\lambda+\mu}$ otherwise
- If $\xi \equiv (deposit, \mathscr{E}_1) \circ (deposit, \mathscr{E}_2) \circ (withdraw, \mathscr{E}_3)$, then for both sets of computations the execution probability is 1 if $\mathscr{E}_2$ does not contain $withdraw$, $\frac{\lambda}{\lambda+\mu}$ otherwise

Since all the other cases are extensions of these four basic cases that comply with the regular expression above, the corresponding extensions of the two sets of computations compatible with the same extended trace still have the same execution probability. Therefore, we can conclude that $PC_{conc,2}^{M} \sim_{MT} ProdCons_{0/2}^{M}$.

3.4.4 Congruence Property

Markovian testing equivalence is a congruence over $\mathbb{P}_{M,pc}$ with respect to all the dynamic and static operators of MPC as well as recursion.

Theorem 3.6. *Let $P_1, P_2 \in \mathbb{P}_{M,pc}$. Whenever $P_1 \sim_{MT} P_2$, then:*

1. $<a,\lambda>.P_1 \sim_{MT} <a,\lambda>.P_2$ *for all $<a,\lambda> \in Act_M$.*
2. $P_1 + P \sim_{MT} P_2 + P$ *and $P + P_1 \sim_{MT} P + P_2$ for all $P \in \mathbb{P}_{M,pc}$.*
3. $P_1 \|_S P \sim_{MT} P_2 \|_S P$ *and $P \|_S P_1 \sim_{MT} P \|_S P_2$ for all $P \in \mathbb{P}_M$ and $S \subseteq Name_v$ such that $P_1 \|_S P, P_2 \|_S P \in \mathbb{P}_{M,pc}$.*
4. $P_1/H \sim_{MT} P_2/H$ *for all $H \subseteq Name_v$.*
5. $P_1 \backslash L \sim_{MT} P_2 \backslash L$ *for all $L \subseteq Name_v$.*
6. $P_1[\varphi] \sim_{MT} P_2[\varphi]$ *for all $\varphi \in Relab$.*

Definition 3.33. Let $P_1, P_2 \in \mathscr{PL}_M$ be guarded process terms containing free occurrences of $k \in \mathbb{N}$ process variables $X_1, \ldots, X_k \in Var$ at most. We define $P_1 \sim_{MT} P_2$ iff there exist $Q_1, \ldots, Q_k \in \mathbb{P}_M$ such that both $P_1\{Q_i \hookrightarrow X_i \mid 1 \le i \le k\}$ and $P_2\{Q_i \hookrightarrow X_i \mid 1 \le i \le k\}$ belong to $\mathbb{P}_{M,pc}$ and, for each such group of process terms $Q_1, \ldots, Q_k \in \mathbb{P}_M$, it holds $P_1\{Q_i \hookrightarrow X_i \mid 1 \le i \le k\} \sim_{MT} P_2\{Q_i \hookrightarrow X_i \mid 1 \le i \le k\}$.

Theorem 3.7. *Let $P_1, P_2 \in \mathscr{PL}_M$ be guarded process terms containing free occurrences of $k \in \mathbb{N}$ process variables $X_1, \ldots, X_k \in Var$ at most. Whenever $P_1 \sim_{MT} P_2$, then $rec X : P_1 \sim_{MT} rec X : P_2$ for all $X \in Var$.*

3.4.5 Sound and Complete Axiomatization

Markovian testing equivalence has a sound and complete axiomatization over the set of nonrecursive process terms of $\mathbb{P}_{M,pc}$, given by the set $\mathscr{X}_{MT}$ of equational laws of Table 3.4.

The main difference with respect to the equational laws for $\sim_{MB}$ shown in Table 3.2 is given by the axiom schema $\mathscr{X}_{MT,4}$, which subsumes axiom $\mathscr{X}_{MB,4}$.

Table 3.4 Equational laws for $\sim_{MT}$

$$(\mathscr{X}_{MT,1}) \qquad P_1 + P_2 = P_2 + P_1$$

$$(\mathscr{X}_{MT,2}) \qquad (P_1 + P_2) + P_3 = P_1 + (P_2 + P_3)$$

$$(\mathscr{X}_{MT,3}) \qquad P + \underline{0} = P$$

$$(\mathscr{X}_{MT,4}) \quad \sum_{i \in I} <a, \lambda_i>. \sum_{j \in J_i} <b_{i,j}, \mu_{i,j}>.P_{i,j} = <a, \sum_{k \in I} \lambda_k>. \sum_{i \in I} \sum_{j \in J_i} <b_{i,j}, \frac{\lambda_i}{\Sigma_{k \in I} \lambda_k} \cdot \mu_{i,j}>.P_{i,j}$$

if: I is a finite index set with $|I| \geq 2$;

for all $i \in I$, index set J_i is finite and its summation is $\underline{0}$ if $J_i = \emptyset$;

for all $i_1, i_2 \in I$ and $b \in Name$:
$$\sum_{j \in J_{i_1}} \{| \mu_{i_1,j} \mid b_{i_1,j} = b |\} = \sum_{j \in J_{i_2}} \{| \mu_{i_2,j} \mid b_{i_2,j} = b |\}$$

$$(\mathscr{X}_{MT,5}) \sum_{i \in I} <a_i, \tilde{\lambda}_i>.P_i \parallel_S \sum_{j \in J} <b_j, \tilde{\mu}_j>.Q_j = \sum_{k \in I, a_k \notin S} <a_k, \tilde{\lambda}_k>. \left(P_k \parallel_S \sum_{j \in J} <b_j, \tilde{\mu}_j>.Q_j \right)$$

$$+ \sum_{h \in J, b_h \notin S} <b_h, \tilde{\mu}_h>. \left(\sum_{i \in I} <a_i, \tilde{\lambda}_i>.P_i \parallel_S Q_h \right)$$

$$+ \sum_{k \in I, a_k \in S, \tilde{\lambda}_k \in \mathbb{R}_{>0}} \sum_{h \in J, b_h = a_k, \tilde{\mu}_h = *_{w_h}} <a_k, \tilde{\lambda}_k \cdot \frac{w_h}{weight(Q, b_h)}>.(P_k \parallel_S Q_h)$$

$$+ \sum_{h \in J, b_h \in S, \tilde{\mu}_h \in \mathbb{R}_{>0}} \sum_{k \in I, a_k = b_h, \tilde{\lambda}_k = *_{v_k}} <b_h, \tilde{\mu}_h \cdot \frac{v_k}{weight(P, a_k)}>.(P_k \parallel_S Q_h)$$

$$+ \sum_{k \in I, a_k \in S, \tilde{\lambda}_k = *_{v_k}} \sum_{h \in J, b_h = a_k, \tilde{\mu}_h = *_{w_h}} <a_k, *_{norm(v_k, w_h, a_k, P, Q)}>.(P_k \parallel_S Q_h)$$

$$(\mathscr{X}_{MT,6}) \qquad \sum_{i \in I} <a_i, \tilde{\lambda}_i>.P_i \parallel_S \underline{0} = \sum_{k \in I, a_k \notin S} <a_k, \tilde{\lambda}_k>.P_k$$

$$(\mathscr{X}_{MT,7}) \qquad \underline{0} \parallel_S \sum_{j \in J} <b_j, \tilde{\mu}_j>.Q_j = \sum_{h \in J, b_h \notin S} <b_h, \tilde{\mu}_h>.Q_h$$

$$(\mathscr{X}_{MT,8}) \qquad \underline{0} \parallel_S \underline{0} = \underline{0}$$

$$(\mathscr{X}_{MT,9}) \qquad \underline{0}/H = \underline{0}$$

$$(\mathscr{X}_{MT,10}) \qquad (<a, \tilde{\lambda}>.P)/H = <\tau, \tilde{\lambda}>.(P/H) \qquad \text{if } a \in H$$

$$(\mathscr{X}_{MT,11}) \qquad (<a, \tilde{\lambda}>.P)/H = <a, \tilde{\lambda}>.(P/H) \qquad \text{if } a \notin H$$

$$(\mathscr{X}_{MT,12}) \qquad (P_1 + P_2)/H = P_1/H + P_2/H$$

$$(\mathscr{X}_{MT,13}) \qquad \underline{0} \backslash L = \underline{0}$$

$$(\mathscr{X}_{MT,14}) \qquad (<a, \tilde{\lambda}>.P) \backslash L = \underline{0} \qquad \text{if } a \in L$$

$$(\mathscr{X}_{MT,15}) \qquad (<a, \tilde{\lambda}>.P) \backslash L = <a, \tilde{\lambda}>.(P \backslash L) \qquad \text{if } a \notin L$$

$$(\mathscr{X}_{MT,16}) \qquad (P_1 + P_2) \backslash L = P_1 \backslash L + P_2 \backslash L$$

$$(\mathscr{X}_{MT,17}) \qquad \underline{0}[\varphi] = \underline{0}$$

$$(\mathscr{X}_{MT,18}) \qquad (<a, \tilde{\lambda}>.P)[\varphi] = <\varphi(a), \tilde{\lambda}>.(P[\varphi])$$

$$(\mathscr{X}_{MT,19}) \qquad (P_1 + P_2)[\varphi] = P_1[\varphi] + P_2[\varphi]$$

The simplest instance of $\mathscr{X}_{\mathrm{MT},4}$ is depicted in the figure below for $P \not\sim_{\mathrm{MB}} Q$:

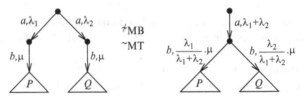

As can be noted, $\sim_{\mathrm{MB}}$ is highly sensitive to branching points, whereas $\sim_{\mathrm{MT}}$ allows choices to be deferred. This happens in the case of branches that start with the same action name (see the two a-branches on the left-hand side) and are followed by sets of actions having the same names and total rates (see $\{<b,\mu>\}$ after each of the two a-branches).

We also point out that axiom $\mathscr{X}_{\mathrm{MT},5}$ applies to non-performance-closed process terms too; e.g., its last addendum is related to reactive–reactive synchronizations.

Theorem 3.8. *Let* $P_1, P_2 \in \mathbb{P}_{\mathrm{M,pc}}$ *be nonrecursive. Then:*

$$P_1 \sim_{\mathrm{MT}} P_2 \iff \mathscr{X}_{\mathrm{MT}} \vdash P_1 = P_2$$

3.4.6 Modal Logic Characterization

Markovian testing equivalence has a modal logic characterization over $\mathbb{P}_{\mathrm{M,pc}}$ based on a modal language comprising true, disjunction, and diamond.

This modal language differs in several aspects from the one for $\sim_{\mathrm{MB}}$ presented in Sect. 3.3.6. First of all, similar to the modal language for $\approx_{\mathrm{T}}$ introduced in Sect. 1.5.5, the modal language for $\sim_{\mathrm{MT}}$ does not include negation and replaces conjunction with disjunction, which is consistent with the decreased discriminating power with respect to $\sim_{\mathrm{MB}}$. Moreover, the considered modal language has a two-level syntax similar to the one for tests, which simplifies the interpretation of formulas. Furthermore, the diamonds occurring at the beginning of subformulas of any disjunction are required to involve distinct sets of action names. This constraint does not reduce the expressiveness of the modal language, as it is consistent with the name-deterministic nature of branches within canonical reactive tests.

Definition 3.34. The set of formulas of the modal language $\mathscr{ML}_{\mathrm{MT}}$ is generated by the following syntax:

$$\begin{aligned} \phi &::= \text{true} \mid \phi' \\ \phi' &::= \langle a \rangle \phi \mid \phi' \vee \phi' \end{aligned}$$

where $a \in \mathit{Name}_{\mathrm{v}}$ and each formula of the form $\phi_1 \vee \phi_2$ satisfies:

$$\mathit{init}(\phi_1) \cap \mathit{init}(\phi_2) = \emptyset$$

with $init(\phi)$ being defined by induction on the syntactical structure of ϕ as follows:

$$\begin{aligned}
init(\text{true}) &= \emptyset \\
init(\phi_1 \vee \phi_2) &= init(\phi_1) \cup init(\phi_2) \\
init(\langle a \rangle \phi) &= \{a\}
\end{aligned}$$

As can be noted, probabilistic and temporal information no longer decorate any operator of the modal language, because in the testing case the focus is on entire computations rather than on step-by-step behavior mimicking. Probability and time come into play through a quantitative interpretation function inspired by [132] that replaces the Boolean satisfaction relation. This interpretation function measures the probability that a process term satisfies a formula quickly enough on average by executing a certain number of actions. The constraint imposed on disjunctions guarantees that their subformulas exercise independent computations of the process term, thus ensuring the correct calculation of the probability of satisfying the overall formula.

Definition 3.35. The interpretation function $[\![\cdot]\!]_{\mathrm{MT}}$ of $\mathscr{M}\mathscr{L}_{\mathrm{MT}}$ over $\mathbb{P}_{\mathrm{M,pc}} \times (\mathbb{R}_{>0})^*$ is defined by letting:

$$[\![\phi]\!]_{\mathrm{MT}}^{|\theta|}(P,\theta) = \begin{cases} 0 & \text{if } |\theta| = 0 \wedge \phi \not\equiv \text{true} \\ & \text{or } |\theta| > 0 \wedge rate_o(P, init(\phi) \cup \{\tau\}, 0) = 0 \\ 1 & \text{if } |\theta| = 0 \wedge \phi \equiv \text{true} \end{cases}$$

otherwise by induction on the syntactical structure of ϕ and on the length of θ as follows:

$$[\![\text{true}]\!]_{\mathrm{MT}}^{|t \circ \theta|}(P, t \circ \theta) = \begin{cases} \displaystyle\sum_{P \overset{\tau,\lambda}{\longrightarrow}_{\mathrm{M}} P'} \frac{\lambda}{rate_o(P,\tau,0)} \cdot [\![\text{true}]\!]_{\mathrm{MT}}^{|\theta|}(P',\theta) & \text{if } \frac{1}{rate_o(P,\tau,0)} \leq t \\[2ex] 0 & \text{if } \frac{1}{rate_o(P,\tau,0)} > t \end{cases}$$

$$\begin{aligned}
[\![\phi_1 \vee \phi_2]\!]_{\mathrm{MT}}^{|t \circ \theta|}(P, t \circ \theta) = {}& p_1 \cdot [\![\phi_1]\!]_{\mathrm{MT}}^{|t_1 \circ \theta|}(P_{no\text{-}init\text{-}\tau}, t_1 \circ \theta) + p_2 \cdot [\![\phi_2]\!]_{\mathrm{MT}}^{|t_2 \circ \theta|}(P_{no\text{-}init\text{-}\tau}, t_2 \circ \theta) \\
& + \sum_{P \overset{\tau,\lambda}{\longrightarrow}_{\mathrm{M}} P'} \frac{\lambda}{rate_o(P, init(\phi_1 \vee \phi_2) \cup \{\tau\}, 0)} \cdot [\![\phi_1 \vee \phi_2]\!]_{\mathrm{MT}}^{|\theta|}(P', \theta)
\end{aligned}$$

$$[\![\langle a \rangle \phi]\!]_{\mathrm{MT}}^{|t \circ \theta|}(P, t \circ \theta) = \begin{cases} \displaystyle\sum_{P \overset{a,\lambda}{\longrightarrow}_{\mathrm{M}} P'} \frac{\lambda}{rate_o(P, \{a,\tau\}, 0)} \cdot [\![\phi]\!]_{\mathrm{MT}}^{|\theta|}(P', \theta) \\ \quad + \displaystyle\sum_{P \overset{\tau,\lambda}{\longrightarrow}_{\mathrm{M}} P'} \frac{\lambda}{rate_o(P, \{a,\tau\}, 0)} \cdot [\![\langle a \rangle \phi]\!]_{\mathrm{MT}}^{|\theta|}(P', \theta) & \text{if } \frac{1}{rate_o(P, \{a,\tau\}, 0)} \leq t \\[2ex] 0 & \text{if } \frac{1}{rate_o(P, \{a,\tau\}, 0)} > t \end{cases}$$

where $P_{no\text{-}init\text{-}\tau}$ is P devoid of all of its computations starting with a τ-transition – which is assumed to be $\underline{0}$ whenever all the computations of P start with a τ-transition – and for $j \in \{1,2\}$:

$$p_j = \frac{rate_o(P,init(\phi_j),0)}{rate_o(P,init(\phi_1 \vee \phi_2) \cup \{\tau\},0)}$$

$$t_j = t + \left(\frac{1}{rate_o(P,init(\phi_j),0)} - \frac{1}{rate_o(P,init(\phi_1 \vee \phi_2) \cup \{\tau\},0)} \right)$$

In the definition above, p_j represents the probability with which P performs actions whose name is in $init(\phi_j)$ rather than actions whose name is in $init(\phi_k) \cup \{\tau\}$, $k = 3 - j$, given that P can perform actions whose name is in $init(\phi_1 \vee \phi_2) \cup \{\tau\}$. These probabilities are used as weights for the correct account of the probabilities with which P satisfies only ϕ_1 or ϕ_2 in the context of the satisfaction of $\phi_1 \vee \phi_2$. If such weights were omitted, then the fact that $\phi_1 \vee \phi_2$ offers a set of initial actions at least as large as the ones offered by ϕ_1 alone and by ϕ_2 alone would be ignored, thus leading to a potential overestimate of the probability of satisfying $\phi_1 \vee \phi_2$.

Similarly, t_j represents the extra average time granted to P for satisfying only ϕ_j. This extra average time is equal to the difference between the average sojourn time in P when only actions whose name is in $init(\phi_j)$ are enabled and the average sojourn time in P when also actions whose name is in $init(\phi_k) \cup \{\tau\}$, $k = 3 - j$, are enabled. Since the latter cannot be greater than the former due to the race policy – more enabled actions means less time spent on average in a state – considering t instead of t_j in the satisfaction of ϕ_j in isolation would lead to a potential underestimate of the probability of satisfying $\phi_1 \vee \phi_2$ within the given average time upper bound, as P may satisfy $\phi_1 \vee \phi_2$ within $t \circ \theta$ even if P satisfies neither ϕ_1 nor ϕ_2 taken in isolation within $t \circ \theta$.

Theorem 3.9. *Let $P_1, P_2 \in \mathbb{P}_{M,pc}$. Then:*

$$P_1 \sim_{MT} P_2 \iff \forall \phi \in \mathcal{ML}_{MT}. \forall \theta \in (\mathbb{R}_{>0})^*. [\![\phi]\!]_{MT}^{|\theta|}(P_1, \theta) = [\![\phi]\!]_{MT}^{|\theta|}(P_2, \theta)$$

3.4.7 Verification Algorithm

Markovian testing equivalence can be decided in polynomial time over $\mathbb{P}_{M,pc}$ by exploiting [121] and the algorithm for probabilistic language equivalence of [191], together with the fact that $\sim_{MT}$ coincides with the Markovian version of ready equivalence as we will see in Sect. 3.7.

The reason is that, given two process terms, their underlying CTMCs in which action names have not been discarded from transition labels are Markovian ready equivalent iff the corresponding embedded DTMCs in which transitions have been labeled with suitably augmented names are related by probabilistic ready equivalence. The latter equivalence is known to be decidable in polynomial time through a suitable reworking of the algorithm for probabilistic language equivalence.

The transformation of a name-labeled CTMC into the corresponding embedded name-labeled DTMC is carried out by simply turning the rate of each transition into the corresponding execution probability. Since, in general, Markovian ready equivalence is strictly finer than probabilistic ready equivalence, in order to make the two equivalences coincide on corresponding models we also need to encode the total exit rate of each state of the original name-labeled CTMC inside the names of all transitions departing from that state in the associated embedded DTMC.

Given $P_1, P_2 \in \mathbb{P}_{\mathrm{M,pc}}$ finite state, the algorithm for checking whether $P_1 \sim_{\mathrm{MT}} P_2$ proceeds as follows:

1. Transform $[\![P_1]\!]_{\mathrm{M}}$ and $[\![P_2]\!]_{\mathrm{M}}$ into their equivalent discrete-time versions:

    (a) Divide the rate of each transition by the total exit rate of its source state.
    (b) Augment the name of each transition with the total exit rate of its source state.

2. Compute the equivalence relation $\mathscr{R}$ that equates any two states of the discrete-time versions of $[\![P_1]\!]_{\mathrm{M}}$ and $[\![P_2]\!]_{\mathrm{M}}$ whenever the two sets of augmented action names labeling the transitions departing from the two states coincide.
3. For each equivalence class R induced by $\mathscr{R}$, consider R as the set of accepting states and check whether the discrete-time versions of $[\![P_1]\!]_{\mathrm{M}}$ and $[\![P_2]\!]_{\mathrm{M}}$ are probabilistic language equivalent.
4. Return yes/no depending on whether all the checks performed in the previous step have been successful or at least one of them has failed.

Each iteration of step 3 above requires the application of the algorithm for probabilistic language equivalence. Denoted by $NameReal_{P_1, P_2}$ the set of augmented action names labeling the transitions of the discrete-time versions of $[\![P_1]\!]_{\mathrm{M}}$ or $[\![P_2]\!]_{\mathrm{M}}$, the algorithm visits in breadth-first order the tree containing a node for each element of $(NameReal_{P_1, P_2})^*$ and studies the linear independence of the state probability vectors associated with a finite subset of the tree nodes:

1. Create an empty set V of state probability vectors.
2. Create a queue whose only element is the empty string ε.
3. While the queue is not empty:

    (a) Remove the first element from the queue, say string ς.
    (b) If the state probability vector of the discrete-time versions of $[\![P_1]\!]_{\mathrm{M}}$ and $[\![P_2]\!]_{\mathrm{M}}$ after reading ς does not belong to the vector space generated by V, then:
        (i) For each $a \in NameReal_{P_1, P_2}$, add $\varsigma \circ a$ to the queue.
        (ii) Add the state probability vector to V.

4. Build a three-valued state vector $\boldsymbol{u}$ whose generic element is:

    (a) 0 if it corresponds to a nonaccepting state
    (b) 1 if it corresponds to an accepting state of the discrete-time version of $[\![P_1]\!]_{\mathrm{M}}$
    (c) -1 if it corresponds to an accepting state of the discrete-time version of $[\![P_2]\!]_{\mathrm{M}}$

5. For each $\boldsymbol{v} \in V$, check whether $\boldsymbol{v} \cdot \boldsymbol{u}^{\mathrm{T}} = 0$.

6. Return yes/no depending on whether all the checks performed in the previous step have been successful or at least one of them has failed.

The time complexity of the overall algorithm is $O(n^5)$, where n is the total number of states of $[[P_1]]_M$ and $[[P_2]]_M$.

3.5 Markovian Trace Equivalence

Markovian trace equivalence relates two process terms whenever they are able to perform computations with the same functional and performance characteristics. In this section, we provide the definition of Markovian trace equivalence over $\mathbb{P}_{M,pc}$ based on quantitative information associated with process term computations, together with a necessary condition and an alternative characterization [194, 31]. Then, we show that Markovian trace equivalence is a congruence with respect to dynamic operators and we present its sound and complete axiomatization, its modal logic characterization, and its verification algorithm [31, 39, 194].

3.5.1 Definition of the Behavioral Equivalence

The basic idea behind the trace approach is to compare process terms on the basis of their computations, thus abstracting from the branching structure of their behavior. In a Markovian framework, we are not only interested in verifying whether process terms have the same computations, but also in measuring the probability and the duration of those computations. More specifically, Markovian trace equivalence relies on comparing the process term probabilities of performing trace-compatible computations within arbitrary sequences of average amounts of time.

Definition 3.36. Let $P \in \mathbb{P}_{M,pc}$, $c \in \mathscr{C}_f(P)$, and $\alpha \in (Name_v)^*$. We say that c is compatible with α iff:

$$trace(c) = \alpha$$

We denote by $\mathscr{C}\mathscr{C}(P, \alpha)$ the multiset of computations in $\mathscr{C}_f(P)$ that are compatible with α.

If a process term $P \in \mathbb{P}_{M,pc}$ has no exponentially timed τ-actions, then for all traces $\alpha \in (Name_v)^*$ it turns out that: (1) all the computations in $\mathscr{C}\mathscr{C}(P, \alpha)$ are independent of each other because of their maximality; (2) the multiset $\mathscr{C}\mathscr{C}(P, \alpha)$ is finite because P is finitely branching. Thus, recalled that all the computations in $\mathscr{C}\mathscr{C}(P, \alpha)$ have finite length by definition, all definitions of Sect. 3.4.1 are applicable to $\mathscr{C}\mathscr{C}(P, \alpha)$ and also to $\mathscr{C}\mathscr{C}_{\leq \theta}(P, \alpha)$ for any sequence $\theta \in (\mathbb{R}_{>0})^*$ of average amounts of time.

Similar to the case of $\sim_{MT}$, in order to cope with the possible presence of exponentially timed τ-actions within P in such a way that all the properties above hold – especially independence – we have to consider subsets of $\mathscr{CC}_{\leq\theta}(P,\alpha)$ including all trace-compatible computations of the same length. This is also necessary to distinguish among process terms comprising only exponentially timed τ-actions – like $<\tau,\lambda>.\underline{0}$ and $<\tau,\mu>.\underline{0}$ with $\lambda \neq \mu$ – as there is a single trace, ε, with which the computations of those process terms are compatible. The only option is to compare them after executing the same number of τ-actions.

Since no element of $\mathscr{CC}_{\leq\theta}(P,\alpha)$ can be longer than $|\theta|$, we should consider every possible subset $\mathscr{CC}^l_{\leq\theta}(P,\alpha)$ for $0 \leq l \leq |\theta|$. However, it is enough to consider $\mathscr{CC}^{|\theta|}_{\leq\theta}(P,\alpha)$, as shorter trace-compatible computations can be taken into account when imposing prefixes of θ as average time upper bounds.

Definition 3.37. Let $P_1, P_2 \in \mathbb{P}_{M,pc}$. We say that P_1 is Markovian trace equivalent to P_2, written $P_1 \sim_{MTr} P_2$, iff for all traces $\alpha \in (Name_v)^*$ and sequences $\theta \in (\mathbb{R}_{>0})^*$ of average amounts of time:

$$prob(\mathscr{CC}^{|\theta|}_{\leq\theta}(P_1,\alpha)) = prob(\mathscr{CC}^{|\theta|}_{\leq\theta}(P_2,\alpha))$$

Using the same examples as Sect. 3.3.2, it is easy to see that $\sim_{MTr}$ is strictly finer than $\approx_{Tr}$ and probabilistic trace equivalence [127].

Example 3.6. Let us consider again $ProdCons^M_{0/2}$ and $PC^M_{conc,2}$, which are defined in Examples 3.1 and 3.3, respectively. Similar to Example 1.6 and as already observed in Example 3.5, the only sequences of visible actions that the two process constants can perform are the prefixes of the strings complying with the following regular expression:

$$(deposit \circ (deposit \circ withdraw)^* \circ withdraw)^*$$

As a consequence, the only significant traces to be considered in this scenario are those coinciding with the previously mentioned prefixes.

If we take one such trace, say α, it is easy to see that any two computations of $ProdCons^M_{0/2}$ and $PC^M_{conc,2}$, respectively, that are compatible with α traverse states that pairwise have the same average sojourn time. Therefore, the stepwise average durations of the considered computations are identical.

As for the execution probabilities of $\mathscr{CC}(ProdCons^M_{0/2},\alpha)$ and $\mathscr{CC}(PC^M_{conc,2},\alpha)$, observed that all these computations have the same length as none of them includes exponentially timed τ-transitions, we have four basic cases corresponding to the four shortest nontrivial prefixes of the strings complying with the regular expression above:

- If $\alpha \equiv deposit$, then for both sets of computations the execution probability is 1
- If $\alpha \equiv deposit \circ withdraw$, then for both sets of computations the execution probability is $\frac{\mu}{\lambda+\mu}$

- If $\alpha \equiv deposit \circ deposit$, then for both sets of computations the execution probability is $\frac{\lambda}{\lambda+\mu}$
- If $\alpha \equiv deposit \circ deposit \circ withdraw$, then for both sets of computations the execution probability is $\frac{\lambda}{\lambda+\mu}$

Since all the other cases are extensions of these four basic cases that comply with the regular expression above, the corresponding extensions of the two sets of computations compatible with the same trace still have the same execution probability. Therefore, we can conclude that $PC^M_{conc,2} \sim_{MTr} ProdCons^M_{0/2}$.

3.5.2 Conditions and Characterizations

A necessary condition for establishing whether two process terms are Markovian trace equivalent is that for each computation of any of the two terms there exists a computation of the other term with the same concrete trace and the same stepwise average duration, such that any pair of corresponding states traversed by the two computations have the same total exit rate. Note that the last constraint is slightly looser than the last constraint of the necessary condition for $\sim_{MT}$ of Proposition 3.4.

Proposition 3.8. Let $P_1, P_2 \in \mathbb{P}_{M,pc}$. Whenever $P_1 \sim_{MTr} P_2$, then for all $c_k \in \mathscr{C}_f(P_k)$ with $k \in \{1,2\}$ there exists $c_h \in \mathscr{C}_f(P_h)$ with $h \in \{1,2\} - \{k\}$ such that:

$$trace_c(c_k) = trace_c(c_h)$$
$$time_a(c_k) = time_a(c_h)$$

and for all $i \in \{0,\ldots,|c_k|\}$:

$$rate_t(P_k^i,0) = rate_t(P_h^i,0)$$

with P_k^i (resp. P_h^i) being the ith state traversed by c_k (resp. c_h).

Markovian trace equivalence has an alternative characterization that establishes that the discriminating power does not change if we consider the probability distribution of executing trace-compatible computations within arbitrary sequences of amounts of time, rather than the probability of executing trace-compatible computations within arbitrary sequences of average amounts of time. Thus, similar to $\sim_{MT}$, considering the (more accurate) stepwise durations of trace-compatible computations leads to the same equivalence as considering the (easier to work with) stepwise average durations.

Definition 3.38. Let $P_1, P_2 \in \mathbb{P}_{M,pc}$. We say that P_1 is Markovian distribution-trace equivalent to P_2, written $P_1 \sim_{MTr,d} P_2$, iff for all traces $\alpha \in (Name_v)^*$ and sequences $\theta \in (\mathbb{R}_{>0})^*$ of amounts of time:

$$prob_d(\mathscr{C}\mathscr{C}^{|\theta|}(P_1,\alpha),\theta) = prob_d(\mathscr{C}\mathscr{C}^{|\theta|}(P_2,\alpha),\theta)$$

Proposition 3.9. *Let $P_1, P_2 \in \mathbb{P}_{M,pc}$. Then:*

$$P_1 \sim_{MTr,d} P_2 \iff P_1 \sim_{MTr} P_2$$

3.5.3 Congruence Property

Markovian trace equivalence is a congruence over $\mathbb{P}_{M,pc}$ with respect to all the dynamic operators of MPC.

Theorem 3.10. *Let $P_1, P_2 \in \mathbb{P}_{M,pc}$. Whenever $P_1 \sim_{MTr} P_2$, then:*

1. $<a, \lambda>.P_1 \sim_{MTr} <a, \lambda>.P_2$ *for all* $<a, \lambda> \in Act_M$.
2. $P_1 + P \sim_{MTr} P_2 + P$ *and* $P + P_1 \sim_{MTr} P + P_2$ *for all* $P \in \mathbb{P}_{M,pc}$.

Similar to the probabilistic case [127], $\sim_{MTr}$ is not a congruence with respect to the parallel composition operator. Consider, for instance, the following two Markovian trace equivalent process terms:

$$<a, \lambda_1>.<b, \mu>.\underline{0} + <a, \lambda_2>.<d, \mu>.\underline{0}$$
$$<a, \lambda_1 + \lambda_2>.(<b, \lambda_1/(\lambda_1 + \lambda_2) \cdot \mu>.\underline{0} + <d, \lambda_2/(\lambda_1 + \lambda_2) \cdot \mu>.\underline{0})$$

where $a, b, d \in Name_v$ and $b \neq d$. If each of the two terms is put in the context $-\|_{\{a,b,d\}} <a, *_1>.<b, *_1>.\underline{0}$, we get two performance-closed process terms, which we call P_1 and P_2, that are no longer Markovian trace equivalent.

In fact, trace $\alpha \equiv a \circ b$ can distinguish between P_1 and P_2. The reason is that the only computation of P_1 compatible with α is formed by a transition labeled with $<a, \lambda_1>$ followed by a transition labeled with $<b, \mu>$, which has execution probability $\frac{\lambda_1}{\lambda_1 + \lambda_2}$ and stepwise average duration $\frac{1}{\lambda_1 + \lambda_2} \circ \frac{1}{\mu}$. In contrast, the only computation of P_2 compatible with α is formed by a transition labeled with $<a, \lambda_1 + \lambda_2>$ followed by a transition labeled with $<b, \frac{\lambda_1}{\lambda_1 + \lambda_2} \cdot \mu>$, which has execution probability 1 and stepwise average duration $\frac{1}{\lambda_1 + \lambda_2} \circ \frac{\lambda_1 + \lambda_2}{\lambda_1 \cdot \mu}$.

3.5.4 Sound and Complete Axiomatization

Markovian trace equivalence has a sound and complete axiomatization over the set of process terms of $\mathbb{P}_{M,pc}$ comprising only dynamic operators, given by the set $\mathscr{X}_{MTr}$ of equational laws of Table 3.5.

The main difference with respect to the equational laws for $\sim_{MT}$ shown in Table 3.4 is given by the axiom schema $\mathscr{X}_{MTr,4}$, which subsumes axiom schema $\mathscr{X}_{MT,4}$. The simplest instance of $\mathscr{X}_{MTr,4}$ is depicted below for $b \neq d$:

Table 3.5 Equational laws for $\sim_{\text{MTr}}$

$(\mathscr{X}_{\text{MTr},1})$	$P_1 + P_2 = P_2 + P_1$
$(\mathscr{X}_{\text{MTr},2})$	$(P_1 + P_2) + P_3 = P_1 + (P_2 + P_3)$
$(\mathscr{X}_{\text{MTr},3})$	$P + \underline{0} = P$

$$(\mathscr{X}_{\text{MTr},4}) \sum_{i \in I} <a,\lambda_i>. \sum_{j \in J_i} <b_{i,j},\mu_{i,j}>.P_{i,j} = <a, \sum_{k \in I} \lambda_k>. \sum_{i \in I} \sum_{j \in J_i} <b_{i,j}, \frac{\lambda_i}{\Sigma_{k \in I} \lambda_k} \cdot \mu_{i,j}>.P_{i,j}$$

if: I is a finite index set with $|I| \geq 2$;

for all $i \in I$, index set J_i is finite and its summation is $\underline{0}$ if $J_i = \emptyset$;

for all $i_1, i_2 \in I$:
$$\sum_{j \in J_{i_1}} \mu_{i_1,j} = \sum_{j \in J_{i_2}} \mu_{i_2,j}$$

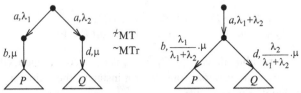

As can be noted, $\sim_{\text{MTr}}$ is less sensitive to branching points than $\sim_{\text{MT}}$, as it allows more choices to be deferred. These are the choices whose branches start with the same action name (see the two a-branches on the left-hand side) and are followed by process terms having the same total exit rate (see the process terms with total exit rate μ after each of the two a-branches).

Theorem 3.11. *Let* $P_1, P_2 \in \mathbb{P}_{\text{M,pc}}$ *comprise only dynamic operators. Then:*

$$P_1 \sim_{\text{MTr}} P_2 \iff \mathscr{X}_{\text{MTr}} \vdash P_1 = P_2$$

3.5.5 Modal Logic Characterization

Markovian trace equivalence has a modal logic characterization over $\mathbb{P}_{\text{M,pc}}$ based on a modal language comprising only true and diamond.

Definition 3.39. The set of formulas of the modal language $\mathscr{M}\mathscr{L}_{\text{MTr}}$ is generated by the following syntax:

$$\phi ::= \text{true} \mid \langle a \rangle \phi$$

where $a \in \textit{Name}_{\text{v}}$.

Like in the case of $\sim_{\text{MT}}$, probability and time do not decorate any operator of the modal language, but come into play through a quantitative interpretation function measuring the probability that a process term satisfies a formula quickly enough on average by executing a certain number of actions.

Definition 3.40. The interpretation function $[\![.]\!]_{\text{MTr}}$ of $\mathscr{M}\mathscr{L}_{\text{MTr}}$ over $\mathbb{P}_{\text{M,pc}} \times (\mathbb{R}_{>0})^*$ is defined by letting:

$$[\![\phi]\!]_{\mathrm{MTr}}^{|\theta|}(P,\theta) = \begin{cases} 0 & \text{if } |\theta| = 0 \wedge \phi \not\equiv \text{true} \\ & \quad \text{or } |\theta| > 0 \wedge rate_t(P,0) = 0 \\ 1 & \text{if } |\theta| = 0 \wedge \phi \equiv \text{true} \end{cases}$$

otherwise by induction on the syntactical structure of ϕ and on the length of θ as follows:

$$[\![\text{true}]\!]_{\mathrm{MTr}}^{|t \circ \theta|}(P, t \circ \theta) = \begin{cases} \displaystyle\sum_{P \xrightarrow{\tau,\lambda}_M P'} \frac{\lambda}{rate_t(P,0)} \cdot [\![\text{true}]\!]_{\mathrm{MTr}}^{|\theta|}(P',\theta) & \text{if } \frac{1}{rate_t(P,0)} \leq t \\[2em] 0 & \text{if } \frac{1}{rate_t(P,0)} > t \end{cases}$$

$$[\![\langle a \rangle \phi]\!]_{\mathrm{MTr}}^{|t \circ \theta|}(P, t \circ \theta) = \begin{cases} \displaystyle\sum_{P \xrightarrow{a,\lambda}_M P'} \frac{\lambda}{rate_t(P,0)} \cdot [\![\phi]\!]_{\mathrm{MTr}}^{|\theta|}(P',\theta) \\[1em] \quad + \displaystyle\sum_{P \xrightarrow{\tau,\lambda}_M P'} \frac{\lambda}{rate_t(P,0)} \cdot [\![\langle a \rangle \phi]\!]_{\mathrm{MTr}}^{|\theta|}(P',\theta) & \text{if } \frac{1}{rate_t(P,0)} \leq t \\[2em] 0 & \text{if } \frac{1}{rate_t(P,0)} > t \end{cases}$$

where a summation is taken to be zero whenever there are no transitions labeled with the considered action name.

Theorem 3.12. *Let $P_1, P_2 \in \mathbb{P}_{\mathrm{M,pc}}$. Then:*

$$P_1 \sim_{\mathrm{MTr}} P_2 \iff \forall \phi \in \mathscr{ML}_{\mathrm{MTr}}. \forall \theta \in (\mathbb{R}_{>0})^*. [\![\phi]\!]_{\mathrm{MTr}}^{|\theta|}(P_1,\theta) = [\![\phi]\!]_{\mathrm{MTr}}^{|\theta|}(P_2,\theta)$$

3.5.6 Verification Algorithm

Markovian trace equivalence can be decided in polynomial time over $\mathbb{P}_{\mathrm{M,pc}}$ by exploiting [121] and the algorithm for probabilistic language equivalence of [191].

Similar to $\sim_{\mathrm{MT}}$, the reason is that, given two process terms, their underlying CTMCs in which action names have not been discarded from transition labels are Markovian trace equivalent iff the corresponding embedded DTMCs in which transitions have been labeled with suitably augmented names are related by probabilistic trace equivalence, which is known to be decidable in polynomial time through the algorithm for probabilistic language equivalence.

As before, the transformation of a name-labeled CTMC into the corresponding embedded name-labeled DTMC is carried out by simply turning the rate of each transition into the corresponding execution probability. Since, in general, $\sim_{\mathrm{MTr}}$ is strictly finer than probabilistic trace equivalence, in order to make the two equivalences coincide on corresponding models we also need to encode the total exit rate of each state of the original name-labeled CTMC inside the names of all transitions departing from that state in the associated embedded DTMC.

Given $P_1, P_2 \in \mathbb{P}_{M,pc}$ finite state, the algorithm for checking whether $P_1 \sim_{MTr} P_2$ proceeds as follows:

1. Transform $[\![P_1]\!]_M$ and $[\![P_2]\!]_M$ into their equivalent discrete-time versions:

   (a) Divide the rate of each transition by the total exit rate of its source state.
   (b) Augment the name of each transition with the total exit rate of its source state.

2. Check whether the discrete-time versions of $[\![P_1]\!]_M$ and $[\![P_2]\!]_M$ are probabilistic language equivalent when all of their states are considered as accepting states.
3. Return yes/no depending on whether the check performed in the previous step has been successful or not.

Step 2 above requires the application of the algorithm for probabilistic language equivalence, which has been described in Sect. 3.4.7. The time complexity of the overall algorithm is $O(n^4)$, where n is the total number of states of $[\![P_1]\!]_M$ and $[\![P_2]\!]_M$.

3.6 Exactness of Markovian Behavioral Equivalences

Every Markovian behavioral equivalence induces aggregations of the CTMCs underlying process terms of $\mathbb{P}_{M,pc}$. Useful CTMC-level aggregations are those that are exact. Given two CTMCs such that the second one is an exact aggregation of the first one, the transient/stationary probability of being in a macrostate of the second CTMC is the sum of the transient/stationary probabilities of being in one of the constituent microstates of the first CTMC. This means that, when going from the first CTMC to the second CTMC, all the performance characteristics are preserved. Therefore, due to its reduced state space, the second CTMC can be exploited for a faster derivation of properties of the first CTMC.

In this section, we show that $\sim_{MB}$, $\sim_{MT}$, and $\sim_{MTr}$ induce exact CTMC-level aggregations; hence, they are all meaningful not only from a functional standpoint, but also from a performance standpoint [118, 58, 31, 32].

Markovian bisimulation equivalence is consistent with an exact aggregation for CTMCs known under the name of ordinary lumping. This fact establishes an important connection between concurrency theory and Markov chain theory. In particular, it implies that ordinary lumpability is entirely characterizable in a process algebraic framework and that a verification/minimization algorithm for it is available.

Definition 3.41. A partition $\mathscr{G}$ of the state space of a CTMC is an ordinary lumping iff, whenever $s_1, s_2 \in G$ for some $G \in \mathscr{G}$, then for all $G' \in \mathscr{G}$:

$$\sum \{\!| \lambda \in \mathbb{R}_{>0} \mid \exists s' \in G'. s_1 \xrightarrow{\lambda} s' |\!\} = \sum \{\!| \lambda \in \mathbb{R}_{>0} \mid \exists s' \in G'. s_2 \xrightarrow{\lambda} s' |\!\}$$

Theorem 3.13. The CTMC-level aggregation induced by $\sim_{MB}$ over $\mathbb{P}_{M,pc}$ is an ordinary lumping, and hence it is exact.

Markovian testing equivalence and Markovian trace equivalence induce the same exact CTMC-level aggregation called T-lumping, which is strictly coarser than ordinary lumping. This aggregation, which was not known in the CTMC field before, can be graphically defined as follows on the basis of the name-abstract variant of the equational laws characterizing $\sim_{\text{MT}}$ and $\sim_{\text{MTr}}$:

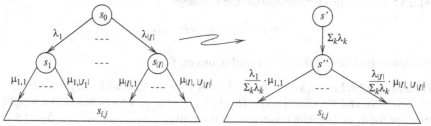

where I is a finite index set with $|I| \geq 2$, k ranges over I, J_i is a nonempty finite index set for all $i \in I$, and for all $i_1, i_2 \in I$:

$$\sum_{j \in J_{i_1}} \mu_{i_1,j} = \sum_{j \in J_{i_2}} \mu_{i_2,j}$$

Theorem 3.14. *The CTMC-level aggregation induced by $\sim_{\text{MT}}$ (resp. $\sim_{\text{MTr}}$) over $\mathbb{P}_{\text{M,pc}}$ is a T-lumping, and hence it is exact.*

3.7 The Markovian Linear-Time/Branching-Time Spectrum

As shown in Sect. 1.7, behavioral equivalences such as bisimulation equivalence, testing equivalence, trace equivalence, and their variants – simulation equivalence, ready-simulation equivalence, completed-trace equivalence, failure equivalence, ready equivalence, failure-trace equivalence, and ready-trace equivalence – form a lattice-like structure when considering their discriminating power.

In this section, we show that, similar to the probabilistic case [127, 121], the linear-time/branching-time spectrum formed by the Markovian versions over $\mathbb{P}_{\text{M,pc}}$ of those behavioral equivalences collapses into a line [24, 194, 31]. With regard to the Markovian behavioral equivalences that we have already encountered, we can easily see from their axiomatizations that $\sim_{\text{MB}}$ is strictly contained in $\sim_{\text{MT}}$, which in turn is strictly contained in $\sim_{\text{MTr}}$.

Let us start with the definition of the Markovian versions of simulation and ready-simulation equivalences. Although simulation of two process terms is defined in terms of simulation of their derivative process terms, in a Markovian setting we need to take rates into account as well. To this purpose, it is convenient to separate time and probability information subsumed by rates and to view the destination of a transition as a probability distribution. Then, we need to lift the simulation relation from states to distributions on states, precisely the next-state distributions encoded by $prob_e(P,a,0,.)$. This can be accomplished through weight functions [126], which relate pairs of distributions in a way that takes into account the simulation relation on states and preserves the probability mass associated with each state.

Definition 3.42. Let S be a countable set. A distribution on set S is a function $d : S \to \mathbb{R}_{[0,1]}$ such that:

$$\sum_{s \in S} d(s) \leq 1$$

which is called a probability distribution whenever:

$$d(\perp) \overset{\Delta}{=} 1 - \sum_{s \in S} d(s) = 0$$

We denote by $Distr(S)$ the set of distributions on S.

Definition 3.43. Let S_1, S_2 be countable sets with $d_1 \in Distr(S_1)$, $d_2 \in Distr(S_2)$, $\mathscr{R} \subseteq S_1 \times S_2$, and $\varpi : (S_1 \cup \{\perp\}) \times (S_2 \cup \{\perp\}) \to \mathbb{R}_{[0,1]}$. We say that ϖ is a weight function for d_1 and d_2 with respect to $\mathscr{R}$ iff for all $s_1 \in S_1 \cup \{\perp\}$ and $s_2 \in S_2 \cup \{\perp\}$:

$$\varpi(s_1, s_2) > 0 \implies (s_1, s_2) \in \mathscr{R} \vee s_1 = \perp$$
$$d_1(s_1) = \sum_{s_2 \in S_2 \cup \{\perp\}} \varpi(s_1, s_2)$$
$$d_2(s_2) = \sum_{s_1 \in S_1 \cup \{\perp\}} \varpi(s_1, s_2)$$

in which case we write $d_1 \sqsubseteq_{\mathscr{R}} d_2$.

Definition 3.44. A binary relation $\mathscr{S}$ over $\mathbb{P}_{M,pc}$ is a Markovian simulation iff, whenever $(P_1, P_2) \in \mathscr{S}$, then for all action names $a \in Name$:

$$rate_o(P_1, a, 0) \leq rate_o(P_2, a, 0)$$
$$prob_e(P_1, a, 0, .) \sqsubseteq_{\mathscr{S}} prob_e(P_2, a, 0, .)$$

Definition 3.45. Markovian simulation preorder, denoted $\precsim_{MS}$, is the largest Markovian simulation.

Definition 3.46. Markovian simulation equivalence, denoted $\sim_{MS}$, is the kernel of Markovian simulation preorder, i.e., $\sim_{MS} = \precsim_{MS} \cap \precsim_{MS}^{-1}$.

Definition 3.47. A binary relation $\mathscr{S}$ over $\mathbb{P}_{M,pc}$ is a Markovian ready simulation iff, whenever $(P_1, P_2) \in \mathscr{S}$, then for all action names $a \in Name$:

$$rate_o(P_1, a, 0) \leq rate_o(P_2, a, 0)$$
$$prob_e(P_1, a, 0, .) \sqsubseteq_{\mathscr{S}} prob_e(P_2, a, 0, .)$$
$$rate_o(P_1, a, 0) = 0 \implies rate_o(P_2, a, 0) = 0$$

Definition 3.48. Markovian ready-simulation preorder, denoted $\precsim_{MRS}$, is the largest Markovian ready simulation.

Definition 3.49. Markovian ready-simulation equivalence, denoted $\sim_{MRS}$, is the kernel of Markovian ready-simulation preorder, i.e., $\sim_{MRS} = \precsim_{MRS} \cap \precsim_{MRS}^{-1}$.

Then, we proceed with the definition of the Markovian versions of completed-trace equivalence, failure equivalence, ready equivalence, failure-trace equivalence, and ready-trace equivalence.

Definition 3.50. Let $P \in \mathbb{P}_{M,pc}$, $c \in \mathscr{C}_f(P)$, and $\alpha \in (Name_v)^*$. We say that c is a maximal computation compatible with α iff $c \in \mathscr{CC}(P, \alpha)$ and the last state reached by c has no outgoing transitions. We denote by $\mathscr{MCC}(P, \alpha)$ the multiset of maximal computations in $\mathscr{C}_f(P)$ that are compatible with α.

Definition 3.51. Let $P_1, P_2 \in \mathbb{P}_{M,pc}$. We say that P_1 is Markovian completed-trace equivalent to P_2, written $P_1 \sim_{MTr,c} P_2$, iff for all traces $\alpha \in (Name_v)^*$ and sequences $\theta \in (\mathbb{R}_{>0})^*$ of average amounts of time:

$$prob(\mathscr{CC}^{|\theta|}_{\leq\theta}(P_1, \alpha)) = prob(\mathscr{CC}^{|\theta|}_{\leq\theta}(P_2, \alpha))$$
$$prob(\mathscr{MCC}^{|\theta|}_{\leq\theta}(P_1, \alpha)) = prob(\mathscr{MCC}^{|\theta|}_{\leq\theta}(P_2, \alpha))$$

Definition 3.52. Let $P \in \mathbb{P}_{M,pc}$, $c \in \mathscr{C}_f(P)$, and $\beta \equiv (\alpha, F) \in (Name_v)^* \times 2^{Name_v}$. We say that computation c is compatible with the failure pair β iff $c \in \mathscr{CC}(P, \alpha)$ and the last state reached by c cannot perform any visible action whose name belongs to the failure set F. We denote by $\mathscr{FCC}(P, \beta)$ the multiset of computations in $\mathscr{C}_f(P)$ that are compatible with β.

Definition 3.53. Let $P_1, P_2 \in \mathbb{P}_{M,pc}$. We say that P_1 is Markovian failure equivalent to P_2, written $P_1 \sim_{MF} P_2$, iff for all failure pairs $\beta \in (Name_v)^* \times 2^{Name_v}$ and sequences $\theta \in (\mathbb{R}_{>0})^*$ of average amounts of time:

$$prob(\mathscr{FCC}^{|\theta|}_{\leq\theta}(P_1, \beta)) = prob(\mathscr{FCC}^{|\theta|}_{\leq\theta}(P_2, \beta))$$

Definition 3.54. Let $P \in \mathbb{P}_{M,pc}$, $c \in \mathscr{C}_f(P)$, and $\rho \equiv (\alpha, R) \in (Name_v)^* \times 2^{Name_v}$. We say that computation c is compatible with the ready pair ρ iff $c \in \mathscr{CC}(P, \alpha)$ and the set of names of visible actions that can be performed by the last state reached by c coincides with the ready set R. We denote by $\mathscr{RCC}(P, \rho)$ the multiset of computations in $\mathscr{C}_f(P)$ that are compatible with ρ.

Definition 3.55. Let $P_1, P_2 \in \mathbb{P}_{M,pc}$. We say that P_1 is Markovian ready equivalent to P_2, written $P_1 \sim_{MR} P_2$, iff for all ready pairs $\rho \in (Name_v)^* \times 2^{Name_v}$ and sequences $\theta \in (\mathbb{R}_{>0})^*$ of average amounts of time:

$$prob(\mathscr{RCC}^{|\theta|}_{\leq\theta}(P_1, \rho)) = prob(\mathscr{RCC}^{|\theta|}_{\leq\theta}(P_2, \rho))$$

Definition 3.56. Let $P \in \mathbb{P}_{M,pc}$, $c \in \mathscr{C}_f(P)$, and $\zeta \in (Name_v \times 2^{Name_v})^*$. We say that computation c is compatible with the failure trace ζ iff c is compatible with the trace projection of ζ and each state traversed by c cannot perform any visible action whose name belongs to the corresponding failure set in the failure projection of ζ. We denote by $\mathscr{FTCC}(P, \zeta)$ the multiset of computations in $\mathscr{C}_f(P)$ that are compatible with ζ.

Definition 3.57. Let $P_1, P_2 \in \mathbb{P}_{M,pc}$. We say that P_1 is Markovian failure-trace equivalent to P_2, written $P_1 \sim_{MFTr} P_2$, iff for all failure traces $\zeta \in (Name_v \times 2^{Name_v})^*$ and sequences $\theta \in (\mathbb{R}_{>0})^*$ of average amounts of time:

$$prob(\mathscr{F}\mathscr{T}\mathscr{C}\mathscr{C}_{\leq\theta}^{|\theta|}(P_1,\zeta)) = prob(\mathscr{F}\mathscr{T}\mathscr{C}\mathscr{C}_{\leq\theta}^{|\theta|}(P_2,\zeta))$$

Definition 3.58. Let $P \in \mathbb{P}_{M,pc}$, $c \in \mathscr{C}_f(P)$, and $\eta \in (Name_v \times 2^{Name_v})^*$. We say that computation c is compatible with the ready trace η iff c is compatible with the trace projection of η and the set of names of visible actions that can be performed by each state traversed by c coincides with the corresponding ready set in the ready projection of η. We denote by $\mathscr{R}\mathscr{T}\mathscr{C}\mathscr{C}(P,\eta)$ the multiset of computations in $\mathscr{C}_f(P)$ that are compatible with η.

Definition 3.59. Let $P_1, P_2 \in \mathbb{P}_{M,pc}$. We say that P_1 is Markovian ready-trace equivalent to P_2, written $P_1 \sim_{MRTr} P_2$, iff for all ready traces $\eta \in (Name_v \times 2^{Name_v})^*$ and sequences $\theta \in (\mathbb{R}_{>0})^*$ of average amounts of time:

$$prob(\mathscr{R}\mathscr{T}\mathscr{C}\mathscr{C}_{\leq\theta}^{|\theta|}(P_1,\eta)) = prob(\mathscr{R}\mathscr{T}\mathscr{C}\mathscr{C}_{\leq\theta}^{|\theta|}(P_2,\eta))$$

Theorem 3.15. *The linear-time/branching-time spectrum over* $\mathbb{P}_{M,pc}$ *is as follows:*

~MB
~MRS
~MS

~MRTr
~MFTr

~MR
~MF
~MT

~MTr,c
~MTr

where arrows denote strict set inclusion.

We conclude by noting that, unlike the nondeterministic case, the trace approach is deadlock sensitive in the Markovian setting because $\sim_{MTr}$ coincides with $\sim_{MTr,c}$. As a consequence, it is not surprising that $\sim_{MTr}$ is not a congruence with respect to the parallel composition operator.

Part II
Process Algebra
for Software Architecture

An important distinction in the software engineering field is the one between programming-in-the-large and programming-in-the-small: structuring a large collection of modules to form a system is an essentially different intellectual activity from that of constructing the individual modules [83]. In the last two decades, the activity of programming-in-the-large and the consequent necessity of separating design from implementation have received an ever increasing attention. This has resulted in a new discipline called software architecture, whose focus is on software components and connectors rather than on algorithms and data structures.

By analogy to building architecture, a model of software architecture can be defined as consisting of elements, form, and rationale [169]. In the software context, architectural elements are processing, data, or connecting elements. The form is expressed through properties and relationships that constrain the choice and the placement of architectural elements. The rationale is the basis for the architecture in terms of the system requirements and provides motivations for the various choices made in defining the architecture.

A software architecture thus emphasizes the elements constituting a system, their interactions, and the constraints on those elements and their interactions that provide a framework in which to satisfy the requirements and serve as a basis for the subsequent development phases. The software architecture level of design is concerned with several issues [184]: organization of a system as a composition of components; global control structures; protocols for communication, synchronization, and data access; assignment of functionality to design elements; composition of design elements; physical distribution; scaling and performance; dimensions of evolution; and selection among design alternatives.

The growing complexity and size of modern software systems can be managed only by adopting architectural notations producing design documents with a precise meaning, which should be used as a guide during software development. Such architectural notations should also enable the rigorous and hopefully automated analysis of system properties [45], in order to avoid delays and costs that may be incurred due to the late discovery of errors in the software development process.

In the second part of this book, we show that process algebra can be usefully employed in the software architecture design phase, as implicitly suggested in [18]. In Chap. 4, we provide a number of guidelines for trasforming process algebra into a fully fledged architectural description language called PADL. In Chap. 5, we illustrate MISMDET, a topological reduction process for the detection of architecture-level mismatches, which relies on behavioral equivalences and exploits their congruence properties for efficiency reasons and their modal logic characterizations for diagnostic purposes. In Chap. 6, we present PERFSEL, a procedure for the performance-driven selection among alternative architectural designs, which is based on equipping process algebraic architectural descriptions with queueing network models allowing for the assessment of system-level and component-level performance measures. Finally, in Chap. 7 we discuss DEPPERF, a methodology for trading dependability features and performance indices in the architectural design phase, which builds on equivalence-checking-based noninterference analysis and performance evaluation techniques.

Chapter 4
Component-Oriented Modeling

Abstract Using process algebra at the software architecture level of design can be beneficial both for enhancing the usability of the formalism and for improving the formality and analyzability of the architectural descriptions. In fact, on the one hand process algebra is forced to support a friendly component-oriented way of modeling systems, while on the other hand the software designer can take advantage of a notation possessing a precise syntax and semantics as well as automated analysis techniques. In this chapter, we provide a number of guidelines for a principled transformation of process algebra into a fully fledged architectural description language called PADL. The guidelines, which favor specification reuse and insist on the elicitation of interfaces and communication features, are exemplified through the modeling of a client–server system and of a pipe–filter system.

4.1 Software Architecture Description Languages

When dealing with nowadays computing systems, designing software soon becomes an unmanageable and error-prone activity if it is not assisted by adequate modeling notations and supporting tools. In this context, the use of process algebra at the software architecture level can be beneficial for several reasons.

On the process algebra side, the maturity of the theory – which we have set out to some extent in the first part of this book – is unfortunately not accompanied by a satisfactory degree of usability of the formalism, as witnessed by the fact that process algebra is rarely adopted in the practice of software development. On the one hand, the technicalities of process algebra often obfuscate the way in which systems are modeled. As an example, in a process term comprising numerous occurrences of the parallel composition operator, it is hard to understand the communication scheme among the various subterms. On the other hand, process algebra is perceived as being difficult to learn and use by practitioners as it is not close enough to the way they think of software systems. For instance, process algebra inherently supports compositionality and abstraction, but it does not support widespread paradigms like

A. Aldini et al., *A Process Algebraic Approach to Software Architecture Design*,
DOI 10.1007/978-1-84800-223-4_4, © Springer-Verlag London Limited 2010

object orientation and component orientation. As a consequence, process algebra cannot compete with commonly accepted notations like UML, although it is more robust than them.

On the software architecture side, what is produced is a document showing the system structure and behavior at a high level of abstraction, which should be shared by all the people contributing to the various phases of the software development process. In many cases, this document boils down to an informal box-and-line diagram, which certainly helps to visualize the system structure and perhaps the functionality of the various units, but its usefulness is rather limited. On the one hand, in the absence of a precise syntax and semantics, the document may turn out to be ambiguous and hence interpretable in different ways, thus leading to potential misunderstandings inside the software development team. On the other hand, an informal document cannot be subject to any check, thus preventing system property analyzability in the early stages of the development process. These drawbacks may negatively affect time-to-market constraints as well as development and maintenance costs.

Adapting process algebra to the software architecture level of design provides a twofold opportunity. Firstly, this can be exploited for increasing the degree of usability of process algebra, as it becomes necessary to support a friendly component-oriented manner of modeling systems with process algebra. In this way, the software designer can reason in terms of composable software units without having to worry about process algebra technicalities. Secondly, this can be exploited for increasing the degree of formality and analyzability of architectural descriptions. In fact, it turns out that the software designer is offered a modeling notation with a completely defined syntax and semantics, which is equipped with various analysis techniques that can be reused at the architectural level.

The purpose of this chapter is to set up an architectural upgrade of process algebra that yields a fully fledged architectural description language called PADL. This transformation is accomplished in a principled way by following a number of guidelines that we deem to be strictly necessary in order to achieve our objective. The guidelines are concerned with: (1) the separation of the behavior description from the topology description, (2) the reuse of the specification of components and connectors, (3) the elicitation of the interface of components and connectors, (4) the classification of the synchronicity of communications, (5) the classification of the multiplicity of communications, (6) the combination of textual and graphical notations, (7) the revision of dynamic operators and the concealment of static operators, and (8) the provision of support for architectural styles.

This chapter is organized as follows. In Sect. 4.2, we introduce a client–server system that is used throughout the chapter as a running example. In Sect. 4.3, we illustrate the first seven guidelines, which lead to the definition of the syntax for PADL. In Sect. 4.4, we present the semantics for PADL, which is given by translation into the process calculus of Sect. 1.3. In Sect. 4.5, we discuss a summarizing example based on a pipe–filter system, which is also used in the rest of the chapter. In Sect. 4.6, we illustrate the eighth guideline after recalling the notion of architectural style. Finally, in Sect. 4.7 we compare the obtained process algebraic architectural description language with the related literature.

4.2 Running Example: Client–Server System

The application of the guidelines is exemplified through the modeling of a client–server system. In general, this is composed of a possibly replicated server and a number of clients. The server provides a set of predefined services and the clients contact it whenever they need some of the available services. The server provides the requested services to the requesting clients according to some predefined discipline.

For the sake of simplicity, we consider a scenario in which there is a single replica of the server, which can be contacted at any time by two identically behaving clients. We assume that the server has no buffer for holding incoming requests and that, after sending a request, a client cannot proceed until it receives a response from the server.

4.3 Architectural Upgrade of Process Algebra: Guidelines

In this section, we illustrate the first seven guidelines, which are related to the modeling of a single software system and lead to the definition of the syntax for PADL.

4.3.1 G1: Separating Behavior and Topology Descriptions

Given a process term comprising numerous occurrences of the parallel composition operator, it is hard to understand which subterms communicate with each other. This is not only a matter of readability. In fact, from the point of view of the designer, selecting the appropriate synchronization sets and the appropriate order for the various subterms is not a trivial task at all. In essence, the problem arises from the fact that the parallel composition operator is not simply a behavioral operator, but encodes both part of the system behavior and the entire system topology.

In order to enhance the usability of process algebra, it is thus necessary to have two distinct sections: one for describing the system behavior and one for describing the system topology. At the architectural level, we call them architectural behavior section and architectural topology section, respectively.

4.3.2 G2: Reusing Component and Connector Specification

In a process algebraic description, there may be several process terms composed in parallel that differ only for the names of some of their actions or process constants. In order to avoid specification redundancy and hence to reduce the modeling time, it is necessary to recognize the presence of repeated behavioral patterns. To this purpose, we introduce the concepts of architectural element type (AET) and architectural element instance (AEI), where by architectural element we mean a component or a connector introduced for gluing components together.

The architectural behavior section contains the definition of as many AETs as there are types of components and connectors in the system. Each of them corresponds to a set of process terms sharing the same behavioral pattern. The architectural topology section contains the declaration of as many AEIs of any previously defined AET as there are components and connectors of that type in the system. They correspond to the process terms exhibiting the same behavioral pattern.

Example 4.1. Let us consider the client–server system introduced in Sect. 4.2. In that case, the architectural behavior section contains the definition of:

- One AET for the server, which we denote by `Server_Type`
- One AET for the two clients, which we denote by `Client_Type`

Notice that a single AET is enough for both clients due to their identical behavior. Then, the architectural topology section contains the declaration of:

- One instance of `Server_Type`, which we denote by `S`
- Two instances of `Client_Type`, which we denote by `C_1` and `C_2`, respectively

Both `C_1` and `C_2` can communicate with `S`.

4.3.3 G3: Eliciting Component and Connector Interface

The actions occurring in a process term do not play the same role from the communication viewpoint. In order to make process algebraic descriptions more readable, it is thus necessary to classify their actions.

First of all, we distinguish between internal actions and interactions. Internal actions model activities related to the implementation of components and connectors, whereas interactions are used for communication purposes and hence constitute the interface of components and connectors. Interactions are further divided into input interactions and output interactions depending on the direction of the information flow. All the interactions occurring in the behavior of an AET have to be explicitly declared within the AET definition as input interactions or output interactions. All the other actions occurring in the behavior of the AET are intended to be internal.

Then, we distinguish between local interactions and architectural interactions. The local interactions of an AEI are the input and output interactions inherited from its AET that are used for communicating with other AEIs inside the system. This is specified in the architectural topology section by declaring architectural attachments between pairs of AEI interactions, which are therefore considered to be local. All the other AEI interactions have to be explicitly declared in the architectural topology section as architectural interactions. This means that they constitute the interface for the whole system and hence can be exploited for hierarchical modeling.

A positive side effect of the elicitation of the interface of components and connectors is the derivation of a number of static checks applicable to the attachments declared in the architectural topology section. Firstly, while any local interaction must be involved at least in one attachment, no internal action or architectural interaction can be involved in attachments. Secondly, every attachment must go from a local output interaction of an AEI to a local input interaction of another AEI. Thirdly, the examination of the attachments reveals whether the topology is connected or there are groups of isolated AEIs.

4.3.4 G4: Classifying Communication Synchronicity

Distinct interactions can participate in different forms of communication. In particular, the interactions occurring in a process term are not necessarily involved in communications with the same synchronicity. In order to improve the readability of process algebraic descriptions, it is thus necessary to classify the degree of synchronicity with which their interactions participate in communications.

We distinguish between synchronous interactions, semi-synchronous interactions, and asynchronous interactions. Synchronous interactions are blocking. An AEI wishing to perform an input synchronous interaction cannot proceed until an output is sent by another AEI. Similarly, an AEI wishing to perform an output synchronous interaction cannot proceed until another AEI is willing to receive.

In contrast, semi-synchronous interactions and asynchronous interactions are not blocking. A semi-synchronous interaction of an AEI succeeds if there is another AEI ready to communicate with it, otherwise it raises an exception and let the first AEI proceed. An example of semi-synchronous communication is the one between a graphical user interface and an underlying software application, as the former must not block whenever the latter cannot do certain tasks requested by the user.

Asynchronous interactions are not blocking because the beginning and the end of the communications in which they are involved are completely decoupled. An example of asynchronous communication is given by event notification services. In this case, the various parties are not synchronized at all as the communication infrastructure basically relies on buffers. Publishers advertise events from time to time by sending messages to a middleware, which in turn delivers event notifications to the appropriate subscribers, which periodically check for the arrival of notifications.

The degree of synchronicity of every input and output interaction must be explicitly declared within the AET definition. For each semi-synchronous interaction, a Boolean variable success is implicitly declared and set, which can be used in the AET behavior in order to check whether the execution of the semi-synchronous interaction succeeds or raises an exception. As far as attachments are concerned, all nine two-by-two combinations are permitted. This means that a local output synchronous, semi-synchronous, or asynchronous interaction of an AEI can be freely attached to a local input synchronous, semi-synchronous, or asynchronous interaction of another AEI.

4.3.5 G5: Classifying Communication Multiplicity

The interactions occurring in a process term are not necessarily involved in communications with the same multiplicity. In order to increase the readability of process algebraic descriptions, it is also necessary to classify the degree of multiplicity of the communications in which their interactions participate.

We distinguish between uni-interactions, and-interactions, and or-interactions. A uni-interaction is mainly involved in one-to-one communications, whereas and-interactions and or-interactions guide inclusive one-to-many communications and selective one-to-many communications, respectively.

A local and-interaction communicates with all the local uni-interactions attached to it, thus realizing a multicast-like communication. In contrast, a local or-interaction communicates with only one of the local uni-interactions attached to it, thus realizing a server–clients-like communication. In order to guarantee that a selective one-to-many output is sent by an AEI to the same AEI from which a certain selective many-to-one input was received, it is necessary to provide support for or-dependences. In this way, the selection performed by a local output or-interaction of an AEI can be constrained by the last selection performed by a certain local input or-interaction of the same AEI.

The degree of multiplicity of every input and output interaction must be explicitly declared within the AET definition. As regards attachments, further static checks come into play. While any local uni-interaction can be attached to only one local interaction, any local and-interaction or or-interaction can be attached only to local uni-interactions each belonging to a different AEI. Moreover, in the case of an output or-interaction that depends on an input or-interaction, the output or-interaction cannot occur before the input or-interaction in the AET behavior, and both or-interactions must be attached to uni-interactions of the same AEIs if local.

Example 4.2. Let us reconsider the client–server system introduced in Sect. 4.2. Following the discussion started in Example 4.1, the definition of `Server_Type` contains:

- One input interaction for receiving requests from the clients, which we denote by `receive_request`
- One internal action modeling the computation of responses, which we denote by `compute_response`
- One output interaction for sending responses to the clients, which we denote by `send_response`

The definition of `Client_Type` contains:

- One internal action modeling the processing of tasks, which we denote by `process`
- One output interaction for sending requests to the server, which we denote by `send_request`
- One input interaction for receiving responses from the server, which we denote by `receive_response`

All the interactions of Server_Type are or-interactions because S is attached to both C_1 and C_2 but can communicate with only one of them at a time. Moreover:

- It is necessary to establish a dependence between send_response and receive_request, because the responses computed by the server have to be sent back to the clients that issued the corresponding requests
- receive_request is synchronous, because the server stays idle as long as it does not receive requests from the clients
- send_response is asynchronous, so that the server can proceed with further requests without being blocked by the unavailability of the client that should receive the response

In contrast, all the interactions of Client_Type are uni-interactions because each of C_1 and C_2 is attached only to S. Moreover:

- send_request is semi-synchronous, so that a client wishing to send a request when the server is busy can keep working instead of passively waiting for the server to become available
- receive_response is synchronous, because after issuing a request a client cannot proceed until it receives a response from the server

All the interactions of S, C_1, and C_2 are local. More precisely:

- Both send_request of C_1 and send_request of C_2 are attached to receive_request of S
- send_response of S is attached to both receive_response of C_1 and receive_response of C_2

4.3.6 G6: Textual and Graphical Notations (PADL Syntax)

Process algebra provides just a textual notation, which may not be enough for the software designer. This is not only a matter of making the textual notation more readable by means of some architectural syntactic sugar based on the previous guidelines. A graphical notation is also necessary, as it provides a visual aid that is not possible with a textual notation. Moreover, it is desirable to permit an integrated use of the two notations: the graphical one for representing the system topology, the textual one for describing the behavior of every architectural element.

Table 4.1 shows the structure of a textual description in the resulting process algebraic architectural description language PADL. The textual description starts with the system name and its formal data parameters initialized with default values (void if absent), then comprises the architectural behavior and topology sections.

The first section describes the behavior of the system by means of its AETs. The definition of each AET, which starts with its name and its formal data parameters (void if absent), consists of the specification of its behavior through simplified process algebraic equations (see Sect. 4.3.7) and of the declaration of its input and output interactions. Every interaction declaration is accompanied by two

Table 4.1 Structure of a PADL textual description

ARCHI_TYPE	◁*name and initialized formal data parameters*▷
ARCHI_BEHAVIOR	
⋮	⋮
ARCHI_ELEM_TYPE	◁*AET name and formal data parameters*▷
BEHAVIOR	◁*sequence of process algebraic equations built from verbose dynamic operators only*▷
INPUT_INTERACTIONS	◁*input synchronous/semi-sync./asynchronous uni/and/or-interactions*▷
OUTPUT_INTERACTIONS	◁*output synchronous/semi-sync./asynchronous uni/and/or-interactions*▷
⋮	⋮
ARCHI_TOPOLOGY	
ARCHI_ELEM_INSTANCES	◁*AEI names and actual data parameters*▷
ARCHI_INTERACTIONS	◁*architecture-level AEI interactions*▷
ARCHI_ATTACHMENTS	◁*attachments between AEI local interactions*▷
END	

qualifiers. The first one establishes whether the interaction is synchronous (qualifier value SYNC), semi-synchronous (qualifier value SSYNC), or asynchronous (qualifier value ASYNC). The second one establishes whether the interaction is a uni-interaction (qualifier value UNI), an and-interaction (qualifier value AND), or an or-interaction (qualifier value OR). Or-dependences can be established by means of keyword DEP.

The second section describes the topology of the system. It is composed of three subsections. Firstly, we have the declaration of the AEIs together with their actual data parameters. Secondly, we have the declaration of the AEI interactions that are architectural (void if absent). Thirdly, we have the declaration of the architectural attachments between pairs of local interactions of the AEIs. In this section, every interaction is expressed through the dot notation; i.e., the name of the interaction is preceded by the name of the AEI to which it belongs. In this way, no ambiguity arises when referring to an interaction of an AET of which several instances have been declared or when interactions of distinct AETs possess the same name.

The graphical notation of PADL is based on enriched flow graphs, an extension of the graphical formalism adopted in [154]. The basic graphical elements are shown in Fig. 4.1. As can be seen, in an enriched flow graph, AEIs are depicted as boxes, local (resp. architectural) interactions are depicted as small black circles (resp. white squares) on the box border, and each attachment is depicted as a directed edge from a local output interaction of an AEI box to a local input interaction of another AEI box. The small circle/square of an interaction is extended inside the AEI box with an arc (resp. a buffer) if the interaction is semi-synchronous (resp. asynchronous). The small circle/square of an interaction is extended outside the AEI box with a triangle (resp. a bisected triangle) if the interaction is an and-interaction (resp. an

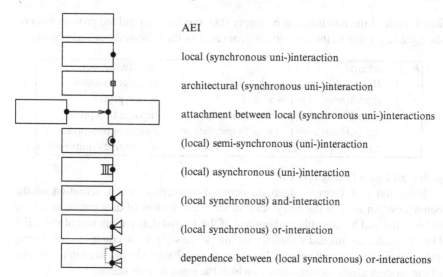

Fig. 4.1 Basic elements of PADL graphical notation

or-interaction). Finally, each or-dependence is depicted as a dotted edge between an input or-interaction and an output or-interaction inside the AEI box.

4.3.7 G7: Dynamic and Static Operators

The behavioral operators provided by process algebra are not all equally easy to use. In particular, static operators like parallel composition, hiding, restriction, and relabeling are harder to use than dynamic operators like action prefix and alternative composition. Therefore, for the sake of usability, it is appropriate to conceal static operators and to make available to the designer only the dynamic operators for describing the behavior of AETs.

Moreover, the operators made available need to be revised. Some of them need to become more verbose. For example, in PADL the inactive process $\underline{0}$ is represented through the more intuitive stop. Other operators need to avoid semantic overloading. For instance, in PADL the alternative composition operator $+$ is more appropriately represented as choice. Similar to process algebra in which communications allow data to be exchanged, in PADL actions are divided into input actions and output actions and can be preceded by Boolean guards establishing conditions under which the actions are enabled. The supported data types are Boolean, (bounded) integer, real, list, array, record, and generic object.

Each process algebraic equation that can occur in the definition of the behavior of an AET has the following form:

$$B(formal\_data\_parameter\_list;\ data\_variable\_list) = P$$

where each of the two lists can be empty (keyword `void`) and the process term on the right-hand side of the equation is generated by the following revised syntax:

$P ::=$ `stop`		inactive process
|	$B(actual\_data\_parameter\_list)$	process constant
|	`cond`$(bool\_expr)$ `->` $a.P$	action prefix
|	`cond`$(bool\_expr)$ `->` $a?(var\_list).P$	input action prefix
|	`cond`$(bool\_expr)$ `->` $a!(expr\_list).P$	output action prefix
|	`choice`$\{P,\ldots,P\}$	alternative composition

with `cond` guard being optional.

Since the first process algebraic equation occurring in the definition of the behavior of an AET is the entry point of the AET, its formal data parameters have to be initialized by possibly making use of the formal data parameters of the AET. Data variables are instead necessary within process algebraic equations for storing values received via input actions. In that case, they have to be declared in the header of the process algebraic equations in which the input actions occur.

As far as static operators are concerned, they are not available for modeling purposes but are somehow present in PADL. Static operators different from parallel composition are implicitly used in the behavioral modification section, the optional third section of a textual description. This section is useful for carrying out certain analyses in which some actions – whose name is expressed in dot notation – have to be hidden, prevented from occurring, or renamed:

`BEHAV_MODIFICATIONS`	
`BEHAV_HIDINGS`	*‹names of actions to be hidden›*
`BEHAV_RESTRICTIONS`	*‹names of actions to be restricted›*
`BEHAV_RENAMINGS`	*‹names of actions to be changed›*

Furthermore, static operators are transparently used in the translation semantics for PADL (see Sect. 4.4). More precisely, the parallel composition operator is used for causing AEIs to communicate with each other according to the declared attachments. This is made possible by the relabeling operator, which is used for converting to the same name local interactions that are attached to each other.

Example 4.3. On the basis of the considerations of Examples 4.1 and 4.2, the PADL textual description of the client–server system introduced in Sect. 4.2 is as follows, where we recall that `void` denotes the absence of formal data parameters in the architectural description header and in the header of all AETs, the absence of formal data parameters and data variables in the header of all process algebraic equations, and the absence of architectural interactions in the architectural topology section:

```
ARCHI_TYPE Client_Server(void)

ARCHI_BEHAVIOR
```

```
ARCHI_ELEM_TYPE Server_Type(void)

  BEHAVIOR
    Server(void; void) =
    receive_request . compute_response .
                                 send_response . Server()

    INPUT_INTERACTIONS  SYNC  OR receive_request
    OUTPUT_INTERACTIONS ASYNC OR send_response
                                        DEP receive_request
ARCHI_ELEM_TYPE Client_Type(void)

  BEHAVIOR
    Client_Internal(void; void) =
    process . Client_Interacting();
    Client_Interacting(void; void) =
    send_request .
      choice
      {
        cond(send_request.success = true) ->
                          receive_response . Client_Internal(),
        cond(send_request.success = false) ->
                          keep_processing . Client_Interacting()
      }

    INPUT_INTERACTIONS  SYNC  UNI receive_response
    OUTPUT_INTERACTIONS SSYNC UNI send_request

  ARCHI_TOPOLOGY

  ARCHI_ELEM_INSTANCES
  S   : Server_Type();
  C_1 : Client_Type();
  C_2 : Client_Type()

  ARCHI_INTERACTIONS
  void

  ARCHI_ATTACHMENTS
  FROM C_1.send_request TO S.receive_request;
  FROM C_2.send_request TO S.receive_request;
  FROM S.send_response  TO C_1.receive_response;
  FROM S.send_response  TO C_2.receive_response

END
```

Note the presence of a further internal action, keep_processing, in the second process algebraic equation of Client_Type.

The corresponding PADL graphical description is shown in Fig. 4.2.

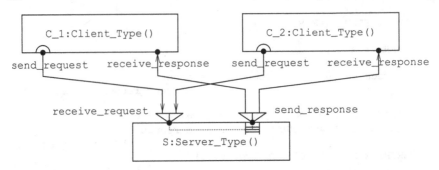

Fig. 4.2 Enriched flow graph of the client–server system

4.4 Translation Semantics for PADL

The semantics for PADL is given by a two-step translation into the process calculus of Sect. 1.3. The meaning of a PADL description is a process term stemming from the parallel composition of the process algebraic specifications of the behavior of the AEIs declared in the description, whose synchronization sets are determined by the attachments declared in the description.

In the first step (Sect. 4.4.1), the focus is on the semantics of each AEI, which is defined to be the behavior of the corresponding AET with all the action occurrences being preceded by the name of the AEI and the AET formal data parameters being substituted for by the corresponding AEI actual data parameters. If the AEI contains local or-interactions, each of them must be replaced by as many fresh local uni-interactions as there are attachments involving the considered or-interaction. Every occurrence of this or-interaction present in the behavior of the AEI must then be suitably rewritten on the basis of the fresh local uni-interactions, in order to reflect the fact that an or-interaction can result in several alternative communications. Moreover, if the AEI contains local asynchronous interactions, each of them must be equipped with as many additional implicit AEIs as there are attachments involving the considered asynchronous interaction, which behave as unbounded buffers.

In the second step (Sect. 4.4.2), the semantics of the whole architectural description is derived by composing in parallel the semantics of its AEIs according to the declared attachments and by taking into account the specified behavioral modifications. This is achieved by transparently exploiting all the static operators: parallel composition, hiding, restriction, and relabeling. Since attached local interactions do not necessarily have the same name while the parallel composition operator of Sect. 1.3 requires that synchronizing actions have the same name, first of all it is necessary to relabel every set of attached local interactions to the same fresh action name. These fresh action names then constitute the synchronization sets among the process terms representing the semantics of the declared AEIs. Additional semantic rules are also introduced for handling exceptions that may be raised by local semi-synchronous interactions. Hiding, restriction, and relabeling operators are finally used for enforcing possible behavioral modifications.

4.4.1 Semantics of Individual Elements

The first step of the translation semantics defines the meaning of any individual AEI. Let $\mathscr{C}$ be an AET with $m \in \mathbb{N}_{\geq 0}$ formal data parameters $fp_1, \ldots, fp_m$ and behavior given by a sequence $\mathscr{E}$ of process algebraic equations obeying the revised syntax. Let C be an AEI of type $\mathscr{C}$ with as many actual data parameters $ap_1, \ldots, ap_m$ consistent by order and type with the formal data parameters. The kernel of the semantics of C is given by $C.\mathscr{E}$, in which every action name a becomes $C.a$. Then, every occurrence of fp_j is substituted for by ap_j, $1 \leq j \leq m$. However, every local or-interaction and every local asynchronous interaction of C requires a specific treatment.

As it guides a selective one-to-many communication, each local or-interaction of C has to be replaced by as many fresh local uni-interactions as there are attachments involving the considered or-interaction. As shown in Fig. 4.3, these fresh uni-interactions are then attached to the local uni-interactions of other AEIs to which the local or-interaction was originally attached. On the behavioral side, a function called *or-rewrite* manipulates the right-hand side of the sequence of process algebraic equations of C on the basis of the fresh uni-interactions.

More precisely, the rewriting is applied only to those local or-interactions of C such that the number *attach-no*($_-$) of attachments involving them is greater than 1. In the rewriting process, or-dependences are dealt with by keeping track of the initially empty set FI of fresh local input uni-interactions currently in force, arising from local input or-interactions on which some local output or-interaction depends. Here are the four essential clauses of the inductive definition of *or-rewrite*, where for simplicity actions are devoid of dot notation, cond guards, and data exchange:

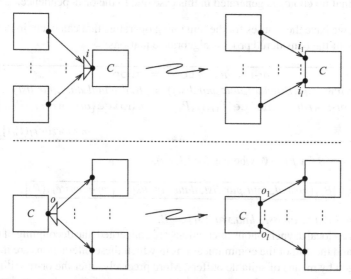

Fig. 4.3 Topological management of local (synchronous) or-interactions

- If a is an or-interaction of C such that $attach\text{-}no(C.a) \leq 1$ (if 0 then architectural) or a uni-/and-interaction or an internal action:

$$\boxed{or\text{-}rewrite_{FI}(a.P) = a.or\text{-}rewrite_{FI}(P)}$$

- If a is a local input or-interaction of C on which no local output or-interaction depends or a local output or-interaction that does not depend on any local input or-interaction and $attach\text{-}no(C.a) = l \geq 2$:

$$\boxed{\begin{aligned} or\text{-}rewrite_{FI}(a.P) = {}& \mathtt{choice}\{a_1.or\text{-}rewrite_{FI}(P), \\ &\qquad\qquad \vdots \\ & a_l.or\text{-}rewrite_{FI}(P)\} \end{aligned}}$$

- If i is a local input or-interaction of C on which a local output or-interaction depends and $attach\text{-}no(C.i) = l \geq 2$:

$$\boxed{\begin{aligned} or\text{-}rewrite_{FI}(i.P) = {}& \mathtt{choice}\{i_1.or\text{-}rewrite_{FI-\{i_j|1\leq j\leq l\}\cup\{i_1\}}(P), \\ &\qquad\qquad \vdots \\ & i_l.or\text{-}rewrite_{FI-\{i_j|1\leq j\leq l\}\cup\{i_l\}}(P)\} \end{aligned}}$$

Note that in this case set FI has to be updated in every branch of the choice due to the or-dependence.

- If o is a local output or-interaction of C that depends on the local input or-interaction i and $attach\text{-}no(C.i) = attach\text{-}no(C.o) \geq 2$ and $i_j \in FI$:

$$\boxed{or\text{-}rewrite_{FI}(o.P) = o_j.or\text{-}rewrite_{FI}(P)}$$

Note that no choice is generated in this case due to the or-dependence.

Then, we have the clauses for the remaining operators that can occur in the right-hand side of the considered process algebraic equations:

$$\boxed{\begin{aligned} or\text{-}rewrite_{FI}(\mathtt{stop}) &= \mathtt{stop} \\ or\text{-}rewrite_{FI}(B(actual\_data\_par\_list)) &= B_{FI}(actual\_data\_par\_list) \\ or\text{-}rewrite_{FI}(\mathtt{choice}\{P_1,\dots,P_n\}) &= \mathtt{choice}\{or\text{-}rewrite_{FI}(P_1), \\ &\qquad\qquad \vdots \\ & or\text{-}rewrite_{FI}(P_n)\} \end{aligned}}$$

where $B_{FI} \equiv B$ for $FI = \emptyset$, whereas for $FI \neq \emptyset$:

$$\boxed{B_{FI}(formal\_data\_par\_list; data\_var\_list) = or\text{-}rewrite_{FI}(P)}$$

if $B(formal\_data\_par\_list; data\_var\_list) = P$.

As far as local asynchronous interactions are concerned, the decoupling of the beginning and the end of the communications in which these interactions are involved is managed by means of suitable buffers. More precisely, after the or-rewriting process, for each local asynchronous uni-/and-interaction of C we have to introduce additional implicit AEIs that behave like unbounded buffers, as shown in Fig. 4.4.

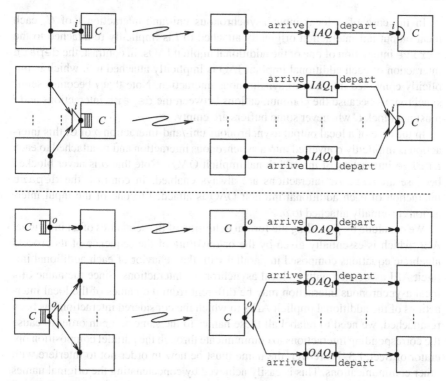

Fig. 4.4 Topological management of local asynchronous uni-/and-interactions

As can be noted, in the case of a local asynchronous and-interaction, it is necessary to introduce as many additional implicit AEIs as there are attachments involving the considered interaction.

Each additional implicit input asynchronous queue (IAQ) and output asynchronous queue (OAQ) is of the following type, where arrive is an always-enabled input synchronous uni-interaction while depart is an output synchronous uni-interaction enabled only if the buffer is not empty:

```
ARCHI_ELEM_TYPE Async_Queue_Type(void)

BEHAVIOR
  Queue(int n := 0;
        void) =
    choice
    {
      cond(true)  -> arrive . Queue(n + 1),
      cond(n > 0) -> depart . Queue(n - 1)
    }

INPUT_INTERACTIONS   SYNC UNI arrive
OUTPUT_INTERACTIONS  SYNC UNI depart
```

In the case of a local input asynchronous uni-/and-interaction i of C, each local output uni-interaction originally attached to i is implicitly re-attached to the arrive interaction of one of the additional implicit IAQs. In contrast, the depart interaction of each additional implicit IAQ is implicitly attached to i, which is implicitly converted into a semi-synchronous interaction. Note that i becomes semi-synchronous because the communications between the depart interactions and i must not block C whenever some buffers are empty.

In the case of a local output asynchronous uni-/and-interaction o of C, this interaction is implicitly converted into a synchronous interaction and re-attached to each arrive interaction of the additional implicit OAQs. Note that o is never blocked because all arrive interactions are always enabled. In contrast, the depart interaction of each additional implicit OAQ is attached to one of the input interactions originally attached to o.

We conclude by providing the formal definition of the semantics of an individual AEI, which is essentially given by the or-rewriting of the sequence of its process algebraic equations composed in parallel with the behavior of each additional implicit AEI associated with its local asynchronous interactions. Since the name of a local asynchronous interaction may be different from the names of the local interactions of the additional implicit AEIs to which the considered interaction has been re-attached, we need to relabel all these names to the same name in order to cause the corresponding interactions to communicate through the parallel composition operator of Sect. 1.3. Moreover, the name must be new in order not to interfere with other communications. This is easily achieved by concatenating the original names of all the involved interactions through symbol #.

Definition 4.1. Let $\mathscr{C}$ be an AET with $m \in \mathbb{N}_{\geq 0}$ formal data parameters $fp_1, \ldots, fp_m$ and behavior given by a sequence $\mathscr{E}$ of process algebraic equations. Let C be an AEI of type $\mathscr{C}$ with $m \in \mathbb{N}_{\geq 0}$ actual data parameters $ap_1, \ldots, ap_m$ consistent by order and type with the formal data parameters and:

- $h \in \mathbb{N}_{\geq 0}$ local input asynchronous uni-interactions $i_1, \ldots, i_h$ handled through the related additional implicit AEIs $IAQ_1, \ldots, IAQ_h$
- $h' \in \mathbb{N}_{\geq 0}$ local input asynchronous and-interactions $i'_1, \ldots, i'_{h'}$, where each i'_j is handled through the $attach\text{-}no(C.i'_j) = il_j$ related additional implicit AEIs $IAQ_{j,1}, \ldots, IAQ_{j,il_j}$
- $k \in \mathbb{N}_{\geq 0}$ local output asynchronous uni-interactions $o_1, \ldots, o_k$ handled through the related additional implicit AEIs $OAQ_1, \ldots, OAQ_k$
- $k' \in \mathbb{N}_{\geq 0}$ local output asynchronous and-interactions $o'_1, \ldots, o'_{k'}$, where each o'_j is handled through the $attach\text{-}no(C.o'_j) = ol_j$ related additional implicit AEIs $OAQ_{j,1}, \ldots, OAQ_{j,ol_j}$

Then the isolated semantics of C is the result of a cascade of function applications:

$$\llbracket C \rrbracket = o\text{-}and_{ol_{k'}}^{k'}(\ldots o\text{-}and_{ol_1}^1(o\text{-}uni_k(i\text{-}and_{il_{h'}}^{h'}(\ldots i\text{-}and_{il_1}^1(i\text{-}uni_h(C))\ldots)))\ldots)$$

where, denoted by $f(C)$ the current result, we define:

$$
\begin{aligned}
i\text{-}uni_0(C) &= or\text{-}rewrite_0(C.\mathcal{E}\{ap_1 \hookrightarrow fp_1, \ldots, ap_m \hookrightarrow fp_m\})[\varphi_{C,\text{async}}] \\
i\text{-}uni_j(C) &= IAQ_j.\texttt{Queue}\,(0)\,[\varphi_{C,\text{async}}] \\
&\quad \parallel_{\{IAQ_j.\text{depart}\#C.i_j\}} (i\text{-}uni_{j-1}(C)) \qquad\qquad 1 \le j \le h
\end{aligned}
$$

$$
\begin{aligned}
i\text{-}and_1^j(f(C)) &= IAQ_{j,1}.\texttt{Queue}\,(0)\,[\varphi_{C,\text{async}}] \qquad\qquad 1 \le j \le h' \\
&\quad \parallel_{\{IAQ_{j,1}.\text{depart}\#\ldots\#IAQ_{j,il_j}.\text{depart}\#C.i'_j\}} (f(C)) \\
i\text{-}and_{j'}^j(f(C)) &= IAQ_{j,j'}.\texttt{Queue}\,(0)\,[\varphi_{C,\text{async}}] \qquad\qquad 2 \le j' \le il_j \\
&\quad \parallel_{\{IAQ_{j,1}.\text{depart}\#\ldots\#IAQ_{j,il_j}.\text{depart}\#C.i'_j\}} \\
&\quad (i\text{-}and_{j'-1}^j(f(C)))
\end{aligned}
$$

$$
\begin{aligned}
o\text{-}uni_0(f(C)) &= f(C) \\
o\text{-}uni_j(f(C)) &= (o\text{-}uni_{j-1}(f(C))) \parallel_{\{C.o_j\#OAQ_j.\text{arrive}\}} \\
&\quad OAQ_j.\texttt{Queue}\,(0)\,[\varphi_{C,\text{async}}] \qquad\qquad 1 \le j \le k
\end{aligned}
$$

$$
\begin{aligned}
o\text{-}and_1^j(f(C)) &= (f(C)) \parallel_{\{C.o'_j\#OAQ_{j,1}.\text{arrive}\#\ldots\#OAQ_{j,ol_j}.\text{arrive}\}} \qquad 1 \le j \le k' \\
&\quad OAQ_{j,1}.\texttt{Queue}\,(0)\,[\varphi_{C,\text{async}}] \\
o\text{-}and_{j'}^j(f(C)) &= (o\text{-}and_{j'-1}^j(f(C))) \\
&\quad \parallel_{\{C.o'_j\#OAQ_{j,1}.\text{arrive}\#\ldots\#OAQ_{j,ol_j}.\text{arrive}\}} \\
&\quad OAQ_{j,j'}.\texttt{Queue}\,(0)\,[\varphi_{C,\text{async}}] \qquad\qquad 2 \le j' \le ol_j
\end{aligned}
$$

with relabeling function $\varphi_{C,\text{async}}$ transforming the originally asynchronous local interactions of C and the local interactions of the additional implicit AEIs attached to them into the respective fresh names occurring in the synchronization sets above.

Example 4.4. In the case of the PADL description of the client–server system shown in Example 4.3, we have that $[\![\texttt{C\_1}]\!]$ (resp. $[\![\texttt{C\_2}]\!]$) coincides with the sequence of process algebraic equations of $\texttt{Client\_Type}$ where action names are preceded by $\texttt{C\_1}$ (resp. $\texttt{C\_2}$). The reason is that there are no formal data parameters, local or-interactions, and local asynchronous interactions.

Instead, due to the presence of two dependent local or-interactions each involved in two attachments, the construction of $[\![\texttt{S}]\!]$ requires first of all the application of function *or-rewrite* to the only process algebraic equation of $\texttt{Server\_Type}$ where action names are preceded by $\texttt{S}$, which thus becomes:

```
Server'(void; void) =
  choice
  {
    S.receive_request_1 . S.compute_response .
                                S.send_response_1 . Server'(),
    S.receive_request_2 . S.compute_response .
                                S.send_response_2 . Server'()
  }
```

Then, it requires two additional implicit OAQs for the two fresh local output asynchronous uni-interactions S.send_response_1 and S.send_response_2. As a consequence:

$$
\begin{aligned}
[\![S]\!] = \ &\texttt{Server}'[\texttt{S.send\_response\_1} \mapsto \texttt{S.send\_response\_1\#OAQ\_1.arrive},\\
&\qquad\quad\ \texttt{S.send\_response\_2} \mapsto \texttt{S.send\_response\_2\#OAQ\_2.arrive}]
\end{aligned}
$$

$$\|_{\{\texttt{S.send\_response\_1\#OAQ\_1.arrive}\}}$$

$$\texttt{OAQ\_1.Queue(0)}\,[\texttt{OAQ\_1.arrive} \mapsto \texttt{S.send\_response\_1\#OAQ\_1.arrive}]$$

$$\|_{\{\texttt{S.send\_response\_2\#OAQ\_2.arrive}\}}$$

$$\texttt{OAQ\_2.Queue(0)}\,[\texttt{OAQ\_2.arrive} \mapsto \texttt{S.send\_response\_2\#OAQ\_2.arrive}]$$

4.4.2 Semantics of Interacting Elements

The second step of the translation semantics defines the meaning of any set of AEIs $\{C_1,\ldots,C_n\}$, and hence of an entire architectural description. Fixed an AEI C_j in the set, let $\mathscr{LI}_{C_j}$ be the set of local interactions of C_j and $\mathscr{LI}_{C_j;C_1,\ldots,C_n} \subseteq \mathscr{LI}_{C_j}$ be the set of local interactions of C_j attached to $\{C_1,\ldots,C_n\}$. Since local or-interactions and local asynchronous interactions have been suitably transformed, here by local interactions of C_j we mean:

- Its original local nonasynchronous uni-/and-interactions
- Its fresh local nonasynchronous uni-interactions that replace its original local nonasynchronous or-interactions
- The local interactions of its additional implicit AEIs that are not attached to its originally asynchronous local interactions

In order to make the process terms representing the semantics of these AEIs communicate in the presence of attached interactions having different names, we need a set $\mathscr{S}(C_1,\ldots,C_n)$ of fresh action names, one for each pair of attached local uni-interactions in $\{C_1,\ldots,C_n\}$ and for each set of local uni-interactions attached to the same local and-interaction in $\{C_1,\ldots,C_n\}$. Similar to Definition 4.1, every fresh name is obtained by concatenating all the original names in a maximal set of attached local interactions. For instance, $C_j.o\#C_g.i$ is the fresh action name for the case in which the local output uni-interaction o of C_j is attached to the local input uni-interaction i of C_g. Then, we need suitable injective relabeling functions $\varphi_{C_j;C_1,\ldots,C_n}$ mapping each set $\mathscr{LI}_{C_j;C_1,\ldots,C_n}$ to $\mathscr{S}(C_1,\ldots,C_n)$ in such a way that $\varphi_{C_j;C_1,\ldots,C_n}(C_j.a_1) = \varphi_{C_g;C_1,\ldots,C_n}(C_g.a_2)$ iff $C_j.a_1$ and $C_g.a_2$ are attached to each other or to the same and-interaction.

Definition 4.2. The interacting semantics of $C_j \in \{C_1,\ldots,C_n\}$ with respect to $\{C_1,\ldots,C_n\}$ is defined as follows:

$$\boxed{[\![C_j]\!]_{C_1,\ldots,C_n} = [\![C_j]\!]\,[\varphi_{C_j;C_1,\ldots,C_n}]}$$

The interacting semantics of $\{C'_1,\ldots,C'_{n'}\}\subseteq\{C_1,\ldots,C_n\}$ with respect to $\{C_1,\ldots,C_n\}$ is the parallel composition of the interacting semantics of the individual AEIs:

$$
\begin{aligned}
[\![C'_1,\ldots,C'_{n'}]\!]_{C_1,\ldots,C_n} = \; & [\![C'_1]\!]_{C_1,\ldots,C_n} \parallel_{\mathscr{S}(C'_1,C'_2;C_1,\ldots,C_n)} \\
& [\![C'_2]\!]_{C_1,\ldots,C_n} \parallel_{\mathscr{S}(C'_1,C'_3;C_1,\ldots,C_n)\cup\mathscr{S}(C'_2,C'_3;C_1,\ldots,C_n)} \\
& \cdots \parallel_{\underset{i=1}{\overset{n'-1}{\cup}}\mathscr{S}(C'_i,C'_{n'};C_1,\ldots,C_n)} [\![C'_{n'}]\!]_{C_1,\ldots,C_n}
\end{aligned}
$$

where $\mathscr{S}(C'_j;C_1,\ldots,C_n) = \varphi_{C'_j;C_1,\ldots,C_n}(\mathscr{LI}_{C'_j;C_1,\ldots,C_n})$ is the synchronization set of C'_j with respect to $\{C_1,\ldots,C_n\}$, $\mathscr{S}(C'_j,C'_g;C_1,\ldots,C_n) = \mathscr{S}(C'_j;C_1,\ldots,C_n)\cap \mathscr{S}(C'_g;C_1,\ldots,C_n)$ is the pairwise synchronization set of C'_j and C'_g with respect to $\{C_1,\ldots,C_n\}$, and the unions of pairwise synchronization sets are consistent with the left associativity of the parallel composition operator of Sect. 1.3.

For a correct management of local semi-synchronous interactions in the interacting semantics, it is necessary to introduce some additional semantic rules. While a local semi-synchronous interaction s executed by an AEI C gives rise to a transition labeled with $C.s$ within $[\![C]\!]$ – and hence to the setting of the related success variable to true (see end of Sect. 4.3.4) – in an interacting context this transition has to be relabeled as an exception if s cannot immediately participate in a communication.

Suppose that the local output interaction o of an AEI C_1 is attached to the local input interaction i of an AEI C_2, where $C_1.o\#C_2.i$ is their fresh name. Let P_1 (resp. P_2) be the process term representing the current state of $[\![C_1]\!]_{C_1,C_2}$ (resp. $[\![C_2]\!]_{C_1,C_2}$) and $S = \mathscr{S}(C_1,C_2;C_1,C_2)$. If o is synchronous and i is semi-synchronous, then the following additional semantic rule is necessary for handling exceptions:

$$
\frac{P_1 \overset{C_1.o\#C_2.i}{\not\longrightarrow} P'_1 \qquad P_2 \overset{C_1.o\#C_2.i}{\longrightarrow} P'_2}{P_1\parallel_S P_2 \overset{C_2.i\_exception}{\longrightarrow} P_1\parallel_S P'_2 \qquad C_2.i.\texttt{success} = \texttt{false}}
$$

In the symmetric case in which o is semi-synchronous and i is synchronous, the following additional semantic rule is necessary for handling exceptions:

$$
\frac{P_1 \overset{C_1.o\#C_2.i}{\longrightarrow} P'_1 \qquad P_2 \overset{C_1.o\#C_2.i}{\not\longrightarrow} P'_2}{P_1\parallel_S P_2 \overset{C_1.o\_exception}{\longrightarrow} P'_1\parallel_S P_2 \qquad C_1.o.\texttt{success} = \texttt{false}}
$$

In the case in which both o and i are semi-synchronous, we need the previous two additional semantic rules together. Note that the two rules encode a context-sensitive variant of the relabeling operator, with respect to which behavioral equivalences are congruent (see Sect. 1.4.1) if corresponding actions have the same qualifiers.

In Fig. 4.5, we summarize the semantic treatment of the nine forms of communications resulting from the attachment of a local output synchronous, semi-synchronous, or asynchronous interaction o of an AEI C_1 whose interacting semantics is process term P_1 to a local input synchronous, semi-synchronous, or asynchronous interaction i of an AEI C_2 whose interacting semantics is process term P_2.

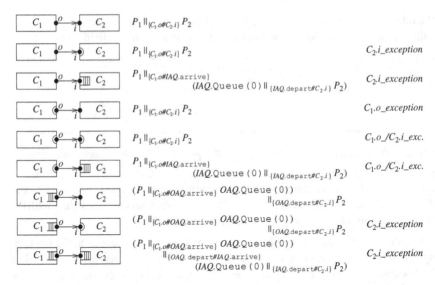

Fig. 4.5 Semantic treatment of the forms of communication synchronicity available in PADL

Definition 4.3. Let $\mathscr{A}$ be an architectural description whose complete set of AEIs is $\{C_1,\dots,C_n\}$, and let $\mathscr{H}$, $\mathscr{R}$, and φ be possible behavioral modifications of $\mathscr{A}$ enforcing action hiding, action restriction, and action renaming, respectively. Then the semantics of $\mathscr{A}$ is defined as follows:

$$\begin{aligned} [\![\mathscr{A}]\!]_{\text{bbm}} &= [\![C_1,\dots,C_n]\!]_{C_1,\dots,C_n} \\ [\![\mathscr{A}]\!]_{\text{abm}} &= [\![\mathscr{A}]\!]_{\text{bbm}} / \mathscr{H} \setminus \mathscr{R}\,[\varphi] \end{aligned}$$

depending on whether it is intended before or after behavioral modifications.

Example 4.5. On the basis of the isolated semantics of the individual AEIs discussed in Example 4.4, the semantics of the entire PADL description of the client–server system shown in Example 4.3 is given by the following process term:

```
[[S]][S.receive_request_1 ↦ C_1.send_request#S.receive_request_1,
     OAQ_1.depart ↦ OAQ_1.depart#C_1.receive_response,
     S.receive_request_2 ↦ C_2.send_request#S.receive_request_2,
     OAQ_2.depart ↦ OAQ_2.depart#C_2.receive_response]

  ||{C_1.send_request#S.receive_request_1,
     OAQ_1.depart#C_1.receive_response}

[[C_1]][C_1.send_request ↦ C_1.send_request#S.receive_request_1,
       C_1.receive_response ↦ OAQ_1.depart#C_1.receive_response]

  ||{C_2.send_request#S.receive_request_2,
     OAQ_2.depart#C_2.receive_response}

[[C_2]][C_2.send_request ↦ C_2.send_request#S.receive_request_2,
       C_2.receive_response ↦ OAQ_2.depart#C_2.receive_response]
```

4.5 Summarizing Example: Pipe–Filter System

Before moving to the last guideline, we illustrate the enhancement of usability with respect to process algebra by means of a further example in which we model a pipe–filter system. In general, this is composed of a number of filters, each of which reads streams of row data on its inputs, applies them a transformation, and produces streams of processed data on its outputs, thus realizing an incremental process. Filters are connected through pipes, each of which transmits outputs of one filter to inputs of another filter. For simplicity, the scenario we consider includes four identical filters, each equipped with a finite buffer. All filters are connected through a single pipe that forwards any item received from the upstream filter to one of the three downstream filters according to the availability of free positions in their buffers.

Let us first model this system with process algebra. The model is given by the parallel composition of five process terms representing the four filters – whose buffers are initially empty and can hold up to ten items – and the pipe:

$$Pipe\_Filter \triangleq Upstream\_Filter_{0/10} \parallel_{\{output\_accept\_item\}}$$
$$Pipe \parallel_{\{forward\_input\_item_1\}}$$
$$Downstream\_Filter^1_{0/10} \parallel_{\{forward\_input\_item_2\}}$$
$$Downstream\_Filter^2_{0/10} \parallel_{\{forward\_input\_item_3\}}$$
$$Downstream\_Filter^3_{0/10}$$

In this model, it is not clear which process term communicates with which process term, nor can there be confidence about the correctness of the synchronization sets associated with the occurrences of the parallel composition operator. Furthermore, the degree of synchronicity and multiplicity of the communications is completely obscure and cannot be easily inferred.

Then, we have the set of equations defining $Upstream\_Filter_{0/10}$ ($1 \leq j \leq 9$):

$$Upstream\_Filter_{0/10} \triangleq input\_item.transform\_item.Upstream\_Filter_{1/10}$$
$$Upstream\_Filter_{j/10} \triangleq input\_item.transform\_item.Upstream\_Filter_{j+1/10}$$
$$+output\_accept\_item.Upstream\_Filter_{j-1/10}$$
$$Upstream\_Filter_{10/10} \triangleq output\_accept\_item.Upstream\_Filter_{9/10}$$

In these equations, it is not clear which actions are part of the interface of the upstream filter and which actions represent internal activities (it can only be guessed). Moreover, the designer is forced to use a name like $output\_accept\_item$ for the action describing the communication between the upstream filter and the pipe, because the parallel composition operator of Sect. 1.3 requires names of synchronizing actions to coincide. A more natural name from the viewpoint of the upstream filter (resp. the pipe) would have been $output\_item$ (resp. $accept\_item$). A solution to this problem could be the use of relabeling functions.

Here is the only equation defining *Pipe*:

$$Pipe \; \overset{\Delta}{=} \; output\_accept\_item \,.\, (forward\_input\_item_1 \,.\, Pipe$$
$$+ forward\_input\_item_2 \,.\, Pipe$$
$$+ forward\_input\_item_3 \,.\, Pipe)$$

Besides the same problem with action names as before, there is a problem with scalability. In fact, for a different number of downstream filters, the intervention of the designer is required in order to modify the part of the defining equation enclosed in parentheses.

The set of equations defining $Downstream\_Filter^1_{0/10}$ $(1 \le j \le 9)$ given by:

$$Downstream\_Filter^1_{0/10} \; \overset{\Delta}{=} \; forward\_input\_item_1 \,.\, transform\_item \,.$$
$$Downstream\_Filter^1_{1/10}$$

$$Downstream\_Filter^1_{j/10} \; \overset{\Delta}{=} \; forward\_input\_item_1 \,.\, transform\_item \,.$$
$$Downstream\_Filter^1_{j+1/10}$$
$$+ output\_item \,.\, Downstream\_Filter^1_{j-1/10}$$

$$Downstream\_Filter^1_{10/10} \; \overset{\Delta}{=} \; output\_item \,.\, Downstream\_Filter^1_{9/10}$$

the set of equations defining $Downstream\_Filter^2_{0/10}$ $(1 \le j \le 9)$ given by:

$$Downstream\_Filter^2_{0/10} \; \overset{\Delta}{=} \; forward\_input\_item_2 \,.\, transform\_item \,.$$
$$Downstream\_Filter^2_{1/10}$$

$$Downstream\_Filter^2_{j/10} \; \overset{\Delta}{=} \; forward\_input\_item_2 \,.\, transform\_item \,.$$
$$Downstream\_Filter^2_{j+1/10}$$
$$+ output\_item \,.\, Downstream\_Filter^2_{j-1/10}$$

$$Downstream\_Filter^2_{10/10} \; \overset{\Delta}{=} \; output\_item \,.\, Downstream\_Filter^2_{9/10}$$

and the set of equations defining $Downstream\_Filter^3_{0/10}$ $(1 \le j \le 9)$ given by:

$$Downstream\_Filter^3_{0/10} \; \overset{\Delta}{=} \; forward\_input\_item_3 \,.\, transform\_item \,.$$
$$Downstream\_Filter^3_{1/10}$$

$$Downstream\_Filter^3_{j/10} \; \overset{\Delta}{=} \; forward\_input\_item_3 \,.\, transform\_item \,.$$
$$Downstream\_Filter^3_{j+1/10}$$
$$+ output\_item \,.\, Downstream\_Filter^3_{j-1/10}$$

$$Downstream\_Filter^3_{10/10} \; \overset{\Delta}{=} \; output\_item \,.\, Downstream\_Filter^3_{9/10}$$

are similar to each other and to the set of equations defining $Upstream\_Filter_{0/10}$, as they differ only for the names of the process constants and of some actions. In order to avoid this redundancy, suitable relabeling functions should have been used. In any case, there is a problem with scalability. For a different number of downstream filters, the intervention of the designer is required in order to add the necessary defining equations or relabeling functions.

Let us now model the same pipe–filter system with PADL. Here is the header:

```
ARCHI_TYPE Pipe_Filter(const integer pf_buffer_size := 10)
```

It provides explicit support for data parameterization at the beginning of the description. The initialization values are the default actual values for the formal data parameters of the whole description. These values can be used in the architectural topology section when passing actual data parameters in the declaration of AEIs.

The architectural behavior section starts with the definition of the filter AET:

```
ARCHI_ELEM_TYPE Filter_Type(const integer buffer_size)

  BEHAVIOR
    Filter(integer(0..buffer_size) item_num := 0;
           void) =
      choice
      {
        cond(item_num < buffer_size) ->
          input_item . transform_item . Filter(item_num + 1),
        cond(item_num > 0) ->
          output_item . Filter(item_num - 1)
      }

  INPUT_INTERACTIONS   SYNC UNI input_item
  OUTPUT_INTERACTIONS  SYNC UNI output_item
```

The definition of a single AET for the four filters is enough, as they are identical. Due to the use of formal data parameters and Boolean guards, a single process algebraic equation suffices. Furthermore, the distinction between interactions and internal actions is made explicit, and their names have been freely chosen.

We also note that the declaration of each formal data parameter of the entire description or of a single AET is preceded by keyword const. This reminds us that the value of such a formal data parameter is constant, whereas this is not the case with formal data parameters of process algebraic equations inside AETs.

Then, we have the definition of the pipe AET:

```
ARCHI_ELEM_TYPE Pipe_Type(void)

  BEHAVIOR
    Pipe(void; void) =
      accept_item . forward_item . Pipe()

  INPUT_INTERACTIONS   SYNC UNI accept_item
  OUTPUT_INTERACTIONS  SYNC OR  forward_item
```

Scalability has been achieved by declaring forward_item as an or-interaction.

Here is the architectural topology section:

```
ARCHI_ELEM_INSTANCES
  F_0 : Filter_Type(pf_buffer_size);
  P   : Pipe_Type();
```

```
F_1 : Filter_Type(pf_buffer_size);
F_2 : Filter_Type(pf_buffer_size);
F_3 : Filter_Type(pf_buffer_size)

ARCHI_INTERACTIONS
F_0.input_item;
F_1.output_item; F_2.output_item; F_3.output_item

ARCHI_ATTACHMENTS
FROM F_0.output_item TO P.accept_item;
FROM P.forward_item  TO F_1.input_item;
FROM P.forward_item  TO F_2.input_item;
FROM P.forward_item  TO F_3.input_item
```

From this description the communication scheme is clear, with F_0 being the upstream filter and F_1, F_2, and F_3 being the downstream filters. We point out that the input_item interaction of the upstream filter and the output_item interactions of the downstream filters have been declared as architectural interactions. This allows for future structural extensions of the pipe–filter system, which will be discussed in Sect. 4.6 together with how to describe the topology more concisely. The topology of the pipe–filter system is even better illustrated by the graphical description shown in Fig. 4.6.

As far as the translation semantics of the PADL description of the pipe–filter system is concerned, it turns out that it closely resembles the process algebraic model of the same system provided at the beginning of this section. Here is the isolated semantics of the various AEIs:

$$[\![\text{F\_0}]\!] = \text{F\_0.Filter}\{10 \hookrightarrow \text{buffer\_size}\}$$
$$[\![\text{F\_1}]\!] = \text{F\_1.Filter}\{10 \hookrightarrow \text{buffer\_size}\}$$
$$[\![\text{F\_2}]\!] = \text{F\_2.Filter}\{10 \hookrightarrow \text{buffer\_size}\}$$
$$[\![\text{F\_3}]\!] = \text{F\_3.Filter}\{10 \hookrightarrow \text{buffer\_size}\}$$
$$[\![\text{P}]\!] = \textit{or-rewrite}_0(\text{P.Pipe})$$

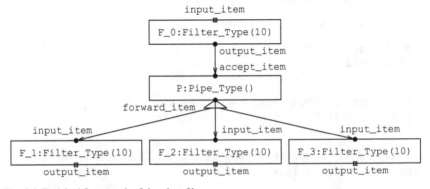

Fig. 4.6 Enriched flow graph of the pipe–filter system

where *or-rewrite$_0$*(P.Pipe) is given by:

```
Pipe'(void; void) =
  P.accept_item . choice
                {
                 P.forward_item_1 . Pipe'(),
                 P.forward_item_2 . Pipe'(),
                 P.forward_item_3 . Pipe'()
                }
```

The semantics of Pipe_Filter(10) is given by the following process term, which is isomorphic to *Pipe_Filter* up to action names:

$[\![$F_0$]\!]$[F_0.output_item ↦ F_0.output_item#P.accept_item]

$\parallel${F_0.output_item#P.accept_item}

  $[\![$P$]\!]$[P.accept_item ↦ F_0.output_item#P.accept_item,
      P.forward_item_1 ↦ P.forward_item_1#F_1.input_item,
      P.forward_item_2 ↦ P.forward_item_2#F_2.input_item,
      P.forward_item_3 ↦ P.forward_item_3#F_3.input_item]

  $\parallel${P.forward_item_1#F_1.input_item}

    $[\![$F_1$]\!]$[F_1.input_item ↦ P.forward_item_1#F_1.input_item]

    $\parallel${P.forward_item_2#F_2.input_item}

      $[\![$F_2$]\!]$[F_2.input_item ↦ P.forward_item_2#F_2.input_item]

      $\parallel${P.forward_item_3#F_3.input_item}

        $[\![$F_3$]\!]$[F_3.input_item ↦ P.forward_item_3#F_3.input_item]

The items processed by the pipe–filter system that we have modeled are all identical. However, it might be the case that the items are different from each other, which can be formalized by giving each of them an identifier. In this case, we have to revise the previous description, as we have to keep track of the order in which items arrive at buffers. This can be accomplished by exploiting the data exchange capability of PADL together with the data types it supports.

Here is the new header, where only the name of the description has changed:

```
ARCHI_TYPE Pipe_Filter_Id(const integer pf_buffer_size := 10)
```

Then, we have the redefinition of the filter AET:

```
ARCHI_ELEM_TYPE Filter_Type(const integer buffer_size)

 BEHAVIOR
  Filter(list(integer) item_list := list_cons();
        local integer id) =
   choice
   {
    cond(length(item_list) < buffer_size) ->
     input_item?(id) . transform_item .
                        Filter(concat(item_list, list_cons(id))),
    cond(length(item_list) > 0) ->
     output_item!(first(item_list)) . Filter(tail(item_list))
   }

  INPUT_INTERACTIONS  SYNC UNI input_item
  OUTPUT_INTERACTIONS SYNC UNI output_item
```

In order to manage items correctly, an initially empty list-typed parameter has been used for holding the identifiers of the various items according to the order of their arrival. Several operations on lists are supported by PADL, among which we mention function `list_cons()` for constructing a list, function `length()` which returns the number of values in a list, function `concat()` for concatenating two lists, function `first()` which returns the first value in a nonempty list, and function `tail()` which returns a list without its first value.

An input action prefix operator has been used for modeling item arrival, whereas an output action prefix operator has been used for modeling item departure. The variable occurring in the input action is declared as a local variable in the header of the process algebraic equation. This declaration is preceded by keyword `local`.

Here is the redefinition of the pipe AET, where a local variable has been used in order to preserve the identity of items throughout the system:

```
ARCHI_ELEM_TYPE Pipe_Type(void)

  BEHAVIOR
   Pipe(void;
        local integer id) =
     accept_item?(id) . forward_item!(id) . Pipe()

  INPUT_INTERACTIONS   SYNC UNI accept_item
  OUTPUT_INTERACTIONS  SYNC OR  forward_item
```

Finally, the architectural topology section, the enriched flow graph, and the structure of the process term formalizing the semantics for this variant of the pipe–filter system are the same as those for the original system.

4.6 G8: Supporting Architectural Styles

Since certain software organizational principles are frequently recurring in practice, they have been classified as architectural styles [169, 184]. Examples of families of software systems sharing specific organizational principles are call-return systems(main program and subroutines, object-oriented programs, hierarchical layers, client–server systems), dataflow systems (pipe–filter systems, compilers), repositories (databases, hypertexts), virtual machines (interpreters), and event-based systems (publish–subscribe systems).

An architectural style defines a vocabulary of components and connectors together with a set of constraints on how they should behave and be combined. Ideally, architectural styles should enable the designer to capitalize on codified principles and experience to specify, analyze, plan, and monitor the construction of software systems with high levels of efficiency and confidence. For this reason, it is important to provide support for architectural styles in PADL.

Unfortunately, the concept of architectural style is hard to formalize. In fact, there are at least two degrees of freedom: the variability of the architectural element behavior and the variability of the architectural topology. These variabilities can be interpreted in different ways, with their interpretation possibly changing from style to style. In order to keep the task manageable, we introduce an approximation of the concept of architectural style, which we call architectural type.

In this section, after introducing the notions of architectural type and architectural invocation (Sect. 4.6.1), we first concentrate on the simplest form of architectural invocation in order to illustrate hierarchical modeling (Sect. 4.6.2). Then, we present the notion of behavioral conformity for architectural invocations comprising actual AETs different from the corresponding formal AETs (Sect. 4.6.3). Finally, we examine the admitted topological variations for architectural invocations including an actual topology different from the formal topology (Sects. 4.6.4, 4.6.5, and 4.6.6). All forms of architectural invocation are exemplified through variants of the client–server system and of the pipe–filter system.

4.6.1 Architectural Types

An architectural type (AT) is a family of software systems in which the behavior of the architectural elements and the overall topology of the system can vary in a controlled way inside the family. The controlled variability of the behavior is achieved by allowing only the internal behavior of corresponding AETs to vary from instance to instance of an AT. The controlled variability of the topology is achieved by admitting only exogenous, endogenous, and multiplicity variations. The first ones permit to add certain AEIs by attaching some of them to architectural interactions. The second ones are concerned with changes of the number of certain AEIs in certain positions of the topology. The third ones allow the number of certain AEIs attached to certain local and-/or-interactions to change from instance to instance of an AT.

The instances of an AT are generated via architectural invocations of the definition of the AT, which consists of a PADL description. An architectural invocation passes both data parameters and architectural parameters, as it comprises:

- Actual values for formal data parameters, which replace the default values
- Actual AETs preserving the observable behavior of the formal AETs
- An actual topology including a group of actual AEIs, a group of actual architectural interactions, a group of actual attachments, and a group of topological variations complying with the formal topology
- Actual behavioral modifications divided into three groups
- Actual names for architectural interactions, needed for hierarchical modeling

Symbol @ is used as separator of groups of actual parameters. When omitted from an architectural invocation, a group of actual architectural parameters is intended to coincide with the corresponding group of formal architectural parameters occurring in the PADL description of the AT. The semantics of an instance of an AT is built in the same way as the semantics of the definition of the AT, by using actual parameters instead of formal ones and relabeling architectural interactions to their actual names.

4.6.2 *Hierarchical Modeling*

In the simplest form of architectural invocation, all the actual architectural parameters coincide with the corresponding formal architectural parameters and only actual data parameters are passed (if any). This form of invocation does not introduce any behavioral or topological variation with respect to the definition of the invoked AT. However, it is useful for hierarchical modeling purposes, if we extend PADL in such a way that an AET can be defined as an instance of a previously defined AT.

In this case, the AET behavior is given by the semantics of the AT instance and the AET interactions are unified with the AT architectural interactions. More precisely, the AET interactions become the actual names for the AT architectural interactions, whose synchronicity and multiplicity qualifiers are overridden. In an enriched flow graph, any instance of this AET is represented as a box with double border and the unification between AEI interactions and AT architectural interactions is represented through dashed edges.

Example 4.6. Let us consider a variant of the client–server system of Sect. 4.2 where the server has the same structure and behavior as the pipe–filter system of Sect. 4.5.

Here is the architectural description header, where formal data parameters are now necessary with respect to the original client–server system modeled in Example 4.3:

```
ARCHI_TYPE H_Client_Server(const integer hcs_buffer_size := 10)
```

In this variant of the client–server system, it is not possible to exploit the or-dependence mechanism. The reason is that this mechanism no longer works inside an architectural element resulting from the combination of other elements, as their interleaving may alter the relationships between local output or-interactions and local input or-interactions. As a consequence, in order to ensure that responses are sent to the clients that issued the corresponding requests, each request needs to carry the client identifier. Hence, the client AET and the server AET are redefined as follows (remind that @ separates groups of actual parameters, which may be empty):

```
ARCHI_ELEM_TYPE Client_Type(const integer id)

BEHAVIOR
  Client_Internal(void; void) =
   process . Client_Interacting();
  Client_Interacting(void; void) =
   send_request!(id) .
    choice
    {
      cond(send_request.success = true) ->
                  receive_response . Client_Internal(),
      cond(send_request.success = false) ->
                  keep_processing . Client_Interacting()
    }
```

```
INPUT_INTERACTIONS   SYNC  UNI receive_response
OUTPUT_INTERACTIONS SSYNC UNI send_request

ARCHI_ELEM_TYPE Server_Type(const integer buffer_size)

BEHAVIOR
 Server(void; void) =
  Pipe_Filter_Id(buffer_size @
                 @       /* reuse formal AETs */
                 @ @ @ @ /* reuse formal topology */
                 @ @ @   /* no behavioral modifications */
                 UNIFY F_0.input_item WITH receive_request;
                 FOR_ALL 1 <= j <= 2
                   UNIFY F_1.output_item!(j),
                         F_2.output_item!(j),
                         F_3.output_item!(j)
                                        WITH send_response[j])

INPUT_INTERACTIONS   SYNC  OR  receive_request
OUTPUT_INTERACTIONS ASYNC UNI send_response[1];
                              send_response[2]
```

The only architectural input interaction of Pipe_Filter_Id has been unified with the only input interaction of Server, thus causing the input_item interaction of the upstream filter to become an or-interaction. In contrast, the three architectural output interactions of Pipe_Filter_Id have been unified with the two output interactions of Server, thus causing the output_item interactions of the three downstream filters to become asynchronous. More precisely, they have been unified with send_response[1] when they output value 1 and with send_response[2] when they output value 2, so as to establish a correct call back. Unification has been expressed concisely thanks to the FOR_ALL construct.

Here is the architectural topology section:

```
ARCHI_ELEM_INSTANCES
 S   : Server_Type(hcs_buffer_size);
 C_1 : Client_Type(1);
 C_2 : Client_Type(2);

ARCHI_INTERACTIONS
 void

ARCHI_ATTACHMENTS
 FROM C_1.send_request    TO S.receive_request;
 FROM C_2.send_request    TO S.receive_request;
 FROM S.send_response[1] TO C_1.receive_response;
 FROM S.send_response[2] TO C_2.receive_response
```

which is graphically illustrated in Fig. 4.7.

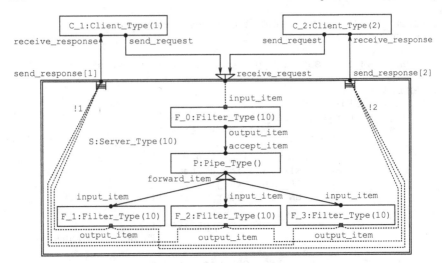

Fig. 4.7 Enriched flow graph of the hierarchical client–server system

4.6.3 Behavioral Conformity

We now abandon the simplest form of architectural invocation and hence we assume that actual architectural parameters are passed that are syntactically different from the corresponding formal architectural parameters of the invoked AT. In particular, we consider the case of actual AETs syntactically different from the corresponding formal AETs, with the actual topology introducing no variations with respect to the formal topology.

According to the definition of AT, an AT instance $\mathscr{A}_1$ behaviorally conforms to another AT instance $\mathscr{A}_2$ if both exhibit the same observable behavior. The concept of behavioral conformity lends itself to be formalized by means of a behavioral equivalence. This should be able to abstract from internal actions, as they play no role in behavioral conformity. The equivalence should also be a congruence with respect to static operators, so as to ease the derivation of AT-level behavioral conformity from AET-level behavioral conformity. Finally, the equivalence should be not too coarse, in order to preserve many properties of interest. A natural candidate turns out to be weak bisimulation equivalence $\approx_B$ (see Sect. 1.4.8).

The properties mentioned above imply that the cost of the AT-level behavioral conformity check is linear in the number of AETs, instead of being exponential in the number of AEIs. Since an actual AET and the corresponding formal AET can give different names to related interactions, during the check it is necessary to find suitable relabeling functions. In contrast, internal actions are simply hidden.

Definition 4.4. Let $\mathscr{C}_1, \mathscr{C}_2$ be two AETs with:

- $\mathscr{D}_1, \mathscr{D}_2$ being the sets of their formal data parameters
- $\mathscr{E}_1, \mathscr{E}_2$ being the sequences of their process algebraic equations

- $\mathcal{N}_1, \mathcal{N}_2$ be the sets of their internal actions
- $\mathcal{I}_1, \mathcal{I}_2$ be the sets of their interactions

Assume that parameters in $\mathcal{D}_1, \mathcal{D}_2$ are consistent by number, order, and type and that interactions in $\mathcal{I}_1, \mathcal{I}_2$ are consistent by number, order, and qualifiers. We say that $\mathscr{C}_1$ behaviorally conforms to $\mathscr{C}_2$ iff there exist two injective relabeling functions φ_1, φ_2 for $\mathcal{I}_1, \mathcal{I}_2$, respectively, which have the same codomain and are qualifier-consistent, such that for all syntactical substitutions σ of $\mathcal{D}_1, \mathcal{D}_2$:

$$(\mathscr{C}_1\,\sigma)\,/\,\mathcal{N}_1\,[\varphi_1] \approx_B (\mathscr{C}_2\,\sigma)\,/\,\mathcal{N}_2\,[\varphi_2]$$

Definition 4.5. Let $\mathscr{A}_1, \mathscr{A}_2$ be two AT instances. We say that $\mathscr{A}_1$ (strictly) behaviorally conforms to $\mathscr{A}_2$ iff:

- Their actual data parameters are consistent by number, order, and type (and value)
- Their AETs are consistent by number, order, and behavioral conformity
- Their AEIs are consistent by number, order, and type and have actual data parameters consistent by number, order, and type (and value)
- Their architectural interactions are consistent by number, order, qualifiers, and AEI membership
- Their attachments are consistent by number, order, and qualifiers and AEI membership of the involved local interactions

Proposition 4.1. *Let $\mathscr{A}_1, \mathscr{A}_2$ be two AT instances with:*

- $\mathcal{N}_1, \mathcal{N}_2$ *being the sets of internal actions of their AEIs*
- $\mathcal{I}_1, \mathcal{I}_2$ *being the sets of interactions of their AEIs*

Whenever $\mathscr{A}_1$ strictly behaviorally conforms to $\mathscr{A}_2$, then there exist two relabeling functions φ_1, φ_2 for $\mathcal{I}_1, \mathcal{I}_2$, which are injective at least on local interactions, have the same codomain, and are qualifier-consistent, such that:

$$[\![\mathscr{A}_1]\!]_{bbm}\,/\,\mathcal{N}_1\,[\varphi_1] \approx_B [\![\mathscr{A}_2]\!]_{bbm}\,/\,\mathcal{N}_2\,[\varphi_2]$$

Example 4.7. Let us consider a variant of the pipe–filter system of Sect. 4.5 in which filters can fail and be subsequently repaired. This can be obtained through the following invocation of AT Pipe_Filter, in which the AET Filter_Type is replaced by the new AET Faulty_Filter_Type passed as actual parameter:

```
Pipe_Filter(@      /* reuse default values of data parameters */
            Faulty_Filter_Type;
            Pipe_Type @
            F_0 : Faulty_Filter_Type(pf_buffer_size);
            P   : Pipe_Type();
            F_1 : Faulty_Filter_Type(pf_buffer_size);
            F_2 : Faulty_Filter_Type(pf_buffer_size);
            F_3 : Faulty_Filter_Type(pf_buffer_size) @
            @ @ @ /* reuse rest of formal topology */
```

```
@ @ @ /* no behavioral modifications */
)       /* reuse names of actual arch. interacts */
```

Suppose that the faulty filter AET is defined as follows:

```
ARCHI_ELEM_TYPE Faulty_Filter_Type(const integer buffer_size)

 BEHAVIOR
  Faulty_Filter(integer(0..buffer_size) item_num := 0;
                void) =
   choice
   {
    cond(item_num < buffer_size) ->
     input_item . transform_item . Faulty_Filter(item_num + 1),
    cond(item_num > 0) ->
     output_item . Faulty_Filter(item_num - 1),
    fail . repair . Faulty_Filter(item_num)
   }

 INPUT_INTERACTIONS  SYNC UNI input_item
 OUTPUT_INTERACTIONS SYNC UNI output_item
```

As can be noted, there are two more internal actions, which are fail and repair.

The question now arises as to whether the architectural invocation generates a legal instance of the AT Pipe_Filter. The answer is positive because, observed that there are no topological variations, the AT instance originated by the architectural invocation strictly behaviorally conforms to the AT instance originated by the AT definition.

In fact, besides having the same data parameters and consistent AEIs, architectural interactions, and attachments, the two AT instances have behaviorally conformant AETs. Apart from the pipe AET, which is the same in both AT instances, it turns out that Faulty_Filter_Type and Filter_Type have the same data parameters and interactions. Moreover, $\approx_B$ relates the process term Faulty_Filter(0)/{transform_item,fail,repair} to process term Filter(0)/{transform_item} for all values assigned to buffer_size. Using the identical relabeling function for interactions is enough in this case.

4.6.4 Exogenous Variations

We finally examine the case of an architectural invocation that, besides possibly passing actual AETs syntactically different from the corresponding formal AETs, introduces topological variations. Here, we consider the addition of AEIs obtained by attaching some of them to the topological frontier of the invoked AT, which is the set of its architectural interactions. This is called an exogenous variation.

Syntactically, an exogenous variation is expressed within the actual topology by means of keyword EXO followed by four parameters:

- A set of additional AEIs, which must be instances of the actual AETs
- A set of replacements of some of the actual architectural interactions with new architectural interactions belonging to the additional AEIs
- A set of additional attachments involving all additional AEIs and all replaced actual architectural interactions, which thus become local
- Possible nested exogenous variations

The resulting AT instance topologically conforms to the invoked AT if, with respect to a portion of the formal topology of the invoked AT, the addendum is complete and contains no new kinds of attachment.

Definition 4.6. An exogenous variation (strictly) topologically conforms to the formal topology of the invoked AT iff there exists an injective function *corr* defined from the set of additional AEIs to the set of actual AEIs such that:

- C and $corr(C)$ have the same type (and the same actual data parameter values)
- For all interactions a of an arbitrary additional AEI C:

  - $C.a$ is local (resp. architectural) iff $corr(C).a$ is local (resp. architectural)
  - There is an additional AEI C' with an additional attachment from $C.a$ to $C'.a'$ (resp. from $C'.a'$ to $C.a$) iff there is an attachment from $corr(C).a$ to $corr(C').a'$ (resp. from $corr(C').a'$ to $corr(C).a$)
  - There is an additional attachment from $C.a$ to the replaced architectural interaction $K.b$ (resp. from $K.b$ to $C.a$) iff there is an actual AEI K' of the same type as K with an attachment from $corr(C).a$ to $K'.b$ (resp. from $K'.b$ to $corr(C).a$)

Example 4.8. Let us extend the pipe–filter system of Sect. 4.5. Its topological frontier is composed of the architectural input interaction F_0.input_item and the architectural output interactions F_1.output_item, F_2.output_item, and F_3.output_item. An exogenous variation at F_0.input_item must replicate the defined topology by viewing F_0 as a downstream filter. Similarly, an exogenous variation at F_1.output_item, F_2.output_item, or F_3.output_item must replicate the defined topology by viewing F_1, F_2, or F_3, respectively, as an upstream filter.

Here is an architectural invocation producing an exogenous variation taking place at F_2.output_item, where an additional pipe P_1 has the already existing AEI F_2 as upstream filter and the new AEIs F_4, F_5, and F_6 as downstream filters:

```
Pipe_Filter(@        /* reuse default values of data params */
            @        /* reuse formal AETs */
            @ @ @    /* reuse formal AEIs, ar. ints, and atts */
            EXO(P_1 : Pipe_Type();
                F_4 : Filter_Type(pf_buffer_size);
                F_5 : Filter_Type(pf_buffer_size);
                F_6 : Filter_Type(pf_buffer_size) @
```

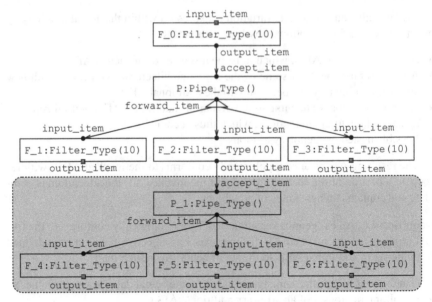

Fig. 4.8 Enriched flow graph of an exogenous variation of the pipe–filter system

```
                REPLACE F_2.output_item WITH F_4.output_item,
                                             F_5.output_item,
                                             F_6.output_item @
                FROM F_2.output_item  TO P_1.accept_item;
                FROM P_1.forward_item TO F_4.input_item;
                FROM P_1.forward_item TO F_5.input_item;
                FROM P_1.forward_item TO F_6.input_item @
                ) @ /* no nested exogenous variations */
        @ @ @   /* no behavioral modifications */
        )       /* reuse names of actual arch. inters */
```

which is graphically illustrated in Fig. 4.8. In this case, function *corr* exists and
maps P_1 to P, F_4 to F_1, F_5 to F_2, and F_6 to F_3.

4.6.5 Endogenous Variations

A different kind of topological variation is the one that takes place inside the topological frontier. We call it an endogenous variation when it changes the number
of AEIs of certain types in certain positions of the topology, without altering the
number of attachments in which local and-/or-interactions are involved.

Syntactically, an endogenous variation is expressed through data parameters of
the AT, each representing the variable number of AEIs of one of the involved types,
together with an indexing mechanism based on the FOR_ALL construct. This can

be used in the architectural topology section of the AT definition for the concise declaration of arbitrarily many AEIs of the same type, of their architectural interactions, and of the attachments involving them.

Unlike exogenous variations, all endogenous variations conform to the formal topology by construction. Moreover, they permit new kinds of attachment with respect to the formal topology, which may be created when varying the number of AEIs of some of the involved types from one to more than one.

Example 4.9. Let us consider a ring of pipe–filter systems, each identical to that of Sect. 4.5. Every pipe–filter system in the ring waits for items from the previous system in the ring, processes them, and then sends them to the next system in the ring. We assume there is an initial component accepting items from the outside and returning them after they have performed an entire traversal of the ring.

When modeling the ring, it is desirable to allow for a variable number of pipe–filter systems. For this reason, the architectural description header includes such a number as a formal data parameter:

```
ARCHI_TYPE Pipe_Filter_R(const integer pfr_system_num  :=  3,
                         const integer pfr_buffer_size := 10)
```

The initial component AET is defined as follows, where in the first state it waits for new items coming from the outside or old items coming from the final pipe–filter system in the ring, while in the second state it sends a new item to the initial pipe–filter system in the ring if the ring has not saturated:

```
ARCHI_ELEM_TYPE Init_Comp_Type(void)

 BEHAVIOR
   Init_Comp_In(void; void) =
    choice
    {
      accept_item . Init_Comp_New(),
      receive_item . return_item . Init_Comp_In()
    };
   Init_Comp_New(void; void) =
    choice
    {
      send_item . Init_Comp_In(),
      receive_item . return_item . Init_Comp_New()
    }

   INPUT_INTERACTIONS  SYNC UNI accept_item; receive_item
   OUTPUT_INTERACTIONS SYNC UNI return_item; send_item
```

The pipe–filter system AET is defined as follows by means of an invocation of the pipe–filter AT:

```
ARCHI_ELEM_TYPE PF_System_Type(const integer buffer_size)

 BEHAVIOR
```

```
PF_System(void; void) =
  Pipe_Filter(buffer_size @
                @        /* reuse formal AETs */
                @ @ @ @ /* reuse formal topology */
                @ @ @    /* no behavioral modifications */
              UNIFY F_0.input_item  WITH receive_item;
              UNIFY F_1.output_item,
                    F_2.output_item,
                    F_3.output_item WITH send_item)

  INPUT_INTERACTIONS  SYNC UNI receive_item
  OUTPUT_INTERACTIONS SYNC UNI send_item
```

The architectural topology section is parameterized with respect to the value of pfr_system_num and is concisely expressed thanks to the FOR_ALL construct already encountered in Example 4.6:

```
ARCHI_ELEM_INSTANCES
  IC : Init_Comp_Type();
  FOR_ALL 1 <= j <= pfr_system_num
  PFS[j] : PF_System_Type(pfr_buffer_size)

ARCHI_INTERACTIONS
  IC.accept_item; IC.return_item

ARCHI_ATTACHMENTS
  FROM IC.send_item TO PFS[1].receive_item;
  FOR_ALL 1 <= j <= pfr_system_num - 1
  FROM PFS[j].send_item TO PFS[j + 1].receive_item;
  FROM PFS[pfr_system_num].send_item TO IC.receive_item
```

Figure 4.9 shows Pipe_Filter_R(4, 10 @ @ @ @ @ @ @ @ @), which is the endogenous variation obtained when changing the number of pipe–filter systems from the default value 3 to 4. Note that a new kind of attachment is created when passing from one pipe–filter system to several pipe–filter systems, which is the attachment from a send_item interaction of a PF_System_Type instance to a receive_item interaction of another PF_System_Type instance.

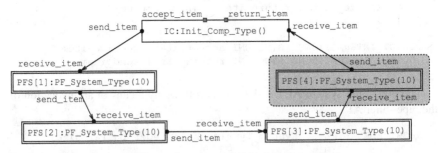

Fig. 4.9 Enriched flow graph of an endogenous variation of the pipe–filter ring

4.6.6 Multiplicity Variations

Another kind of topological variation taking place inside the topological frontier is the one that changes the number of AEIs of certain types that are attached to certain local and-/or-interactions. This is called a multiplicity variation.

Syntactically, a multiplicity variation is expressed in the same way as an endogenous variation; i.e., through data parameters of the AT representing the variable numbers of involved AEIs and an indexing mechanism based on the FOR_ALL construct to be used in the architectural topology section of the AT definition.

With respect to endogenous variations, multiplicity variations cannot create new kinds of attachment when changing the number of involved AEIs. Moreover, a multiplicity variation is admissible iff the involved local and-/or-interactions support variability. We say that a local and-/or-interaction of an AEI supports variability if the AEI is not attached with uni-interactions to any of the AEIs attached to the considered local and-/or-interaction. If this were not the case, when increasing the number of AEIs attached to the local and-/or-interaction, the new AEIs could not be attached to the uni-interactions.

Example 4.10. Let us consider once more the pipe–filter system of Sect. 4.5. When modeling this system, it is desirable to allow for a variable number of downstream filters. This can be achieved by introducing topological variability at the or-interaction forward_item of the pipe.

Here is the new architectural description header:

```
ARCHI_TYPE OV_Pipe_Filter(const integer ovpf_downstr_num := 3,
                          const integer ovpf_buffer_size := 10)
```

Observed that the definitions of the filter AET and of the pipe AET do not change, the architectural topology section is expressed as follows:

```
ARCHI_ELEM_INSTANCES
  F[0] : Filter_Type(ovpf_buffer_size);
  P    : Pipe_Type();
  FOR_ALL 1 <= j <= ovpf_downstr_num
   F[j] : Filter_Type(ovpf_buffer_size)

ARCHI_INTERACTIONS
  F[0].input_item;
  FOR_ALL 1 <= j <= ovpf_downstr_num
   F[j].output_item

ARCHI_ATTACHMENTS
  FROM F[0].output_item TO P.accept_item;
  FOR_ALL 1 <= j <= ovpf_downstr_num
   FROM P.forward_item TO F[j].input_item
```

It is worth noting that the FOR_ALL construct could have been exploited in Sect. 4.5 already for getting a more concise description of the topology of the original pipe–filter system.

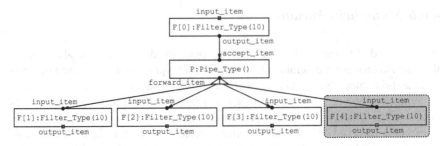

Fig. 4.10 Enriched flow graph of a multiplicity variation of the pipe–filter system

Figure 4.10 shows `OV_Pipe_Filter(4, 10 @ @ @ @ @ @ @ @ @)`, which is the multiplicity variation obtained when changing the number of down-stream filters from the default value 3 to 4.

4.7 Comparisons

The design choices and the guidelines leading to the development of the syntax and of the semantics for the process algebraic architectural description language presented in this chapter are taken from [41, 7, 38]. In order to highlight the features of PADL with respect to the related literature, in this section we perform a comparison with process algebra (Sect. 4.7.1), parallel composition operators (Sect. 4.7.2), and other software architecture description languages (Sect. 4.7.3).

4.7.1 Comparison with Process Algebra

PADL has been specifically structured on the basis of a set of guidelines aimed at improving usability with respect to process algebra. Perhaps the most important guideline is the one prescribing the presence of two distinct sections for behavior description and topology description. This significantly eases the task of the designer, as the two descriptions are no longer intertwinedly encoded through the parallel composition operator, but are sharply separated.

Another remarkable difference with respect to process algebra is that in PADL the intended use of every action is made clear via a set of explicit qualifiers, so that in particular the actions modeling interaction activities have no longer to be inferred from the occurrences of the parallel composition operator. This is then complemented by the fact that communicating interactions have to be explicitly related by means of attachments, thus removing any constraint on synchronizing action names. As a consequence of the interface elicitation and of the explicit communication scheme, error-prone situations can be easily detected via static checks.

Among the various behavioral operators offered by process algebra, PADL makes available to the designer only dynamic operators as they are simpler to use, whereas static operators are implicitly employed in the behavioral modification section and transparently exploited in the translation semantics. The textual notation is then accompanied by a graphical notation based on enriched flow graphs. We also mention the higher degree of specification reuse achieved at the component level through the concept of AET and at the system level through the concept of AT.

4.7.2 Comparison with Parallel Composition Operators

Depending on the qualifiers associated with the interactions, the communication mechanism of PADL implements one-to-one or inclusive/selective one-to-many connections where each of the involved parties can communicate in synchronous, semi-synchronous, or asynchronous mode. Due to its simplicity and its expressiveness, this mechanism turns out to be more adequate for modeling purposes than typical parallel composition operators.

In fact, the parallel composition operator of CCS [154] supports only two-way synchronizations, where the two synchronizing actions are required to have complementary names. The use of the restriction operator is then necessary to enforce synchronization, as having complementary names is not enough for two actions to synchronize. The parallel composition operator of CSP [119] supports multiway synchronizations, but synchronizing actions are required to have the same name. In order to establish which actions must synchronize, explicit synchronization sets have then to be associated with the occurrences of the parallel composition operator, whose contents depend on the operator associativity and the order of the subterms composed in parallel. The parallel composition operator of ACP [22] overcomes the previously mentioned drawbacks by means of the definition of a communication function over the set of action names. However, the use of the restriction operator is again necessary to enforce synchronization.

In [94], a more friendly parallel composition operator has been proposed, which is n-ary instead of binary and requires the explicit declaration of interfaces. The operator is then extended in order to deal with m-among-n synchronizations $(2 \leq m \leq n)$, which take place when n process terms synchronize m by m on the same action. It is worth noting that an inclusive one-to-many communication coincides with an n-among-n synchronization, whereas a selective one-to-many communication coincides with a 2-among-n synchronization.

In [103], an alternative approach has been taken, which requires the specification of the sets of actions that can synchronize with each other and, within each set, the indication of those groups of actions that result in complete synchronizations. Although more flexible, this approach cannot enforce m-among-n synchronizations, because it assumes that complete synchronizations are closed with respect to set inclusion and adopts a rule that favors the largest complete synchronizations.

4.7.3 Comparison with Other Software Architecture Languages

We conclude by comparing PADL with other process algebraic architectural description languages that have appeared in the literature, among which we mention Wright [18, 17], Darwin/FSP [141, 142], LEDA [61], and π-ADL [166]. First of all, PADL deals only with static architectures, whereas the other languages can manage dynamic architectures – in which architectural elements can be created/destroyed and attachments can be reconfigured at run time – and some of them also mobile architectures – in which architectural elements can migrate at run time. The choice of restricting PADL to static architectures is motivated by the need of developing effective analysis techniques like those of the next three chapters, so as to achieve an acceptable balance between expressiveness and analyzability.

We then observe that the textual notation and the translation semantics for PADL are inspired by Wright. However, there is a couple of differences that are worth mentioning. First, Wright distinguishes between components and connectors, while in PADL there are just architectural elements, each of which can be interpreted as a component or a connector depending on the specific system. This avoids the presence of trivial connectors in the architectural descriptions. Second, in Wright the representation of each component/connector is accompanied by the specification of its ports/roles, whereas in PADL the interface of each architectural element is simply expressed through actions. Since ports/roles can be retrieved by applying the hiding operator to the behavior of the related components/connectors, avoiding their specification simplifies the architectural descriptions.

Furthermore, PADL introduces a number of new features with respect to the mentioned process algebraic architectural description languages. One of them is the adoption of specific qualifiers for eliciting interaction synchronicity and multiplicity and keywords for declaring dependences between interactions. Then, we have the possibility of expressing behavioral modifications, which is useful for conducting certain kinds of analysis. Another important characteristic is the notion of AT, which opens the way to the formal description of families of software systems and provides support for hierarchical modeling via the architectural invocation mechanism. This approximation of the notion of architectural style limits the variability within any system family to internal behavioral variations respecting behavioral conformity and to a restricted number of topological variations. Once again, the reason for these limitations is related to analyzability.

The process algebraic formalization of architectural styles based on ATs is quite different from other approaches. For instance, in [1] a formal framework has been provided for precisely defining architectural styles and analyzing within and between different architectural styles. This is accomplished by means of a small set of mappings from the syntactic domain of architectural descriptions to the semantic domain of architectural meanings, following the standard denotational approach developed for programming languages. As another example, in [81] a syntactic theory of software architecture has been presented that is based on set theory, regular expressions, and context-free grammars. Architectural styles have been categorized through the typing of the nodes and of the connections in the diagrammatic syntax, which is accompanied by a pattern matching mechanism. A different direction has been taken in [159], where architectural styles have been represented as logical theories and a method has been introduced for the stepwise refinement of an abstract architecture into a relatively correct lower level architecture. As a final example, in [138] architectural styles have been formalized as context-free graph grammars, which produce all the architectures topologically conforming to the various styles. In this setting, software architectures have to be described as graphs whose nodes represent computational entities and whose edges represent communication links, then a coordinator has to be expressed in terms of conditional graph rewriting in order to manage the creation and the removal of entities and links.

For the sake of completeness, we point out that many architectural description languages have been proposed that are not process algebraic. We have for instance Aesop [95], UniCon [183], Rapide [140], SADL [159], C2 [148], and Acme [97], as well as approaches based on Z [1], CHAM [123], UML [149], and Java [16]. Comparing PADL – or the class of process algebraic architectural description languages – with each of these different architectural description languages is outside the scope of this chapter. We rather refer the interested reader to survey papers like [150].

Chapter 5
Component-Oriented Functional Verification

Abstract Enhancing the usability of process algebra on the modeling side must be accompanied by an analogous effort on the verification side. At the architectural design level, it is important to detect mismatches stemming from the inappropriate assembly of several software units, which are correct when considered in isolation. In this chapter, we present a topological reduction process based on behavioral equivalences called MISMDET, which exploits their congruence properties for efficiency reasons and their modal logic characterizations for diagnostic purposes. It investigates the absence of architectural mismatches in a component-oriented fashion by examining star-shaped and cycle-shaped topological portions. The application of the two techniques corresponding to the two topological formats, called architectural compatibility check and architectural interoperability check, is exemplified through the verification of a compressing proxy system and of a cruise control system.

5.1 MISMDET: Architecture-Level Mismatch Detection

As argued at the end of the previous chapter, for modeling purposes PADL is much easier to use than process algebra. As far as the verification of functional properties is concerned, PADL inherits all the analysis techniques applicable to process algebraic descriptions, like equivalence checking [71] and model checking [67]. However, what we need to verify at the software architecture level of design is the absence of mismatches stemming from the inappropriate assembly of several software units, which are correct when considered in isolation. If these architectural mismatches are not revealed in the early design stages, then a lack of coordination among architectural elements will emerge at run time [96].

For efficiency reasons, the detection of architectural mismatches should proceed in a component-oriented manner. In other words, the absence of architectural mismatches within the description of a software system should be inferred from the properties of its individual architectural elements. Whenever an architectural mismatch is encountered, diagnostic information should be produced in order to enable

A. Aldini et al., *A Process Algebraic Approach to Software Architecture Design*,
DOI 10.1007/978-1-84800-223-4_5, © Springer-Verlag London Limited 2010

the identification of the architectural elements responsible for well-formedness violations. In the case of component-based software systems, this should then lead to the modification of the design of in-house components or to the synthesis of models of wrappers/adaptors for off-the-shelf components [198, 53, 190].

In this chapter, we tackle the problem introduced above by means of a topological reduction process called MISMDET. Given an architectural description, MISMDET relies on an architectural compatibility check for star-shaped portions of the topology and on an architectural interoperability check for cycle-shaped portions of the topology, both of which are based on behavioral equivalences (see Chap. 1). Each portion of the topology passing the related check is replaced by a single architectural element whose observable behavior is equivalent to that of the original portion, then the application of the two checks continues on the reduced topology.

The various basic portions of the topology can be considered in isolation – and hence the generation of the entire state space underlying the architectural description can be avoided – provided that the employed behavioral equivalence is a congruence with respect to static operators. Whenever a check is not passed, the modal logic characterization of the employed behavioral equivalence can be exploited in order to derive diagnostic information. As can be noted, the activity of architectural mismatch detection conducted with MISMDET makes use of process algebraic machinery only.

An important characteristic of MISMDET is scalability. In fact, under certain conditions, the absence of architectural mismatches verified in basic portions of the topology extends to the whole topology and also to the entire architectural type.

This chapter is organized as follows. In Sect. 5.2, we outline the class of properties we are interested in verifying, together with the detection strategy on which MISMDET is based. In Sect. 5.3, we introduce the architectural compatibility check for star-shaped topologies, which is exemplified through the verification of a compressing proxy system. In Sect. 5.4, we present the architectural interoperability check for cycle-shaped topologies, which is exemplified through the verification of a cruise control system. In Sects. 5.5 and 5.6, we generalize the previous process algebraic techniques for mismatch detection to arbitrary topologies and to architectural types, respectively. Finally, in Sect. 5.7 we compare the considered equivalence-checking-based topological reduction process with the related literature.

5.2 Class of Properties and Detection Strategy

Properties related to the absence of architectural mismatches can be formalized in terms of the possibility/necessity of executing certain local interactions in a certain order. The reason is that internal actions and architectural interactions are not involved in communications; hence, architectural mismatches can be generated only by the wrong interplay of local interactions. An action-based modal or temporal logic is thus a good candidate for specifying such properties. We restrict ourselves to logical formulas in which negation does not occur, as this simplifies the derivation of the validity of a property for an architectural description – where certain actions may not be hidden – from a topologically reduced variant of that description – where the same actions may be hidden.

MISMDET focuses on the class Ψ of properties $\mathscr{P}$ expressible in terms of the possibility/necessity of executing certain local interactions in a certain order, for which there exist behavioral equivalences $\approx_{\mathscr{P}}$ satisfying the following constraints:

- $\approx_{\mathscr{P}}$ must preserve $\mathscr{P}$ – i.e., it cannot relate two models such that one of them enjoys $\mathscr{P}$ whereas the other one does not – which is fundamental for enabling the topological reduction process.
- $\approx_{\mathscr{P}}$ must be a congruence with respect to static operators, which allows the topological reduction process to be applied to single portions of the topology of an architectural description without affecting the possible validity of $\mathscr{P}$.
- $\approx_{\mathscr{P}}$ must be weak, which permits to get rid of unimportant activities, especially the ones that are not local interactions.
- $\approx_{\mathscr{P}}$ must have a modal logic characterization, which is necessary for producing diagnostic information in case of failure of the topological reduction process.

A typical example of property related to architectural well-formedness is deadlock freedom. It is included in Ψ because it is preserved by weak bisimulation equivalence $\approx_B$, which is congruent with respect to static operators and characterized by weak Hennessy–Milner logic (see Sect. 1.4.8). Since any negation-free formula of weak Hennessy–Milner logic is preserved by $\approx_B$, the considered class Ψ also includes all properties expressible through such formulas.

Given an architectural description, MISMDET works on an abstract variant of its enriched flow graph, where vertices correspond to AEIs and two vertices are linked by an edge iff attachments have been declared among the interactions of their corresponding AEIs. In other words, MISMDET abstracts from the direction and the number of the attachments between any two AEIs. The resulting graph is an arbitrary combination of possibly intersecting stars and cycles, which are thus viewed as basic topological formats. This graph is assumed to be strongly connected.

The detection strategy of MISMDET consists of applying specific checks locally to all stars/cycles of AEIs occurring in the abstract graph. Given a property $\mathscr{P} \in \Psi$, each check verifies whether the star/cycle contains an AEI that is $\approx_{\mathscr{P}}$-equivalent to the whole star/cycle, in which case the star/cycle can be replaced by that AEI. MISMDET successfully terminates when the whole graph has been reduced to a single $\approx_{\mathscr{P}}$-equivalent AEI, as at that point it is sufficient to verify whether that AEI satisfies $\mathscr{P}$ or not. In case of failure, the mentioned checks provide diagnostic information through a formula of the modal logic characterizing $\approx_{\mathscr{P}}$, which is useful to pinpoint AEIs responsible for possible mismatches within a single star/cycle.

Before applying the check to a star/cycle given by the set of AEIs $\{C_1, \ldots, C_n\}$, for each AEI C_j in the set we have to hide all of its internal actions and architectural interactions as well as all of its local interactions that are not attached to $\{C_1, \ldots, C_n\}$. The reason is that these actions cannot result in mismatches within the star/cycle, but may hamper the topological reduction process if left visible. For each AEI C_j in the set we also have to exclude all of its additional implicit AEIs that are not attached to $\{C_1, \ldots, C_n\}$, as those additional implicit AEIs are necessary only in the presence of the AEIs not in $\{C_1, \ldots, C_n\}$ to which they are attached.

Therefore, the only actions that remain observable are those in $\mathscr{L}\mathscr{I}_{C_j;C_1,\ldots,C_n}$ (see beginning of Sect. 4.4.2) and those in $\mathscr{O}\mathscr{A}\mathscr{L}\mathscr{I}_{C_j}$. The latter set contains the originally asynchronous local interactions of C_j together with the local interactions of the related additional implicit AEIs to which they have been re-attached, including the exceptions that may be raised by the local input semi-synchronous interactions in the set corresponding to local input asynchronous interactions. We point out that $\mathscr{O}\mathscr{A}\mathscr{L}\mathscr{I}_{C_j}$ is disjoint from $\mathscr{L}\mathscr{I}_{C_j}$, as it essentially comprises the action names forming the composite names occurring in the synchronization sets of Definition 4.1.

In order to set the visibility of each action according to the needs of MISMDET, we introduce a partially closed variant of the interacting semantics of Definition 4.2. Since in many cases we also have to hide all the actions in $\mathscr{O}\mathscr{A}\mathscr{L}\mathscr{I}_{C_j}$, we introduce a totally closed variant too. Both variants are parameterized with respect to a set of AEIs $\{C_1'', \ldots, C_{n''}''\}$, $n'' \in \mathbb{N}$, determining the additional implicit AEIs to be included.

Definition 5.1. Let $\mathscr{C}$ be an AET with $m \in \mathbb{N}_{\geq 0}$ formal data parameters $fp_1, \ldots, fp_m$ and behavior given by a sequence $\mathscr{E}$ of process algebraic equations. Let $C_j \in \{C_1, \ldots, C_n\}$ be an AEI of type $\mathscr{C}$ with $m \in \mathbb{N}_{\geq 0}$ actual data parameters $ap_1, \ldots, ap_m$ consistent by order and type with the formal data parameters. The interacting semantics of C_j with respect to $\{C_1, \ldots, C_n\}$ without buffers for its originally asynchronous local interactions is defined as follows:

$$\llbracket C_j \rrbracket^{\text{wob}}_{C_1,\ldots,C_n} = \text{or-rewrite}_\emptyset(C_j.\mathscr{E}\{ap_i \hookrightarrow fp_i \mid 1 \leq i \leq m\})\,[\varphi_{C_j,\text{async}}]\,[\varphi_{C_j;C_1,\ldots,C_n}]$$

We denote by $\llbracket C_j \rrbracket^{\#C_1'',\ldots,C_{n''}''}_{C_1,\ldots,C_n}$ the variant of $\llbracket C_j \rrbracket^{\text{wob}}_{C_1,\ldots,C_n}$ including the buffers for the originally asynchronous local interactions of C_j attached to $\{C_1'', \ldots, C_{n''}''\}$.

Definition 5.2. The partially closed interacting semantics of $C_j \in \{C_1, \ldots, C_n\}$ with respect to $\{C_1, \ldots, C_n\}$ including its buffers attached to $\{C_1'', \ldots, C_{n''}''\}$ is defined as:

$$\llbracket C_j \rrbracket^{\text{pc};\#C_1'',\ldots,C_{n''}''}_{C_1,\ldots,C_n} = \llbracket C_j \rrbracket^{\#C_1'',\ldots,C_{n''}''}_{C_1,\ldots,C_n} / (Name - \mathscr{V}_{C_j;C_1,\ldots,C_n})$$

with $\mathscr{V}_{C_j;C_1,\ldots,C_n} = \varphi_{C_j;C_1,\ldots,C_n}(\mathscr{L}\mathscr{I}_{C_j;C_1,\ldots,C_n}) \cup \varphi_{C_j,\text{async}}(\mathscr{O}\mathscr{A}\mathscr{L}\mathscr{I}_{C_j})$ and we write $\llbracket C_j \rrbracket^{\text{pc};\text{wob}}_{C_1,\ldots,C_n}$ if $n'' = 0$. The partially closed interacting semantics of $\{C_1', \ldots, C_{n'}'\} \subseteq \{C_1, \ldots, C_n\}$ with respect to $\{C_1, \ldots, C_n\}$ including their buffers attached to $\{C_1'', \ldots, C_{n''}''\}$ is defined as follows:

$$\begin{aligned}
\llbracket C_1', \ldots, C_{n'}' \rrbracket^{\text{pc};\#C_1'',\ldots,C_{n''}''}_{C_1,\ldots,C_n} = {} & \llbracket C_1' \rrbracket^{\text{pc};\#C_1'',\ldots,C_{n''}''}_{C_1,\ldots,C_n} \,\|_{\mathscr{S}(C_1',C_2';C_1,\ldots,C_n)} \\
& \llbracket C_2' \rrbracket^{\text{pc};\#C_1'',\ldots,C_{n''}''}_{C_1,\ldots,C_n} \,\|_{\mathscr{S}(C_1',C_3';C_1,\ldots,C_n)\cup\mathscr{S}(C_2',C_3';C_1,\ldots,C_n)} \\
& \cdots \,\|_{\bigcup_{i=1}^{n'-1}\mathscr{S}(C_i',C_{n'}';C_1,\ldots,C_n)} \llbracket C_{n'}' \rrbracket^{\text{pc};\#C_1'',\ldots,C_{n''}''}_{C_1,\ldots,C_n}
\end{aligned}$$

where the synchronization sets are built as in Definition 4.2.

Definition 5.3. The totally closed interacting semantics of $C_j \in \{C_1,\ldots,C_n\}$ with respect to $\{C_1,\ldots,C_n\}$ including its buffers attached to $\{C_1'',\ldots,C_{n''}''\}$ is defined as:

$$[\![C_j]\!]_{C_1,\ldots,C_n}^{\mathrm{tc};\#C_1'',\ldots,C_{n''}''} = [\![C_j]\!]_{C_1,\ldots,C_n}^{\mathrm{pc};\#C_1'',\ldots,C_{n''}''} / \varphi_{C_j,\mathrm{async}}(\mathscr{OALSI}_{C_j})$$

and we write $[\![C_j]\!]_{C_1,\ldots,C_n}^{\mathrm{tc};\mathrm{wob}}$ if $n'' = 0$. The totally closed interacting semantics of $\{C_1',\ldots,C_{n'}'\} \subseteq \{C_1,\ldots,C_n\}$ with respect to $\{C_1,\ldots,C_n\}$ including their buffers attached to $\{C_1'',\ldots,C_{n''}''\}$ is defined as follows:

$$
\begin{aligned}
[\![C_1',\ldots,C_{n'}']\!]_{C_1,\ldots,C_n}^{\mathrm{tc};\#C_1'',\ldots,C_{n''}''} &= [\![C_1']\!]_{C_1,\ldots,C_n}^{\mathrm{tc};\#C_1'',\ldots,C_{n''}''} \parallel_{\mathscr{S}(C_1',C_2';C_1,\ldots,C_n)} \\
&\quad [\![C_2']\!]_{C_1,\ldots,C_n}^{\mathrm{tc};\#C_1'',\ldots,C_{n''}''} \parallel_{\mathscr{S}(C_1',C_3';C_1,\ldots,C_n)\cup\mathscr{S}(C_2',C_3';C_1,\ldots,C_n)} \\
&\quad \cdots \parallel_{\bigcup_{i=1}^{n'-1}\mathscr{S}(C_i',C_{n'}';C_1,\ldots,C_n)} [\![C_{n'}']\!]_{C_1,\ldots,C_n}^{\mathrm{tc};\#C_1'',\ldots,C_{n''}''}
\end{aligned}
$$

where the synchronization sets are built as in Definition 4.2. The variant totally closed up to $\{C_1''',\ldots,C_{n'''}'''\} \subset \{C_1',\ldots,C_{n'}'\}$, i.e., in which $[\![C_j''']\!]_{C_1,\ldots,C_n}^{\mathrm{pc};\#C_1'',\ldots,C_{n''}''}$ is considered in place of $[\![C_j''']\!]_{C_1,\ldots,C_n}^{\mathrm{tc};\#C_1'',\ldots,C_{n''}''}$, is denoted by $[\![C_1',\ldots,C_{n'}']\!]_{C_1,\ldots,C_n}^{\mathrm{tc};\#C_1'',\ldots,C_{n''}'';C_1''',\ldots,C_{n'''}'''}$.

5.3 Architectural Compatibility of Star-Shaped Topologies

A star is a portion of the abstract enriched flow graph of an architectural description $\mathscr{A}$, which is not part of a cyclic subgraph. It is formed by a central AEI K and a border $\mathscr{B}_K = \{C_1,\ldots,C_n\}$ including all the AEIs attached to K. In the case of a star, MISMDET investigates the validity of a property $\mathscr{P} \in \Psi$ by analyzing the interplay between the central AEI K and each of the AEIs in the border, as there cannot be attachments among AEIs in the border. In order to achieve a correct coordination between K and $C_j \in \mathscr{B}_K$, the actual observable behavior of C_j should coincide with the observable behavior expected by K. In other words, the observable behavior of K should not be altered by the insertion of C_j into the border of the star.

Definition 5.4. Given an architectural description $\mathscr{A}$ and a property $\mathscr{P} \in \Psi$, let K be the central AEI of a star of $\mathscr{A}$, $\mathscr{B}_K = \{C_1,\ldots,C_n\}$ be the border of the star, C_j be an AEI in $\mathscr{B}_K$, H_{K,C_j} be the set of interactions of additional implicit AEIs of K that are attached to interactions of C_j, and E_{K,C_j} be the set of exceptions that may be raised by semi-synchronous interactions involved in attachments between K and C_j. We say that K is $\mathscr{P}$-compatible with C_j iff:

$$([\![K]\!]_{\mathscr{A}}^{\mathrm{pc};\#C_j} \parallel_{\mathscr{S}(K,C_j;\mathscr{A})} [\![C_j]\!]_{K,\mathscr{B}_K}^{\mathrm{tc};\#K}) / (H_{K,C_j} \cup E_{K,C_j}) \approx_{\mathscr{P}} [\![K]\!]_{\mathscr{A}}^{\mathrm{pc};\mathrm{wob}}$$

All possible originally asynchronous local interactions of C_j and all of its interactions possibly attached to AEIs outside the star have been hidden by taking the totally closed interacting semantics of C_j with respect to the AEIs inside the star. We also observe that $H_{K,C_j} \bigcup E_{K,C_j} = \emptyset$ whenever there are no nonsynchronous interactions involved in attachments inside the star, in which case all partially closed interacting semantics between $[\![K]\!]_{\mathscr{A}}^{pc;\#\mathscr{A}}$ and $[\![K]\!]_{\mathscr{A}}^{pc;wob}$ coincide with $[\![K]\!]_{\mathscr{A}}^{tc;wob}$.

Proposition 5.1. *Given an architectural description $\mathscr{A}$ and a property $\mathscr{P} \in \Psi$, let K be the central AEI of a star of $\mathscr{A}$, $\mathscr{B}_K = \{C_1, \ldots, C_n\}$ be the border of the star, and H_{K,C_j} and E_{K,C_j} be the same sets as Definition 5.4. Whenever K is $\mathscr{P}$-compatible with every $C_j \in \mathscr{B}_K$, then:*

$$[\![K, \mathscr{B}_K]\!]_{K,\mathscr{B}_K}^{tc;\#K,\mathscr{B}_K;K} \Big/ \bigcup_{j=1}^{n} (H_{K,C_j} \bigcup E_{K,C_j}) \approx_{\mathscr{P}} [\![K]\!]_{\mathscr{A}}^{pc;wob}$$

hence $[\![K, \mathscr{B}_K]\!]_{K,\mathscr{B}_K}^{tc;\#K,\mathscr{B}_K;K} / \bigcup_{j=1}^{n}(H_{K,C_j} \bigcup E_{K,C_j})$ satisfies $\mathscr{P}$ iff so does $[\![K]\!]_{\mathscr{A}}^{pc;wob}$.

Based on the sufficient condition established by the proposition above, in the case of a star the architectural compatibility check for a property $\mathscr{P} \in \Psi$ is applied to any pair of AEIs composed of the central AEI K and one of the AEIs in $\mathscr{B}_K$. If the check is passed by all such pairs of AEIs, then the whole star can be reduced to its central AEI K and the validity of $\mathscr{P}$ can be verified on this single AEI. In contrast, if the check is not passed with respect to some $C_g \in \mathscr{B}_K$, then this reveals a potential lack of coordination between K and C_g.

We observe that the cost of the compatibility-check-based verification of $\mathscr{P}$ grows linearly with the size of $\mathscr{B}_K$, while the cost of directly verifying the whole star against $\mathscr{P}$ grows exponentially with the size of $\{K\} \bigcup \mathscr{B}_K$.

5.3.1 Case Study: Compressing Proxy System

We now illustrate an application of the architectural compatibility check to the compressing proxy system examined in [124]. The purpose of this system is to improve the performance of a Unix-based web browser over a slow network by causing the HTTP server to compress data with the gzip program before sending them across the network. Since this system is the result of the combination of an HTTP server with the gzip program, it must be designed in such a way to ensure deadlock freedom.

The HTTP server is a series of filters strung together, which communicate through a function-call-based stream interface that allows an upstream filter to push data into a downstream filter. The gzip program is instead a Unix filter communicating through pipes. An important difference between the two software units is that the gzip program explicitly chooses when to get data, while the HTTP filters are forced to read when data are pushed to them. Moreover, the gzip program may attempt to output a portion of the compressed data before finishing getting all the input data, which may happen when its internal buffer becomes full.

The compressing proxy system must be assembled from the existing HTTP server and the gzip program without modifying them. The only solution is to implement a software adaptor between two consecutive filters of the HTTP server, which redirects to the gzip program data coming from the upstream filter and delivers to the downstream filter compressed data produced by the gzip program.

Let us model the system with PADL. Here is the architectural description header:

```
ARCHI_TYPE Compressing_Proxy(void)
```

As far as the HTTP server is concerned, it is enough to consider the upstream filter and the downstream filter between which data compression takes place via the gzip program; hence, the definition of the following two AETs:

```
ARCHI_ELEM_TYPE U_Filter_Type(void)

BEHAVIOR
 U_Filter(void; void) =
  write_data . U_Filter()

INPUT_INTERACTIONS   void
OUTPUT_INTERACTIONS SYNC UNI write_data

ARCHI_ELEM_TYPE D_Filter_Type(void)

BEHAVIOR
 D_Filter(void; void) =
  read_data . D_Filter()

INPUT_INTERACTIONS   SYNC UNI read_data
OUTPUT_INTERACTIONS void
```

The adaptor can be in one of the following states: waiting for data from the upstream filter, passing packets of data to be compressed to the gzip program, waiting for packets of compressed data from the gzip program, or sending compressed data to the downstream filter. Here is the definition of the adaptor AET:

```
ARCHI_ELEM_TYPE Adaptor_Type(void)

BEHAVIOR
 Adaptor_From_Filter(void; void) =
  receive_from_filter . put_to_gzip . Adaptor_To_Gzip();
 Adaptor_To_Gzip(void; void) =
  choice
  {
   put_to_gzip . Adaptor_To_Gzip(),
   put_eoi_gzip . get_from_gzip . Adaptor_From_Gzip()
  };
 Adaptor_From_Gzip(void; void) =
  choice
  {
   get_from_gzip . Adaptor_From_Gzip(),
   get_eoo_gzip . Adaptor_To_Filter()
  };
```

```
Adaptor_To_Filter(void; void) =
  send_to_filter . Adaptor_From_Filter()

INPUT_INTERACTIONS   SYNC UNI receive_from_filter;
                              get_from_gzip; get_eoo_gzip
OUTPUT_INTERACTIONS  SYNC UNI send_to_filter;
                              put_to_gzip; put_eoi_gzip
```

Then, we have the definition of the gzip AET, whose state changes upon receiving end-of-input messages and upon sending end-of-output messages:

```
ARCHI_ELEM_TYPE Gzip_Type(void)

BEHAVIOR
 Gzip(void; void) =
  get_data . Gzip_In();
 Gzip_In(void; void) =
  choice
  {
   get_data . Gzip_In(),
   get_eoi . compress . put_data . Gzip_Out(),
   saturate_buffer . compress . put_data . Gzip_Out()
  };
 Gzip_Out(void; void) =
  choice
  {
   put_data . Gzip_Out(),
   put_eoo . Gzip()
  }

INPUT_INTERACTIONS   SYNC UNI get_data; get_eoi
OUTPUT_INTERACTIONS  SYNC UNI put_data; put_eoo
```

Finally, we have the architectural topology section, which is graphically illustrated in Fig. 5.1:

```
ARCHI_ELEM_INSTANCES
 UF : U_Filter_Type();
 DF : D_Filter_Type();
 A  : Adaptor_Type();
 G  : Gzip_Type()

ARCHI_INTERACTIONS
 void

ARCHI_ATTACHMENTS
 FROM UF.write_data    TO A.receive_from_filter;
 FROM A.put_to_gzip    TO G.get_data;
 FROM A.put_eoi_gzip   TO G.get_eoi;
 FROM G.put_data       TO A.get_from_gzip;
 FROM G.put_eoo        TO A.get_eoo_gzip;
 FROM A.send_to_filter TO DF.read_data
```

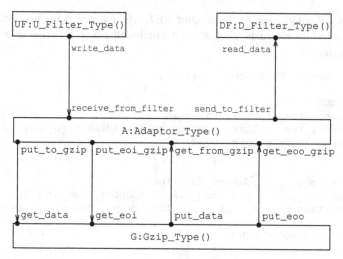

Fig. 5.1 Enriched flow graph of the compressing proxy system

Having formalized the architecture of the compressing proxy system with PADL, we can proceed with deadlock freedom analysis. First of all, we observe that the abstract variant of the enriched flow graph in Fig. 5.1 subsumes all the attachments between A and G with a single edge, so that its topology precisely coincides with a star whose central AEI is A. Based on the considerations of Sect. 5.2, we apply the architectural compatibility check by exploiting weak bisimulation equivalence $\approx_B$. Since there are no local nonsynchronous interactions, the check can be applied by taking the totally closed interacting semantics without buffers of the various AEIs.

Unfortunately, it turns out that A is not deadlock-freedom-compatible with G because $[\![A]\!]_{A,UF,DF,G}^{tc;wob} \parallel_{\mathscr{S}(A,G;A,UF,DF,G)} [\![G]\!]_{A,UF,DF,G}^{tc;wob} \not\approx_B [\![A]\!]_{A,UF,DF,G}^{tc;wob}$. In order to understand the origin of the potential architectural mismatch, we can exploit the following distinguishing formula of weak Hennessy–Milner logic generated when checking for weak bisimulation equivalence:

$$\langle\langle \texttt{UF.write\_data\#A.receive\_from\_filter} \rangle\rangle$$
$$\langle\langle \texttt{A.put\_to\_gzip\#G.get\_data} \rangle\rangle$$
$$\neg\langle\langle \texttt{A.put\_eoi\_gzip\#G.get\_eoi} \rangle\rangle \text{ true}$$

The formula above says that it may happen that the adaptor, after receiving some data from the upstream filter, starts sending data packets to the gzip program but is not able to send the end-of-input message. Since this can only be due to the saturation of the internal buffer of the gzip program, the current description of the compressing proxy system can deadlock when G autonomously decides to start sending compressed data back to A. In fact, this creates a circular waiting because G can send compressed data to A iff A has signaled end of input to G.

In order to solve this problem, A must be redesigned in order to account for the possibility of receiving compressed data from G before signaling end of input. On the other hand, G must inform A about its intention to start sending compressed data in advance.

Here is the redefinition of the adaptor AET, where a new state has been added in which activities are suspended in order to allow the gzip program to empty its internal buffer:

```
ARCHI_ELEM_TYPE Adaptor_Type(void)

 BEHAVIOR
  Adaptor_From_Filter(void; void) =
   receive_from_filter . put_to_gzip . Adaptor_To_Gzip();
  Adaptor_To_Gzip(void; void) =
   choice
   {
    put_to_gzip . Adaptor_To_Gzip(),
    put_eoi_gzip . get_from_gzip . Adaptor_From_Gzip(),
    notified_buffer_full . get_from_gzip . Adaptor_Suspended()
   };
  Adaptor_Suspended(void; void) =
   choice
   {
    get_from_gzip . Adaptor_Suspended(),
    get_eoo_gzip . put_to_gzip . Adaptor_To_Gzip()
   };
  Adaptor_From_Gzip(void; void) =
   choice
   {
    get_from_gzip . Adaptor_From_Gzip(),
    get_eoo_gzip . Adaptor_To_Filter()
   };
  Adaptor_To_Filter(void; void) =
   send_to_filter . Adaptor_From_Filter()

  INPUT_INTERACTIONS   SYNC UNI receive_from_filter;
                                get_from_gzip; get_eoo_gzip;
                                notified_buffer_full
  OUTPUT_INTERACTIONS  SYNC UNI send_to_filter;
                                put_to_gzip; put_eoi_gzip
```

Then, we have the redefinition of the gzip AET, where a new interaction has been elicited:

```
ARCHI_ELEM_TYPE Gzip_Type(void)

 BEHAVIOR
  Gzip(void; void) =
   get_data . Gzip_In();
  Gzip_In(void; void) =
   choice
   {
    get_data . Gzip_In(),
    get_eoi . compress . put_data . Gzip_Out(),
    notify_buffer_full . compress . put_data . Gzip_Out()
   };
```

```
Gzip_Out(void; void) =
  choice
  {
   put_data . Gzip_Out(),
   put_eoo . Gzip()
  }

INPUT_INTERACTIONS   SYNC UNI get_data; get_eoi
OUTPUT_INTERACTIONS  SYNC UNI put_data; put_eoo;
                              notify_buffer_full
```

Finally, we have the redeclaration of the attachments:

```
ARCHI_ATTACHMENTS
  FROM UF.write_data         TO A.receive_from_filter;
  FROM A.put_to_gzip         TO G.get_data;
  FROM A.put_eoi_gzip        TO G.get_eoi;
  FROM G.notify_buffer_full  TO A.notified_buffer_full;
  FROM G.put_data            TO A.get_from_gzip;
  FROM G.put_eoo             TO A.get_eoo_gzip;
  FROM A.send_to_filter      TO DF.read_data
```

With this revised description of the compressing proxy system, it turns out that A is deadlock-freedom-compatible with G. Since A is also deadlock-freedom-compatible with UF and DF, we can conclude that Compressing_Proxy is deadlock free from the fact that A is deadlock free, without having to generate the state space underlying the entire architectural description.

5.4 Architectural Interoperability of Cycle-Shaped Topologies

The architectural compatibility check is not enough when dealing with cycles. As shown in the following example inspired by [124], the AEIs in a cycle cannot be considered two-by-two because each of them may interfere with any of the others.

Example 5.1. A party involves three kinds of actor: guest, host, and waiter. For instance, suppose that after arriving at the party place, the guest can ask the host for an orange juice or a pineapple juice. Of course, the host is expected to tell the waiter to bring the requested drink. What if the host is absentminded or malicious, and hence tells the waiter to bring a drink different from the one requested by the guest? This scenario is depicted in Fig. 5.2.

The question arises as to whether the party can deadlock. This corresponds to the embarrassing situation in which the guest receives a drink different from the requested one, as the guest may then be led to refrain from asking for further drinks. If we apply the architectural compatibility check, it turns out that H is deadlock-freedom-compatible both with W and with G. From the fact that H is deadlock free, we should then conclude that the party cannot deadlock. Unfortunately, this is not true, as can be seen in Fig. 5.2 by considering the case in which G asks H for an orange juice but H tells W to bring a pineapple juice to G.

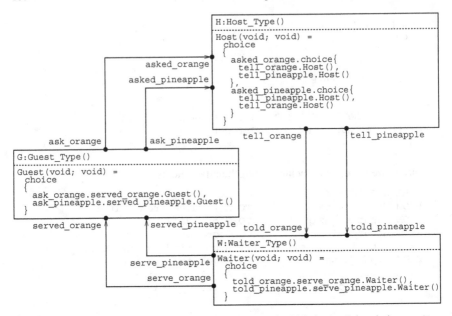

Fig. 5.2 Enriched flow graph of the guest analogy integrated with behavioral description

The point is that in this case the abstract enriched flow graph is a cycle, whereas Proposition 5.1 holds under the constraint that the considered AEIs form a star. In conclusion, this example demonstrates that the architectural compatibility check does not suffice in the presence of cycles.

A cycle is a closed simple path in the abstract enriched flow graph of an architectural description $\mathscr{A}$, which traverses a set $\mathscr{Y} = \{C_1, \ldots, C_n\}$ of $n \geq 3$ AEIs. In the case of a cycle, MISMDET cannot investigate the validity of a property $\mathscr{P} \in \Psi$ by analyzing the interplay between pairs of AEIs, because of the possible presence of arbitrary interferences among the various AEIs in the cycle. In order to achieve a correct coordination inside the cycle, the actual observable behavior of any AEI C_j in the cycle should coincide with the observable behavior expected by the rest of the cycle. In other words, the observable behavior of C_j should not be altered by the insertion of C_j itself into the cycle.

Definition 5.5. Given an architectural description $\mathscr{A}$ and a property $\mathscr{P} \in \Psi$, let $\mathscr{Y} = \{C_1, \ldots, C_n\}$ be the set of AEIs traversed by a cycle of $\mathscr{A}$, C_j be an AEI in the cycle, $H_{C_j, \mathscr{Y}}$ be the set of interactions of additional implicit AEIs of C_j that are attached to $\mathscr{Y}$, and $E_{C_j, \mathscr{Y}}$ be the set of exceptions that may be raised by semi-synchronous interactions involved in attachments between C_j and $\mathscr{Y}$. We say that C_j $\mathscr{P}$-interoperates with the other AEIs in the cycle iff:

$$[\![\mathscr{Y}]\!]_{\mathscr{A}}^{\mathrm{tc};\#\mathscr{Y};C_j} / (Name - \mathscr{V}_{C_j;\mathscr{A}}) / (H_{C_j,\mathscr{Y}} \cup E_{C_j,\mathscr{Y}}) \approx_{\mathscr{P}} [\![C_j]\!]_{\mathscr{A}}^{\mathrm{pc};\mathrm{wob}}$$

Similar to Definition 5.4, all possible originally asynchronous local interactions of the other AEIs in the cycle and all of their interactions that are not attached to C_j have been hidden by taking the totally closed interacting semantics of those AEIs and by leaving visible only the actions in $\mathcal{V}_{C_j;\mathcal{A}}$. We also observe that, whenever C_j has no local nonsynchronous interactions and is not attached to semi-synchronous interactions of other AEIs in the cycle, then $H_{C_j,\mathcal{Y}} \cup E_{C_j,\mathcal{Y}} = \emptyset$ and both $[\![C_j]\!]_{\mathcal{A}}^{\text{pc};\#\mathcal{Y}}$ and $[\![C_j]\!]_{\mathcal{A}}^{\text{pc};\text{wob}}$ coincide with $[\![C_j]\!]_{\mathcal{A}}^{\text{tc};\text{wob}}$.

Interoperability is an adaptation of compatibility to cycles, as can be viewed by developing for all $1 \leq j \leq n$ the equivalence established in Definition 5.5:

$$([\![C_1]\!]_{\mathcal{A}}^{\text{pc};\#\mathcal{Y}} \|_{\overline{S}_{1,n}} [\![C_2,\dots,C_n]\!]_{\mathcal{A}}^{\text{tc};\#\mathcal{Y}}) / NV_1 \approx_{\mathcal{P}} [\![C_1]\!]_{\mathcal{A}}^{\text{pc};\text{wob}}$$

$$\vdots \qquad \qquad \vdots \qquad \qquad \vdots$$

$$([\![C_1,\dots,C_{j-1}]\!]_{\mathcal{A}}^{\text{tc};\#\mathcal{Y}} \|_{S_{j-1}} [\![C_j]\!]_{\mathcal{A}}^{\text{pc};\#\mathcal{Y}} \|_{\overline{S}_{j,n}} [\![C_{j+1},\dots,C_n]\!]_{\mathcal{A}}^{\text{tc};\#\mathcal{Y}}) / NV_j \approx_{\mathcal{P}} [\![C_j]\!]_{\mathcal{A}}^{\text{pc};\text{wob}}$$

$$\vdots \qquad \qquad \vdots \qquad \qquad \vdots$$

$$([\![C_1,\dots,C_{n-1}]\!]_{\mathcal{A}}^{\text{tc};\#\mathcal{Y}} \|_{S_{n-1}} [\![C_n]\!]_{\mathcal{A}}^{\text{pc};\#\mathcal{Y}}) / NV_n \approx_{\mathcal{P}} [\![C_n]\!]_{\mathcal{A}}^{\text{pc};\text{wob}}$$

where:

- $\overline{S}_{j,n} = \bigcup\limits_{f=1}^{j} \bigcup\limits_{g=j+1}^{n} \mathcal{S}(C_f, C_g; \mathcal{A})$
- $S_j = \bigcup\limits_{g=1}^{j} \mathcal{S}(C_g, C_{j+1}; \mathcal{A})$
- $NV_j = (Name - \mathcal{V}_{C_j;\mathcal{A}}) \cup (H_{C_j,\mathcal{Y}} \cup E_{C_j,\mathcal{Y}})$

Proposition 5.2. *Given an architectural description $\mathcal{A}$ and a property $\mathcal{P} \in \Psi$, let $\mathcal{Y} = \{C_1,\dots,C_n\}$ be the set of AEIs traversed by a cycle of $\mathcal{A}$. Whenever there exists $C_j \in \mathcal{Y}$ that $\mathcal{P}$-interoperates with the other AEIs in the cycle, then $[\![\mathcal{Y}]\!]_{\mathcal{A}}^{\text{tc};\#\mathcal{Y};C_j} / (Name - \mathcal{V}_{C_j;\mathcal{A}}) / (H_{C_j,\mathcal{Y}} \cup E_{C_j,\mathcal{Y}})$ satisfies $\mathcal{P}$ iff so does $[\![C_j]\!]_{\mathcal{A}}^{\text{pc};\text{wob}}$, where $H_{C_j,\mathcal{Y}}$ and $E_{C_j,\mathcal{Y}}$ are the same sets as Definition 5.5.*

Based on the sufficient condition established by the proposition above, in the case of a cycle the architectural interoperability check for a property $\mathcal{P} \in \Psi$ is applied to any AEI in the cycle. As soon as an AEI $C_j \in \mathcal{Y}$ is found that passes the check, then the whole cycle can be reduced to C_j and the validity of $\mathcal{P}$ can be verified on this single AEI. In contrast, if the check is not passed by any $C_g \in \mathcal{Y}$, then this reveals a potential lack of coordination among the AEIs in the cycle.

The cost of the interoperability-check-based verification of $\mathcal{P}$ grows exponentially with the size of $\mathcal{Y}$. However, due to the numerous actions that have to be hidden in the cycle, this cost can be mitigated if the state space of the cycle is built compositionally and minimized at each step with respect to $\approx_{\mathcal{P}}$ by taking into account the interfaces of the various AEIs in the cycle [105].

Different from the architectural compatibility check, whenever no AEI in a cycle passes the architectural interoperability check, it is not immediately clear which

AEIs are responsible for possible well-formedness violations. In this case, the following cycle shrinking algorithm can be employed:

- Consider an AEI $C_g \in \mathscr{Y}$ that does not $\mathscr{P}$-interoperate with the other AEIs in the cycle.
- Use the modal-logic diagnostic information coming from the failure of the $\mathscr{P}$-interoperability check for C_g in order to determine where the source of a potential well-formedness violation is.
- If the source is within C_g, modify C_g and repeat the $\mathscr{P}$-interoperability check.
- Otherwise shrink the cycle by replacing C_{g-1}, C_g, and C_{g+1} with a new AEI whose behavior is the parallel composition of the interacting semantics of the three original AEIs, then repeat the $\mathscr{P}$-interoperability check.

The principle at the basis of the cycle shrinking algorithm, i.e., considering sets of adjacent AEIs in a cycle instead of single AEIs, can be exploited in order to improve the effectiveness of the architectural interoperability check.

Example 5.2. Let us revisit the guest analogy scenario of Example 5.1. Suppose that the party now involves four kinds of actor: couple of guests, host, and waiter. As before, whenever a guest wants something to drink, the guest has to ask the host. Different from before, the drink mentioned to the waiter by the host always coincides with the drink requested by the guest.

Some conflicts may arise in this new scenario: one inside the couple of guests and another one between the host and the waiter. The first conflict happens if the wife wants to dance with her husband, whereas her husband wants to go home. We assume that this conflict can be solved by means of an agreement on having another drink, which will be ordered by the husband. The second conflict takes place if the host asks the waiter to work one more hour because the couple has no intention to leave the party yet, whereas the waiter asks the host to quit working earlier due to tiredness. We assume that this conflict cannot be solved, but drink requests are always satisfied in spite of possible disagreements between the host and the waiter. The new scenario is depicted in Fig. 5.3, where only the conflictual part of the behavior of the various actors is exposed.

Let us investigate whether the party can deadlock. If we apply the architectural interoperability check, it turns out that none of the AEIs deadlock-freedom-interoperates with the other AEIs in the cycle because of the wife–husband and host–waiter conflicts. However, the AEI obtained from the combination of G1 and G2 – by taking the parallel composition of their interacting semantics – deadlock-freedom-interoperates with H and W, from which we derive that the party does not deadlock. In conclusion, this example demonstrates that the outcome of the architectural interoperability check depends on the number of adjacent AEIs that are considered during the application of the check.

The architectural interoperability check can be generalized as follows when considering sets of adjacent AEIs in a cycle. For symmetry reasons, the size of each such set can be limited to half of the number of AEIs traversed by the cycle.

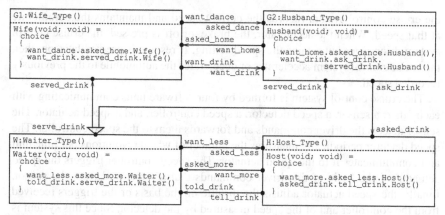

Fig. 5.3 Enriched flow graph of the revisited guest analogy integrated with behavioral description

Definition 5.6. Given an architectural description $\mathscr{A}$ and a property $\mathscr{P} \in \Psi$, let $\mathscr{Y} = \{C_1, \ldots, C_n\}$ be the set of AEIs traversed by a cycle of $\mathscr{A}$, $\mathscr{J} = \{C_1', \ldots, C_l'\}$ be a set of $1 \le l \le n/2$ adjacent AEIs in the cycle, $\mathscr{T} = \mathscr{Y} - \mathscr{J}$ be the set of the other AEIs in the cycle, $H_{C_j', \mathscr{T}}$ be the set of interactions of additional implicit AEIs of $C_j' \in \mathscr{J}$ that are attached to $\mathscr{T}$, and $E_{C_j', \mathscr{T}}$ be the set of exceptions that may be raised by semi-synchronous interactions involved in attachments between $C_j' \in \mathscr{J}$ and $\mathscr{T}$. We say that $\mathscr{J} = \{C_1', \ldots, C_l'\}$ $\mathscr{P}$-interoperates with the other AEIs in the cycle iff:

$$[\![\mathscr{Y}]\!]_{\mathscr{A}}^{\text{tc};\#\mathscr{Y};\mathscr{J}} \bigg/ \left(Name - \bigcup_{j=1}^{l} \mathscr{V}_{C_j';\mathscr{A}}\right) \bigg/ \bigcup_{j=1}^{l} (H_{C_j', \mathscr{T}} \cup E_{C_j', \mathscr{T}}) \approx_{\mathscr{P}} [\![\mathscr{J}]\!]_{\mathscr{A}}^{\text{pc};\#\mathscr{J}}$$

Proposition 5.3. *Given an architectural description $\mathscr{A}$ and a property $\mathscr{P} \in \Psi$, let $\mathscr{Y} = \{C_1, \ldots, C_n\}$ be the set of AEIs traversed by a cycle of $\mathscr{A}$. Whenever there exists $\mathscr{J} = \{C_1', \ldots, C_l'\} \subseteq \mathscr{Y}$, $1 \le l \le n/2$, that $\mathscr{P}$-interoperates with the other AEIs in the cycle, then $[\![\mathscr{Y}]\!]_{\mathscr{A}}^{\text{tc};\#\mathscr{Y};\mathscr{J}} / (Name - \bigcup_{j=1}^{l} \mathscr{V}_{C_j';\mathscr{A}}) / \bigcup_{j=1}^{l} (H_{C_j', \mathscr{T}} \cup E_{C_j', \mathscr{T}})$ satisfies $\mathscr{P}$ iff so does $[\![\mathscr{J}]\!]_{\mathscr{A}}^{\text{pc};\#\mathscr{J}}$, where $\mathscr{T}$, $H_{C_j', \mathscr{T}}$, and $E_{C_j', \mathscr{T}}$ are the same sets as Definition 5.6.*

5.4.1 Case Study: Cruise Control System

We now illustrate an application of the architectural interoperability check to the cruise control system examined in [131]. Once the engine has been turned on, this system is governed by the two standard pedals of the automobile – accelerator and brake – and by three additional buttons – on, off, and resume. When on is pressed, the cruise control system records the current speed and maintains the automobile at that speed. When the accelerator, the brake, or off is pressed, the cruise control system disengages but retains the speed setting. If resume is pressed later on, then the cruise control system accelerates or decelerates the automobile to the previously recorded speed.

The cruise control system is formed by four software units communicating with each other: a sensor, a speed detector, a speed controller, and a speed actuator. The sensor detects the driver commands and forwards them to the speed controller. The speed detector periodically measures the number of wheel revolutions per time unit and communicates it to the speed actuator. The speed controller triggers the speed actuator on the basis of the driver commands that are received from the sensor. Finally, the speed actuator adjusts the throttle on the basis of the triggers received from the controller and of the speed measured by the detector. Since this system is the result of the combination of several software units, it must be designed in such a way to ensure deadlock freedom.

Let us model the system with PADL. Here is the architectural description header:

```
ARCHI_TYPE Cruise_Control(void)
```

The sensor AET is defined as follows, where two states are distinguished depending on whether the engine is off or on:

```
ARCHI_ELEM_TYPE Sensor_Type(void)

  BEHAVIOR
  Sensor_Off(void; void) =
    detected_engine_on . turn_engine_on . Sensor_On();
  Sensor_On(void; void) =
    choice
    {
    detected_accelerator . press_accelerator . Sensor_On(),
    detected_brake . press_brake . Sensor_On(),
    detected_on . press_on . Sensor_On(),
    detected_off . press_off . Sensor_On(),
    detected_resume . press_resume . Sensor_On(),
    detected_engine_off . turn_engine_off . Sensor_Off()
    }

  INPUT_INTERACTIONS   SYNC UNI detected_engine_on;
                                detected_engine_off;
                                detected_accelerator;
                                detected_brake;
                                detected_on; detected_off;
                                detected_resume
  OUTPUT_INTERACTIONS SYNC UNI press_accelerator; press_brake;
                                press_on; press_off; press_resume
                            AND turn_engine_on; turn_engine_off
```

The speed detector AET is defined as follows, where once again two states are distinguished depending on whether the engine is off or on:

```
ARCHI_ELEM_TYPE Detector_Type(void)

  BEHAVIOR
   Detector_Off(void; void) =
    turned_engine_on . Detector_On();
   Detector_On(void; void) =
    choice
    {
     measure_speed . signal_speed . Detector_On(),
     turned_engine_off . Detector_Off()
    }

  INPUT_INTERACTIONS   SYNC UNI turned_engine_on;
                                turned_engine_off
  OUTPUT_INTERACTIONS SYNC UNI signal_speed
```

The speed controller can be in one of the following states: inactive (when the engine is off), active (when the engine is on), cruising (after pressing the on button in the active/suspended state or the resume button in the suspended state), or suspended (after pressing any pedal or button different from on/resume in the cruising state). Here is the definition of the speed controller AET:

```
ARCHI_ELEM_TYPE Controller_Type(void)

  BEHAVIOR
   Inactive(void; void) =
    turned_engine_on . Active();
   Active(void; void) =
    choice
    {
     pressed_accelerator . Active(),
     pressed_brake . Active(),
     pressed_on . trigger_record . Cruising(),
     pressed_off . Active(),
     pressed_resume . Active(),
     turned_engine_off . Inactive()
    };
   Cruising(void; void) =
    choice
    {
     pressed_accelerator . trigger_disable . Suspended(),
     pressed_brake . trigger_disable . Suspended(),
     pressed_on . Cruising(),
     pressed_off . trigger_disable . Suspended(),
     pressed_resume . Cruising(),
     turned_engine_off . Inactive()
    };
   Suspended(void; void) =
    choice
    {
```

```
        pressed_accelerator . Suspended(),
        pressed_brake . Suspended(),
        pressed_on . trigger_record . Cruising(),
        pressed_off . Suspended(),
        pressed_resume . trigger_resume . Cruising(),
        turned_engine_off . Inactive()
      }

  INPUT_INTERACTIONS  SYNC UNI turned_engine_on;
                               turned_engine_off;
                               pressed_accelerator;
                               pressed_brake;
                               pressed_on; pressed_off;
                               pressed_resume
  OUTPUT_INTERACTIONS SYNC UNI trigger_record; trigger_resume;
                               trigger_disable
```

The speed actuator can be in one of the following states: disabled (until the on/resume button is pressed) or enabled (until any pedal or button different from on/resume is pressed). Here is the definition of the speed actuator AET:

```
ARCHI_ELEM_TYPE Actuator_Type(void)

  BEHAVIOR
   Disabled(void; void) =
    choice
    {
     signaled_speed . Disabled(),
     triggered_record . record_speed . Enabled(),
     triggered_resume . resume_speed . Enabled()
    };
   Enabled(void; void) =
    choice
    {
     signaled_speed . adjust_throttle . Enabled(),
     triggered_disable . disable_control . Disabled()
    }

  INPUT_INTERACTIONS  SYNC UNI triggered_record;
                               triggered_resume;
                               triggered_disable;
                               signaled_speed
  OUTPUT_INTERACTIONS void
```

Finally, we have the architectural topology section, which is graphically illustrated in Fig. 5.4:

```
ARCHI_ELEM_INSTANCES
  S : Sensor_Type();
  D : Detector_Type();
  C : Controller_Type();
  A : Actuator_Type()
```

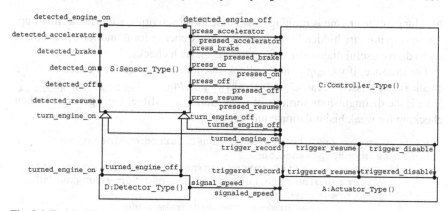

Fig. 5.4 Enriched flow graph of the cruise control system

```
ARCHI_INTERACTIONS
  S.detected_engine_on; S.detected_engine_off;
  S.detected_accelerator; S.detected_brake;
  S.detected_on; S.detected_off; S.detected_resume

ARCHI_ATTACHMENTS
  FROM S.turn_engine_on     TO D.turned_engine_on;
  FROM S.turn_engine_on     TO C.turned_engine_on;
  FROM S.turn_engine_off    TO D.turned_engine_off;
  FROM S.turn_engine_off    TO C.turned_engine_off;
  FROM S.press_accelerator  TO C.pressed_accelerator;
  FROM S.press_brake        TO C.pressed_brake;
  FROM S.press_on           TO C.pressed_on;
  FROM S.press_off          TO C.pressed_off;
  FROM S.press_resume       TO C.pressed_resume;
  FROM D.signal_speed       TO A.signaled_speed;
  FROM C.trigger_record     TO A.triggered_record;
  FROM C.trigger_resume     TO A.triggered_resume;
  FROM C.trigger_disable    TO A.triggered_disable
```

Having formalized the architecture of the cruise control system with PADL, we can proceed with deadlock freedom analysis. First of all, we observe that the abstract variant of the enriched flow graph in Fig. 5.4 subsumes all the attachments between S and D, between S and C, and between C and A with a single edge, respectively, so that its topology precisely concides with a cycle. Based on the considerations of Sect. 5.2, we apply the architectural interoperability check by exploiting weak bisimulation equivalence $\approx_B$. Since there are no local nonsynchronous interactions, the check can be applied by taking the totally closed interacting semantics without buffers of the various AEIs.

Although all the AEIs are deadlock free, none of them deadlock-freedom-interoperates with the others; hence, we can suspect that some mismatch exists. Looking carefully at the PADL description, we discover that Cruise_Control is deadlock free because speed signaling activities take place endlessly between D and

A as long as the engine is running. If we hide those activities, a deadlock shows up. Those activities are hidden in the interoperability checks for S and for C, so we can try to derive useful diagnostic information from such checks.

For instance, if we apply the deadlock-freedom-interoperability check to S, the check is not passed because $[[S,D,C,A]]_{S,D,C,A}^{tc;wob} / (Name - \mathcal{V}_{S;S,D,C,A}) \not\approx_B [[S]]_{S,D,C,A}^{tc;wob}$. Here is the distinguishing formula of weak Hennessy–Milner logic generated when checking for weak bisimulation equivalence:

$\langle\!\langle$S.turn_engine_on#D.turned_engine_on#C.turned_engine_on$\rangle\!\rangle$
    $\langle\!\langle$S.press_on#C.pressed_on$\rangle\!\rangle$
        $\langle\!\langle$S.turn_engine_off#D.turned_engine_off#C.turned_engine_off$\rangle\!\rangle$
            $\langle\!\langle$S.turn_engine_on#D.turned_engine_on#C.turned_engine_on$\rangle\!\rangle$
                $\langle\!\langle$S.press_on#C.pressed_on$\rangle\!\rangle$
                    $\neg\langle\!\langle$S.press_brake#C.pressed_brake$\rangle\!\rangle$ true

The formula above says that, if we turn the engine on and off and in the meanwhile we press on, then the speed actuator remains enabled instead of being disengaged. This may result in an extremely dangerous situation in which the cruise control system is no longer sensitive to brake pressure.

This problem can be solved by modifying the cruising behavior of the speed controller AET so that a disabling trigger is sent also when the engine is turned off, as shown below:

```
Cruising(void; void) =
 choice
 {
  pressed_accelerator . trigger_disable . Suspended(),
  pressed_brake . trigger_disable . Suspended(),
  pressed_on . Cruising(),
  pressed_off . trigger_disable . Suspended(),
  pressed_resume . Cruising(),
  turned_engine_off . trigger_disable . Inactive()
 }
```

With this modification of the cruise control system, it turns out that S deadlock-freedom-interoperates with the other AEIs. Since S is deadlock free, we can conclude that Cruise_Control is now deadlock free even if we hide the speed signaling activities.

5.5 Generalization to Arbitrary Topologies

The abstract enriched flow graph underlying an architectural description may contain arbitrarily many stars and cycles. In accordance with the detection strategy outlined in Sect. 5.2, in that case MISMDET applies the compatibility and interoperability checks several times in a way that hopefully converges towards the reduction of the entire topology to a single architectural element, which is finally checked against some property $\mathscr{P} \in \Psi$ of interest.

In this general setting, a prominent role is played by AEIs that belong to the intersection of cycles with acyclic portions of the topology or other cycles, where acyclic portions are intended not to be in cyclic subgraphs. The reason is that each of these AEIs is part of the frontier of the cycle to which it belongs; hence, it can be exploited for reduction purposes. In contrast, the reduction to any AEI in a cycle that does not interact with AEIs outside the cycle leads the process to a dead end.

Definition 5.7. Let $\mathscr{A}$ be an architectural description and $\{C_1, \ldots, C_n\}$ be a set of AEIs of $\mathscr{A}$. The frontier of $\{C_1, \ldots, C_n\}$ is defined as follows:

$$\boxed{\mathscr{F}_{C_1,\ldots,C_n} = \{C_j \in \{C_1,\ldots,C_n\} \mid \mathscr{LI}_{C_j;C_1,\ldots,C_n} \neq \mathscr{LI}_{C_j}\}}$$

Moreover, we denote by $\mathscr{CU}_{C_j}$ the cyclic union of C_j, which is the union of the sets of AEIs traversed by a cycle that traverses also C_j.

The topological reduction process for an arbitrary topology can take place in several different ways depending on the interleaving of applications of the architectural compatibility and interoperability checks. In turn, this depends on the order in which the various stars and cycles of the topology are considered by MISMDET. In any case, all cycles have to be taken into account sooner or later, as the reduction process tends to transform an arbitrary topology into an acyclic topology.

The cycles of an architectural description $\mathscr{A}$ can be managed by means of a cycle covering algorithm like the following, which relies on the notion of cyclic union:

1. All the AEIs of $\mathscr{A}$ are initially unmarked.
2. While there are unmarked AEIs in the cycles of the abstract enriched flow graph of $\mathscr{A}$:

   (a) Pick out one such AEI, say C.
   (b) Mark all the AEIs in $\mathscr{CU}_C$.

The result of a cycle covering algorithm κ is a set $\mathscr{CU}(\kappa)$ of cyclic unions that include every AEI belonging to a cycle in the abstract enriched flow graph of $\mathscr{A}$. Any two cyclic unions in $\mathscr{CU}(\kappa)$ are connected at most through a single shared AEI or through the attachments between a single AEI of one cyclic union and a single AEI of the other cyclic union. The cycle covering algorithm is said to be total iff the topology becomes acyclic after replacing every cyclic union $\mathscr{Y} = \{C_1, \ldots, C_n\} \in \mathscr{CU}(\kappa)$ with an AEI whose behavior is given by:

$$[\![\mathscr{Y}]\!]_{\mathscr{A}}^{\text{tc};\#\mathscr{Y};\mathscr{F}_{C_1,\ldots,C_n}} \Big/ \Big(Name - \bigcup_{C_j \in \mathscr{F}_{C_1,\ldots,C_n}} \mathscr{V}_{C_j;\mathscr{A}}\Big) \Big/ \bigcup_{C_j \in \mathscr{F}_{C_1,\ldots,C_n}} (H_{C_j,\mathscr{Y}} \cup E_{C_j,\mathscr{Y}})$$

Given a property $\mathscr{P} \in \Psi$, MISMDET addresses arbitrary topologies by combining the sufficient condition for stars given by Proposition 5.1 with the sufficient condition for cycles given by Proposition 5.2, as formalized by the theorem below. The importance of AEIs belonging to the frontier of cyclic unions is emphasized by the fact that each of these AEIs must be $\mathscr{P}$-compatible with every AEI attached to it that belongs to an acyclic portion of the topology and, at the same time, must

$\mathscr{P}$-interoperate with the other AEIs in the cyclic union to which it belongs. Although appropriate for certain properties like deadlock freedom, it is not required that all the AEIs satisfy $\mathscr{P}$ in order for the entire architectural description to satisfy $\mathscr{P}$. In fact, it is sufficient for $\mathscr{P}$ to be satisfied by some suitable AEI – the one obtained at the end of the topological reduction process.

Theorem 5.1. *Let $\mathscr{A}$ be an architectural description and $\mathscr{P} \in \Psi$ be a property for which the following two conditions hold:*

1. *For each $K \in \mathscr{A}$ belonging to an acyclic portion or to the intersection of some cycle with acyclic portions of the abstract enriched flow graph of $\mathscr{A}$, K is $\mathscr{P}$-compatible with every $C \in \mathscr{B}_K - \mathscr{C}\mathscr{U}_K$*
2. *If $\mathscr{A}$ is cyclic, then there exists a total cycle covering algorithm κ such that for each cyclic union $\{C_1, \ldots, C_n\} \in \mathscr{C}\mathscr{U}(\kappa)$:*

   (a) *If $\mathscr{F}_{C_1,\ldots,C_n} = \emptyset$, then there exists $C_j \in \{C_1, \ldots, C_n\}$ that $\mathscr{P}$-interoperates with the other AEIs in the cyclic union*
   (b) *If $\mathscr{F}_{C_1,\ldots,C_n} \neq \emptyset$, then every $C_j \in \mathscr{F}_{C_1,\ldots,C_n}$ $\mathscr{P}$-interoperates with the other AEIs in the cyclic union*
   (c) *If no $C_j \in \mathscr{F}_{C_1,\ldots,C_n}$ is such that $[\![C_j]\!]_{\mathscr{A}}^{\mathrm{pc;wob}}$ satisfies $\mathscr{P}$ and there exists $C_g \in \{C_1, \ldots, C_n\} - \mathscr{F}_{C_1,\ldots,C_n}$ such that $[\![C_g]\!]_{\mathscr{A}}^{\mathrm{pc;wob}}$ satisfies $\mathscr{P}$, then at least one such C_g $\mathscr{P}$-interoperates with the other AEIs in the cyclic union*

Then $[\![\mathscr{A}]\!]_{\mathrm{bbm}}^{\mathrm{pc;\#}\mathscr{A}}$ satisfies $\mathscr{P}$ iff so does $[\![C]\!]_{\mathscr{A}}^{\mathrm{pc;wob}}$ for some $C \in \mathscr{A}$.

5.5.1 Case Study: Simulator for the Cruise Control System

We now illustrate an application of the generalization of the architectural compatibility and interoperability checks to arbitrary topologies, in which we consider the design of an applet-based simulator for the cruise control system examined in Sect. 5.4.1. The applet must contain a panel with seven software buttons – corresponding to turning the engine on/off, the two pedals, and the three hardware buttons – and a text area showing the sequence of buttons successfully pressed so far. Each of the seven software buttons can be pressed at any time. When pressing one of them, the corresponding operation either succeeds or fails. In the first case, the panel can interact with the sensor and the text area is updated accordingly. In the second case – think, e.g., of pressing the accelerator button when the engine is off – the panel cannot interact with the sensor, rather it emits a beep. Also for this cruise control system simulator, the objective is to ensure deadlock freedom.

Let us model the simulator with PADL. Here is the architectural description header:

```
ARCHI_TYPE Cruise_Control_Simulator(void)
```

Thanks to the architectural interactions provided by the sensor, the definition of the architectural type `Cruise_Control` of Sect. 5.4.1 can be reused through the following architectural invocation, where the only actual parameters that occur are the actual names of the previously mentioned architectural interactions:

```
ARCHI_ELEM_TYPE Cruise_Control_System_Type(void)

  BEHAVIOR
    Cruise_Control_System(void; void) =
     Cruise_Control(@        /* no data parameters */
                    @        /* reuse formal AETs */
                    @ @ @ @  /* reuse formal topology */
                    @ @ @    /* no behavioral modifications */
                    UNIFY S.detected_engine_on   WITH engine_on;
                    UNIFY S.detected_engine_off  WITH engine_off;
                    UNIFY S.detected_accelerator WITH accelerator;
                    UNIFY S.detected_brake       WITH brake;
                    UNIFY S.detected_on          WITH on;
                    UNIFY S.detected_off         WITH off;
                    UNIFY S.detected_resume      WITH resume)

  INPUT_INTERACTIONS   SYNC UNI engine_on; engine_off;
                                accelerator; brake;
                                on; off; resume
  OUTPUT_INTERACTIONS void
```

As far as the applet is concerned, interactions have to be provided in order to allow the user to start/stop the applet itself. Its panel has to send the user commands to the sensor, which then propagates them inside the cruise control system. In order not to block the simulator when the pressure of a software button fails, certain interactions have to be semi-synchronous, as shown below:

```
ARCHI_ELEM_TYPE Panel_Type(void)

  BEHAVIOR
    Unallocated(void; void) =
     init_applet . start_applet . Active();
    Active(void; void) =
     choice
     {
      signal_engine_on . Checking(signal_engine_on.success),
      signal_accelerator . Checking(signal_accelerator.success),
      signal_brake . Checking(signal_brake.success),
      signal_on . Checking(signal_on.success),
      signal_off . Checking(signal_off.success),
      signal_resume . Checking(signal_resume.success),
      signal_engine_off . Checking(signal_engine_off.success),
      stop_applet . Inactive()
     };
```

```
Checking(boolean success; void) =
 choice
  {
   cond(success = true)   -> update . Active(),
   cond(success = false) -> beep . Active()
  };
 Inactive(void; void) =
  choice
  {
   start_applet . Active(),
   destroy_applet . Unallocated()
  }
```

```
INPUT_INTERACTIONS   SYNC  UNI  init_applet; start_applet;
                                 stop_applet; destroy_applet
OUTPUT_INTERACTIONS SSYNC UNI  signal_engine_on;
                                 signal_engine_off;
                                 signal_accelerator;
                                 signal_brake; signal_on;
                                 signal_off; signal_resume
```

Finally, we have the architectural topology section, which is depicted in Fig. 5.5:

```
ARCHI_ELEM_INSTANCES
 P   : Panel_Type();
 CCS : Cruise_Control_System_Type()
```

```
ARCHI_INTERACTIONS
 P.init_applet; P.start_applet; P.stop_applet; P.destroy_applet
```

```
ARCHI_ATTACHMENTS
 FROM P.signal_engine_on   TO CCS.engine_on;
```

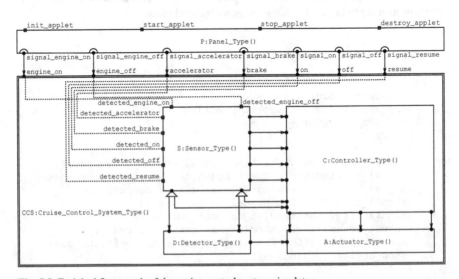

Fig. 5.5 Enriched flow graph of the cruise control system simulator

```
FROM P.signal_engine_off   TO CCS.engine_off;
FROM P.signal_accelerator  TO CCS.accelerator;
FROM P.signal_brake        TO CCS.brake;
FROM P.signal_on           TO CCS.on;
FROM P.signal_off          TO CCS.off;
FROM P.signal_resume       TO CCS.resume
```

As far as deadlock freedom analysis is concerned, we observe that all the AEIs are deadlock free and that the abstract variant of the flattened version of the enriched flow graph in Fig. 5.5 is an intersection of a cycle and a star, where the cycle traverses AEIs S, D, C, and A. From Sect. 5.4.1 we know that S deadlock-freedom-interoperates with D, C, A; hence, the cycle can be reduced to $[\![S]\!]_{P,S,D,C,A}^{tc;wob}$. Moreover, it is easy to see that the only AEI in the frontier of the cycle, i.e., S, is deadlock-freedom-compatible with P, the only AEI in the only acyclic portion of the topology – remember that all exceptions that P may raise are hidden when applying the check. Therefore, we can conclude that Cruise_Control_Simulator is deadlock free from the fact that S is deadlock free.

5.6 Generalization to Architectural Types

The process algebraic techniques for architectural mismatch detection discussed so far are not only useful for deriving information about the correct coordination within an arbitrary architectural description from star-shaped and cycle-shaped portions of its topology. In fact, these techniques can also be exploited for deducing information about the correct coordination within an entire architectural type from one of its instances. This avoids the cost resulting from the application of the architectural compatibility and interoperability checks to every single instance of the considered architectural type.

In this section, we show the conditions under which the absence of architectural mismatches investigated by means of MISMDET scales from a single architectural description to the architectural type of the description. More precisely, we present suitable extensions of Theorem 5.1 dealing with internal behavioral variations (Sect. 5.6.1) as well as with exogenous variations (Sect. 5.6.2), endogenous variations (Sect. 5.6.3), and multiplicity variations (Sect. 5.6.4). All the extensions of the theorem are illustrated through the corresponding examples of Sect. 4.6 based on variants of the pipe–filter system.

5.6.1 Generalization to Internal Behavioral Variations

Two AT instances behaviorally conform to each other if they exhibit the same observable behavior according to weak bisimulation equivalence $\approx_B$. When introducing internal behavioral variations, the absence of architectural mismatches is then preserved for each property $\mathscr{P} \in \Psi$ such that $\approx_{\mathscr{P}}$ is coarser than $\approx_B$.

Corollary 5.1. *Let $\mathscr{A}$ be an AT instance and $\mathscr{P} \in \Psi$ be a property for which the two conditions of Theorem 5.1 hold. Whenever $\approx_B \subseteq \approx_{\mathscr{P}}$, then for each AT instance $\mathscr{A}'$ that strictly behaviorally conforms to $\mathscr{A}$ it turns out that $[\![\mathscr{A}']\!]_{bbm}^{pc;\#\mathscr{A}'}$ satisfies $\mathscr{P}$ iff so does $[\![C]\!]_{\mathscr{A}}^{pc;wob}$ for some $C \in \mathscr{A}$.*

Example 5.3. Let us consider the architectural type `Pipe_Filter` of Sect. 4.5. This is deadlock free, because from the topological viewpoint it is a star and its central AEI P is deadlock free and deadlock-freedom-compatible with F_0, F_1, F_2, and F_3. Then we can immediately derive that its strictly behaviorally conformant instance of Example 4.7, in which the AET `Filter_Type` is replaced by the new AET `Faulty_Filter_Type`, is deadlock free too.

5.6.2 Generalization to Exogenous Variations

An exogenous variation of an AT instance consists of adding AEIs outside the topological frontier, with some of these AEIs being attached to architectural interactions.

In this case, there are two issues to be taken into account. The first issue is that all the architectural interactions at which an exogenous variation takes place become local interactions; hence, they must be left visible when applying the architectural compatibility and interoperability checks. This is accomplished by introducing suitable variants of the partially and totally closed interacting semantics and of the notion of frontier, which coincide with the respective original definitions in the absence of architectural interactions. Then, the notions of architectural compatibility and interoperability have to be revised accordingly, in such a way that the new ones imply the respective original ones when hiding architectural interactions, thanks to the congruence property of $\approx_{\mathscr{P}}$, $\mathscr{P} \in \Psi$, with respect to static operators. In the following, we denote by $\mathscr{A}\mathscr{I}_{C_j}$ the set of architectural interactions of C_j.

Definition 5.8. The partially semi-closed interacting semantics of $C_j \in \{C_1, \ldots, C_n\}$ with respect to $\{C_1, \ldots, C_n\}$ including its buffers attached to $\{C_1'', \ldots, C_{n''}''\}$ is defined as follows:

$$\left[[\![C_j]\!]_{C_1,\ldots,C_n}^{psc;\#C_1'',\ldots,C_{n''}''} = [\![C_j]\!]_{C_1,\ldots,C_n}^{\#C_1'',\ldots,C_{n''}''} / (Name - \mathscr{V}_{C_j;C_1,\ldots,C_n} - \mathscr{A}\mathscr{I}_{C_j}) \right]$$

and we write $[\![C_j]\!]_{C_1,\ldots,C_n}^{psc;wob}$ if $n'' = 0$. The partially semi-closed interacting semantics of $\{C_1', \ldots, C_{n'}'\} \subseteq \{C_1, \ldots, C_n\}$ with respect to $\{C_1, \ldots, C_n\}$ including their buffers attached to $\{C_1'', \ldots, C_{n''}''\}$ is defined as follows:

$$\left[[\![C_1', \ldots, C_{n'}']\!]_{C_1,\ldots,C_n}^{psc;\#C_1'',\ldots,C_{n''}''} = [\![C_1']\!]_{C_1,\ldots,C_n}^{psc;\#C_1'',\ldots,C_{n''}''} \, \|_{\mathscr{S}(C_1',C_2';C_1,\ldots,C_n)} \right. $$
$$[\![C_2']\!]_{C_1,\ldots,C_n}^{psc;\#C_1'',\ldots,C_{n''}''} \, \|_{\mathscr{S}(C_1',C_3';C_1,\ldots,C_n) \cup \mathscr{S}(C_2',C_3';C_1,\ldots,C_n)}$$
$$\left. \cdots \, \|_{\bigcup_{i=1}^{n'-1} \mathscr{S}(C_i',C_{n'}';C_1,\ldots,C_n)} [\![C_{n'}']\!]_{C_1,\ldots,C_n}^{psc;\#C_1'',\ldots,C_{n''}''} \right]$$

where the synchronization sets are built as in Definition 4.2.

Definition 5.9. The totally semi-closed interacting semantics of $C_j \in \{C_1, \ldots, C_n\}$ with respect to $\{C_1, \ldots, C_n\}$ including its buffers attached to $\{C_1'', \ldots, C_{n''}''\}$ is defined as follows:

$$[\![C_j]\!]_{C_1,\ldots,C_n}^{\text{tsc};\#C_1'',\ldots,C_{n''}''} = [\![C_j]\!]_{C_1,\ldots,C_n}^{\text{psc};\#C_1'',\ldots,C_{n''}''} / \varphi_{C_j,\text{async}}(\mathcal{OALI}_{C_j})$$

and we write $[\![C_j]\!]_{C_1,\ldots,C_n}^{\text{tsc};\text{wob}}$ if $n'' = 0$. The totally semi-closed interacting semantics of $\{C_1', \ldots, C_{n'}'\} \subseteq \{C_1, \ldots, C_n\}$ with respect to $\{C_1, \ldots, C_n\}$ including their buffers attached to $\{C_1'', \ldots, C_{n''}''\}$ is defined as follows:

$$\begin{aligned}
[\![C_1', \ldots, C_{n'}']\!]_{C_1,\ldots,C_n}^{\text{tsc};\#C_1'',\ldots,C_{n''}''} = [\![C_1']\!]_{C_1,\ldots,C_n}^{\text{tsc};\#C_1'',\ldots,C_{n''}''} &\parallel_{\mathcal{S}(C_1',C_2';C_1,\ldots,C_n)} \\
[\![C_2']\!]_{C_1,\ldots,C_n}^{\text{tsc};\#C_1'',\ldots,C_{n''}''} &\parallel_{\mathcal{S}(C_1',C_3';C_1,\ldots,C_n) \cup \mathcal{S}(C_2',C_3';C_1,\ldots,C_n)} \\
\cdots \parallel_{\bigcup_{i=1}^{n'-1} \mathcal{S}(C_i',C_{n'}';C_1,\ldots,C_n)} &[\![C_{n'}']\!]_{C_1,\ldots,C_n}^{\text{tsc};\#C_1'',\ldots,C_{n''}''}
\end{aligned}$$

where the synchronization sets are built as in Definition 4.2. The variant totally semi-closed up to $\{C_1''', \ldots, C_{n'''}'''\} \subset \{C_1', \ldots, C_{n'}'\}$, i.e., in which $[\![C_j''']\!]_{C_1,\ldots,C_n}^{\text{psc};\#C_1'',\ldots,C_{n''}''}$ is considered in place of $[\![C_j''']\!]_{C_1,\ldots,C_n}^{\text{tsc};\#C_1'',\ldots,C_{n''}''}$, is denoted by $[\![C_1', \ldots, C_{n'}']\!]_{C_1,\ldots,C_n}^{\text{tsc};\#C_1'',\ldots,C_{n''}'';C_1''',\ldots,C_{n'''}'''}$.

Definition 5.10. Given an architectural description $\mathcal{A}$ and a property $\mathcal{P} \in \Psi$, let K be the central AEI of a star of $\mathcal{A}$, $\mathcal{B}_K = \{C_1, \ldots, C_n\}$ be the border of the star, C_j be an AEI in $\mathcal{B}_K$, H_{K,C_j} be the set of interactions of additional implicit AEIs of K that are attached to interactions of C_j, and E_{K,C_j} be the set of exceptions that may be raised by semi-synchronous interactions involved in attachments between K and C_j. We say that K is $\mathcal{P}$-semi-compatible with C_j iff:

$$([\![K]\!]_{\mathcal{A}}^{\text{psc};\#C_j} \parallel_{\mathcal{S}(K,C_j;\mathcal{A})} [\![C_j]\!]_{K,\mathcal{B}_K}^{\text{tc};\#K}) / (H_{K,C_j} \cup E_{K,C_j}) \approx_{\mathcal{P}} [\![K]\!]_{\mathcal{A}}^{\text{psc};\text{wob}}$$

Definition 5.11. Given an architectural description $\mathcal{A}$ and a property $\mathcal{P} \in \Psi$, let $\mathcal{Y} = \{C_1, \ldots, C_n\}$ be the set of AEIs traversed by a cycle of $\mathcal{A}$, C_j be an AEI in the cycle, $H_{C_j,\mathcal{Y}}$ be the set of interactions of additional implicit AEIs of C_j that are attached to $\mathcal{Y}$, and $E_{C_j,\mathcal{Y}}$ be the set of exceptions that may be raised by semi-synchronous interactions involved in attachments between C_j and $\mathcal{Y}$. We say that C_j $\mathcal{P}$-semi-interoperates with the other AEIs in the cycle iff:

$$[\![\mathcal{Y}]\!]_{\mathcal{A}}^{\text{tsc};\#\mathcal{Y};C_j} / (Name - \mathcal{V}_{C_j;\mathcal{A}} - \mathcal{AI}_{C_j}) / (H_{C_j,\mathcal{Y}} \cup E_{C_j,\mathcal{Y}}) \approx_{\mathcal{P}} [\![C_j]\!]_{\mathcal{A}}^{\text{psc};\text{wob}}$$

Definition 5.12. Let $\mathscr{A}$ be an architectural description and $\{C_1, \ldots, C_n\}$ be a set of AEIs of $\mathscr{A}$. The semi-frontier of $\{C_1, \ldots, C_n\}$ is defined as follows:

$$\mathscr{S}\mathscr{F}_{C_1,\ldots,C_n} = \{C_j \in \{C_1,\ldots,C_n\} \mid \mathscr{L}\mathscr{I}_{C_j;C_1,\ldots,C_n} \neq \mathscr{L}\mathscr{I}_{C_j} \vee \mathscr{A}\mathscr{I}_{C_j} \neq \emptyset\}$$

which coincides with $\mathscr{F}_{C_1,\ldots,C_n}$ plus other AEIs having architectural interactions.

The second issue to be taken into account is that an exogenous variation may alter the set of original cyclic unions, in which case nothing can be deduced from the absence of architectural mismatches in the original AT instance whenever new kinds of cycle are generated. Think, e.g., of an exogenous variation of a pipe–filter system whose only pipe has not only several downstream filters, but also several upstream filters. Below we introduce the concept of topological equivalence for cyclic unions.

Definition 5.13. Given an architectural description $\mathscr{A}$, let $\mathscr{C}\mathscr{U}_1$ and $\mathscr{C}\mathscr{U}_2$ be two cyclic unions of $\mathscr{A}$. We say that $\mathscr{C}\mathscr{U}_1$ is (strictly) topologically equivalent to $\mathscr{C}\mathscr{U}_2$ iff there exists a bijection between them that preserves the type (and the actual data parameter values), the attachments within the cyclic union, and the membership to the frontier of the cyclic union of corresponding AEIs.

The cycles of an AT instance $\mathscr{A}'$ resulting from a strictly topologically conformant exogenous variation of an AT instance $\mathscr{A}$ can be managed by means of the following exogenous variation of a total cycle covering algorithm κ for $\mathscr{A}$:

1. All the AEIs of $\mathscr{A}'$ are initially unmarked.
2. For each cyclic union $\mathscr{C}\mathscr{U}_C^{\mathscr{A}} \in \mathscr{C}\mathscr{U}^{\mathscr{A}}(\kappa)$:

   (a) Pick out C.
   (b) Mark all the AEIs in $\mathscr{C}\mathscr{U}_C^{\mathscr{A}'}$.

3. While there is an unmarked additional AEI C in the cycles of the abstract enriched flow graph of $\mathscr{A}'$ such that there exists $\mathscr{C}\mathscr{U}_{C'}^{\mathscr{A}} \in \mathscr{C}\mathscr{U}^{\mathscr{A}}(\kappa)$ with $C' = corr(C)$ and $\mathscr{C}\mathscr{U}_C^{\mathscr{A}'}$ strictly topologically equivalent to $\mathscr{C}\mathscr{U}_{C'}^{\mathscr{A}}$:

   (a) Pick out C.
   (b) Mark all the AEIs in $\mathscr{C}\mathscr{U}_C^{\mathscr{A}'}$.

We say that $\mathscr{A}'$ is exo-coverable by κ iff all the AEIs in the cycles of the abstract enriched flow graph of $\mathscr{A}'$ are marked, the exogenous variation of κ is total, and for each $C \in \mathscr{A}$ such that $\mathscr{C}\mathscr{U}_C^{\mathscr{A}} \in \mathscr{C}\mathscr{U}^{\mathscr{A}}(\kappa)$ it holds $\mathscr{C}\mathscr{U}_C^{\mathscr{A}'} = \mathscr{C}\mathscr{U}_C^{\mathscr{A}}$. In that case, each cyclic union generated by the exogenous variation of κ for $\mathscr{A}'$ is strictly topologically equivalent to a cyclic union generated by κ for $\mathscr{A}$. Therefore, if $\mathscr{A}$ is acyclic, then none of its cyclic exogenous variations is exo-coverable. Moreover, no exo-coverable exogenous variation of $\mathscr{A}$ can be a cyclic union with empty frontier.

Corollary 5.2. *Let $\mathscr{A}$ be an AT instance and $\mathscr{P} \in \Psi$ be a property for which the two conditions of Theorem 5.1 hold. Let $\mathscr{A}'$ be an AT instance resulting from a strictly topologically conformant exogenous variation of $\mathscr{A}$ for which the following additional conditions hold:*

3. *For each $K \in \mathscr{A}$ belonging to an acyclic portion or to the intersection of some cycle with acyclic portions of the abstract enriched flow graph of $\mathscr{A}$, if K is of the same type as an AEI having architectural interactions at which the exogenous variation takes place, then K is $\mathscr{P}$-semi-compatible with every $C \in \mathscr{B}_K - \mathscr{C}\mathscr{U}_K^{\mathscr{A}}$.*
4. *If $\mathscr{A}'$ is cyclic, then $\mathscr{A}'$ is exo-coverable by κ and for each $C_j \in \mathscr{S}\mathscr{F}_{C_1,\ldots,C_n}$ with $\{C_1,\ldots,C_n\} \in \mathscr{C}\mathscr{U}^{\mathscr{A}}(\kappa)$, if C_j is of the same type as an AEI having architectural interactions at which the exogenous variation takes place, then C_j $\mathscr{P}$-semi-interoperates with the other AEIs in $\{C_1,\ldots,C_n\}$.*

Then $[\![\mathscr{A}']\!]_{bbm}^{pc;\#\mathscr{A}'}$ satisfies $\mathscr{P}$ iff so does $[\![C]\!]_{\mathscr{A}}^{pc;wob}$ for some $C \in \mathscr{A}$.

Example 5.4. Consider again the architectural type `Pipe_Filter` of Sect. 4.5. Then, we can immediately derive that its exogenous variation of Example 4.8, which takes place at `F_2.output_item` by means of an additional pipe `P_1` having the already existing AEI `F_2` as upstream filter and the new AEIs `F_4`, `F_5`, and `F_6` as downstream filters, is deadlock free too.

5.6.3 Generalization to Endogenous Variations

An endogenous variation of an AT instance consists of changing the number of AEIs of certain types in certain positions of the original topology – without altering the number of attachments in which local and-/or-interactions are involved – by adding new AEIs of those types or removing existing AEIs of those types.

Also in this case, there are two issues to be taken into account. The first issue is that an endogenous variation may create new kinds of attachment that are not present in the original topology, which may compromise compatibility within some altered acyclic portion. Similarly, an endogenous variation may cancel existing attachments – like those involving removed AEIs or those broken to allow for added AEIs – that are important for the validity of $\mathscr{P} \in \Psi$. In such situations, nothing can be deduced from the absence of architectural mismatches in the original AT instance.

The second issue is that an endogenous variation may alter the set of original cyclic unions, in which case nothing can be deduced from the absence of architectural mismatches in the original AT instance whenever new kinds of cycle are generated or interoperability is compromised along some altered cycle.

The cycles of an AT instance $\mathscr{A}'$ resulting from an endogenous variation of an AT instance $\mathscr{A}$ can be managed by means of the following endogenous variation of a total cycle covering algorithm κ for $\mathscr{A}$:

1. All the AEIs of $\mathscr{A}'$ are initially unmarked.
2. For each cyclic union $\mathscr{C}\mathscr{U}_C^{\mathscr{A}} \in \mathscr{C}\mathscr{U}^{\mathscr{A}}(\kappa)$:

   (a) Pick out C.
   (b) Mark all the AEIs in $\mathscr{C}\mathscr{U}_C^{\mathscr{A}'}$.

3. While there is an unmarked additional AEI C in the cycles of the abstract enriched flow graph of $\mathscr{A}'$ such that there exists $\mathscr{C}\mathscr{U}_{C'}^{\mathscr{A}} \in \mathscr{C}\mathscr{U}^{\mathscr{A}}(\kappa)$ with C' of the same type as C and $\mathscr{C}\mathscr{U}_{C}^{\mathscr{A}'}$ strictly topologically equivalent to $\mathscr{C}\mathscr{U}_{C'}^{\mathscr{A}}$:

   (a) Pick out C.
   (b) Mark all the AEIs in $\mathscr{C}\mathscr{U}_{C}^{\mathscr{A}'}$.

We say that $\mathscr{A}'$ is endo-coverable by κ iff all the AEIs in the cycles of the abstract enriched flow graph of $\mathscr{A}'$ are marked, the endogenous variation of κ is total, and for each $C \in \mathscr{A}$ such that $\mathscr{C}\mathscr{U}_{C}^{\mathscr{A}} \in \mathscr{C}\mathscr{U}^{\mathscr{A}}(\kappa)$ it holds $\mathscr{C}\mathscr{U}_{C}^{\mathscr{A}'} = \mathscr{C}\mathscr{U}_{C}^{\mathscr{A}}$ up to added/removed AEIs.

Corollary 5.3. *Let $\mathscr{A}$ be an AT instance and $\mathscr{P} \in \Psi$ be a property for which the two conditions of Theorem 5.1 hold. Let $\mathscr{A}'$ be an AT instance resulting from an endogenous variation of $\mathscr{A}$ for which the following additional conditions hold:*

$\bar{3}$. *For each attachment in $\mathscr{A}'$ from interaction o of an AEI C_1', which belongs to an acyclic portion or to the intersection of some cycle with acyclic portions of the abstract enriched flow graph of $\mathscr{A}'$, to interaction i of an AEI $C_2' \in \mathscr{B}_{C_1'} - \mathscr{C}\mathscr{U}_{C_1'}^{\mathscr{A}'}$, there exists an attachment in $\mathscr{A}$ from interaction o of an AEI C_1 of the same type as C_1', with C_1 belonging to an acyclic portion or to the intersection of some cycle with acyclic portions of the abstract enriched flow graph of $\mathscr{A}$, to interaction i of an AEI $C_2 \in \mathscr{B}_{C_1} - \mathscr{C}\mathscr{U}_{C_1}^{\mathscr{A}}$ of the same type as C_2'.*

$\bar{4}$. *No local interaction occurring in $\mathscr{P}$ is involved in attachments canceled by the endogenous variation.*

$\bar{5}$. *If $\mathscr{A}$ or $\mathscr{A}'$ is cyclic, then $\mathscr{A}'$ is endo-coverable by κ and for each cyclic union $\mathscr{C}\mathscr{U}_{C}^{\mathscr{A}'}$ generated by the endogenous variation of κ:*

   (a) *No local interaction of the AEIs of $\mathscr{C}\mathscr{U}_{C}^{\mathscr{A}}$ that $\mathscr{P}$-interoperate with the other AEIs in $\mathscr{C}\mathscr{U}_{C}^{\mathscr{A}}$ by virtue of condition 2 of Theorem 5.1 is involved in attachments canceled by the endogenous variation.*
   (b) *No possibly added AEI in $\mathscr{C}\mathscr{U}_{C}^{\mathscr{A}'}$ belongs to the frontier of $\mathscr{C}\mathscr{U}_{C}^{\mathscr{A}'}$.*
   (c) *If $C \in \mathscr{A}$, then $[\![\mathscr{C}\mathscr{U}_{C}^{\mathscr{A}'}]\!]_{\mathscr{C}\mathscr{U}_{C}^{\mathscr{A}'}}^{\mathrm{pc};\#\mathscr{C}\mathscr{U}_{C}^{\mathscr{A}'}} / H \approx_{\mathscr{P}} [\![\mathscr{C}\mathscr{U}_{C}^{\mathscr{A}}]\!]_{\mathscr{C}\mathscr{U}_{C}^{\mathscr{A}}}^{\mathrm{pc};\#\mathscr{C}\mathscr{U}_{C}^{\mathscr{A}}} / H$ where H contains all local interactions of the added/removed AEIs as well as those attached to them.*

Then $[\![\mathscr{A}']\!]_{\mathrm{bbm}}^{\mathrm{pc};\#\mathscr{A}'}$ satisfies $\mathscr{P}$ iff so does $[\![C]\!]_{\mathscr{A}}^{\mathrm{pc};\mathrm{wob}}$ for some $C \in \mathscr{A}$.

Example 5.5. Let us consider the architectural type `Pipe_Filter_R` of Example 4.9, which is given by a ring of systems each having the same structure and behavior as the architectural type `Pipe_Filter` of Sect. 4.5. This ring is deadlock free, because from the topological viewpoint it is a cyclic union and each of its instances of AET `Pipe_Type` is deadlock free and deadlock-freedom-interoperates with the other AEIs in the cyclic union. Then, we can immediately derive that its endogenous variation of Example 4.9, in which the number of pipe–filter systems changes from 3 to 4, is deadlock free too.

5.6.4 Generalization to Multiplicity Variations

A multiplicity variation of an AT instance consists of changing the number of AEIs of certain types that are attached to certain local and-/or-interactions, by adding new AEIs of those types or removing existing AEIs of those types.

In this case, there are various issues to be taken into account. A multiplicity variation may cancel existing attachments that are important for the validity of $\mathscr{P} \in \Psi$. Moreover, when involving or-interactions, it may not support the scaling of architectural well-formedness. This happens when those or-interactions are attached to uni-interactions that may raise exceptions or are enabled a number of times that does not allow all the uni-interactions attached to them to be executed.

Similar to exogenous and endogenous variations, a multiplicity variation may alter the set of original cyclic unions. When that happens, nothing can be deduced from the absence of architectural mismatches in the original AT instance.

Corollary 5.4. *Let $\mathscr{A}$ be an AT instance and $\mathscr{P} \in \Psi$ be a property for which the two conditions of Theorem 5.1 hold. Let $\mathscr{A}'$ be an AT instance resulting from a multiplicity variation of $\mathscr{A}$ for which the following additional conditions hold:*

$\tilde{3}$. *No local interaction occurring in $\mathscr{P}$ is involved in attachments canceled by the multiplicity variation.*

$\tilde{4}$. *No local or-interaction involved in the multiplicity variation is attached to a semi-synchronous uni-interaction or to an input asynchronous uni-interaction.*

$\tilde{5}$. *Each local or-interaction involved in the multiplicity variation is enabled infinitely often.*

$\tilde{6}$. *If $\mathscr{A}$ or $\mathscr{A}'$ is cyclic, then $\mathscr{C}\mathscr{U}^{\mathscr{A}}(\kappa) = \mathscr{C}\mathscr{U}^{\mathscr{A}'}(\kappa)$.*

Then $[\![\mathscr{A}']\!]_{\text{bbm}}^{\text{pc};\#\mathscr{A}'}$ satisfies $\mathscr{P}$ iff so does $[\![C]\!]_{\mathscr{A}}^{\text{pc;wob}}$ for some $C \in \mathscr{A}$.

Example 5.6. Let us consider the architectural type OV_Pipe_Filter of Example 4.10. This is a variant of the architectural type Pipe_Filter of Sect. 4.5 allowing for a variable number of downstream filters; hence, it can be shown to be deadlock free with the same argument used in Example 5.3. Then, we can immediately derive that its multiplicity variation of Example 4.10, in which the number of downstream filters changes from 3 to 4, is deadlock free too.

5.7 Comparisons

The equivalence-checking-based topological reduction process presented in this chapter is taken from [41, 7, 38]. Apart from [62], where a generic notion of composability has been addressed, other mismatch detection techniques based on behavioral equivalences are specifically concerned with deadlock freedom. In contrast, the techniques discussed in this chapter are more general because they focus on an entire class of properties – including deadlock freedom – rather than on individual properties. These techniques are also more flexible, as they make use of property-specific behavioral equivalences instead of a single general behavioral equivalence and exploit the hiding operator in order to highlight only the parts of the system behavior that are important for well-formedness verification.

MISMDET can be viewed as a generalization of other techniques previously proposed in the literature. For instance, the topological format that has been addressed in [18] is limited to pairs of software units from the point of view of a specific communication involving both of them. In that case, the activity of mismatch detection is conducted by comparing any two software units each projected onto one of its interactions, where the two selected interactions are attached to each other. In this way it is only possible to check for the correct combination of two software units with respect to individual communications.

In [124, 122], a more liberal topological format has been investigated, in which pairs of software units are viewed from the standpoint of all the communications involving both of them. Mismatch detection is carried out by extracting from the description of each software unit the assumptions made about the behavior of the rest of the system and by trying to match expected behaviors with actual behaviors. In this way, it becomes possible to check for the presence of interferences among the various communications in which two software units are involved. As an example, in the compressing proxy system, the adaptor and the gzip program seem to interact properly as long as the information flow from the adaptor to the gzip program and the information flow from the gzip program to the adaptor are examined separately. However, a mismatch is revealed as soon as the interplay between the two information flows is taken into account.

The natural generalization of the latter topological format is the star, which has been handled through the introduction in MISMDET of the architectural compatibility check. As demonstrated by the guest analogy scenario, this check is not sufficient when dealing with cycles, as each of the various software units may interfere with any of the others. This has led to the introduction in MISMDET of the architectural interoperability check. Both checks rely on suitable variants of the interacting semantics of a software unit and take care of details related to nonsynchronous communications. Afterwards, the scalability to arbitrary topologies and to architectural types, respectively, of the absence of architectural mismatches inferred from the application of architectural compatibility and interoperability checks to single stars and cycles have been studied.

We conclude by mentioning that the architectural checks constituting MISMDET can provide useful information to be exploited in the subsequent stages of the software development process.

As an example, in [36, 37, 52] an architecture-driven code generation approach has been set up, which translates PADL descriptions into multithreaded Java programs by respecting the communication model adopted in PADL. Due to the different levels of abstraction characterizing an architectural description language like PADL and an object-oriented programming language like Java, the code synthesis cannot be complete. For instance, while interactions are fully handled by the translation process, internal actions are managed by generating stubs that the software developer will have to fill in. In that case, conditions have been obtained that guarantee the preservation at the code level of the absence of well-formedness mismatches demonstrated at the architectural level through the application of compatibility and interoperability checks.

As another example, in [46,47] an architecture-driven approach to the generation of integration tests has been proposed, which derives test plans from the labeled transition system underlying an architectural description. The identification of classes of behaviors that are important for testing purposes is conducted by creating abstract views of the labeled transition system. Each such view corresponds to an abstract path in the labeled transition system, which emphasizes communications among certain software units while hiding other communications. The concrete paths related to the abstract path are then retrieved and refined into code-level integration tests. In that case, the diagnostic information returned by the application of compatibility and interoperability checks can be employed in order to single out critical paths in the labeled transition system, which are worth testing.

Chapter 6
Component-Oriented Performance Evaluation

Abstract The functional verification of software systems should not be separate from system performance evaluation. Any software architecture should be designed by having in mind the satisfaction of functional and nonfunctional requirements, and efforts should be made in order to understand whether the performance of a specific design can be improved. In addition to that, performance criteria should guide the choice among several alternative designs each of which is functionally correct. In this chapter, we present a procedure for the prediction, improvement, and comparison of the performance of architectural designs called PERFSEL. It relies on the combined use of process algebraic architectural descriptions and queueing network models for assessing typical performance indices both at the system level and at the component level. Its application is exemplified through the performance comparison of three different architectures for a compiler system.

6.1 PERFSEL: Performance-Driven Architectural Selection

A crucial issue in the software development process is that of taking into account nonfunctional aspects since the early stages, which is motivated by several reasons. As an example, for a given system a number of alternative architectural designs may be developed, each of which is functionally correct. In that case, we need to establish criteria for deciding which architectural design is more appropriate. Similarly, for a given set of functionalities there may be several off-the-shelf components that provide what is required. Also in that case, some suitable criterion is necessary.

Performance requirements and constraints are certainly among the most influential factors that drive design choices in the cases mentioned above. Moreover, also a specific architectural design may be subject to an investigation based on performance criteria. In order for the performance investigation to be effective, similar to functional verification it should proceed in a component-oriented fashion and should return diagnostic information useful for determining whether, how, and to what extent the performance of the considered design can be improved.

A. Aldini et al., *A Process Algebraic Approach to Software Architecture Design*,
DOI 10.1007/978-1-84800-223-4_6, © Springer-Verlag London Limited 2010

In this chapter, we present a procedure for the prediction, improvement, and comparison of the performance of architectural designs called PERFSEL. The procedure consists of a number of phases at the end of which typical performance indices are assessed in different scenarios for the various architectural designs both at the system level and the component level. On the basis of those indices, it can be decided to discard some designs, improve others, or select the one to be implemented.

In order to achieve component orientation, PERFSEL relies on the combined use of process algebraic architectural descriptions and queueing networks. Different from MISMDET, it does not make use of behavioral equivalences, because these are qualitative means for establishing whether distinct elements possess the same properties or not. PERFSEL needs instead to quantify the extent to which properties are satisfied. This is accomplished by equipping process algebraic architectural descriptions with quantitative semantics.

On the modeling side, PERFSEL employs a performance-aware variant of PADL called ÆMILIA, which builds on the Markovian process calculus of Sect. 3.2 extended as in Sect. 3.3.8. On the analysis side, PERFSEL instead employs queueing networks [130, 137], as they are structured performance models providing support for establishing a correspondence between their constituent elements and the components of architectural descriptions. Moreover, some families of queueing networks, called product-form queueing networks [27], are equipped with efficient solution algorithms that do not require the construction of the underlying state space.

The combined use of the two formalisms in PERFSEL is made possible by a transformation that associates a queueing network model with every ÆMILIA description satisfying certain constraints. The presence of such constraints has a twofold motivation. Firstly, although they share a certain degree of component orientation, the two formalisms are quite different from each other. On the one hand, ÆMILIA is a completely formal, general-purpose architectural description language handling both functional and performance aspects, whose basic ingredients are actions and behavioral operators. On the other hand, queueing networks are instances of a queue-based graphical notation for performance modeling purposes only, in which some details like the queueing disciplines are usually expressed in natural language. Secondly, the components of an ÆMILIA description cannot be precisely mapped to the service centers of a queueing network model, but on finer parts that we call queueing network basic elements and represent arrival processes, buffers, service processes, fork processes, join processes, and routing processes.

This chapter is organized as follows. In Sect. 6.2, we outline the class of performance indices we are interested in assessing, together with the selection strategy on which PERFSEL is based. In Sect. 6.3, we define ÆMILIA as an extension of PADL with performance aspects. In Sect. 6.4, we recall some of the most important concepts and properties in the field of queueing systems and queueing networks. In Sect. 6.5, we present the transformation of ÆMILIA descriptions into queueing networks that enables the combined use of the two formalisms. In Sect. 6.6, we illustrate an application of PERFSEL to the performance comparison of three different architectures for a compiler system. Finally, in Sect. 6.7 we compare the considered performance-driven architectural selection procedure with the related literature.

6.2 Class of Measures and Selection Strategy

PERFSEL focuses on the following four typical average indicators, which refer to both system level and component level and give insights into the overall performance:

- Throughput, which is the mean number of tasks executed by a system/component per unit of time. This is a measure of the productivity of a system/component. It provides information useful for singling out bottleneck components, i.e., components that are responsible for degrading the system performance and hence must be redesigned.
- Utilization, which is the mean fraction of time during which a system/component is running. This is a measure of the relative usage of the computational resources by a system/component. It provides information useful at deployment time for a balanced distribution of the workload among the computational resources.
- Mean queue length, which is the mean number of items in a system/component handling data. This is a measure of the space complexity of data repositories. It provides information useful for setting their dimension in such a way to avoid component execution blocking due to under-sized buffers as well as waste of memory due to over-sized buffers.
- Mean response time, which is the mean time needed by a system/component to complete or repeat its execution. This is a measure of the time complexity of a system/component. It provides information useful for predicting the quality of service that will be perceived by the software user on average.

The selection strategy of PERFSEL is illustrated in Fig. 6.1. It is composed of the following nine phases, which support the prediction, improvement, and comparison of the performance of alternative architectural designs of a certain system:

1. Given a set of functional and performance requirements that should be satisfied by the software system to be implemented, the designer devises a certain number $d \in \mathbb{N}_{>0}$ of alternative designs, which we assume to be functionally correct.
2. Each such architectural design is then formalized as an ÆMILIA description in order to enable the evaluation of its performance.
3. The ÆMILIA description of some of the considered software architectures may not obey the constraints that make it possible to transform the description into a queueing network model. In that case, the ÆMILIA description is replaced by an approximating ÆMILIA description obeying the constraints. The approximation may result in the modification of the behavior of certain AEIs as well as in the replacement of existing AEIs with groups of new AEIs.
4. The possibly approximate ÆMILIA description of each architectural design is subsequently transformed into a queueing network model.
5. The queueing network model associated with some of the considered software architectures may not be in product form, thus hampering a quick computation of the four average performance indicators. In that case, the queueing network model is replaced by an approximating product-form queueing network model.

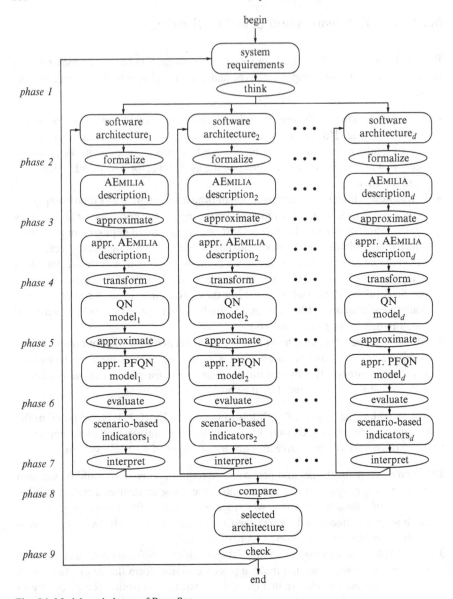

Fig. 6.1 Models and phases of PERFSEL

The approximation may result in the modification of interarrival time distributions, buffer capacities, service time distributions, and customer classes.

6. The possibly approximate product-form queueing network model associated with each architectural design is then evaluated in order to derive the four average performance indicators both at the system level and the component level. The evaluation is done in several different scenarios considered significant

for the assessment of the various architectural designs. This requires the parameterization of the derived product-form queueing network model and the characterization of its workload, which in turn may require the introduction in the corresponding ÆMILIA description of suitable AEIs representing arrival processes. As examples of scenarios, it is interesting to study the differences in the value of the four average performance indicators under light load and heavy load conditions. Similarly, it is worth investigating those differences when the service centers provide service at the same rate and when one of them is slower/faster than the others.

7. The previously obtained performance figures are subsequently interpreted on the ÆMILIA description of the various architectural designs. For each of them a decision has to be made as to whether the design is satisfactory, should be discarded, or can be improved. In the last case, it is necessary to go back to phase 2.

8. When the predict–improve cycle is terminated for all the considered architectural designs, a comparison takes place in the various scenarios among the last groups of performance figures obtained for the architectural designs that have not been discarded. The comparison should be fair, in the sense that the alternative designs should be given comparable workloads in each scenario. Since the outcome of the comparison may be different from scenario to scenario, in order to select the architecture to be implemented it may be necessary to take into account the frequency with which every examined scenario can arise in practice.

9. The selected architecture is finally checked against the specific performance requirements of the system to be implemented. Such requirements can be formalized through different notations like those mentioned in [66, 23, 8], which rely on logical formulas combined with reward structures [120, 180, 109]. If the outcome of the check is positive, then the application of PERFSEL terminates, otherwise the designer has to go back to step 1 and also reconsider the performance requirements, as they may have turned out to be impossible to meet.

We conclude by noting that the final check is necessary for at least two reasons. Firstly, the selection is made on the basis of general performance indicators, which are not necessarily connected in any way to the specific performance requirements. Secondly, the product-form queueing network model associated with the selected architecture or the ÆMILIA description from which it has been derived may have been subject to approximations. Although the perturbation of the four performance indicators introduced by the approximations cannot be easily quantified, it is worth recalling from [137] that queueing network models are in general robust, in the sense that even their approximate analysis is in any case useful to get some insights about the performance of the systems they represent.

The consideration of a restricted set of general performance indicators and the possibility of introducing approximations are justified at the architectural design level by the fact that the objective is that of getting a quick feedback about how to improve the performance of a certain design, or making a rapid comparison of the performance of alternative designs, rather than a precise performance evaluation. This is conducted anyhow, but only in the last phase and only on the selected architecture, so as to achieve a tradeoff between saving time and ensuring that the selected architecture actually meets the specified performance requirements.

6.3 ÆMILIA: Extending PADL with Performance Aspects

PERFSEL enables the modeling of nonfunctional aspects of architectural designs by resorting to a performance-aware variant of PADL called ÆMILIA. This is an architectural description language based no longer on the process calculus of Sect. 1.3, but on the Markovian process calculus of Sect. 3.2 extended as in Sect. 3.3.8 by introducing immediate actions together with priorities for passive actions.

In ÆMILIA, every action is thus composed of a name – like in PADL – and a rate – which determines the speed of the action. Actions are divided into exponentially timed, immediate, and passive. An exponentially timed action is denoted by `<a, exp(r)>`, where a is the name of the action and r is a positive real number expressing the rate of the exponentially distributed random variable that quantifies the duration of the action. An immediate action is denoted by `<a, inf(l, w)>`, where l is a positive natural number representing the priority level of the action and w is a positive real number representing the weight of the action. A passive action is denoted by `<a, _(l, w)>`, where l is a natural number representing the reactive priority constraint of the action and w is a positive real number representing the reactive weight of the action. Passive actions with reactive priority constraint 0 can synchronize only with exponentially timed actions, while passive actions with reactive priority constraint l greater than 0 can synchronize only with immediate actions having priority level equal to l. The use of inf and _ alone is permitted, in which case priorities and weights assume their default value 1.

ÆMILIA descriptions can be parameterized also with respect to rates, priorities, and weights. The corresponding parameters are preceded by the keywords `rate`, `prio`, and `weight`, respectively, in the architectural header and in the headers of the AETs. The occurrences of an action name within the behavior of an AET must be all exponentially timed, all immediate, or all passive. Moreover, every set of local interactions attached to each other can contain at most one nonpassive local interaction, due to the synchronization discipline adopted by the parallel composition operator of the underlying Markovian process calculus.

ÆMILIA inherits from PADL the structure of the descriptions, which comprises an architectural behavior section, an architectural topology section, and an optional behavioral modification section. As a consequence, ÆMILIA also inherits the construction of the translation semantics, which starts with the various AEIs in isolation and then makes them interact on the basis of the attachments through suitable applications of the relabeling operator and of the parallel composition operator.

With regard to the functional verification techniques of Chap. 5, they can be applied as they are to ÆMILIA descriptions that cannot execute immediate actions. For the other ÆMILIA descriptions, it is necessary to take into account the preemption possibly exercised by immediate actions on lower priority actions. Performance analysis can instead be conducted only in the case of performance-closed ÆMILIA descriptions. The stochastic process governing the time behavior of each such architectural description turns out to be a continuous-time Markov chain. This is obtained by discarding rates from the transitions of the labeled multitransition system underlying the architectural description, and can be solved as explained in Sect. 3.2.1.

Example 6.1. Let us consider a performance-aware variant of the pipe–filter system of Example 4.10, which has one upstream filter, a connecting pipe, and an arbitrary number of downstream filters.

In this system, there is only one activity that introduces nonnegligible delays, which is item transformation. For a correct performance modeling, item transformation must be separated from item buffering. This can be accomplished by means of two distinct AETs for representing a single filter, where one AET is for the item buffering and the other AET is for the item transformation.

As far as performance parameters are concerned, we assume different transformation rates for the various filters. Moreover, we assume different forward probabilities towards downstream filters as a consequence of the fact that the pipe is most likely to forward items to faster downstream filters with free positions.

Here is the architectural description header, where function `array_cons` constructs an array:

```
ARCHI_TYPE PA_Pipe_Filter(const integer papf_downstr_num := 3,
                          const integer papf_buffer_size := 10,
                          const rate    papf_tran_rate_0 := 60,
                          const weight  papf_forw_prob_0 :=  1,
                          const array(papf_downstr_num, rate)
                          papf_tran_rate := array_cons(70,
                                                       45,
                                                       30),
                          const array(papf_downstr_num, weight)
                          papf_forw_prob := array_cons(0.5,
                                                       0.3,
                                                       0.2))
```

The filter buffer AET is defined as follows, where parameter `forward_prob` is used as weight in a passive action and interaction `pass_item` is used for communicating with the transformation part of the filter:

```
ARCHI_ELEM_TYPE Filter_Buffer_Type(const integer buffer_size,
                                   const weight  forward_prob)

BEHAVIOR
  Filter_Buffer(integer(0..buffer_size) item_num := 0;
                void) =
  choice
  {
    cond(item_num < buffer_size) ->
    <input_item, _(1, forward_prob)> . Filter(item_num + 1),
```

```
  cond(item_num > 0) ->
   <pass_item, _> . Filter(item_num - 1)
 }

INPUT_INTERACTIONS  SYNC UNI input_item
OUTPUT_INTERACTIONS SYNC UNI pass_item
```

While all the actions occurring in the previous AET are passive to reflect the fact that the activities involving a buffer are originated from the outside, every action occurring in the filter core AET is exponentially timed or immediate:

```
ARCHI_ELEM_TYPE Filter_Core_Type(const rate transf_rate)

BEHAVIOR
 Filter_Core(void; void) =
   <select_item, inf> . <transform_item, exp(transf_rate)> .
                        <output_item, inf> . Filter_Core()

INPUT_INTERACTIONS  SYNC UNI select_item
OUTPUT_INTERACTIONS SYNC UNI output_item
```

The definition of the pipe AET is as in Sect. 4.5, with the difference that interaction accept_item is passive and interaction forward_item is immediate:

```
ARCHI_ELEM_TYPE Pipe_Type(void)

BEHAVIOR
 Pipe(void; void) =
   <accept_item, _> . <forward_item, inf> . Pipe()

INPUT_INTERACTIONS  SYNC UNI accept_item
OUTPUT_INTERACTIONS SYNC OR  forward_item
```

It is worth observing that forward probabilities towards downstream filters have been encoded in some of the passive actions of those filters rather than in the pipe, so that a single output or-interaction is still enough when modeling the pipe. The possibility of associating weights both to immediate actions and to passive actions is thus convenient for exploiting or-interactions in a performance-aware setting.

Finally, we have the architectural topology section:

```
ARCHI_ELEM_INSTANCES
 FB[0] : Filter_Buffer_Type(papf_buffer_size,
                            papf_forw_prob_0);
 FC[0] : Filter_Core_Type(papf_tran_rate_0);
 P     : Pipe_Type();
 FOR_ALL 1 <= j <= papf_downstr_num
  FB[j] : Filter_Buffer_Type(papf_buffer_size,
                             papf_forw_prob[j]);
 FOR_ALL 1 <= j <= papf_downstr_num
  FC[j] : Filter_Core_Type(papf_tran_rate[j])
```

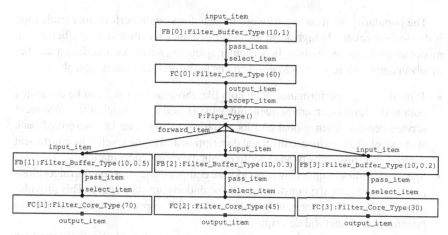

Fig. 6.2 Enriched flow graph of the performance-aware variant of the pipe–filter system

```
ARCHI_INTERACTIONS
  FB[0].input_item;
  FOR_ALL 1 <= j <= papf_downstr_num
  FC[j].output_item

ARCHI_ATTACHMENTS
  FROM FB[0].pass_item   TO FC[0].select_item;
  FROM FC[0].output_item TO P.accept_item;
  FOR_ALL 1 <= j <= papf_downstr_num
    FROM P.forward_item TO FB[j].input_item;
  FOR_ALL 1 <= j <= papf_downstr_num
    FROM FB[j].pass_item TO FC[j].select_item
```

This is graphically illustrated in Fig. 6.2.

6.4 Queueing Systems and Queueing Networks

Any performance-closed ÆMILIA description can be analyzed from a quantitative viewpoint by studying the associated continuous-time Markov chain. However, the latter is a state-based model that does not keep track of the component-based structure of the ÆMILIA description; hence, it is not suited for the architectural design level. For this reason, PERFSEL evaluates nonfunctional aspects of architectural designs by resorting to queueing network models.

A queueing network [130, 137] is a collection of interacting service centers that represent resources shared by classes of customers, where customer competition for resources corresponds to queueing into the service centers. Queueing networks are structured performance models because they elucidate system components and their connectivity; hence, they can be employed for representing architectural descriptions in a way that preserves their topology.

The popularity of queueing network models for system performance evaluation is due to their relatively high accuracy in performance results and their efficiency in model analysis and evaluation. In particular, queueing networks introduce a number of advantages with respect to Markov chains in the architectural design phase:

- Typical average performance indicators like those of Sect. 6.2 can be computed both at the level of an entire queueing network and at the level of its constituent service centers. Such global and local indicators can then be interpreted back at the level of an entire architectural description and at the level of its constituent components, respectively, in order to obtain diagnostic information.
- Specific families of queueing networks are equipped with fast solution algorithms that do not require the construction of the underlying state space. This provides support for a performance analysis that scales with respect to the number of components in architectural descriptions.
- The solution of a queueing network can be expressed symbolically in the case of certain topologies. This feature is useful in the early stages of the software development cycle, since the actual values of system performance parameters may be unknown at that time.

The simplest queueing network consists of a single service center and is called queueing system. As depicted below, it includes a source of arrivals, a queue, and a set of independent servers:

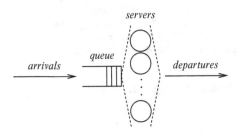

Every customer needing a certain service arrives at the queueing system, waits in the queue for a while, is served by one of the servers, and finally leaves the queueing system. A queueing system is said to be single class or multiclass depending on the number of classes of customers, with each class possibly characterized by different arrival processes and different service demands.

Every queueing system is completely described by the customer interarrival time distribution, the customer service time distribution, the number of independent servers, the queue capacity, the customer population size, and the queueing discipline. The first five parameters are summarized by using the following notation:

$$A/B/m/c/p$$

with A and B ranging over the set of probability distributions – M for memoryless distributions, D for deterministic distributions, PH for phase-type distributions, and

G for general distributions – and m, c, and p being natural numbers. If c and p are unspecified, they are assumed to be ∞, i.e., to describe an unlimited queue capacity and an unlimited customer population, respectively.

The sixth parameter, i.e., the queueing discipline, is an algorithm that determines the order in which the customers in the queue have to be served. Such a scheduling algorithm may depend on the order in which the customers arrive at the queueing system, the priorities assigned to the customers, or the amounts of service already provided to the customers. Here are some commonly adopted queueing disciplines:

- First come first served (FCFS): the customers are served in the order of their arrival. This is the default queueing discipline.
- Last come first served (LCFS): the customers are served in the reverse order of their arrival.
- Last come first served with preemptive resume (LCFS-PR): same as LCFS, but each arriving customer interrupts the current service, if any, and begins to be served; the interrupted service of a customer is resumed when all customers arrived later than that customer have departed.
- Service in random order (SIRO): the next customer to be served is chosen probabilistically, with equal probabilities assigned to all the waiting customers.
- Nonpreemptive priority (NP): customers are assigned fixed priorities; the waiting customer with the highest priority is served first; if several waiting customers have the same highest priority, they are served in the order of their arrival; once begun, a service cannot be interrupted by the arrival of a higher priority customer.
- Preemptive priority (PP): same as NP, but each arriving higher priority customer interrupts the current service, if any, and begins to be served; a customer whose service was interrupted resumes service when there are no higher priority customers to be served.
- Round robin (RR): each customer is given continuous service for a maximum interval of time called a quantum; if the customer service demand is not satisfied during the quantum, the customer reenters the queue and waits to receive an additional quantum, repeating this process until the service demand is satisfied; the waiting customers are served in the order in which they last entered the queue.
- Processor sharing (PS): all the waiting customers receive service simultaneously with equal shares of the service rate. This is an approximation of RR.
- Infinite server (IS): no queueing takes place as each arriving customer always finds an available server. In this case, an unbounded number of servers is needed.

The quantitative behavior of a queueing system can be analyzed during a given time interval (transient analysis) or after the system has reached a stability condition (steady-state analysis). The solution of a queueing system is the probability distribution of the number of customers in the system, which is computed on the basis of the underlying stochastic process. This solution can then be exploited for calculating the average indicators of Sect. 6.2, which represent the mean number of customers leaving the system per unit of time, the mean fraction of time during which the servers are used, the mean number of customers in the system, and the mean response time experienced by the customers visiting the system.

The stability condition enabling steady-state analysis requires, in general, that the customer arrival rate be less than the service rate, so as not to saturate the queueing system. In the specific case of a queueing system M/M/1 with arrival rate $\lambda \in \mathbb{R}_{>0}$ and service rate $\mu \in \mathbb{R}_{>0}$, the stability condition is $\lambda < \mu$. Although the stochastic process underlying this queueing system is an infinite-state continuous-time Markov chain, the birth–death structure of such a stochastic process implies that the number N_1 of customers in the system is geometrically distributed with the parameter given by the traffic intensity $\rho_1 = \lambda/\mu$ under FCFS, LCFS, LCFS-PR, SIRO, and PS. Therefore, the probability that there are $k \in \mathbb{N}$ customers in the system is:

$$\Pr\{N_1 = k\} = \rho_1^k \cdot (1 - \rho_1)$$

The average indicators for the queueing system M/M/1 above can then be easily derived in symbolic form as follows:

- The throughput is given by the service rate multiplied by the probability that there is at least one customer in the system, which turns out to coincide with the arrival rate:

$$\boxed{\overline{T}_1 = \mu \cdot \Pr\{N_1 > 0\} = \mu \cdot \rho_1 = \lambda}$$

- The utilization is given by the probability that there is at least one customer in the system:

$$\boxed{\overline{U}_1 = 1 - \Pr\{N_1 = 0\} = \rho_1}$$

- The mean number of customers in the system is the expected value of the geometrically distributed random variable for the number of customers in the system:

$$\boxed{\overline{N}_1 = \sum_{k=0}^{\infty} k \cdot \Pr\{N_1 = k\} = \frac{\rho_1}{1-\rho_1}}$$

- The mean response time is obtained from Little's law as the ratio of the mean number of customers in the system to the arrival rate:

$$\boxed{\overline{R}_1 = \overline{N}_1/\lambda = \frac{1}{\mu \cdot (1-\rho_1)}}$$

In the slightly more general case of a queueing system M/M/m with arrival rate $\lambda \in \mathbb{R}_{>0}$, there are $m \in \mathbb{N}_{>0}$ identical servers that operate independently and in parallel each with service rate $\mu \in \mathbb{R}_{>0}$. In this case, the traffic intensity is defined by $\rho_m = \lambda/(m \cdot \mu)$ and, under the stability condition $\rho_m < 1$ and the same queueing disciplines as before, the average indicators in symbolic form are given by:

$$\overline{T}_m = \sum_{k=1}^{m-1} k \cdot \mu \cdot \Pr\{N_m = k\} + m \cdot \mu \cdot \Pr\{N_m \geq m\} = \lambda$$

$$\overline{U}_m = 1 - \Pr\{N_m = 0\} = 1 - \left(\sum_{k=0}^{m-1} \frac{(m \cdot \rho_m)^k}{k!} + \frac{(m \cdot \rho_m)^m}{m! \cdot (1 - \rho_m)} \right)^{-1}$$

$$\overline{N}_m = \sum_{k=0}^{\infty} k \cdot \Pr\{N_m = k\} = m \cdot \rho_m + \frac{\Pr\{N_m = 0\} \cdot \rho_m \cdot (m \cdot \rho_m)^m}{m! \cdot (1 - \rho_m)^2}$$

$$\overline{R}_m = \overline{N}_m / \lambda = \frac{1}{\mu} \cdot \left(1 + \frac{\Pr\{N_m = 0\} \cdot \rho_m \cdot (m \cdot \rho_m)^{m-1}}{m! \cdot (1 - \rho_m)^2} \right)$$

A queueing network is a set of interconnected service centers, which are queueing systems when considered in isolation and hence for each of them it is necessary to specify the six parameters mentioned before. In order to complete the description of a queueing network, it is also necessary to specify its topology by means of a matrix of routing probabilities governing the customer flow through the network.

Similar to queueing systems, a queueing network is said to be single class or multiclass depending on the number of classes of customers, with each class possibly characterized by different arrival processes, different service demands, and different routing probabilities. Moreover, a queueing network is said to be open, closed, or mixed depending on the extent to which external arrivals and departures are allowed for the various classes of customers. In an open queueing network, all customers arrive from the outside and every customer that completes service at a service center immediately enters another service center, reenters the same service center, or leaves the network. In a closed queueing network, instead, a fixed number of customers circulate indefinitely among the service centers.

The solution of a queueing network is the probability distribution of the number of customers in the network. This number is actually expressed as a tuple holding the numbers of customers in the various service centers, so as to reflect the structure of the queueing network. Since the state space of the underlying stochastic process grows exponentially with the number of service centers, solving a queueing network can often become unfeasible.

However, there exist families of queueing networks that can be solved compositionally, for which efficient algorithms have been devised. These queueing networks are called product-form queueing networks because the probability that each such queueing network contains a given number of customers $(k_1, k_2, \ldots, k_n)$, with n being the number of its service centers, is the product of the probabilities that every service center i contains k_i customers, up to a normalizing constant in the case of closed queueing networks. In other words, it is possible to solve each service center in isolation and then combine their solutions via multiplications.

An important property of product-form queueing networks is exact aggregation, which allows subnetworks to be replaced with single service centers in such a way that the resulting queueing network has the same quantitative behavior as the original one. Exact aggregation can be exploited for evaluating the average performance indicators of Sect. 6.2 at different abstraction levels. More precisely, the average

indicators can be easily obtained at the global level and at the local level for an open
product-form queueing network composed of M/M service centers by using for each
center the corresponding formulas shown earlier. The arrival rates for the various
service centers can be computed by solving the linear system of traffic equations
defined by the routing probabilities. In the case of closed or mixed product-form
queueing networks, the same average indicators can be derived at the global level
and at the local level by applying suitable algorithms [60, 175, 63, 72].

A well known characterization of product-form queueing networks is given
by the BCMP theorem [27], which establishes that an open/closed/mixed single-
class/multiclass queueing network is product form if it has Poisson arrivals (i.e.,
exponentially distributed interarrival times) with possibly state-dependent rates,
Markovian (i.e., history-independent) routing, and service centers featuring a combination of the following queueing disciplines and service time distributions:

- FCFS with the same exponentially distributed service time for all classes of customers
- LCFS-PR, PS, or IS with phase-type distributed service time possibly different
  for the various classes of customers

In the second case, the values of the average performance indicators do not
change if the phase-type distributed service times are replaced by exponentially distributed service times with the same expected values. The figure below shows basic
examples of phase-type distributions [161], which describe the time to absorption
in finite-state continuous-time Markov chains having exactly one absorbing state:

Exp. distrib.   Hypoexponential distribution   Hyperexponential distribution

Due to the linearity of the expected value operator, it is easy to compute the expected
value of a phase-type distribution. For instance, the expected value of a hypoexponential distribution is the sum of the expected values of its exponentially distributed
consecutive phases. As another example, the expected value of a hyperexponential
distribution is the sum of the expected values of its exponentially distributed alternative phases, each multiplied by the corresponding initial-state probability.

6.5 From ÆMILIA Descriptions to Queueing Networks

PERFSEL employs ÆMILIA descriptions for representing functional and nonfunctional aspects of architectural designs and queueing networks for evaluating their
performance. In this section, we define a transformation that associates queueing
networks with ÆMILIA descriptions.

Apart from producing structured models, we observe that the two formalisms are
quite different from each other. On the one hand, ÆMILIA is a completely formal,

general-purpose architectural description language handling functional and performance aspects, whose basic ingredients are actions and behavioral operators. On the other hand, queueing networks are instances of a queue-based graphical notation for performance modeling purposes only, in which some details like the queueing disciplines are usually expressed in natural language.

As a consequence, only some ÆMILIA descriptions can be transformed into queueing networks, depending on whether they follow a queue-like pattern or not. In order to single out a reasonably wide family of ÆMILIA descriptions from which queueing networks can be derived, we impose a number of general syntactical restrictions (Sect. 6.5.1).

Another issue to be taken into account is that, even though an ÆMILIA description obeys all general syntactical restrictions, it is not necessarily the case that its AEIs can be precisely mapped to the service centers of some queueing network. It is more reasonable to expect to be able to map groups of AEIs to service centers of the form PH/PH/m/c/p or, equivalently, to map each AEI to some basic element of a queueing network. Therefore, we also introduce a number of specific syntactical restrictions in order to single out those AEIs that can be mapped to queueing network basic elements representing arrival processes, buffers, service processes, fork processes, join processes, and routing processes (Sect. 6.5.2).

For each ÆMILIA description obeying both the general and the specific syntactical restrictions, the transformation is accomplished by first mapping the various AEIs into the corresponding queueing network basic elements and then composing such elements according to the attachments declared in the ÆMILIA description. Formally, the transformation is defined through a set of documental functions (Sect. 6.5.3) and a set of characterizing functions (Sect. 6.5.4).

6.5.1 General Syntactical Restrictions

The aim of the general syntactical restrictions is that of identifying ÆMILIA descriptions from which it is possible to derive queueing networks. Given an ÆMILIA description, the first general syntactical restriction requires that every AEI conforms to a queueing network basic element and is suitably connected to the other AEIs in order to yield a well-formed queueing network, as formalized in more detail by the specific syntactical restrictions.

The second general syntactical restriction requires that every interaction is immediate or passive. This restriction simplifies the detection of AEIs representing arrival or service processes, as such processes are built around sets of exponentially timed activities related to customer arrivals or services.

The third general syntactical restriction requires that no AEI contains exponentially timed actions alternative to each other. This restriction avoids the application of the race policy within arrival or service processes, which would not be natural due to the sequential nature of such processes.

The fourth general syntactical restriction requires that no AEI contains exponentially timed actions alternative to immediate or passive actions, immediate actions alternative to passive actions, or interactions alternative to internal actions. This restriction simplifies the detection of the phase-type distributed delays associated with arrival or service processes.

All these restrictions can be automatically checked at the syntax level, without constructing the state space underlying the ÆMILIA description. They preserve much of the modeling power of ÆMILIA, without hampering the representation of typical situations like parallel executions, synchronization constraints, prioritized/probabilistic choices, and activities whose duration is or can be approximated with a phase-type distribution.

On the other hand, such restrictions introduce some limitations on the admitted ÆMILIA descriptions. As an example, preemption cannot be dealt with, as it is not possible to express the fact that the service of a customer of a certain class is interrupted by the arrival of a customer of another class having higher service priority. In general, it is possible to address only queueing disciplines with noninterruptable service for a fixed number of servers, like FCFS, LCFS, SIRO, and NP. We thus exclude policies in which the service of a customer can be interrupted (LCFS-PR, PP) or divided into several rounds (RR, PS) as well as policies in which no queueing takes place as every incoming customer always finds an available server (IS).

6.5.2 Queueing Network Basic Elements

We now present the specific syntactical restrictions by examining the various queueing network basic elements to which the AEIs of an ÆMILIA description should conform. For the sake of simplicity, these elements are represented graphically, with the understanding that the interactions occurring in them are part of process algebraic equations obeying the general syntactical restrictions.

An arrival process is a generator of arrivals of customers of a certain class, whose interarrival times follow a phase-type distribution. As depicted in Fig. 6.3, we distinguish between two kinds of arrival process depending on whether the related customer population is unbounded or finite.

In the first case, the customer interarrival time distribution refers to the whole population. Therefore, it is not necessary to model explicitly the return of customers after they have been served. In the second case, the customer interarrival time distribution varies proportionally to the number of customers that are not requesting any service, hence the return of customers must be explicitly modeled through passive input interactions. In order to achieve a correct scaling of the interarrival time distribution, the various customers of the considered class have to be represented through as many instances of the AET associated with the arrival process. The immediate output (resp. passive input) interactions of these AET instances must consequently be attached to passive input (resp. immediate output) or-interactions of the same AEIs. In both cases, the f alternative immediate output interactions modeling the

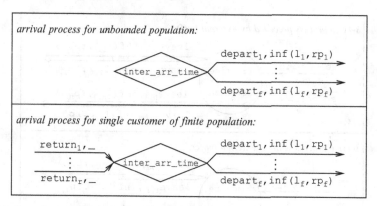

Fig. 6.3 Queueing network basic elements representing arrival processes

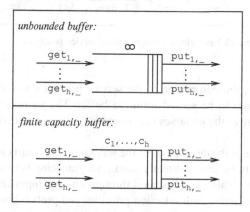

Fig. 6.4 Queueing network basic elements representing buffers

departure of customers towards the queueing network comprise routing priorities and probabilities. Departure can be alternatively represented through a single immediate output or-interaction.

A buffer is a repository of customers of different classes that are waiting to be served according to some noninterruptable queueing discipline like FCFS, LCFS, SIRO, or NP. As depicted in Fig. 6.4, we distinguish between two kinds of buffer depending on the buffer capacity.

In the first case, incoming customers of the h different classes can always be accommodated inside the buffer. In the second case, incoming customers of class i can be accommodated only if the buffer capacity c_i for that class is not exceeded. In both cases, all the interactions are passive and no exponentially timed internal action can occur within the behavior of the AET associated with the buffer.

A service process is a server for customers of different classes, whose service times follow a phase-type distribution for each class. As depicted in Fig. 6.5, we distinguish between two kinds of service process depending on the presence or the absence of a buffer – modeled by another AEI – where customers can wait before being served.

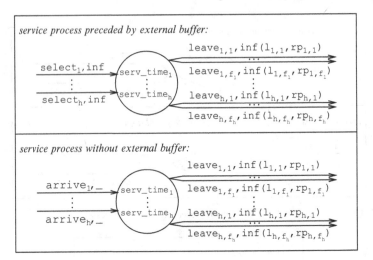

Fig. 6.5 Queueing network basic elements representing service processes

In the first case, the description of the service process starts with the selection of the next customer to be served from the buffer. The immediate input interactions corresponding to the h classes may comprise different selection priorities and probabilities.

In the second case, the description of the service process starts with the arrival of the next customer to be served directly from some queueing network basic element other than a buffer. This is represented through passive input interactions corresponding to the h classes, with selection priorities and probabilities for the various classes possibly encoded within the attached immediate output interactions.

In both cases, the $f_1 + \cdots + f_h$ alternative immediate output interactions modeling the departure of customers comprise routing priorities and probabilities. Some of these interactions are absent if they are related to the return of customers to their unbounded populations. Departure can be alternatively represented through a single immediate output or-interaction. We also observe that the case of a service center composed of several servers corresponds to having several instances of the same AET associated with the service process, with these instances attached to or-interactions of the same AEIs and sharing the same buffer if present.

A fork process splits requests coming from customers of a certain class into subrequests directed to different service centers. As depicted in Fig. 6.6, we distinguish between two kinds of fork process depending on the presence or the absence of a buffer – modeled by another AEI – where requests can wait before being split.

In the first case, an immediate input interaction describes the selection of the next request to be split from the buffer. In the second case, a passive input interaction describes the arrival of the next request to be split directly from some queueing network basic element other than a buffer. In both cases, the departure of subrequests from the fork process can be expressed through f consecutive immediate output

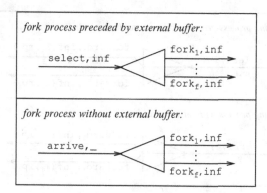

Fig. 6.6 Queueing network basic elements representing fork processes

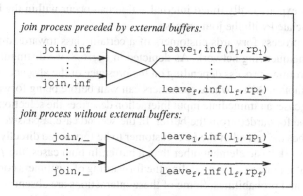

Fig. 6.7 Queueing network basic elements representing join processes

uni-interactions or through a single immediate output and-interaction. Moreover, no exponentially timed internal action can occur within the behavior of the AET associated with the fork process.

A join process merges subrequests coming from customers of a certain class after they have been served at different service centers. As depicted in Fig. 6.7, we distinguish between two kinds of join process depending on the presence or the absence of buffers – modeled by other AEIs – where subrequests can wait before being merged.

In the first case, an immediate input and-interaction describes the selection of the next subrequests to be merged from the buffers. In the second case, a passive input and-interaction describes the arrival of the next subrequests to be merged directly from queueing network basic elements other than buffers. In both cases, the f alternative immediate output interactions modeling the departure of customers comprise routing priorities and probabilities. Some of these interactions are absent if they are related to the return of customers to their unbounded populations. Departure can be alternatively represented through a single immediate output or-interaction.

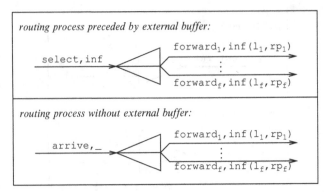

Fig. 6.8 Queueing network basic elements representing routing processes

Moreover, no exponentially timed internal action can occur within the behavior of the AET associated with the join process.

A routing process forwards customers of a certain class towards different destinations in the queueing network. As depicted in Fig. 6.8, we distinguish between two kinds of routing process depending on the presence or the absence of a buffer – modeled by another AEI – where customers can wait before being forwarded.

In the first case, an immediate input interaction describes the selection of the next customer to be forwarded from the buffer. In the second case, a passive input interaction describes the arrival of the next customer to be forwarded directly from some queueing network basic element other than a buffer. In both cases, the f alternative immediate output interactions modeling the forwarding of customers comprise routing priorities and probabilities. Some of these interactions are absent if they are related to the return of customers to their unbounded populations. Forwarding can be alternatively represented through a single immediate output or-interaction. Moreover, no exponentially timed internal action can occur within the behavior of the AET associated with the routing process.

The attachments declared in an ÆMILIA description must be such that the queueing network basic elements derivable from the various AEIs result in a well-formed queueing network. This is formalized by imposing the following additional specific restrictions on connections:

- An arrival process can be followed only by a service or fork process, possibly preceded by a buffer.
- A buffer can be followed only by a service, fork, join, or routing process.
- A service process can be followed by any queueing network basic element.
- A fork process can be followed only by a service process or another fork process, possibly preceded by a buffer.
- A join process can be followed by any queueing network basic element.
- A routing process can be followed by any queueing network basic element.

6.5.3 Documental Functions

Whenever an ÆMILIA description satisfies all general and specific syntactical restrictions, then each of its AEIs is transformed into a queueing network basic element. This is formalized by means of two groups of functions, which provide the attributes that label the resulting queueing network basic elements as depicted in the figures of Sect. 6.5.2.

The four functions of the first group play a documental role for each AEI and are subsequently used to assemble the derived queueing network basic elements according to the attachments declared in the ÆMILIA description:

- Function *qnbe* specifies the kind of queueing network basic element into which the AEI is transformed.
- Function *name* associates the name of the AEI with the corresponding queueing network basic element.
- Function *input* associates the local input interactions of the AEI with the incoming arcs of the corresponding queueing network basic element.
- Function *output* associates the local output interactions of the AEI with the outgoing arcs of the corresponding queueing network basic element.

Example 6.2. Let us consider the performance-aware pipe–filter system of Example 6.1. Observed that its ÆMILIA description satisfies all the syntactical restrictions, function *qnbe* establishes that:

- FB[0], FB[1], FB[2], and FB[3] are buffers
- FC[0], FC[1], FC[2], and FC[3] are service processes each preceded by a buffer
- P is a routing process not preceded by a buffer

The other functions, i.e., *name*, *input*, and *output*, label the above identified queueing network basic elements as expected.

6.5.4 Characterizing Functions

The five functions of the second group characterize the quantitative aspects of the queueing network basic elements derived from the AEIs of an ÆMILIA description obeying all syntactical restrictions:

- Function *inter_arr_time* computes the phase-type distribution governing the interarrival times of the customers of a certain class for an AEI transformed into an arrival process.
- Function *capacity* computes the capacity for an AEI transformed into a buffer.
- Function *queueing_disc* establishes the queueing discipline for an AEI transformed into a buffer.

- Function *serv_time* computes the phase-type distribution governing the service times related to the customers of a certain class for an AEI transformed into a service process.
- Function *routing_prob* computes the routing probabilities of the customers of a certain class for an AEI transformed into an arrival, service, join, or routing process. It also assigns a value to the return of customers to unbounded populations.

Example 6.3. Let us consider again the performance-aware pipe-filter system of Example 6.1. Based on the documental functions of Example 6.2, we have that:

- *capacity* and *queueing_disc* establish that FB[0], FB[1], FB[2], and FB[3] are finite-capacity FCFS buffers for a single class of customers
- *serv_time* establishes that FC[0], FC[1], FC[2], and FC[3] provide service according to an exponential distribution for a single class of customers
- *routing_prob* determines the routing probabilities out of P and assigns value 1 everywhere else

The open single-class queueing network resulting from the application of the various documental and characterizing functions discussed before is shown in Fig. 6.9. We point out that an additional arrival process would be necessary in order to

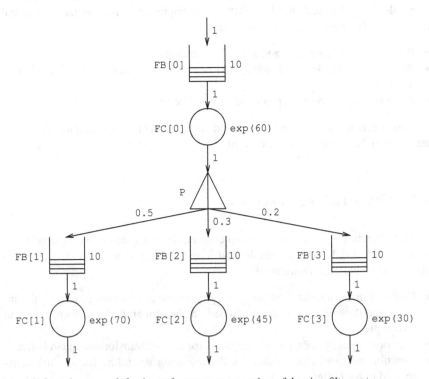

Fig. 6.9 Queueing network for the performance-aware variant of the pipe–filter system

characterize the workload, so that the model would become performance closed, and hence the value of the average performance indicators of Sect. 6.2 could then be calculated.

6.6 Case Study: Selecting Compiler Architectures

We now illustrate an application of PERFSEL to the performance comparison of the three different architectures for a compiler system examined in [19]. This system translates programs written in some programming language into executable code by means of six well-known phases: lexical analysis, parsing, type checking, intermediate code generation, intermediate code optimization, and code synthesis. Not all the programs have to undergo the same sequence of phases. In particular, we distinguish between programs that have to be optimized and programs that do not need to be optimized.

In this section, we consider a sequential architecture (Sect. 6.6.1), a pipeline architecture (Sect. 6.6.2), and a concurrent architecture (Sect. 6.6.3) for the compiler system, by providing for each of them an ÆMILIA description and the corresponding queueing network. Then, we compare their performance in various scenarios on the basis of the usual average indicators (Sect. 6.6.4).

6.6.1 Sequential Architecture

In the case of the sequential architecture, only one program at a time can be compiled. The system thus comprises a buffer in which incoming programs of the two classes wait before being compiled. We assume that each compilation phase introduces an exponentially distributed delay, that the buffer is unbounded, and that the program interarrival times follow an exponential distribution for each class.

Let us model the sequential architecture with ÆMILIA. Here is the architectural description header:

```
ARCHI_TYPE Sequential_Compiler(const rate sc_lambda_1  :=    ,
                               const rate sc_lambda_2  :=    ,
                               const rate sc_mu_1      :=    ,
                               const rate sc_mu_p      :=    ,
                               const rate sc_mu_c      :=    ,
                               const rate sc_mu_g      :=    ,
                               const rate sc_mu_o      :=    ,
                               const rate sc_mu_s      :=   )
```

Note that the description is parameterized with respect to the rates of the various exponential distributions; however, their default actual values have not been specified because the performance comparison can be conducted symbolically. In the following, we use λ_1 and λ_2 as symbolic actual values for the arrival rates of the two classes of programs and $1/\mu_1$, $1/\mu_p$, $1/\mu_c$, $1/\mu_g$, $1/\mu_o$, and $1/\mu_s$ as symbolic actual values for the average durations of the six compilation phases.

The program generator AET is parameterized with respect to the arrival rate of the specific class of customers:

```
ARCHI_ELEM_TYPE Program_Generator_Type(const rate lambda)

  BEHAVIOR
   Program_Generator(void; void) =
    <generate_prog, exp(lambda)> . <deliver_prog, inf> .
                                              Program_Generator()

  INPUT_INTERACTIONS   void
  OUTPUT_INTERACTIONS SYNC UNI deliver_prog
```

The program buffer AET for the two classes of programs is defined as follows:

```
ARCHI_ELEM_TYPE Program_Buffer_2C_Type(void)

  BEHAVIOR
   Program_Buffer_2C(integer n_1 := 0,
                     integer n_2 := 0;
                     void) =
    choice
    {
     <get_prog_1, _> . Program_Buffer_2C(n_1 + 1, n_2),
     <get_prog_2, _> . Program_Buffer_2C(n_1, n_2 + 1),
     cond(n_1 > 0) ->
            <put_prog_1, _> . Program_Buffer_2C(n_1 - 1, n_2),
     cond(n_2 > 0) ->
            <put_prog_2, _> . Program_Buffer_2C(n_1, n_2 - 1)
    }

  INPUT_INTERACTIONS   SYNC UNI get_prog_1; get_prog_2
  OUTPUT_INTERACTIONS SYNC UNI put_prog_1; put_prog_2
```

The sequential compiler AET is parameterized with respect to the service rates of the six compilation phases:

```
ARCHI_ELEM_TYPE Seq_Compiler_Type(const rate mu_1,
                                  const rate mu_p,
                                  const rate mu_c,
                                  const rate mu_g,
                                  const rate mu_o,
                                  const rate mu_s)

  BEHAVIOR
   Seq_Compiler(void; void) =
    choice
    {
     <select_prog_1, inf> .
```

```
                    <recognize_tokens, exp(mu_1)> .
                    <parse_phrases, exp(mu_p)> .
                    <check_phrases, exp(mu_c)> .
                    <generate_icode, exp(mu_g)> .
                    <optimize_icode, exp(mu_o)> .
                    <synthesize_code, exp(mu_s)> . Seq_Compiler(),
            <select_prog_2, inf> .
                    <recognize_tokens, exp(mu_1)> .
                    <parse_phrases, exp(mu_p)> .
                    <check_phrases, exp(mu_c)> .
                    <generate_icode, exp(mu_g)> .
                    <synthesize_code, exp(mu_s)> . Seq_Compiler()
        }

INPUT_INTERACTIONS   SYNC UNI select_prog_1;
                              select_prog_2
OUTPUT_INTERACTIONS void
```

Finally, we have the architectural topology section:

```
ARCHI_ELEM_INSTANCES
  PG_1 : Program_Generator_Type(sc_lambda_1);
  PG_2 : Program_Generator_Type(sc_lambda_2);
  PB   : Program_Buffer_2C_Type();
  SC   : Seq_Compiler_Type(sc_mu_1, sc_mu_p, sc_mu_c,
                           sc_mu_g, sc_mu_o, sc_mu_s)

ARCHI_INTERACTIONS
  void

ARCHI_ATTACHMENTS
  FROM PG_1.deliver_prog TO PB.get_prog_1;
  FROM PG_2.deliver_prog TO PB.get_prog_2;
  FROM PB.put_prog_1     TO SC.select_prog_1;
  FROM PB.put_prog_2     TO SC.select_prog_2
```

Since the ÆMILIA description satisfies all the syntactical restrictions of Sect. 6.5, from it we can derive a queueing network, which is shown in Fig. 6.10. This is

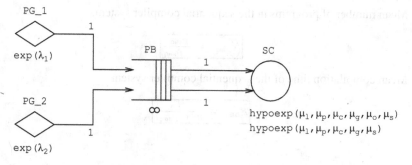

Fig. 6.10 Queueing network for the sequential compiler

a queueing system M/PH/1 for two classes of customers, where PG_1 and PG_2 are two exponential arrival processes, PB is an unbounded FCFS buffer for two classes of customers, and SC is a hypoexponential service process for two classes of customers.

In order to exploit the formulas given in Sect. 6.4 for single-class queueing systems M/M/1, we have to merge the two classes into a single one and then introduce some average-preserving exponential distributions on the service side. More precisely, the two arrival processes can be aggregated consistently with the race policy by taking $\lambda = \lambda_1 + \lambda_2$ as cumulative arrival rate. Then, the two hypoexponential service times can be converted into two average-preserving exponential service times with average durations given respectively by

$$\frac{1}{\mu_1} = \frac{1}{\mu_1} + \frac{1}{\mu_p} + \frac{1}{\mu_c} + \frac{1}{\mu_g} + \frac{1}{\mu_o} + \frac{1}{\mu_s}$$

and

$$\frac{1}{\mu_2} = \frac{1}{\mu_1} + \frac{1}{\mu_p} + \frac{1}{\mu_c} + \frac{1}{\mu_g} + \frac{1}{\mu_s}$$

The last step consists of converting the convex combination of the two derived exponential service times into a single average-preserving exponential service time, whose average duration is given by

$$\frac{1}{\mu} = \frac{\lambda_1}{\lambda} \cdot \left(\frac{1}{\mu_1}\right) + \frac{\lambda_2}{\lambda} \cdot \left(\frac{1}{\mu_2}\right)$$

Under the stability condition $\rho_{seq} = \lambda/\mu < 1$, the value of the average performance indicators of Sect. 6.2 is determined as follows:

- Throughput of the sequential compiler system:

$$\boxed{\overline{T}_{seq} = \lambda}$$

- Utilization of the sequential compiler system:

$$\boxed{\overline{U}_{seq} = \rho_{seq}}$$

- Mean number of programs in the sequential compiler system:

$$\boxed{\overline{N}_{seq} = \frac{\rho_{seq}}{1-\rho_{seq}}}$$

- Mean compilation time of the sequential compiler system:

$$\boxed{\overline{R}_{seq} = \frac{1}{\mu \cdot (1-\rho_{seq})}}$$

6.6.2 Pipeline Architecture

In the case of the pipeline architecture, the simultaneous compilation of several programs at different advancing stages is possible. This is achieved by decoupling the compilation phases by means of intermediate buffers and having the various phases working on a different program.

Let us model the pipeline architecture with ÆMILIA. Here is the architectural description header:

```
ARCHI_TYPE Pipeline_Compiler(const rate pc_lambda_1 :=  ,
                             const rate pc_lambda_2 :=  ,
                             const rate pc_mu_l     :=  ,
                             const rate pc_mu_p     :=  ,
                             const rate pc_mu_c     :=  ,
                             const rate pc_mu_g     :=  ,
                             const rate pc_mu_o     :=  ,
                             const rate pc_mu_s     :=  )
```

where we use the same symbolic actual values as before.

As far as AETs are concerned, we observe that Program_Generator_Type and Program_Buffer_2C_Type are unchanged, while Seq_Compiler_Type needs to be replaced by six new AETs, with each of them corresponding to a different compilation phase.

Since intermediate code optimization deals only with the first class of programs, we also have to introduce a program buffer AET for one class of programs, which is defined as follows:

```
ARCHI_ELEM_TYPE Program_Buffer_1C_Type(void)

  BEHAVIOR
  Program_Buffer_1C(integer n := 0;
                           void) =
  choice
  {
   <get_prog, _> . Program_Buffer_1C(n + 1),
   cond(n > 0) -> <put_prog, _> . Program_Buffer_1C(n - 1)
  }

  INPUT_INTERACTIONS   SYNC UNI get_prog
  OUTPUT_INTERACTIONS  SYNC UNI put_prog
```

The AETs for the compilation phases have basically the same structure, as each of them selects the next program to process from its buffer, works on the program, and then sends it to the buffer of the next phase.

The lexical analyzer AET is defined as follows:

```
ARCHI_ELEM_TYPE Lexer_Type(const rate mu)
```

```
BEHAVIOR
 Lexer(void; void) =
  choice
  {
    <select_prog_1, inf> . <recognize_tokens, exp(mu)> .
                            <deliver_tokens_1, inf> . Lexer(),
    <select_prog_2, inf> . <recognize_tokens, exp(mu)> .
                            <deliver_tokens_2, inf> . Lexer()
  }

INPUT_INTERACTIONS  SYNC UNI select_prog_1;
                             select_prog_2
OUTPUT_INTERACTIONS SYNC UNI deliver_tokens_1;
                             deliver_tokens_2
```

The parser AET is defined as follows:

```
ARCHI_ELEM_TYPE Parser_Type(const rate mu)

 BEHAVIOR
  Parser(void; void) =
   choice
   {
     <select_tokens_1, inf> . <parse_phrases, exp(mu)> .
                             <deliver_phrases_1, inf> . Parser(),
     <select_tokens_2, inf> . <parse_phrases, exp(mu)> .
                             <deliver_phrases_2, inf> . Parser()
   }

 INPUT_INTERACTIONS  SYNC UNI select_tokens_1;
                              select_tokens_2
 OUTPUT_INTERACTIONS SYNC UNI deliver_phrases_1;
                              deliver_phrases_2
```

The type checker AET is defined as follows:

```
ARCHI_ELEM_TYPE Checker_Type(const rate mu)

 BEHAVIOR
  Checker(void; void) =
   choice
   {
     <select_phrases_1, inf> . <check_phrases, exp(mu)> .
                      <deliver_cphrases_1, inf> . Checker(),
     <select_phrases_2, inf> . <check_phrases, exp(mu)> .
                      <deliver_cphrases_2, inf> . Checker()
   }

 INPUT_INTERACTIONS  SYNC UNI select_phrases_1;
                              select_phrases_2
 OUTPUT_INTERACTIONS SYNC UNI deliver_cphrases_1;
                              deliver_cphrases_2
```

The intermediate code generator AET is defined as follows:

```
ARCHI_ELEM_TYPE Generator_Type(const rate mu)

  BEHAVIOR
   Generator(void; void) =
    choice
    {
     <select_cphrases_1, inf> . <generate_icode, exp(mu)> .
                        <deliver_icode_1, inf> . Generator(),
     <select_cphrases_2, inf> . <generate_icode, exp(mu)> .
                        <deliver_icode_2, inf> . Generator()
    }

  INPUT_INTERACTIONS   SYNC UNI select_cphrases_1;
                                select_cphrases_2
  OUTPUT_INTERACTIONS SYNC UNI deliver_icode_1;
                                deliver_icode_2
```

The code synthesizer AET is defined as follows:

```
ARCHI_ELEM_TYPE Synthesizer_Type(const rate mu)

  BEHAVIOR
   Synthesizer(void; void) =
    choice
    {
     <select_oicode_1, inf> .
            <synthesize_code, exp(mu)> . Synthesizer(),
     <select_icode_2, inf> .
            <synthesize_code, exp(mu)> . Synthesizer()
    }

  INPUT_INTERACTIONS  SYNC UNI select_oicode_1;
                               select_icode_2
  OUTPUT_INTERACTIONS void
```

Slightly different is the intermediate code optimizer AET:

```
ARCHI_ELEM_TYPE Optimizer_Type(const rate mu)

  BEHAVIOR
   Optimizer(void; void) =
    <select_icode, inf> . <optimize_icode, exp(mu)> .
                          <deliver_oicode, inf> . Optimizer()

  INPUT_INTERACTIONS  SYNC UNI select_icode
  OUTPUT_INTERACTIONS SYNC UNI deliver_oicode
```

Finally, we have the architectural topology section:

```
ARCHI_ELEM_INSTANCES
  PG_1 : Program_Generator_Type(pc_lambda_1);
```

```
PG_2  :  Program_Generator_Type(pc_lambda_2);
PB_L  :  Program_Buffer_2C_Type();
L     :  Lexer_Type(pc_mu_l);
PB_P  :  Program_Buffer_2C_Type();
P     :  Parser_Type(pc_mu_p);
PB_C  :  Program_Buffer_2C_Type();
C     :  Checker_Type(pc_mu_c);
PB_G  :  Program_Buffer_2C_Type();
G     :  Generator_Type(pc_mu_g);
PB_O  :  Program_Buffer_1C_Type();
O     :  Optimizer_Type(pc_mu_o);
PB_S  :  Program_Buffer_2C_Type();
S     :  Synthesizer_Type(pc_mu_s)

ARCHI_INTERACTIONS
void

ARCHI_ATTACHMENTS
FROM PG_1.deliver_prog        TO PB_L.get_prog_1;
FROM PG_2.deliver_prog        TO PB_L.get_prog_2;
FROM PB_L.put_prog_1          TO L.select_prog_1;
FROM PB_L.put_prog_2          TO L.select_prog_2;
FROM L.deliver_tokens_1       TO PB_P.get_prog_1;
FROM L.deliver_tokens_2       TO PB_P.get_prog_2;
FROM PB_P.put_prog_1          TO P.select_tokens_1;
FROM PB_P.put_prog_2          TO P.select_tokens_2;
FROM P.deliver_phrases_1      TO PB_C.get_prog_1;
FROM P.deliver_phrases_2      TO PB_C.get_prog_2;
FROM PB_C.put_prog_1          TO C.select_phrases_1;
FROM PB_C.put_prog_2          TO C.select_phrases_2;
FROM C.deliver_cphrases_1     TO PB_G.get_prog_1;
FROM C.deliver_cphrases_2     TO PB_G.get_prog_2;
FROM PB_G.put_prog_1          TO G.select_cphrases_1;
FROM PB_G.put_prog_2          TO G.select_cphrases_2;
FROM G.deliver_icode_1        TO PB_O.get_prog;
FROM G.deliver_icode_2        TO PB_S.get_prog_2;
FROM PB_O.put_prog            TO O.select_icode;
FROM O.deliver_oicode         TO PB_S.get_prog_1;
FROM PB_S.put_prog_1          TO S.select_oicode_1;
FROM PB_S.put_prog_2          TO S.select_icode_2
```

Since the ÆMILIA description satisfies all the syntactical restrictions of Sect. 6.5, from it we can derive a queueing network, which is shown in Fig. 6.11. This is an open network of five queueing systems M/M/1 for two classes of customers and one queueing system M/M/1 for one class of customers. In particular, PG_1 and PG_2 are two exponential arrival processes; PB_L, PB_P, PB_C, PB_G, and PB_S are unbounded FCFS buffers for two classes of customers; PB_O is an unbounded FCFS buffer for one class of customers; L, P, C, G, and S are exponential service processes for two classes of customers; and O is an exponential service process for one class of customers.

In order to exploit the BCMP theorem and the formulas given in Sect. 6.4 for single-class queueing systems M/M/1, we simply have to merge the two classes into a single one. Observed that the service rate is uniquely defined for each phase, the

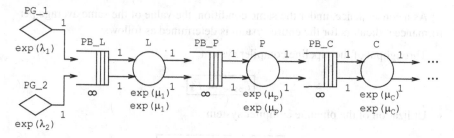

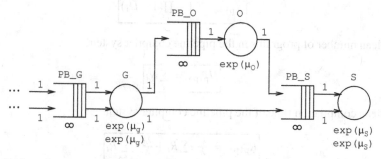

Fig. 6.11 Queueing network for the pipeline compiler

cumulative arrival rate for all phases excluding optimization is given by $\lambda = \lambda_1 + \lambda_2$, whereas the arrival rate for the optimization phase is λ_1. Moreover, we also have to take into account that the probability that a program leaving the code generator enters the optimizer (resp. the synthesizer) is λ_1/λ (resp. λ_2/λ).

The stability conditions for the phases involving both classes are $\rho_1 = \lambda/\mu_1 < 1$, $\rho_p = \lambda/\mu_p < 1$, $\rho_c = \lambda/\mu_c < 1$, $\rho_g = \lambda/\mu_g < 1$, and $\rho_s = \lambda/\mu_s < 1$, whereas for the optimization phase it is $\rho_o = \lambda_1/\mu_o < 1$. Therefore, the overall stability condition for the entire system is given by $\lambda < \min(\mu_1, \mu_p, \mu_c, \mu_g, \mu_o \cdot \lambda/\lambda_1, \mu_s)$.

Under this condition, the value of the average performance indicators of Sect. 6.2 for each phase i is determined as follows:

- Throughput of phase i:

$$\boxed{\begin{aligned} \overline{T}_i &= \lambda \qquad \text{if } i \in \{1, \text{p}, \text{c}, \text{g}, \text{s}\} \\ \overline{T}_o &= \lambda_1 \end{aligned}}$$

- Utilization of phase i:

$$\boxed{\overline{U}_i = \rho_i}$$

- Mean number of programs in phase i:

$$\boxed{\overline{N}_i = \frac{\rho_i}{1 - \rho_i}}$$

- Mean processing time of phase i:

$$\boxed{\overline{R}_i = \frac{1}{\mu_i \cdot (1 - \rho_i)}}$$

As a consequence, under the same condition, the value of the same average performance indicators for the entire system is determined as follows:

- Throughput of the pipeline compiler system:

$$\boxed{\overline{T}_{\mathtt{pipe}} = \overline{T}_{\mathtt{s}}}$$

- Utilization of the pipeline compiler system:

$$\boxed{\overline{U}_{\mathtt{pipe}} = 1 - \prod_{i}(1 - \overline{U}_i)}$$

- Mean number of programs in the pipeline compiler system:

$$\boxed{\overline{N}_{\mathtt{pipe}} = \sum_{i}\overline{N}_i}$$

- Mean compilation time of the pipeline compiler system:

$$\boxed{\overline{R}_{\mathtt{pipe}} = \frac{\lambda_1}{\lambda} \cdot \sum_{i}\overline{R}_i + \frac{\lambda_2}{\lambda} \cdot \sum_{i \neq o}\overline{R}_i}$$

6.6.3 Concurrent Architecture

In the case of the concurrent architecture, the simultaneous compilation of several programs is possible, thanks to the presence of several replicas of the sequential compiler. These replicas work independent of each other and share the same buffer for incoming programs.

Let us model the concurrent architecture with ÆMILIA. Here is the architectural description header:

```
ARCHI_TYPE Concurrent_Compiler(const integer cc_seq_num  := 2,
                               const rate    cc_lambda_1 :=  ,
                               const rate    cc_lambda_2 :=  ,
                               const rate    cc_mu_1     :=  ,
                               const rate    cc_mu_p     :=  ,
                               const rate    cc_mu_c     :=  ,
                               const rate    cc_mu_g     :=  ,
                               const rate    cc_mu_o     :=  ,
                               const rate    cc_mu_s     :=  )
```

where we use the same symbolic actual values as before and we have an additional parameter for the number of replicas of the sequential compiler.

This description has the same AETs as the description for the sequential architecture, with the only difference that the output interactions put_prog_1 and put_prog_2 of the program buffer AET are declared as or-interactions in order to support multiplicity variations that arise when changing the number of replicas of the sequential compiler.

Then, we have the architectural topology section:

```
ARCHI_ELEM_INSTANCES
  PG_1 : Program_Generator_Type(cc_lambda_1);
  PG_2 : Program_Generator_Type(cc_lambda_2);
  PB   : Program_Buffer_2C_Type();
  FOR_ALL 1 <= j <= cc_seq_num
    SC[j] : Seq_Compiler_Type(cc_mu_1, cc_mu_p, cc_mu_c,
                              cc_mu_g, cc_mu_o, cc_mu_s)

ARCHI_INTERACTIONS
  void

ARCHI_ATTACHMENTS
  FROM PG_1.deliver_prog TO PB.get_prog_1;
  FROM PG_2.deliver_prog TO PB.get_prog_2;
  FOR_ALL 1 <= j <= cc_seq_num
   FROM PB.put_prog_1 TO SC[j].select_prog_1;
  FOR_ALL 1 <= j <= cc_seq_num
   FROM PB.put_prog_2 TO SC[j].select_prog_2
```

Since the ÆMILIA description satisfies all the syntactical restrictions of Sect. 6.5, from it we can derive a queueing network, which is shown in Fig. 6.12. This is a queueing system M/PH/2 for two classes of customers, where PG_1 and PG_2 are two exponential arrival processes, PB is an unbounded FCFS buffer for two classes of customers, and SC[1] and SC[2] are two identical hypoexponential service processes for two classes of customers.

In order to exploit the formulas given in Sect. 6.4 for single-class QSs M/M/2, we have to merge the two classes into a single one and then introduce some average-preserving exponential distributions on the service side. After making manipulations similar to those for the sequential compiler, we get $\lambda = \lambda_1 + \lambda_2$ as cumulative arrival rate together with

$$\frac{1}{\mu} = \frac{\lambda_1}{\lambda} \cdot \left(\frac{1}{\mu_1} + \frac{1}{\mu_p} + \frac{1}{\mu_c} + \frac{1}{\mu_g} + \frac{1}{\mu_o} + \frac{1}{\mu_s} \right) + \frac{\lambda_2}{\lambda} \cdot \left(\frac{1}{\mu_1} + \frac{1}{\mu_p} + \frac{1}{\mu_c} + \frac{1}{\mu_g} + \frac{1}{\mu_s} \right)$$

as average service duration.

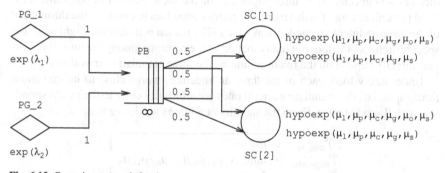

Fig. 6.12 Queueing network for the concurrent compiler

Under the stability condition $\rho_{\text{conc}} = \lambda/(2 \cdot \mu) < 1$, the value of the average performance indicators of Sect. 6.2 is determined as follows:

- Throughput of the concurrent compiler system:

$$\boxed{\overline{T}_{\text{conc}} = \lambda}$$

- Utilization of the concurrent compiler system:

$$\boxed{\overline{U}_{\text{conc}} = \frac{2 \cdot \rho_{\text{conc}}}{1 + \rho_{\text{conc}}}}$$

- Mean number of programs in the concurrent compiler system:

$$\boxed{\overline{N}_{\text{conc}} = \frac{2 \cdot \rho_{\text{conc}}}{1 - \rho_{\text{conc}}^2}}$$

- Mean compilation time of the concurrent compiler system:

$$\boxed{\overline{R}_{\text{conc}} = \frac{1}{\mu_{\text{conc}} \cdot (1 - \rho_{\text{conc}}^2)}}$$

6.6.4 Scenario-Based Performance Selection

In order to select which of the three architectural designs is more appropriate to implement, as prescribed by PERFSEL we compare the values of their average performance indicators in various scenarios of interest.

First of all, we point out that the comparison must be fair. This means that identical actual values of service rates have to be used for each compilation phase across the three architectures. Moreover, the actual values of the arrival rates for each class of programs can be different from architecture to architecture, but must ensure that the frequencies p_1 and p_2 of the two classes of programs do not vary across the three architectures. For instance, fairness is simply achieved by using the same symbolic actual values λ_1, λ_2, μ_1, μ_p, μ_c, μ_g, μ_o, and μ_s that have already been introduced.

For the sake of simplicity, among the four considered average performance indicators we concentrate on throughput, i.e., on the mean number of programs compiled per unit of time. Furthermore, we restrict ourselves to compare the throughput of the three architectures under heavy load. The reason is that, under light load, the specific architecture does not really matter, as the relations among the three throughputs directly depend on the relations among the three cumulative arrival rates.

Under heavy load, each of the three architectures works close to its maximum throughput, i.e., the cumulative arrival rates are arbitrarily close to their corresponding overall service rates. From the stability conditions we derive that:

$$\boxed{\begin{aligned} \overline{T}_{\text{seq,max}} &= \mu \\ \overline{T}_{\text{pipe,max}} &= \min(\mu_1, \mu_p, \mu_c, \mu_g, \mu_o/p_1, \mu_s) \\ \overline{T}_{\text{conc,max}} &= 2 \cdot \mu \end{aligned}}$$

In this setting, the performance comparison is conducted symbolically by examining three scenarios. In the first one, we assume that all compilation phases have the same average duration μ_{avg}^{-1}. In this case:

$$
\begin{aligned}
\overline{T}_{seq,max} &= (5+p_1)^{-1} \cdot \mu_{avg} \\
\overline{T}_{pipe,max} &= \mu_{avg} \\
\overline{T}_{conc,max} &= 2 \cdot (5+p_1)^{-1} \cdot \mu_{avg}
\end{aligned}
$$

hence:

$$
\begin{aligned}
\overline{T}_{pipe,max}/\overline{T}_{seq,max} &= 5+p_1 \\
\overline{T}_{pipe,max}/\overline{T}_{conc,max} &= 2.5+0.5 \cdot p_1 \\
\overline{T}_{conc,max}/\overline{T}_{seq,max} &= 2
\end{aligned}
$$

which implies that the pipeline architecture is the most convenient one under the assumption above.

In the second scenario, we assume that there is a compilation phase whose average duration is several orders of magnitude greater than the average duration of the other phases. Suppose, e.g., that lexical analysis is the bottleneck. In this case:

$$
\begin{aligned}
\overline{T}_{seq,max} &= \mu_1 \\
\overline{T}_{pipe,max} &= \mu_1 \\
\overline{T}_{conc,max} &= 2 \cdot \mu_1
\end{aligned}
$$

hence:

$$
\begin{aligned}
\overline{T}_{conc,max}/\overline{T}_{pipe,max} &= 2 \\
\overline{T}_{conc,max}/\overline{T}_{seq,max} &= 2 \\
\overline{T}_{pipe,max}/\overline{T}_{seq,max} &= 1
\end{aligned}
$$

which implies that the concurrent architecture is the most convenient one under the assumption above.

Finally, in the third scenario we assume that the average duration of all phases ranges between μ_{max}^{-1} and μ_{min}^{-1}, with the two endpoints possibly being several orders of magnitude apart. In this case:

$$
\begin{aligned}
(5+p_1)^{-1} \cdot \mu_{min} &\leq \overline{T}_{seq,max} \leq (5+p_1)^{-1} \cdot \mu_{max} \\
\mu_{min} &\leq \overline{T}_{pipe,max} \leq \mu_{min} \\
2 \cdot (5+p_1)^{-1} \cdot \mu_{min} &\leq \overline{T}_{conc,max} \leq 2 \cdot (5+p_1)^{-1} \cdot \mu_{max}
\end{aligned}
$$

hence:

$$
\begin{aligned}
(5+p_1) \cdot \frac{\mu_{min}}{\mu_{max}} &\leq \overline{T}_{pipe,max}/\overline{T}_{seq,max} \leq 5+p_1 \\
(2.5+0.5 \cdot p_1) \cdot \frac{\mu_{min}}{\mu_{max}} &\leq \overline{T}_{pipe,max}/\overline{T}_{conc,max} \leq 2.5+0.5 \cdot p_1 \\
2 &\leq \overline{T}_{conc,max}/\overline{T}_{seq,max} \leq 2
\end{aligned}
$$

Therefore, in general, the concurrent architecture is twice more productive than the sequential one and the pipeline architecture can perform better/worse than the other two depending on the distance between μ_{min} and μ_{max}.

6.7 Comparisons

The performance-driven architectural selection procedure presented in this chapter is taken from [43, 25]. On the modeling side, PERFSEL makes use of process algebraic architectural descriptions extended with performance information. Such descriptions provide an integrated view of functional and nonfunctional aspects, which overcomes the well-known drawbacks related to the insularity of performance modeling [88] and, at the same time, ensures the consistency of the results obtained from functional verification with the results derived from performance evaluation. In particular, it enables the application of the architecture-level techniques for mismatch detection discussed in Chap. 5.

On the analysis side, PERFSEL resorts to queueing networks as they are structured performance models and hence provide support for relating their constituent parts with system components. The existence of fast solution algorithms for certain families of queueing networks and their capability of giving insights both at the system level and at the component level make them an effective tool in the software performance engineering field, as already recognized, e.g., in [186, 195].

PERFSEL is not aimed at precisely assessing the performance of architectural designs. Rather, it focuses on a restricted number of typical average performance indicators as a means for the rapid prediction, improvement, and comparison of the quantitative behavior of alternative designs. In order to achieve a tradeoff between efficiency and accuracy, the verification of the specific performance requirements is done in detail in the last phase of PERFSEL, once a specific architectural design has been selected and optimized with respect to the average performance indicators.

With regard to the transformation of process algebraic architectural descriptions into queueing network models, this is similar in spirit to the derivation of the same kind of models proposed in [19]. The difference is that queueing networks are extracted from labeled transition systems rather than process algebraic architectural descriptions. The advantage is that in this way the transformation method is independent from the architectural description language adopted by the software designer. The disadvantage is that the transformation method is more complicated as it is applied to a low-level model that does not elucidate the component-based structure of the system it represents.

Chapter 7
Trading Dependability and Performance

Abstract Modern software systems are often subject to dependability and performance requirements in conflict with each other. Since it is common to carry out separately dependability analysis and performance evaluation, the study of a tradeoff becomes hard to accomplish. In this chapter, we present DEPPERF, a component-oriented methodology that can be used at the architectural design level for predicting the qualitative and quantitative impact of individual components on system dependability and performance. The methodology encompasses the behavioral equivalence approach to noninterference analysis and standard performance evaluation techniques, in order to reveal functional and nonfunctional dependences among components and then pinpoint the metrics to investigate for achieving a balanced tradeoff. The methodology is illustrated through its application to a secure routing system and to a power-manageable system.

7.1 DEPPERF: Mixed View of Dependability and Performance

In the previous two chapters, we have considered component-oriented analysis techniques for functional verification and performance evaluation, respectively, which represent two consolidated tasks contributing to the assessment of the dependability and the efficiency of software architectures. While performance evaluation concentrates on measures of the quality of service like system productivity, resource usage, and response time for a properly working system, dependability analysis focuses on different aspects such as reliability, safety, security, and availability, which are related to the ability of delivering a service that can be justifiably trusted [135]. In particular, reliability expresses the continuity of the delivery of correct service, safety regards the absence of catastrophic consequences in case of improper service, security determines the robustness against malicious intruders, and availability refers to the promptness of the provision of proper service.

All together, the above mentioned measures and aspects concur in an orthogonal way to the definition of the performability profile of a system. Performability,

intended as the ability to perform in the presence of faults, was originally motivated by the needs of degradable systems, which are highly dependable systems
that can possibly undergo a tolerable degradation of performance in order to ensure
the provision of service under negative circumstances [151]. The integration of the
assessment of dependability aspects with the evaluation of performance measures
can provide a clear understanding of the interrelations between dependability and
performance requirements.

Achieving a reasonable balance between these often conflicting requirements is
of utmost importance in component-based software design. Components that run
perfect, either in isolation or in a particular configuration, can cause problems in
other combinations or under partial system faults, mainly because of resource dependences, constraint conflicts, and information flow interferences. A systematic
treatment of these problems in the software design process is a major challenge
that requires the combination of several analysis techniques. Unfortunately, different
aspects are usually dealt with by heterogeneous analysis techniques that are applied
separately and, even worse, consider different descriptions of the software architecture, without a clear comprehension of how to validate mutually such descriptions,
how to combine the results obtained through the various analysis techniques, and,
most importantly, how to evaluate the correlation among such results.

These problems are exacerbated in the case of modern computing systems, which
are characterized by interacting software components executing orthogonal activities over wide-area networks composed of devices performing their tasks in a col-
laborative way. A single component may be dedicated to a sole specific aspect in a
one-to-one fashion, as in the case of power-consumption control [29], or else crosscutting aspects may be handled by several different components, as happens for
fault tolerance reasons [152]. In any case, the involved components may interfere
with each other when working for satisfying different requirements. For instance,
mechanisms for controlling power-consumption are typically designed in such a
way to avoid any observable interference with service reliability and, in particular,
with performance indices like response time.

Along the same line, it is commonly recognized that lightweight security is necessary in systems such as mobile computing platforms and wireless networks, where
the securing mechanisms must meet the security needs in face of strict resource constraints. Lightweight securing infrastructures like those employed for access control
in the setting of the IEEE 802.11 standard for wireless local area networks [196]
are able to mitigate the impact of the securing mechanisms on quality of service parameters, such as system throughput and response time, still preserving to a specific
extent the properties for which they are introduced.

These and other examples highlight the importance of integrating the different
qualitative and quantitative views of a system in order to understand whether a reasonable balance can be achieved between the expected quality of service and the
satisfaction of dependability requirements. An integrated view can then be at the
base of a predictive methodology combining both dependability analysis and performance evaluation, with the aim of guiding the system design towards the desired
tradeoff among all the various aspects.

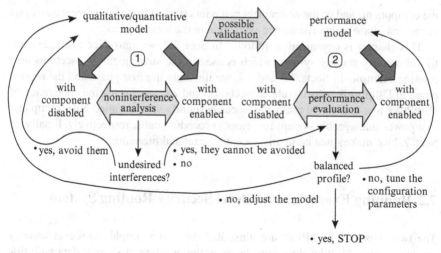

Fig. 7.1 Models and phases of DEPPERF

In this chapter, we present a methodology called DEPPERF for predicting the existence, estimating the impact, and mitigating the effect of interferences caused by some components on the behavior of other components. For this purpose, the methodology employs an integrated system view and combines different techniques for dependability analysis and performance evaluation. As illustrated in Fig. 7.1, the methodology DEPPERF consists of the following two phases:

1. Noninterference analysis, which is carried out to predict the influence of specific components on system dependability properties, so as to establish the absence of undesired, direct and indirect information flows through the system [101,89]. Essentially, it reduces to verify whether system projections in which certain components are enabled or disabled are equivalent to each other by applying variants of the architectural checks of Chap. 5.
2. Performance evaluation, which is conducted to estimate the impact of the previously revealed interferences and the effect of the corresponding mitigating strategies on the quality of service. To this aim, standard performance techniques are employed, including the numerical solution of Markov chain models [188] or the analysis of queueing network models [130] as discussed in Chap. 6.

The results returned by each phase should help the designer to pinpoint the causes of system crosscutting anomalies, change the system model, and configure system parameters, depending on the requirements that should be met.

Each of the two phases of DEPPERF works on a component-oriented formal description of the system at hand expressed in ÆMILIA, the process algebraic architectural description language introduced in Chap. 6. The choice of ÆMILIA guarantees by construction the consistency between functional and performance models obtained from its descriptions. Moreover, it facilitates the identification of the components and of the component behaviors subject to noninterference analysis in the first phase and performance evaluation in the second phase.

This chapter is organized as follows. In Sect. 7.2, we introduce a simple multilevel security routing system, which is used in the subsequent two sections as a running example. In Sects. 7.3 and 7.4, we illustrate the first phase and the second phase of DEPPERF, respectively. In Sects. 7.5 and 7.6, we discuss the application of DEPPERF to a real-world multilevel security routing system called NRL pump and to a power-manageable system for remote procedure calls, respectively. Finally, in Sect. 7.7 we make some comparisons with the related literature.

7.2 Running Example: Multilevel Security Routing System

The two phases of DEPPERF are illustrated through a simple multilevel security routing system. Multilevel security refers to the problem of sharing data with different access clearances in the same system or network. The goal is permitting information to flow freely among users having appropriate security clearances while preventing leaks to unauthorized users.

For the sake of simplicity, we consider only two access clearance levels, high and low, and users playing only two different roles, sender and receiver. The communication between these users is controlled by a router that regulates the exchange of messages among senders and receivers on the basis of their level. We also assume that there is only one high (resp. low) sender and only one high (resp. low) receiver.

Let us model this system with ÆMILIA. Here is the architectural description header:

```
ARCHI_TYPE ML_Sec_Routing(const rate mlsr_sending_high := 4
                          const rate mlsr_sending_low  := 4
                          const rate mlsr_trans_high   := 5
                          const rate mlsr_trans_low    := 5)
```

The formal data parameters specify rates expressed in s^{-1} that are concerned with the duration of system activities. The average sending time for high and low senders is 250 ms, while the average transmission time from the routing system to each receiver is 200 ms. We use four different parameters because when conducting performance evaluation we will make them vary in different ranges.

The system comprises four AETs: the sender, the buffer, the router, and the receiver. The sender AET, which repeatedly sends messages, is defined as follows:

```
ARCHI_ELEM_TYPE Sender_Type(const rate sending_rate)

  BEHAVIOR
   Sender(void; void) =
   <send, exp(sending_rate)> . Sender()

  INPUT_INTERACTIONS  void
  OUTPUT_INTERACTIONS SYNC UNI send
```

and the receiver AET, which is waiting for incoming messages, is defined as follows:

```
ARCHI_ELEM_TYPE Receiver_Type(void)

  BEHAVIOR
   Receiver(void; void) =
    <receive, _(0, 1)> . Receiver()

  INPUT_INTERACTIONS   SYNC UNI receive
  OUTPUT_INTERACTIONS void
```

The routing system is made of two one-position buffers – one for each level – and a shared router. The buffer AET is defined as follows:

```
ARCHI_ELEM_TYPE Buffer_Type(void)

  BEHAVIOR
   Buffer(void; void) =
    <deposit, _(0, 1)> . <withdraw, _(1, 1)> . Buffer()

  INPUT_INTERACTIONS   SYNC UNI deposit
  OUTPUT_INTERACTIONS SYNC UNI withdraw
```

The router accepts messages arriving from high and low senders and then transmits them to receivers of the corresponding level. The router AET is as follows:

```
ARCHI_ELEM_TYPE Router_Type(const rate trans_rate_high,
                            const rate trans_rate_low)

  BEHAVIOR
   Router(void; void) =
    choice
    {
     <get_high, inf(1, 1)> .
      <trans_high, exp(trans_rate_high)> . Router(),
     <get_low, inf(1, 1)> .
      <trans_low, exp(trans_rate_low)> . Router()
    }

  INPUT_INTERACTIONS   SYNC UNI get_high; get_low
  OUTPUT_INTERACTIONS SYNC UNI trans_high; trans_low
```

The architectural topology section, which is illustrated by the enriched flow graph of Fig. 7.2, is as follows:

```
ARCHI_ELEM_INSTANCES
S_High : Sender_Type(mlsr_sending_high);
S_Low  : Sender_Type(mlsr_sending_low);
B_High : Buffer_Type();
B_Low  : Buffer_Type();
U      : Router_Type(mlsr_trans_high,
                     mlsr_trans_low);
R_High : Receiver_Type();
R_Low  : Receiver_Type()
```

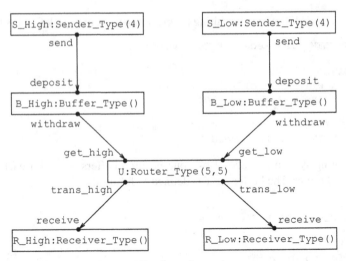

Fig. 7.2 Enriched flow graph of the multilevel security routing system

```
ARCHI_INTERACTIONS
  void

ARCHI_ATTACHMENTS
  FROM S_High.send      TO B_High.deposit;
  FROM S_Low.send       TO B_Low.deposit;
  FROM B_High.withdraw  TO U.get_high;
  FROM B_Low.withdraw   TO U.get_low;
  FROM U.trans_high     TO R_High.receive;
  FROM U.trans_low      TO R_Low.receive
```

7.3 First Phase of DEPPERF: Noninterference Analysis

The objective of the first phase of DEPPERF is to reveal potential interferences among system components that may affect the satisfaction of dependability requirements. Such interferences arise whenever some components behave in a way that hampers some other components that intend to ensure dependability. For example, the first phase can be used for studying the influence of faults triggered by a component upon the behavior of other components performing safety-critical applications, or else for determining the influence of events caused by nontrusted components upon the behavior of components performing security-critical applications [189].

In this section, we introduce the basics of noninterference theory (Sect. 7.3.1), we show how to apply it to the general setting of the first phase (Sect. 7.3.2), we discuss how to make it component oriented (Sect. 7.3.3), and finally we explain how to interpret the feedback it provides (Sect. 7.3.4).

7.3.1 Noninterference Theory

The noninterference approach to information flow theory [101] was originally proposed for the formal verification of security properties (see, e.g., [147] and the references therein) and is essentially implemented by resorting to equivalence checking (see, e.g., [90] and the references therein).

The basic idea behind noninterference applies to multilevel security systems and can be illustrated as follows. A group of high security level users, who perform confidential operations only, does not interfere with a group of low security level users, who observe public operations only, if what the former group of users can do with the confidential operations has no effect on what the latter group of users can see. Noninterference analysis can reveal direct and indirect information flows that violate the security policies based on the access clearances assigned to different user groups. These illegal flows represent a leakage of information from high security level users to low security level users.

In order to formalize what a user at a certain security level can see, the activities performed by the system are divided into two disjoint sets: *High*, representing system activities at high security level, and *Low*, representing system activities at low security level. Then, independent of the specific formalization of the notion of noninterference, checking noninterference is actually verifying the indistinguishability of the different low-level views of the system that are obtained by changing the high-level behavior.

Several notions of noninterference have been designed to analyze sequential programs and concurrent systems (see, e.g., [193, 92, 144, 125]), in particular also in the setting of process algebra (see, e.g., [89, 178, 139]). Without loss of generality, the first phase of DEPPERF concentrates on (variants of) strong nondeterministic noninterference [89]. This establishes whether the view of the system behavior as observed by a low-level user when the system interacts with high-level users is the same – according to weak bisimulation equivalence $\approx_B$ (see Sect. 1.4.8) – as that observed by the low-level user in the absence of high-level users.

Formally, a process term P representing the behavior of a system has no illegal information leakage if the low system view where the high-level activities are made unobservable is indistinguishable from the low system view where these activities are prevented from execution:

$$P/High \approx_B P \backslash High$$

A weak behavioral equivalence is needed because the noninterference comparison requires the ability of abstracting from the high-level activities that a low-level user cannot see directly. In particular, $\approx_B$ is sufficiently expressive to be sensitive to high-level interferences causing, e.g., deadlock or violations of properties that depend on the branching structure of the models. If the two system views to compare do not behave the same, then a low-level user can detect indirectly the behavior of the high-level part of the system by observing what happens at the low level. In other words, an indirect information flow from high level to low level, called covert channel, is set up by exploiting the distinguishing power of the low-level user.

Moving to a quantitative framework including fine-grain information, such as probability distributions associated with event execution, augments the distinguishing power of the observer, as recognized in [146, 106, 179, 11, 12]. A quantitative notion of noninterference can be based not only on probabilistic information, but also on temporal information. Several proposals concerned with timed extensions of noninterference have been made, e.g., in the setting of deterministically timed process algebra [87, 91], probabilistic timed automata [134, 85], and stochastically timed process algebra [10], while other time-based aspects of noninterference have been investigated, e.g., in the context of information theory [145]. As an example, a stochastic variant of noninterference that takes into account the exponentially distributed timing of events can be defined in terms of weak Markovian bisimulation equivalence $\approx_{MB}$ (see Sect. 3.3.8).

In general, the more information is added to a system model, the higher the number of vulnerabilities revealed through fine-grain notions of noninterference. In this case, some covert channels that are revealed cannot be completely eliminated without introducing complicated (and perhaps invasive) securing strategies.

7.3.2 Noninterference Verification

The noninterference approach to security analysis can be reused in other frameworks in order to verify system dependability. The intuition is that a covert channel reveals an information flow, from a part of the system to another one, which can unexpectedly alter the behavior of system components. In essence, the basic idea of noninterference can be generalized by viewing a system execution as an information flow. As a consequence, we can say that a group of system components does not interfere with another group of system components if the behavior of the former group has no effect on the behavior of the latter group.

The above mentioned reuse of noninterference for dependability assessment purposes is embodied in the first phase of DEPPERF. In fact, first of all the parts of the component behavior related to the chosen dependability aspect are elucidated. Then, by rephrasing the security-based classification of activities mentioned in Sect. 7.3.1, the local interactions occurring in the relevant parts of the component behavior are divided into two sets, *High* and *Low*.

In particular, *High* contains the interfering local interactions of which we intend to evaluate the impact, while *Low* contains the local interactions related to the behavior we intend to monitor. *High* and *Low* are disjoint sets, while all the remaining, unclassified activities are simply disregarded by hiding them. Among the unclassified activities we include the internal actions and the architectural interactions, as they do not contribute to describe the information flowing through the components within the system. Moreover, for each pair of attached interactions $C_1.o$ and $C_2.i$, we assume that if one of them is declared to be high (resp. low), then the other is automatically considered high (resp. low). The reason is that attaching a high interaction to a low interaction would violate the policy that prohibits any direct information flow from high level to low level. For instance, if the aim is to evaluate the impact of a component C_1 on the behavior of a component C_2, then the local interactions of C_1 (and those of C_2 that are attached to C_1) have to be declared high, while all the remaining local interactions of C_2 have to be declared low.

Due to the way in which the semantics of interacting elements has been defined in Sect. 4.4, the local interactions of every component are subject to relabeling and also to rewriting in the case of or-interactions, so that it is important to define carefully how the high/low classification is inherited by the semantics of an architectural description. Formally, with each AEI K of an architectural description $\mathscr{A}$ we associate the sets $High_K$ and Low_K of its high and low interactions, respectively. The set $High_K$ is defined as the smallest set satisfying the following conditions (Low_K is defined similarly):

- If $K.a \in \mathscr{LI}_K$ is a local nonasynchronous uni-/and-interaction and $K.a \in High$, then $\varphi_{K;\mathscr{A}}(K.a) \in High_K$
- If $K.a_i \in \mathscr{LI}_K$ is a fresh local nonasynchronous uni-interaction among those replacing the original local nonasynchronous or-interaction $K.a$ and $K.a \in High$, then $\varphi_{K;\mathscr{A}}(K.a_i) \in High_K$
- If $K.a$ is an originally asynchronous local input interaction and $K.a \in High$, then $\varphi_{K,\mathrm{async}}(K.a) \in High_K$

In the following, we define $High_{C_1,\ldots,C_n} = \bigcup_{i=1}^{n} High_{C_i}$ and $Low_{C_1,\ldots,C_n} = \bigcup_{i=1}^{n} Low_{C_i}$. Moreover, we denote with $High_{K\#C}$ (resp. $Low_{K\#C}$) the subset of $High_K$ (resp. Low_K) containing the high (resp. low) actions that are obtained from attachments involving K and C.

In order to clarify, consider the nine attachments reported in Fig. 4.5 and assume that $C_1.o, C_2.i \in High$. Then, each action of the form $\_\#C_2.i$ is in $High_{C_2}$, while each action of the form $C_1.o\#\_$ is in $High_{C_1}$ iff $C_1.o$ is not asynchronous. If $C_1.o$ is asynchronous, then $C_1.o\#OAQ.\mathtt{arrive}$ and $OAQ.\mathtt{depart}\#\_$ are not included in $High_{C_1}$. The reason is that asynchronous outputs are nonblocking, and hence do not reveal any information flow until the completion of the communication [6].

By rephrasing the noninterference property, after classifying the appropriate local interactions DEPPERF compares the two system views that can be seen by a low observer whenever the interfering activities are enabled/disabled. The derivation of these two views requires in principle the application of hiding and restriction operators, but in ÆMILIA they can be easily expressed by adding behavioral modifications to two copies of the architectural description of the system. The comparison is carried out according to the weak behavioral equivalence, denoted $\approx_{NI}$, underlying the chosen notion of noninterference. If the comparison establishes that the two views behave the same, then the absence of any information flow from high level to low level is guaranteed with respect to $\approx_{NI}$, otherwise the modal logic formula returned by the equivalence check can be employed to determine the causes of the revealed interference, and hence the countermeasures to adopt.

Definition 7.1. Let $\mathscr{A}$ be an architectural description and $C_1,\ldots,C_n$ be some of its AEIs. Let $\{C_1^h,\ldots,C_g^h\}$ and $\{C_1^l,\ldots,C_j^l\}$ be two subsets of $\{C_1,\ldots,C_n\}$. We say that $\{C_1,\ldots,C_n\}$ is $\approx_{NI}$-noninterfering with respect to $High_{C_1^h,\ldots,C_g^h}$ and $Low_{C_1^l,\ldots,C_j^l}$ iff:

$$[\![C_1, \ldots, C_n]\!]_{C_1, \ldots, C_n}^{pc; \#C_1, \ldots, C_n} / (Name - Low_{C_1^l, \ldots, C_j^l})$$

$$\approx_{NI}$$

$$[\![C_1, \ldots, C_n]\!]_{C_1, \ldots, C_n}^{pc; \#C_1, \ldots, C_n} \backslash High_{C_1^h, \ldots, C_g^h} / (Name - Low_{C_1^l, \ldots, C_j^l})$$

The first phase of DEPPERF relies on a wide range of fine-grain notions of non-interference including deterministic ones, nondeterministic ones, probabilistic ones, timed ones, or a combination of these, whose choice is left to the designer and depends on how strict the dependability requirements are. For example, as already mentioned the nondeterministic noninterference check is based on weak bisimulation equivalence $\approx_B$, while the stochastically timed noninterference check is defined in terms of weak Markovian bisimulation equivalence $\approx_{MB}$.

Example 7.1. Let us analyze the multilevel security routing system presented in Sect. 7.2. One dependability aspect of interest is security against the interference of the high sender on the low receiver. In order to study possible dependences from component S_High to component R_Low, we assume that the following classification of local interactions accompanies the ÆMILIA description:

```
HIGH  S_High.send
LOW   R_Low.receive
```

Then, supposing to be interested in purely functional covert channels, we check whether ML_Sec_Routing is $\approx_B$-noninterfering with respect to $High_{S\_High}$ and Low_{R_Low}. The result is positive; i.e., the two system views to compare behave the same. Intuitively, the availability to transmit low messages is never compromised, so that the low receiver cannot deduce anything about the behavior of the high sender in spite of the fact that they interact with the same router.

Now, suppose that fine-grain information based on time is important for security requirements. The motivation for this stronger verification is that the low receiver may capture the behavior of the high sender by observing the time needed to receive a message. The introduction of this fine-grain information causes an information flow, which is revealed by the violation of the $\approx_{MB}$-noninterference check with respect to $High_{S\_High}$ and Low_{R_Low}. In particular, the diagnostic information returned by this check intuitively reveals two interferences.

Firstly, the presence of S_High is detected by the low receiver by observing the time passage. Indeed, the version of this component with hiding describes a working process that, according to the race policy, competes with the other durational processes, while the version of the same component with restriction does not. Secondly, from the viewpoint of the low receiver, the time spent by the router to transmit high messages describes an observable busy-waiting phase. In the following, we show how to interpret these results in order to make the system secure.

7.3.3 Component-Oriented Noninterference Check

The formalization of noninterference provided in Definition 7.1 is not adequate to implement a component-oriented check in the first phase of DEPPERF. For efficiency reasons, the absence of architectural interferences within the description of a software system should be inferred from the properties of its individual architectural elements. Most importantly, under certain conditions, the absence of architectural interferences verified in basic portions of the topology should scale to the entire topology. Since the noninterference check is based on behavioral equivalences, it can be turned into an architectural check like the compatibility and interoperability checks of Chap. 5. This can be accomplished whenever $\approx_{NI}$ is a congruence with respect to static operators, so as to enable the topological reduction process.

Let us start with acyclic topologies. Observing that Definition 7.1 is based on a global notion of noninterference, where the set of components under investigation is considered as a whole, we need a local notion of noninterference that analyzes the interplay between pairs of components. Consider the central AEI K of a star including AEIs that perform high activities. While the noninterference notion of Definition 7.1 establishes the impact of the border of the star, taken as a whole, on the low behavior of K, the local noninterference notion is intended to verify the interference of each AEI in the border of the star on the behavior of K.

Definition 7.2. Given an architectural description $\mathscr{A}$, let K be the central AEI of a star of $\mathscr{A}$ and C_i be an AEI in $\mathscr{B}_K$ performing high activities. We say that C_i does not locally $\approx_{NI}$-interfere with K iff:

$$[\![K,C_i]\!]_{K,\mathscr{B}_K}^{\mathrm{pc};\#K,C_i} / High_{K\#C_i} \approx_{NI} [\![K,C_i]\!]_{K,\mathscr{B}_K}^{\mathrm{pc};\#K,C_i} \backslash High_{K\#C_i}$$

Based on the notion of local noninterference, the following proposition addresses star-shaped topologies where some AEIs in the border of the central AEI K are high components. The proposition states sufficient conditions for ensuring that the interactions among K and these high components do not interfere with the low behavior of the star by examining local noninterference.

Proposition 7.1. *Given an architectural description $\mathscr{A}$, let K be the central AEI of a star of $\mathscr{A}$ and $\mathscr{B}_K = \{C_1^h, \ldots, C_g^h, C_1, \ldots, C_n\}$ be the border of the star, such that $High_K = \bigcup_{i=1}^g High_{K\#C_i^h}$ and $High_{K\#C_i^h} \cap High_{K\#C_j^h} = \emptyset$ for $i \neq j$. If every C_i^h does not locally $\approx_{NI}$-interfere with K, then $\{K\} \cup \mathscr{B}_K$ is $\approx_{NI}$-noninterfering with respect to $High_K$ and $Low_{K,C_1,\ldots,C_n}$.*

If local noninterference is satisfied by each pair of AEIs composed of the central AEI K and one of the high AEIs in the border, then we can infer the absence of interferences in the entire star. This result can be viewed as the counterpart of Proposition 5.1 for star-shaped topologies.

For these topologies, local noninterference and compatibility are similar – both are intended to check whether the way in which the central AEI of a star interacts with its border is safe – but not related in any formal way. However, the compatibility check can help to conduct component-oriented noninterference analysis.

Essentially, in order to verify whether the border of a star $\approx_{\text{NI}}$-interferes with the central AEI K of the star it is sufficient to analyze the interacting semantics of K alone, provided that K is $\mathscr{P}_{\text{NI}}$-compatible with every AEI in the border. Here, $\mathscr{P}_{\text{NI}}$ is any property belonging to the class Ψ outlined in Sect. 5.2 that is characterized by $\approx_{\text{NI}}$. We thus derive the following sufficient condition for noninterference based on compatibility.

Proposition 7.2. *Given an architectural description $\mathscr{A}$, let K be the central AEI of a star of $\mathscr{A}$ and $\mathscr{B}_K = \{C_1, \ldots, C_n\}$ be the border of the star. If K is $\mathscr{P}_{\text{NI}}$-compatible with every AEI in $\mathscr{B}_K$, then $\{K\} \cup \mathscr{B}_K$ is $\approx_{\text{NI}}$-noninterfering with respect to $High_K$ and Low_K iff:*

$$[\![K]\!]_{K,\mathscr{B}_K}^{\text{pc;wob}} / (Name - Low_K) \approx_{\text{NI}} [\![K]\!]_{K,\mathscr{B}_K}^{\text{pc;wob}} \backslash High_K / (Name - Low_K)$$

The application of the component-oriented noninterference check based on a combination of local noninterference and compatibility can be generalized to arbitrary acyclic topologies in order to reveal undesired interferences from a component K^h to a component K^l. In accordance with the topological reduction process of Chap. 5, the compatibility check is applied several times to reduce the entire acyclic topology to the path from K^h to K^l, which is unique because the topology is acyclic. Afterwards, we exploit a variant of the local noninterference check in order to establish the absence of any interfering information flow from K^h to K^l. In particular, if there exists a prefix of this path that is noninterfering with respect to the high activities of K^h and the interactions with the remaining portion of the path, then we can deduce that no illegal information flow goes from K^h to K^l.

Theorem 7.1. *Given an acyclic architectural description $\mathscr{A}$, let K^h and K^l be two AEIs of $\mathscr{A}$ such that $C_1, \ldots, C_n$, with $n \geq 0$, are the AEIs constituting a path connecting K^h to K^l in the abstract enriched flow graph of $\mathscr{A}$. If every AEI of $\mathscr{A}$ is $\mathscr{P}_{\text{NI}}$-compatible with each AEI attached to it and there exists $C_i \in \{C_1, \ldots, C_n, C_{n+1}\}$, with $C_{n+1} = K^l$, such that:*

$$[\![K^h, C_1, \ldots, C_i]\!]_{\mathscr{A}}^{\text{pc};\#K^h, C_1, \ldots, C_i} / (Name - Low'_{C_i})$$
$$\approx_{\text{NI}}$$
$$[\![K^h, C_1, \ldots, C_i]\!]_{\mathscr{A}}^{\text{pc};\#K^h, C_1, \ldots, C_i} \backslash High_{K^h} / (Name - Low'_{C_i})$$

where $Low'_{C_i} = \mathscr{V}_{C_i;C_{i+1}}$ for $1 \leq i \leq n$ and $Low'_{C_i} = Low_{K^l}$ for $i = n+1$, then $\mathscr{A}$ is $\approx_{\text{NI}}$-noninterfering with respect to $High_{K^h}$ and Low_{K^l}.

Intuitively, the presence of an AEI C_i that satisfies the hypothesis of the theorem above ensures that every information flow starting from K^h stops without reaching K^l. From a methodological standpoint, the noninterference check is applied in an incremental way by starting from C_1 and stopping as soon as C_i is found that satisfies the noninterference condition. If this verification propagates to K^l without success, then K^h may be able to interfere with the low behavior of K^l.

Example 7.2. Let us reconsider the analysis of the multilevel security routing system of Sect. 7.2 from the viewpoint of the component-based verification of nondeterministic noninterference. Since the architectural topology of this system is acyclic, we can apply Theorem 7.1 in order to analyze the potential interference of component S_High on component R_Low. According to the theorem, the path to analyze is represented by the AEIs S_High, B_High, U, and R_Low. As can be easily seen, S_High $\approx_B$-interferes with B_High, but this pair of components does not $\approx_B$-interfere with the view of U interacting with R_Low. Hence, the sufficient condition of Theorem 7.1 holds and the information flow starting from S_High stops in U without reaching R_Low.

In the case of cyclic topologies, noninterference can still be analyzed in a component-oriented fashion if we exploit the interoperability results of Sect. 5.4. The following proposition establishes sufficient conditions ensuring that the interactions within a cycle do not interfere with respect to the high behavior of the cycle and the low behavior of an AEI C_j in the cycle.

Proposition 7.3. *Given an architectural description $\mathscr{A}$, let $\mathscr{Y} = \{C_1,\dots,C_n\}$ be the set of AEIs traversed by a cycle of $\mathscr{A}$, such that all the high and low local interactions of $\mathscr{Y}$ are involved in attachments between AEIs in $\mathscr{Y}$. For each $C_j \in \mathscr{Y}$ that $\mathscr{P}_{NI}$-interoperates with the other AEIs in the cycle, we have that $\mathscr{Y}$ is $\approx_{NI}$-noninterfering with respect to $High_{C_1,\dots,C_n}$ and Low_{C_j} iff:*

$$[\![C_j]\!]_{\mathscr{A}}^{pc;wob} / (Name - Low_{C_j})$$
$$\approx_{NI}$$
$$[\![\mathscr{Y}]\!]_{\mathscr{A}}^{pc;\#\mathscr{Y}} \setminus High_{C_1,\dots,C_n} / (Name - Low_{C_j})$$

From a methodological standpoint, we observe that it may not be necessary to consider the interacting semantics of the whole cycle. Indeed, let us assume that there exists an AEI C_i in the cycle such that all of its local interactions belong to *High*. Then, when preventing the high activities from being executed, C_i turns out to be isolated from the other AEIs in the cycle, i.e., the cycle becomes a chain because of the removal of C_i. Under this assumption, verifying the condition stated in Proposition 7.3 reduces to check the compatibility of C_j with respect to such a chain. Hence, it is sufficient to apply repeatedly the compatibility check for acyclic topologies in order to shrink the chain and reduce it to C_j.

The application of the component-oriented noninterference check can be generalized to arbitrary topologies in order to reveal undesired interferences from a component K^h to a component K^l. The following theorem combines the sufficient conditions for stars and cycles introduced in this section with those of Theorem 5.1. In particular, in accordance with the topological reduction process of Chap. 5, the compatibility and interoperability checks are applied several times until the entire topology is reduced either to a single cyclic union – including both K^h and K^l – that satisfies Proposition 7.3, or to a path from K^h to K^l that satisfies Theorem 7.1. In the latter case, observed that some consecutive AEIs in the path from K^h to K^l may be adjacent AEIs in a cyclic union, we can reduce the cyclic union to these adjacent AEIs iff such AEIs $\mathscr{P}_{NI}$-interoperate with the other AEIs in the cyclic union.

Theorem 7.2. *Let $\mathscr{A}$ be an architectural description, K^h, K^l be two of its AEIs, and κ be a total cycle covering algorithm for $\mathscr{A}$ if $\mathscr{A}$ is cyclic. Assume that the following conditions hold:*

1. *For each $C \in \mathscr{A}$ belonging to an acyclic portion or to the intersection of some cycle with acyclic portions of the abstract enriched flow graph of $\mathscr{A}$, C is $\mathscr{P}_{NI}$-compatible with every $C' \in \mathscr{B}_C - \mathscr{C}\mathscr{U}_C$.*
2. *For each cyclic union $\{C_1, \ldots, C_n\} \in \mathscr{C}\mathscr{U}(\kappa)$, every $C_j \in \mathscr{F}_{C_1, \ldots, C_n}$ $\mathscr{P}_{NI}$-interoperates with the other AEIs in the cyclic union.*
3. *If both K^h and K^l belong to a cyclic union $\mathscr{Y} \in \mathscr{C}\mathscr{U}(\kappa)$, then $\mathscr{Y}$ satisfies the equality of Proposition 7.3 with respect to $High_{K^h}$ and Low_{K^l}, otherwise there exists a path connecting K^h to K^l through $n \geq 0$ AEIs $C_1, \ldots, C_n$ in the abstract enriched flow graph of $\mathscr{A}$ such that:*

   (a) *For each $\{C_1', \ldots, C_g'\} \subseteq \{K^h, C_1, \ldots, C_n, K^l\}$ such that $\{C_1', \ldots, C_g'\}$ are adjacent AEIs in a cyclic union of $\mathscr{C}\mathscr{U}(\kappa)$, it holds that $\{C_1', \ldots, C_g'\}$ $\mathscr{P}_{NI}$-interoperate with the other AEIs in the cyclic union,*
   (b) *There is an AEI in $\{C_1, \ldots, C_n, K^l\}$ satisfying the equality of Theorem 7.1.*

Then $\mathscr{A}$ is $\approx_{NI}$-noninterfering with respect to $High_{K^h}$ and Low_{K^l}.

7.3.4 Interpretation and Feedback

In the previous section, we have shown that, under certain conditions, the noninterference check can proceed in a component-oriented manner. Independent of the efficiency with which this check can be implemented, its goal is to reveal information flows within a system, with the ultimate objective of understanding whether the interfering components can compromise the functionalities of the rest of the system. Consider, e.g., an architectural description with AEIs $C_1, \ldots, C_n$ and analyze the impact of C_j on the behavior of C_i. Based on the chosen notion of noninterference, if an undesired, direct or indirect, information flow from C_j to C_i is revealed, then we have the proof that C_j interferes with the monitored behavior of C_i. In this case, diagnostic information, in the form of a modal logic formula returned by the equivalence check, reveals the causes of the interference.

   If the information flow can be eliminated, then this diagnostic information can be employed by the designer to modify C_j, C_i, and possibly the rest of the system. Obviously, such modifications must be validated also from a performance standpoint, in the sense that they should not cause a intolerable degradation of the quality of service. This performance-based validation is mandatory even if the two system views to compare satisfy the strongest property based on the finest information details. For instance, the satisfaction of the stochastically timed noninterference property ensures that no kind of covert channel occurs, but does not provide specific information about the delivered quality of service, which may be unsatisfactory because of the strategies adopted to remove the covert channels.

In contrast, due to their intrinsic nature many covert channels are either unavoidable or tolerated, because they would require impractical revisions of the system. In this case, we have to estimate the impact of these interferences on the system performance and dependability. For instance, if the system does not satisfy the stochastically timed noninterference property, it holds that the two system views to compare do not behave the same from the viewpoint of a performance-aware notion of equivalence. Hence, they offer different performance measures that must be estimated.

In any case, it is necessary to move on to the second phase of DEPPERF, where quality of service metrics are evaluated in order to assess the impact on these metrics of any residual information flow and of any mechanism implemented to minimize each such flow.

Example 7.3. Let us see how to interpret the feedback obtained in Example 7.1 from the application of the stochastic noninterference check to the multilevel security routing system of Sect. 7.2.

The first interference that has been captured in Example 7.1 shows that S_High reveals its behavior when executing high durational activities. To avoid this covert channel, it is necessary to confine the behavior of the component in order to hide its impact on the timing of low activities. This can be done by defining a sort of black box that limits and controls the activities performed by the high sender. Formally, S_High becomes an instance of the high sender AET illustrated in Table 7.1, where we assume that $h > k > 2$. The initial τ-action denotes the activation of the black box and is technically needed because it allows $\approx_{MB}$ to abstract from the subsequent immediate τ-actions (see Sect. 3.3.8). Action high_interaction $\in$ *High* denotes the intention by the high sender of sending a message, while action no_high_interaction represents the absence of any activity by the high sender. Because of the chosen priorities, the branch guarded by no_high_interaction, which is internal and, therefore, unobservable when applying the noninterference check, is enabled iff the high sender is prevented from any interaction with the routing system. The role of this branch is to simulate, from a temporal standpoint, the presence of the high sender in a way that makes its absence invisible to the low receiver.

This is not enough to hide completely the interference. Whenever the high sender is blocked because the high buffer is full and hence not willing to accept further messages, then the black box does not compete for the resource time. Indeed, in this case the high sender declares its intention of sending a message and then waits for the transmission of the message. This observable behavior would reveal to the low receiver that the high buffer is full. This covert channel can be avoided by introducing the high buffer AET, of which B_High becomes an instance. Such an AET is shown in Table 7.1, where we assume that the actual rate passed to B_High is the same as that passed to S_High, because its role is to simulate the durational activities of the high sender whenever it is blocked because of buffer saturation.

Table 7.1 Multilevel security routing system: securing the high sender/buffer types

```
ARCHI_ELEM_TYPE High_Sender_Type(const rate sending_rate,
                                 const prio h,
                                 const prio k)

  BEHAVIOR
   High_Sender(void; void) =
    <tau, inf(2,1)> .
     choice
     {
      <high_interaction, inf(h, 1)> .
       <send, exp(sending_rate)> . High_Sender(),
      <no_high_interaction, inf(k, 1)> .
       <tau, exp(sending_rate)> . High_Sender()
     }

  INPUT_INTERACTIONS   void
  OUTPUT_INTERACTIONS SYNC UNI send; high_interaction

ARCHI_ELEM_TYPE High_Buffer_Type(const rate waiting_rate)

  BEHAVIOR
   High_Buffer(void; void) =
   <deposit, _(0, 1)> .
     choice
     {
      <withdraw, _(1, 1)> . High_Buffer(),
      <tau, exp(waiting_rate)> . High_Buffer()
     }

  INPUT_INTERACTIONS   SYNC UNI deposit
  OUTPUT_INTERACTIONS SYNC UNI withdraw
```

The second interference that has been captured in Example 7.1 shows that the AEI U forces a busy-waiting phase for the low receiver whenever transmitting high messages. The router can be made transparent to the low receiver by following an approach borrowed from round-robin scheduling strategies. The intuition is similar to that underlying the definition of the black box. The routing activities are divided into temporal slots, each one dedicated to a class of senders in a round-robin fashion. Independent of the presence of a pending message from a sender of the currently managed class, the temporal slot is spent. In this way, a low receiver cannot deduce whether the high slot has been actively exploited. Formally, we replace the AET Router_Type with the round-robin router type of Table 7.2, of which U becomes an instance.

With these modifications, the system ML_Sec_Routing now passes the stochastic noninterference check.

Table 7.2 Multilevel security routing system: securing the router type

```
ARCHI_ELEM_TYPE RR_Router_Type(const rate trans_rate_high,
                               const rate trans_rate_low)

BEHAVIOR
  Low_Round(void; void) =
  choice
    {
     <get_low, inf(1, 1)> .
      <trans_low, exp(trans_rate_low)> . High_Round(),
      <tau, exp(trans_rate_low)> . High_Round()
    };
  High_Round(void; void) =
  choice
    {
     <get_high, inf(1, 1)> .
      <trans_high, exp(trans_rate_high)> . Low_Round(),
      <tau, exp(trans_rate_high)> . Low_Round()
    }

INPUT_INTERACTIONS  SYNC UNI get_high; get_low
OUTPUT_INTERACTIONS SYNC UNI trans_high; trans_low
```

7.4 Second Phase of DEPPERF: Performance Evaluation

The objective of the second phase of DEPPERF is to provide a performance profile of the system. The motivations for moving to a quantitative setting are twofold. On the one hand, all the unavoidable information flows that have been revealed in the first phase by the noninterference check must be quantitatively analyzed in order to estimate their negative impact on dependability requirements. For this purpose, the bandwidth of the covert channels detected in the first phase is quantitatively assessed in terms of information leakage per unit of time. On the other hand, even in the case that every covert channel has been eliminated by means of adequate strategies, the application of these possibly invasive modifications could be made impractical by hard quality of service constraints.

Therefore, in this phase we trade performance aspects with covert channel bandwidth and with each possible solution proposed to mitigate the information leakage. This is done by observing the performance behavior of the system when disabling and enabling the interfering components.

In this section, we first discuss how to relate the models considered in the two phases of DEPPERF (Sect. 7.4.1). Then, we show how to conduct the performance analysis and exploit the obtained results for tuning system configuration parameters in order to achieve the desired tradeoff (Sect. 7.4.2). Finally, we introduce the companion notation of ÆMILIA for the component-oriented specification of performance measures (Sect. 7.4.3).

7.4.1 Model Validation

Depending on the chosen fine-grain notion of noninterference, the system model considered in the first phase of DEPPERF can be nondeterministic, probabilistic, or timed. In contrast, the second phase relies on a performance model that can be analyzed through standard performance techniques. In particular, in the following we consider an approach based on the numerical solution of Markov chains [188].

When applying DEPPERF, it is necessary to ensure the consistency of the performance model used in the second phase with respect to the model analyzed in the first phase in order to preserve the same noninterference outcome. Obviously, if the performance model is already used in the first phase of DEPPERF to check stochastically timed noninterference, then the same model is analyzed in the second phase and no validation is actually needed. Instead, validation may be needed if in the first phase a model different from the performance model has been employed.

In this case, if all the activity durations are expressed through exponentially distributed random variables, the performance model turns out to be a continuous-time Markov chain, which is valid by construction against the corresponding functional model considered in the first phase. In fact, the nondeterministic and stochastically timed models have isomorphic state spaces, up to the fine-grain information attached to state transitions. On the other hand, if the performance model contains general distributions for a better characterization of some delays, then the consistency with the untimed model used in the first phase is not guaranteed. Indeed, the use of general distributions no longer having infinite support may alter the state space, thus invalidating the noninterference check. Hence, in order to ensure consistency of the analysis, the noninterference check should be repeated in the second phase if some activities are characterized through distributions with finite support.

7.4.2 Analysis and Tuning

In the second phase of DEPPERF, the analysis is governed by the results obtained in the first phase. Should the first phase reveal undesired information flows that are unavoidable or whose elimination is impractical, an estimate of the related information leakage is provided in the second phase by evaluating the performance metrics that are directly related to the bandwidth of each information flow. These metrics provide different results for the two system views corresponding to the presence and the absence of the interfering components, respectively, and the difference between such results represents the amount of information leakage. Similarly, quality of service metrics are assessed by analyzing the same system views in order to measure the impact of any residual covert channel on such metrics.

The output of this performance comparison is given by the value of some important efficiency measures of the system together with the bandwidth of its covert channels, expressed as the amount of information leaked per unit of time. Such performance figures can be used in the second phase of DEPPERF as a feedback to tune system configuration parameters, in a way that lowers the covert channel bandwidth under a tolerable threshold without jeopardizing the quality of service delivered by the system. In the case that a reasonable tradeoff cannot be obtained, it is necessary to adjust the model and restart the analysis.

Since the designer may have to face different requirements such as strict/relaxed dependability needs or loose/tight quality of service constraints, the adjustment activity can follow opposite strategies. If the main objective is to preserve dependability requirements, the designer can modify the system behavior until the resulting model suffers only from unavoidable covert channels that are quantitatively negligible. In this respect, different dependability aspects may again require opposite strategies. As an example, aiming at perfect security might compromise service availability, which is one of the most critical factors for the success of network-based applications. Hence, balancing these different dependability aspects is of paramount importance, and for this purpose tuning configuration parameters can be useful to keep the quality of service as high as possible without significantly altering the dependability constraints.

If instead ensuring quality of service is more important than dealing with dependability issues, the designer can determine a threshold for the performance indices and then modify the functional and performance system behavior until the resulting model meets the desired quality of service. In this case, tuning the configuration parameters is needed to keep the bandwidth of the potential covert channels as low as possible without jeopardizing the quality of service. In this respect, controlling the kind and the amount of illegal information flows might be necessary to ensure dependability properties like, e.g., service availability.

Another significant scenario considers the case in which dependability has been achieved at the chosen grain level. This means that either the noninterference check does not reveal any information flow, or all the unwanted interferences among components have been eliminated. In complex systems, the strategies adopted to guarantee the dependability requirements have an impact on the system performance. In this case, we need to estimate the impact of these strategies on quality of service metrics. This performance analysis can be exploited to tune the frequency of the component activities, in such a way that a reasonable overall system efficiency can be achieved.

In any case, independent of the particular scenario, the outcome resulting from the second phase of DEPPERF reveals whether a balanced tradeoff between dependability – in terms of influence of each covert channel upon aspects like, e.g., safety and security – and performance – in terms of indices like system productivity and response time – is met or not.

7.4.3 Measure Specification Language

As far as the specification of performance measures is concerned, in Chap. 6 we have
seen that ÆMILIA is equipped with a translation semantics into a Markovian process
calculus whose underlying stochastic process is a continuous-time Markov chain.
In order to enable the specification of performance metrics in a component-oriented
fashion, ÆMILIA is endowed with a companion notation called Measure Specification Language (MSL). This notation builds on a simple first-order logic by means
of which reward structures [120] are associated with the continuous-time Markov
chains underlying component-oriented system models expressed in ÆMILIA. The
notation itself is component oriented because it includes a mechanism for defining
measures that are parameterized with respect to component activities and component behaviors. Such a mechanism allows performance metrics to be defined in a
transparent way in terms of the activities that individual components or parts of
their behavior can carry out, or in terms of specific local behaviors that describe the
components of interest, thus facilitating the task for nonexperts.

As an example, the use of the measure expressing system throughput simply requires the designer to specify the component activities contributing to the throughput. In fact, the measure is defined in MSL as follows:

```
MEASURE throughput (C₁.a₁,...,Cₙ.aₙ)
    IS ◁body▷
```

where *body* is a first-order logic formula specifying how the component activities
$C_1.a_1, \ldots, C_n.a_n$ contribute to the reward structure associated with the metric. In particular, the throughput formula establishes that each state transition labeled with an
activity in $\{C_1.a_1, \ldots, C_n.a_n\}$ is given a unit reward, which specifies the instantaneous gain implied by the execution of the related transition.

MSL provides support for the incremental definition of performance measures.
Basic measures like system throughput can be combined to define derived measures.
The body of a derived measure definition is an expression involving identifiers of
previously defined metrics each denoting the value of the corresponding measure,
as well as arithmetic operators and mathematical functions.

Example 7.4. Let us examine the quantitative impact of the interfering information flow from S_High to R_Low detected in Example 7.1 via the application of
the stochastic noninterference check to the multilevel security routing system of
Sect. 7.2.

From a performance perspective, this interference affects the system productivity
as observed by the low receiver, expressed by the number of actions trans_low
executed per unit of time. Hence, the first analysis we conduct aims at estimating
the amount of information leakage for the original version of the multilevel security
routing system. The value of this measure is obtained by evaluating the following
MSL definition:

```
MEASURE low_prod(U.trans_low)
    IS throughput(U.trans_low)
```

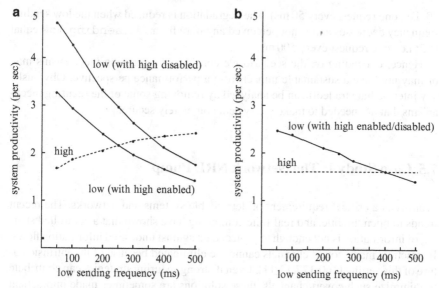

Fig. 7.3 Performance evaluation of different versions of the multilevel security routing system

in the presence and in the absence of high interferences. The results are depicted in Fig. 7.3a, where we also report, for the sake of comparison, the number of messages transmitted to the high receiver whenever the high activities are enabled, which is a metric expressed by the following MSL definition:

```
MEASURE high_prod(U.trans_high)
    IS throughput(U.trans_high)
```

The curves refer to the scenario in which the average sending time for the low sender varies in the range [50, 500] ms. The influence of the undesired information flow is easily estimated by comparing the two thicked curves that are related to the low system productivity in the presence and in the absence of high interferences.

As shown in Example 7.3, the removal of each covert channel requires the application of control mechanisms that, as expected, aim at degrading the performance of the system in order to make the behavior of the high sender transparent to the low receiver. In Fig. 7.3b, we estimate the system productivity when activating all the securing strategies described in Example 7.3. Thanks to these strategies, the two thick curves of Fig. 7.3a collapse into the same curve– i.e., the low system productivity is independent of the high sender behavior– while the high system productivity becomes constant. However, it is easy to observe the cost that is paid in terms of decrease of the low system productivity with respect to the scenario of Fig. 7.3a. In this respect, it is interesting to compare the low system productivity with that of Fig. 7.3a in the presence of high interferences. The performance degradation experienced by the low receiver when activating the securing mechanisms is remarkable if the low sending frequency is high (about 23% for mlsr_sending_low equal to

20; i.e., one request every 50 ms). The degradation is reduced when the low sending frequency decreases and is not perceived anymore for $mlsr\_sending\_low$ equal to 2; i.e., one request every 500 ms.

Hence, depending on the scenario we consider, the securing mechanisms may or may not have a sustainable impact from a performance perspective. Obviously, any intermediate tradeoff can be analyzed by removing some of the securing mechanisms that are needed to make the system completely secure.

7.5 Case Study I: The Network NRL Pump

Security is a critical requirement of dependable systems and networks. The recent trends to open, mobile, and real-time computing have shown that a controlled sharing of information is not enough to protect data against undesired information flows. In practice, many covert channels cannot be eliminated because of the intrinsic nature of this setting [160,177,13,11]. Even if strong securing strategies can contribute to minimize such covert channels, these solutions are sometimes made impractical by hard quality of service constraints.

In this section, we apply DEPPERF to a secure routing mechanism called network NRL pump [129]. This is a trusted device used in multilevel security architectures to offer replication of information from low security level systems (L for short) to high security level systems (H for short) with adequate assurance security guarantees. Data replication is a proven approach to strengthen availability [165] and has a beneficial impact also on security, as users at different security levels access the same data through different repositories without interfering with each other.

The objective of the NRL pump is thus to ensure data replication by controlling each possible security risk with a minor impact on other aspects such as service availability. Hence, it represents an ideal case study for the application of DEPPERF, through which we can formally verify the existence of unavoidable covert channels and their relation with dependability aspects. In the following, we illustrate the NRL pump system (Sect. 7.5.1), we present its formal description in ÆMILIA (Sect. 7.5.2), and then we apply the first phase (Sect. 7.5.3) and the second phase (Sect. 7.5.4) of DEPPERF to this description.

7.5.1 Informal Specification

The NRL pump is configured as a single hardware device that interfaces a low security level LAN with a high security level LAN. Such an intermediate role played by the pump is necessary to avoid any insecure information flow in the message exchange from L to H. Typically, message exchanges in this direction suffer from subtle covert channels that depend on the feedback that is usually required by the sender. In fact, in order to offer reliable communications, an acknowledgement (ack

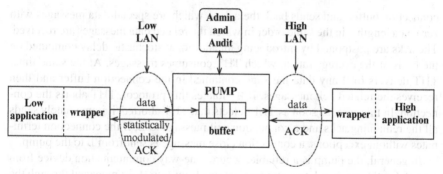

Fig. 7.4 Architecture of the network NRL pump

for short) is sent for each message that is successfully received. The transmission of an ack from H to L is more than enough to set up a covert communication channel if the timing of the ack is under the control of H. The main role of the pump is to act as a delaying buffer between H and L, which pumps data from L to H and then probabilistically modulates the timing of the ack from H to L in order to make such a timed covert channel negligible.

The architecture of the NRL pump is illustrated in Fig. 7.4. Each enclave at a given security level interacts with the pump through an interfacing software called wrapper, which supports the set of functionalities satisfying application-specific requirements. The pump is not a general-purpose network router, because an uncontrolled behavior would cause both security and availability problems. On the availability side, any low-level application may request to connect to any high-level repository thus wasting the pump resources. On the security side, a low-level Trojan horse application could ask high-level Trojan horse processes to reveal their behavior. To avoid these risks, each process that uses the pump is subject to authentication, which is managed by the pump administration system by means of a connection table containing registration information. The pump provides both recoverable and nonrecoverable services. Recoverability safely assumes that any sent message is delivered to H, even if connection failures occur. For the sake of simplicity, we concentrate on nonrecoverable applications (like, e.g., FTP), which provide best-effort reliability of connection.

A connection between L and H through the pump is established as follows. Initially, L sends a connection request message to the main thread (MT) of the pump, which authenticates the sending process and the address of the final destination. If authentication fails, a connection reject message is sent back, otherwise MT sends a connection valid message to L and then activates a trusted low thread (TLT) and a trusted high thread (THT), which represent the pump interfaces with L and H, respectively. Registered H processes are always ready to accept a connection from the pump through the same handshake mechanism described above.

Once a new connection is established, the pump sends a connection grant message to both systems with initialization parameters for the communication. During the connection lifetime, TLT receives data messages from L, stores them in the connection buffer, and sends back the acks – which are special data messages with zero data length – in the same order in which the related data messages are received. The acks are postponed by introducing an additional stochastic delay computed on the basis of the average rate at which THT consumes messages. At the same time, THT delivers to H any data message contained in the connection buffer and then receives the related ack messages. If H violates this protocol, THT aborts the connection. In this case, as soon as TLT detects that THT aborted, it immediately sends all the remaining acks and a connection exit message to L. If the connection terminates without exceptions, a connection close message is sent from L to the pump.

In general, the pump is a reliable, secure, one-way communication device from L to H. On the one hand, the communications from L to H are managed through the connection buffer by different pump components, each one separately interacting with enclaves at different security levels. On the other hand, the communications from H to L are limited to the transmission of the acks. Any dependence between the transmission of an ack from H and the delivery of an ack to L is broken by the pump, which also eliminates the related timed covert channel, as formally recognized in [133].

Hence, apparently the pump does not suffer from any security problem. In the following, we apply DEPPERF in order to refuse formally this claim and study the consequences of interferences that violate the security requirements.

7.5.2 Architectural Description

The ÆMILIA description of the NRL pump starts with its name and the definition of its formal parameters:

```
ARCHI_TYPE NRL_Pump_Type(const integer buffer_size :=      1,
                         const rate    conn_gen     :=    500,
                         const rate    conn_init    :=     62.5,
                         const rate    data_trans   :=    125,
                         const rate    ack_trans    :=   1306.12,
                         const rate    ack_delay    :=    435.37,
                         const rate    timeout      :=     57.04,
                         const weight  valid_prob   :=      0.99)
```

The formal parameters describe the size of the connection buffer, some rates modeling exponentially distributed delays, and the probability associated with valid connection requests.

Since the amount of data sent from L to H does not alter the kind of communications between them through the pump, without loss of generality we assume that a single message is to be sent from L to H. Hence, we assume buffer_size = 1.

As far as activity durations are concerned, we suppose that all the transmission delays of messages exchanged by the pump and the wrappers through the network are modeled as exponentially distributed random variables, while internal communications among pump components are modeled by immediate actions. This is because the duration of an activity internally performed by the pump is negligible with respect to the transmission delay of a message.

The rates of exponentially distributed delays are expressed in s^{-1}. In the following, we assume that the pump uses two 64 Kbps full-duplex lines and, according to the NRL pump protocol specification, the mean length of data (resp. ack) messages is 512 (resp. 49) bits, so that the data (resp. ack) message transmission rate data_trans (resp. ack_trans) is equal to 125 (resp. 1306.12), while the connection initialization rate conn_init is equal to 62.5. The connection request generation rate conn_gen corresponds to 2 requests/s. The rate ack_delay of the stochastic delay added by the pump to the transmission of acks to L is assumed to be equal to 435.37, which corresponds to the transmission time of three ack messages. This is long enough to hide the fluctuations of the transmission delays of ack messages propagating from the high wrapper to the pump. The rate timeout, which is the inverse of the maximum amount of time that the pump waits for an expected ack, is equal to 57.04, corresponding to doubling the average time needed to send a data message and to receive the related ack, i.e., about 17 ms.

As far as the last parameter is concerned, for each connection request we abstract from the authentication operations and we assume valid_prob to be 0.99.

The first AET we present is the low wrapper type – see Table 7.3 – which models the behavior of the low security level wrapper. It sends a connection request to the

Table 7.3 NRL pump model: low wrapper type

```
ARCHI_ELEM_TYPE LW_Type(const rate conn_gen,
                        const rate data_trans)

BEHAVIOR
  LW(void; void) =
   <send_conn_request, exp(conn_gen)> .
    choice
     {
      <receive_conn_valid, _(0, 1)> .
       <receive_conn_grant, _(0, 1)> .
        <send_msg, exp(data_trans)> .
         <receive_low_ack, _(0, 1)> .
          choice
           {
            <receive_conn_exit, _(0, 1)> . LW(),
            <send_conn_close, exp(data_trans)> . LW()
           },
        <receive_conn_reject, _(0, 1)> . LW()
     }

  INPUT_INTERACTIONS   SYNC UNI receive_conn_valid;
                                receive_conn_grant;
                                receive_conn_reject;
                                receive_low_ack;
                                receive_conn_exit
  OUTPUT_INTERACTIONS SYNC UNI send_conn_request;
                               send_msg;
                               send_conn_close
```

Table 7.4 NRL pump model: main thread type

```
ARCHI_ELEM_TYPE MT_Type(const rate data_trans,
                        const weight valid_prob)

  BEHAVIOR
  MT(void; void) =
  <receive_conn_request, _(0, 1)> .
    choice
    {
     <conn_is_valid, inf(1, valid_prob)> .
       <wakeup_tht, inf(1, 1)> .
         <send_conn_valid, exp(data_trans)> . MT(),
       <conn_not_valid, inf(1, 1 - valid_prob)> .
         <send_conn_reject, exp(data_trans)> . MT()
    }

  INPUT_INTERACTIONS  SYNC UNI receive_conn_request
  OUTPUT_INTERACTIONS SYNC UNI wakeup_tht;
                              send_conn_valid;
                              send_conn_reject
```

pump and then is ready to accept either a connection valid message or a connection reject message. If a connection is established, the low wrapper receives a grant message, sends a data message to TLT, and then waits for the related ack. After the reception of this ack, the low wrapper can either receive a connection exit message in the case that the connection is aborted, or send a connection close message in the case that the connection is correctly terminated.

The AET modeling the MT – see Table 7.4 – describes the initial handshaking phase between the pump and the low wrapper. In order not to have to introduce a definition of the pump administrator, the verification of an incoming request is abstracted away by means of a probabilistic choice between two immediate actions, which is governed by parameter valid_prob. In response to a request, either MT activates THT and sends back a connection valid message, or it sends back a connection reject message.

The initialization of a new connection to the high wrapper is conducted by the AET modeling the THT – see Table 7.5 – which is spawned by MT during the initial setup phase. Upon the initialization of THT, the connection setup handshake between THT and the high wrapper is modeled by means of a single action. Afterwards, THT awakens TLT. When a connection is active, THT checks the buffer for new incoming data messages. Upon reading a message from the buffer, THT outputs it to the high communication channel. Then, THT waits for the reception of the ack from the high wrapper. The arrival of an ack message competes with the timeout defined by THT. If the ack is received before the end of the timeout, THT removes the message from the buffer and notifies TLT about the correct connection status. On the other hand, if the timeout expires before the reception of the ack, THT notifies the timeout expiration, removes the message from the buffer, and informs TLT about the connection failure.

Table 7.5 NRL pump model: trusted high thread type

```
ARCHI_ELEM_TYPE THT_Type(const rate conn_init,
                         const rate timeout)

BEHAVIOR
 THT(void; void) =
  choice
  {
    <receive_high_wakeup, _(1, 1)> .
     <init_high_conn, exp(conn_init)> .
      <wakeup_tlt, inf(1, 1)> . THT(),
    <read_msg, inf(1, 1)> . <forward_msg, inf(1, 1)> .
     choice
     {
       <receive_high_ack, _(0, 1)> . <delete_msg, inf(1, 1)> .
        <send_ok_to_tlt, inf(1, 1)> . THT(),
       <wait_for_timeout, exp(timeout)> .
        <comm_timeout, inf(1, 1)> . <delete_msg, inf(1, 1)> .
         <send_abort_to_tlt, inf(1, 1)>. THT()
     }
  }

INPUT_INTERACTIONS   SYNC UNI receive_high_wakeup;
                              receive_high_ack
OUTPUT_INTERACTIONS  SYNC UNI wakeup_tlt;
                              read_msg;
                              forward_msg;
                              delete_msg;
                              send_ok_to_tlt;
                              comm_timeout;
                              send_abort_to_tlt
```

The AET modeling the TLT is illustrated in Table 7.6. TLT waits for THT to awaken it and then establishes the connection from L to the pump by sending a connection grant message to the low wrapper. Whenever a connection is activated, TLT is ready to receive data messages from the low wrapper. Upon receiving a data message, TLT stores it in the connection buffer and then sends back the related ack after a certain delay. At any moment, TLT may receive a message from THT concerning the status of the connection. In the case of failure, TLT sends a connection exit message to the low wrapper. Alternatively, TLT can accept a connection close message from the low wrapper. If TLT detects the connection failure before sending back the ack, then TLT immediately transmits the ack and the connection exit message to the low wrapper.

TLT and THT share the communication buffer, through which data messages coming from the low wrapper are forwarded to the high wrapper. The definition of the buffer AET – see Table 7.7 – is parameterized with respect to the maximum size of the buffer, while its behavior is characterized by the number of messages that are currently stored, ranging from 0 to the maximum size. The buffer is initially

Table 7.6 NRL pump model: trusted low thread type

```
ARCHI_ELEM_TYPE TLT_Type(const rate data_trans,
                         const rate ack_trans,
                         const rate ack_delay)

BEHAVIOR
 TLT(void; void) =
  <receive_low_wakeup, _(1, 1)> .
   <send_conn_grant, exp(data_trans)> .
    <receive_msg, _(0, 1)> . <store_msg, inf(1, 1)> .
     choice
     {
      <wait_delay, exp(ack_delay)> .
       <send_low_ack, exp(ack_trans)> .
        choice
        {
         <receive_abort_from_tht, _(1, 1)> .
          <send_conn_exit, exp(data_trans)> . TLT(),
         <receive_ok_from_tht, _(1, 1)> .
          <receive_conn_close, _(0, 1)> . TLT()
        },
      <receive_abort_from_tht, _(1, 1)> .
       <send_low_ack, exp(ack_trans)> .
        <send_conn_exit, exp(data_trans)> . TLT(),
      <receive_ok_from_tht, _(1, 1)> .
       <wait_delay, exp(ack_delay)> .
        <send_low_ack, exp(ack_trans)> .
         <receive_conn_close, _(0, 1)> . TLT()
     }

INPUT_INTERACTIONS   SYNC UNI receive_low_wakeup;
                              receive_msg;
                              receive_abort_from_tht;
                              receive_ok_from_tht;
                              receive_conn_close
OUTPUT_INTERACTIONS SYNC UNI send_conn_grant;
                              store_msg;
                              send_low_ack;
                              send_conn_exit
```

empty and is accessed by TLT and THT only. When the buffer is not full, i.e., the condition msg_num < buffer_size holds, a new data message can be accepted from TLT. When the buffer is not empty, i.e., the condition msg_num > 0 holds, a data message can be read or deleted from THT.

The communication link between THT and the high wrapper is explicitly described through an AET modeling the high channel – see the upper part of Table 7.8 – because the round-trip delay of a message exchange between THT and the high wrapper competes with the timeout set by THT. Initially, the high channel is ready to accept a data message from THT, which is then transmitted to the high

Table 7.7 NRL pump model: buffer type

```
ARCHI_ELEM_TYPE Buffer_Type(const integer buffer_size)

BEHAVIOR
  Buffer(integer(0..buffer_size) msg_num := 0;
         void) =
   choice
   {
    cond(msg_num < buffer_size) ->
     <accept_msg, _(1, 1)> . Buffer(msg_num + 1),
    cond(msg_num > 0) ->
     choice
     {
      <read_msg, _(1, 1)> . Buffer(msg_num),
      <delete_msg, _(1, 1)> . Buffer(msg_num - 1),
     }
   }

INPUT_INTERACTIONS  SYNC UNI accept_msg;
                             read_msg;
                             delete_msg
OUTPUT_INTERACTIONS SYNC UNI void
```

wrapper. After the delivery of the message, the high channel waits for the related ack to be sent to THT. Such a handshake competes with the notification of the timeout from THT, which represents a connection abort. In the case of abort, we assume that the high channel loses each pending message.

The last AET is the high wrapper type – see the lower part of Table 7.8 – which models the behavior of the high security level wrapper. The high wrapper can accept a data message from the high channel and, in this case, is expected to transmit an ack message. It is worth noting that the high wrapper does not execute other operations, as we abstract away from the communications concerning the high connection initialization/termination.

The architectural topology of the NRL pump description – see Table 7.9 – is illustrated by the enriched flow graph of Fig. 7.5, whose abstract variant is made of a cyclic union – with constituent AEIs LW, MT, THT, B, and TLT – attached to a star – with constituent AEIs HC and HW.

7.5.3 Noninterference Analysis

We now apply the first phase of DEPPERF to the ÆMILIA description of the NRL pump, ranging from the $\approx_B$-noninterference analysis of the functional behavior to the interpretation of a more detailed check based on the timing of events.

Table 7.8 NRL pump model: high channel type and high wrapper type

```
ARCHI_ELEM_TYPE HC_Type(const rate data_trans,
                        const rate ack_trans)

 BEHAVIOR
  HC(void; void) =
   <accept_msg, _(1, 1) .
    choice
    {
     <receive_timeout, _(0, 1)> . HC(),
     <transmit_msg, exp(data_trans)> .
      choice
      {
       <receive_timeout, _(0, 1)> . HC(),
       <accept_high_ack, _(1, 1)> .
        choice
        {
         <receive_timeout, _(0, 1)> . HC(),
         <transmit_high_ack, exp(ack_trans)> . HC()
        }
      }
    }

 INPUT_INTERACTIONS  SYNC UNI accept_msg;
                              receive_timeout;
                              accept_high_ack
 OUTPUT_INTERACTIONS SYNC UNI transmit_msg;
                              transmit_high_ack


ARCHI_ELEM_TYPE HW_Type(void)

 BEHAVIOR
  HW(void; void) =
   <receive_msg, _(0, 1)> . <send_high_ack, inf(1, 1)> . HW()

 INPUT_INTERACTIONS  SYNC UNI receive_msg
 OUTPUT_INTERACTIONS SYNC UNI send_high_ack
```

The first dependability aspect of interest for the NRL pump system is security. More precisely, we concentrate on the analysis of any insecure information flow that reveals to the low security level enclave L the behavior of the high security level enclave H. As already mentioned, among the potential covert channels, a specific behavior of H that we intend to avoid is the so-called denial-of-service attack, which is related to the second important dependability aspect of interest, i.e., service availability. In particular, the NRL pump should be always able to manage incoming requests of L independently of the behavior of H. To sum up, the goal of the noninterference check is to establish whether the behavior of H is transparent with respect to the observations of L.

Table 7.9 NRL pump model: architectural topology

```
ARCHI_ELEM_INSTANCES
  LW  : LW_Type(conn_gen, data_trans);
  MT  : MT_Type(data_trans, valid_prob);
  THT : THT_Type(conn_init, timeout);
  TLT : TLT_Type(data_trans, ack_trans, ack_delay);
  B   : Buffer_Type(buffer_size);
  HC  : HC_Type(data_trans, ack_trans);
  HW  : HW_Type()

ARCHI_INTERACTIONS
  void

ARCHI_ATTACHMENTS
  FROM LW.send_conn_request     TO MT.receive_conn_request;
  FROM MT.send_conn_valid       TO LW.receive_conn_valid;
  FROM MT.send_conn_reject      TO LW.receive_conn_reject;
  FROM MT.wakeup_tht            TO THT.receive_high_wakeup;
  FROM THT.wakeup_tlt           TO TLT.receive_low_wakeup;
  FROM TLT.send_conn_grant      TO LW.receive_conn_grant;
  FROM LW.send_msg              TO TLT.receive_msg;
  FROM TLT.store_msg            TO B.accept_msg;
  FROM TLT.send_low_ack         TO LW.receive_low_ack;
  FROM THT.read_msg             TO B.read_msg;
  FROM THT.forward_msg          TO HC.accept_msg;
  FROM HC.transmit_msg          TO HW.receive_msg;
  FROM THT.comm_timeout         TO HC.receive_timeout;
  FROM HW.send_high_ack         TO HC.accept_high_ack;
  FROM HC.transmit_high_ack     TO THT.receive_high_ack;
  FROM THT.delete_msg           TO B.delete_msg;
  FROM THT.send_abort_to_tlt    TO TLT.receive_abort_from_tht;
  FROM THT.send_ok_to_tlt       TO TLT.receive_ok_from_tht;
  FROM TLT.send_conn_exit       TO LW.receive_conn_exit;
  FROM LW.send_conn_close       TO TLT.receive_conn_close
```

From an architectural description standpoint, the unique AEI including activities of L is given by the low wrapper LW. Similarly, the unique AEI including activities of H is given by the high wrapper HW. All the other AEIs model activities internally performed by the pump like, e.g., the synchronizations between MT and THT, or between TLT and the buffer.

Formally, we assume that all the action names representing activities performed by LW belong to *Low*, while all the action names representing activities performed by HW belong to *High*. This is expressed in ÆMILIA as follows:

```
HIGH HW.receive_msg;
     HW.send_high_ack
LOW  LW.send_conn_request;
     LW.receive_conn_valid;
     LW.receive_conn_reject;
     LW.receive_conn_grant;
     LW.send_msg;
```

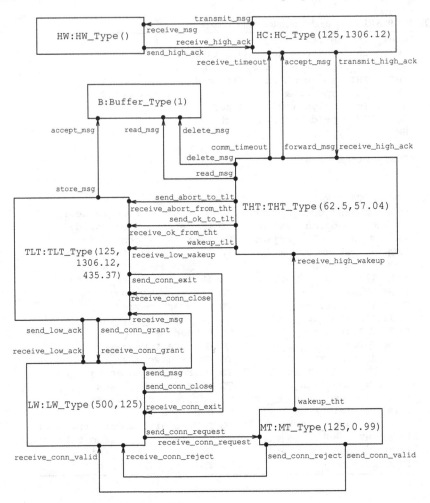

Fig. 7.5 Enriched flow graph of the NRL pump

```
LW.receive_low_ack;
LW.receive_conn_exit;
LW.send_conn_close
```

The first noninterference check is intended to reveal nondeterministic covert channels and, therefore, is based on $\approx_B$ and is applied to the functional behavior of the NRL pump architectural description. On the basis of the topology illustrated in Fig. 7.5, we apply Theorem 7.2 and we obtain that condition 3 is not satisfied. Intuitively, we observe that the pair of AEIs (HW, HC) interferes with the frontier of the cyclic union to which LW belongs, and such an information flow is propagated to LW. Hence, we do not have any guarantee that the security property is satisfied by the whole system. Indeed, the result of the noninterference check is negative and the distinguishing modal logic formula shows what follows.

If the AEI HW is enabled then each connection can either terminate correctly (synchronization of LW.send_conn_close with TLT.receive_conn_close) or abort because of the timeout mechanism implemented by THT (synchronization of LW.receive_conn_exit with TLT.send_conn_exit). On the other hand, whenever the interfering component HW is disabled, then each connection is aborted so that LW.send_conn_close cannot synchronize anymore.

The covert channel revealed by the nondeterministic noninterference check is caused by the unavoidable notification feedback from the pump to L, through which the low wrapper is made aware of the way in which every connection terminates. In fact, H can manipulate this notification procedure to set up a 1-bit covert channel guided by the connection status. Because of its functional nature, such an information flow cannot be eliminated by simply tuning system configuration parameters. However, it is worth noting that if we prevent L from observing the result of each connection (by hiding the actions modeling the connection close/exit messages), we obtain that the system is secure. This means that the covert channel described above is the unique nondeterministic information leakage that occurs in the NRL pump.

As far as other dependability issues are concerned, the nondeterministic noninterference check highlights the availability of the NRL pump in terms of its ability to deliver the required service under intentional faults caused by H. In this respect, the noninterference check has pointed out that the unique difference between the presence and the absence of H is given by the result of the notification procedure. Hence, the behavior of H, which can be either trusted or nontrusted, cannot compromise the NRL pump functionalities. Independent of the current connection, the NRL pump is eventually available to accept and manage new incoming connection requests. More precisely, in the case H cheats by performing a denial-of-service attack, as modeled by the system view preventing the execution of high actions, the pump is able to abort the connection by exploiting the timeout mechanism, thus becoming ready for new incoming requests. In other words, the service offered by the NRL pump satisfies the availability property, even if the functional analysis is not sufficient to evaluate efficiency issues.

The second noninterference check we apply is intended to reveal stochastically timed covert channels and, therefore, is based on $\approx_{MB}$. Since the functional model of the NRL pump description is not secure, it is obvious that the performance model cannot pass a stronger verification based on stochastic noninterference. However, the interesting result in this richer setting is that the stochastic noninterference check is passed not even after removing the communication to L concerning the connection status. The intuitive reason is that the average time elapsing between two consecutive connections changes depending on the behavior of H. This means that the covert channel affects the quality of service delivered by the NRL pump in a way that can be perceived by the low security level enclave.

In conclusion, the lesson we learn from the noninterference analysis is that the NRL pump suffers from a functional covert channel whose elimination is impractical. The bandwidth of this unavoidable information flow and its impact on efficiency issues can be estimated by moving on to the second phase of DEPPERF.

7.5.4 Performance Evaluation

We then apply the second phase of DEPPERF to the ÆMILIA description of the
NRL pump. The first phase has revealed that H interferes by influencing the
termination/abortion of each connection and, as a consequence, the average time
elapsing between two consecutive connections. Therefore, the number of connections that can be closed/aborted because of the behavior/misbehavior of H represents
the amount of bits that can be leaked from H to L through this 1-bit covert channel.

From a performance perspective, the indices that represent the covert channel
bandwidth are given by the system throughput in terms of number of connections
that are either closed or aborted per unit of time. These performance metrics can be
expressed through the measure definition mechanism of MSL as follows:

```
MEASURE closed_connections(LW.send_conn_close)
    IS throughput(LW.send_conn_close)

MEASURE aborted_connections(TLT.send_conn_exit)
    IS throughput(TLT.send_conn_exit)
```

The experiments have been conducted by making the connection request generation
rate conn_gen vary in the range $[1, 1000]$; i.e., from 1 request/s to 1 request/ms.
Moreover, the timeout delay used by the pump when waiting for the ack from the
high wrapper varies from 2 s to 10 ms. Therefore, the corresponding rate timeout
varies in the range $[0.5, 100]$.

Figure 7.6 reports the number of connection close/exit messages observed
per second. In particular, Fig. 7.6a refers to the scenario in which H is enabled.

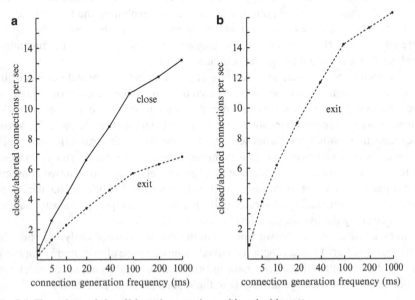

Fig. 7.6 Throughput of closed/aborted connections with and without H

Therefore, most connections are normally closed, while aborted connections occur because of the expiration of the timeout set by the pump. Figure 7.6b refers to the scenario in which H is disabled, i.e., all the connections abort. For both scenarios, as the connection request rate increases, the number of closed/aborted connections increases as well. Note that abortions occur in both figures independently of the behavior of H. As a consequence, a connection exit message does not reveal the presence/absence of H. Instead, L deduces the presence of H if a connection is correctly closed, which is an event that occurs in Fig. 7.6a only. In particular, from Fig. 7.6a we derive that H succeeds in leaking its presence to L up to 13 times/s. Note that the difference between the curve of Fig. 7.6b and the corresponding curve of Fig. 7.6a shows that the number of aborted connections observed per second is appreciably altered by the absence of H. This means that L can deduce the presence of H by simply measuring the average number of connection exit messages received per second.

The number of connections that abort because of the timeout expiration can be limited by increasing the timeout duration. In Fig. 7.7, we show the tradeoff between the timeout duration and the pump throughput in terms of the number of connections served per second. We consider a scenario where both L and H execute correctly the protocol, a connection request takes place every 50 ms, and the timeout duration varies in the interval [10,2000] ms, i.e., timeout varies from 100 to 0.5. The curves show that as the timeout duration increases, the number of connection exit messages tends to zero, while the number of connection close messages rises up to 9/s. The most interesting result is that, whenever the timeout expires after at least 200 ms, it is very likely that an ack sent by H arrives before the expiration of the timeout. More precisely, if timeout is set to 5 we have 0.412051 abortions/s, while in the limiting scenario where the timeout duration is 2 s we observe 0.0425696 abortions/s, corresponding to 2.554176 abortions/min. In other words, it is reasonable to predict with good approximation that an aborted connection occurs

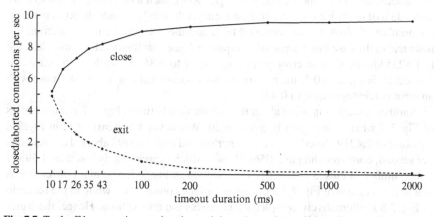

Fig. 7.7 Tradeoff between timeout duration and throughput of closed/aborted connections

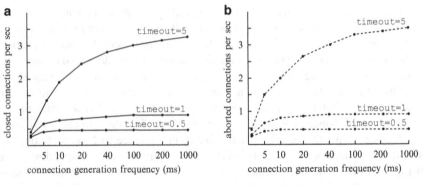

Fig. 7.8 Throughput of closed/aborted connections for different configuration parameters

because of a misbehavior of H rather than a timeout expiration. Hence, H may exploit the connection exit message to leak a bit to L, meaning that each connection really leaks a bit from H to L (e.g., 0 if it succeeds, 1 if it fails).

In order to measure the bandwidth of this 1-bit covert channel, in Fig. 7.8 we report the number of connections served per second whenever H alternatively completes and blocks (with equal probabilities) each connection in order to express a sequence of bits to be sent to L. We make the connection request rate conn_gen vary from 1/s to 1/ms. Moreover, the timeout duration is chosen to be long enough to ensure an exact interpretation of the information leakage; i.e., timeout $\in \{0.5, 1, 5\}$. With a timeout duration of 200 ms, we observe a number of closed connections between 0.41382 and 3.23043, and a number of aborted connections between 0.45022 and 3.51459. This means that if L interprets each connection termination as a leaked bit, in the worst case the maximum information leakage is 6.77633 bits/s. However, we know from the analysis of Fig. 7.7 that some abortions depend on the timeout expiration. As a consequence, a percentage of the bit sequence deduced by L in a second is wrong. In the scenario above (timeout equal to 5 and conn_gen $\in [1,1000]$), such a percentage is 4.043% independent of the connection request frequency. Obviously, a tradeoff exists between the number of bits/s that are deduced by L and the accuracy of the deduction. For instance, in the case that timeout is equal to 1, the maximum information leakage is 1.82353 bits/s with an error percentage equal to 0.862%, while in the case that timeout is equal to 0.5, the maximum information leakage is 0.95383 bits/s with an error percentage equal to 0.435%.

Another remark is in order about the comparison between Fig. 7.7 and the curves of Fig. 7.8 when conn_gen is equal to 20. Whenever timeout is 5, in Fig. 7.8 we observe 2.4219 closed connections per second and 2.63493 aborted connections per second, corresponding to 5.05683 bits/s, which is appreciably less than 9.59341 – the number of closed connections per second in Fig. 7.7. The main difference is that in the scenario of Fig. 7.7 H completes all the connections, while in the scenario of Fig. 7.8 H alternatively completes and blocks the connections. Hence, the bandwidth of the covert channel also depends on the sequence of bits that are leaked from H to L.

In general, we can quantitatively assess the relation between the amount of information leaked from H to L and the value of each configuration parameter that influences the quality of service delivered by the NRL pump. For instance, covert channel bandwidth and pump throughput intended as the number of connections served per second are directly proportional. Therefore, the availability of the NRL pump, expressed in terms of efficiency in responding to incoming requests, is inversely proportional to the security degree offered by the NRL pump. As another example, there is a relation between the timeout duration chosen by the pump and the amount of information flowing from H to L. The longer the timeout duration, the more an aborted connection may be interpreted as a leaked bit with high accuracy.

A strategy to reduce the covert channel bandwidth consists of enforcing a minimum delay to elapse between subsequent connection establishments. This policy, which has been suggested in [129], aims at minimizing the effects of connections that restart their execution with a suspicious frequency. In order to verify formally this strategy we add an extra delay, exponentially distributed with rate λ/s, after the abortion of a connection and before its reestablishment. In Fig. 7.9, we report the effect of this extra delay in the case that H alternatively completes and blocks (with equal probabilities) the connections, a connection request takes place every 5 ms, and timeout $\in \{1, 5\}$. The extra delay varies from 2 s to 10 ms; i.e., $\lambda \in [0.5, 100]$. As expected, the total number of closed/aborted connections per second decreases when the artificial delay increases. For instance, in the case that timeout is 5, the covert channel bandwidth ranges from an upper bound of 6.48454 bits/s to a lower bound of 0.84203 bits/s. We recall that the covert channel bandwidth in the corresponding scenario of Fig. 7.8 is 6.56608 bits/s. Hence, the bandwidth reduction is proportional to the extra delay duration. In the case that timeout is 1, the connections are equally divided into aborted and closed. The information leakage ranges from 1.80413 bits/s to 0.643281 bits/s.

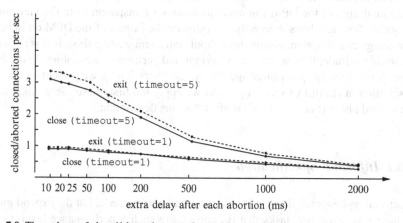

Fig. 7.9 Throughput of closed/aborted connections with extra delay

In conclusion, the covert channel bandwidth can be reduced under any threshold in spite of a reduction of the quality of service. In practice, a tradeoff exists between the robustness against the 1-bit covert channel and other dependability issues such as service availability. To reduce the unfavorable side effect of the proposed strategy, which could be unacceptably burdensome, the extra delay mechanism should be carefully activated, e.g., in the case of frequent abortions, which are an evidence of the misbehavior of H. Hence, an acceptable quality of service can be guaranteed by monitoring the kind of traffic with the aim of reducing the waiting time for the trusted users that behave correctly and, instead, adopting the delay mechanism for the suspicious connections that try to exploit the 1-bit covert channel.

7.6 Case Study II: Power-Manageable System

A fundamental issue in the design of mobile computing devices is reducing their power consumption. A commonly used technique is the adoption of a dynamic power management (DPM) policy, which modifies the power consumption of battery-powered devices based on certain run-time conditions (see, e.g., [29] and the references therein). The introduction of DPM may not be transparent, as it may alter the dependability and performance requirements of the device. Therefore, it is of paramount importance to assess such an impact before the DPM is introduced, in order to make sure that the dependability properties required by the system will not be significantly altered and that the quality of service will not go below an acceptable threshold.

In this section, we apply DEPPERF to a battery-powered system for remote procedure calls (RPC) implementing a DPM policy. Firstly, we predict the effect of the DPM on dependability requirements like reliability. In this respect, we show that an accurate design of the DPM can make its behavior transparent from the viewpoint of system functionalities. Secondly, we estimate the impact of the DPM on indices like energy consumption, system throughput, and client waiting time. In this respect, we study the tradeoff between energy savings and performance penalties. In the following, we show the power-manageable system (Sect. 7.6.1), we present its formal description in ÆMILIA (Sect. 7.6.2), and we apply the first phase (Sect. 7.6.3) and the second phase (Sect. 7.6.4) of DEPPERF to this description.

7.6.1 Informal Specification

Electronic systems are designed to deliver peak performance, but they spend most of their time executing tasks that do not require such a performance level, as in the case of cellular phones, which are reactive systems that are usually idle waiting for incoming calls or user commands. In general, these systems are subject to time-varying workloads. Since there is a close relation between power consumption and performance, the capability of tuning at run time the performance of a system to its workload provides great opportunity to save power. DPM techniques dynamically reconfigure an electronic system by changing its operating mode and by turning its components on and off in order to provide at any time the minimum performance/functionality required by the workload while consuming the minimum amount of power. Whatever scheme is adopted, the application of DPM techniques requires power-manageable components providing multiple operating modes, a power manager having run-time control of the operating mode of the power-manageable components, and a DPM policy specifying the control rules to be implemented by the power manager.

The simplest example of power-manageable hardware is a device that can be dynamically turned on and off by a power manager that issues shutdown and wakeup commands according to a given policy. When turned on, the device is active and provides a given performance at the cost of a given power consumption. When turned off, the device is inactive, hence provides no performance and consumes no power. The workload of the device is a sequence of service requests issued by a generic client. The particular power-manageable system that we consider is concerned with a battery-powered server for RPC. The overall system is depicted in Fig. 7.10.

The client (C) synchronously interacts with the server (S) through a full-duplex radio channel implemented by two half-duplex radio channels: RCS, from C to S, and RSC, from S to C. Channel RCS is used by the client to send remote procedure calls to the server, while channel RSC is used by the server to send the results back to the client. The server also interacts with the DPM, which issues shutdown commands in order to put the server in a low power inactive state whenever appropriate. Two more signals, idle and busy, are used by the server to notify the DPM about every change of its service state.

In its easiest implementation, the blocking client issues a call, waits for the results, then takes some time to process the results before issuing the next call. A simple timeout mechanism can be employed by the client to resend a call whenever the waiting time exceeds a given threshold. This can happen because the half-duplex radio channels are not ideal; hence, they may introduce both a long propagation delay and a packet loss probability.

The behavior of the server is characterized through the following four states:

- Idle: the server is waiting for a call to arrive.
- Busy: the server is processing a call.

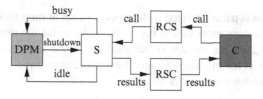

Fig. 7.10 Power-manageable system for remote procedure calls

- Sleeping: the server has been shut down by the DPM.
- Awaking: the server has been woken up by the arrival of a call.

The server is sensitive to shutdown commands in the idle state. However, the server may also be sensitive to shutdown commands when busy, in which case a shutdown can interrupt the call processing. In the sleeping state, the server consumes no power. The awaking state is a power consuming state in which the server temporarily resides while going from sleeping to busy.

Finally, the DPM sends shutdown commands to the server at certain time instants, possibly based on the knowledge of the current state of the server. There are two different policies:

- Trivial policy: the DPM issues shutdown commands with a given frequency, independent of the current state of the server.
- Timeout policy: shutdown commands are issued by the DPM upon the expiration of a fixed or random timeout after the server has entered the idle state.

In the following, we apply DEPPERF in order to assess formally the impact of different DPM policies on system dependability and performance. The objective is to check that the DPM does not significantly change the system functionality and does not cause an intolerable degradation of the system efficiency.

7.6.2 Architectural Description

Initially, we consider a simplified version of the power-manageable system in which the radio channels are perfect (so that the blocking client does not need to use any timeout mechanism), the DPM sends shutdown commands independent of the current state of the server (hence, the server does not need to notify the DPM about its state changes), and the server is sensitive to shutdown commands both in the idle state and in the busy state.

The ÆMILIA description of this system starts with its name and the definition of its formal parameters:

```
ARCHI_TYPE RPC_DPM(const rate server_proc    := 5,
                   const rate server_awaking := 0.333,
                   const rate packet_prop    := 1.25,
                   const rate client_proc    := 0.103,
                   const rate dpm_shutdown   := 0.1)
```

The description is parameterized with respect to a set of rates modeling exponentially distributed delays expressed in ms^{-1}. We assume that the average server processing time is 0.2 ms, the average server awaking time is 3 ms, the average packet propagation time is 0.8 ms, the average client processing time is 9.7 ms, and the average DPM shutdown timeout is 10 ms.

The blocking client synchronously communicates with the power-manageable server through the radio channel by repeatedly issuing a call, waiting for the results, and processing them. The corresponding AET is thus defined as follows:

```
ARCHI_ELEM_TYPE Client_Type(const rate client_proc)

  BEHAVIOR
    Client(void; void) =
     <send_rpc_packet, inf(1, 1)> .
      <receive_result_packet, _(1, 1)> .
       <process_result_packet, exp(client_proc)> . Client()

  INPUT_INTERACTIONS   SYNC UNI receive_result_packet
  OUTPUT_INTERACTIONS  SYNC UNI send_rpc_packet
```

The half-duplex radio channel is a perfect link – it does not lose any packet – so it repeatedly waits for a packet, propagates it, and delivers it. The corresponding AET is as follows:

```
ARCHI_ELEM_TYPE Radio_Channel_Type(const rate packet_prop)

  BEHAVIOR
    Radio_Channel(void; void) =
     <get_packet, _(1, 1)> .
      <propagate_packet, exp(packet_prop)> .
       <deliver_packet, inf(1, 1)> . Radio_Channel()

  INPUT_INTERACTIONS   SYNC UNI get_packet
  OUTPUT_INTERACTIONS  SYNC UNI deliver_packet
```

The behavior of the server AET is given by five process algebraic equations:

```
ARCHI_ELEM_TYPE Server_Type(const rate server_proc,
                            const rate server_awaking)

  BEHAVIOR
    Idle_Server(void; void) =
      choice
      {
       <receive_rpc_packet, _(1, 1)> . Busy_Server(),
       <receive_shutdown, _(0, 1)> . Sleeping_Server()
      };
    Busy_Server(void; void) =
      choice
      {
       <prepare_result_packet, exp(server_proc)> .
        Responding_Server(),
       <receive_shutdown, _(0, 1)> . Sleeping_Server()
      };
    Responding_Server(void; void) =
      choice
      {
       <send_result_packet, inf(1, 1)> . Idle_Server(),
       <receive_shutdown, _(0, 1)> . Sleeping_Server()
```

```
    };
  Sleeping_Server(void; void) =
    <receive_rpc_packet, _(1, 1)> . Awaking_Server();
  Awaking_Server(void; void) =
    <awake, exp(server_awaking)> . Busy_Server()

  INPUT_INTERACTIONS   SYNC UNI receive_rpc_packet;
                                receive_shutdown
  OUTPUT_INTERACTIONS SYNC UNI send_result_packet
```

The first equation is associated with the idle state, while the second and third ones represent the busy state. Two equations are necessary for this state because two activities are carried out – processing the call and sending the results back to the client – each of which can be interrupted by the reception of a shutdown command from the DPM. The fourth and the fifth equations are concerned with the sleeping and the awaking states, respectively.

The DPM issues shutdown commands that are periodically sent to the server even when this is busy. The corresponding AET is defined as follows:

```
ARCHI_ELEM_TYPE DPM_Type(const rate dpm_shutdown)

  BEHAVIOR
   DPM(void; void) =
     <send_shutdown, exp(dpm_shutdown)> . DPM()

   INPUT_INTERACTIONS   void
   OUTPUT_INTERACTIONS SYNC UNI send_shutdown
```

In the architectural topology section, we declare one instance for the server, client, and DPM types together with two instances of the half-duplex radio channel type. The declaration of the attachments between the interactions of such AEIs is as prescribed by Fig. 7.10 up to the busy and idle triggers, which are left out:

```
ARCHI_ELEM_INSTANCES
  C   : Client_Type(client_proc);
  RCS : Radio_Channel_Type(packet_prop);
  RSC : Radio_Channel_Type(packet_prop);
  S   : Server_Type(server_proc, server_awaking);
  DPM : DPM_Type(dpm_shutdown)

ARCHI_INTERACTIONS
  void

ARCHI_ATTACHMENTS
  FROM C.send_rpc_packet      TO RCS.get_packet;
  FROM RCS.deliver_packet     TO S.receive_rpc_packet;
  FROM S.send_result_packet   TO RSC.get_packet;
  FROM RSC.deliver_packet     TO C.receive_result_packet;
  FROM DPM.send_shutdown      TO S.receive_shutdown
```

We conclude the presentation of the architectural description of the power-manageable system by illustrating in Fig. 7.11 its enriched flow graph. The abstract version of this graph is made of a cycle – with constituent AEIs C, RCS, S, and RSC – attached to the AEI DPM through the frontier AEI S.

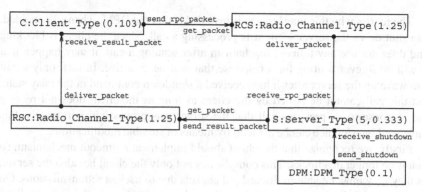

Fig. 7.11 Enriched flow graph of the power-manageable system

7.6.3 Noninterference Analysis

We now apply the first phase of DEPPERF to the ÆMILIA description of the power-manageable system for RPC. With respect to the case study of Sect. 7.5, the noninterference analysis reveals both covert channels that can be repaired and covert channels whose quantitative impact needs to be estimated in the second phase.

In the setting of the power-manageable system for RPC, the main dependability aspect is reliability, expressed in terms of the absence of any interference from the DPM to the client. In other words, we want to assess the transparency of the DPM from the viewpoint of the client.

From an architectural standpoint, the interfering AEI is DPM, while C is the unique AEI including the activities that an external observer can monitor in order to assess the transparency of the DPM. Formally, we assume that the actions representing the interactions of C belong to *Low*, while the action send_shutdown representing the only activity performed by DPM belongs to *High*. This is expressed in ÆMILIA as follows:

```
HIGH DPM.send_shutdown
LOW  C.send_rpc_packet;
     C.receive_result_packet
```

The first noninterference check we apply, which is based on $\approx_B$, provides a negative result. With respect to the topology illustrated in Fig. 7.11, we observe that the system does not satisfy the conditions of Theorem 7.2. The modal logic formula stating the interference intuitively shows that, whenever the interfering component is active, then it is possible to observe a computation along which no results are returned to the client (synchronization of RSC.deliver_packet with C.receive_result_packet) after that the client has issued a call (synchronization of C.send_rpc_packet with RCS.get_packet), while this computation does not exist when the AEI DPM is disabled.

The reason why this interference is revealed is that the DPM, whenever enabled, can shut down the server while it is processing a call. Since the client is blocking and does not use any timeout mechanism after sending a call, it may happen that it will be forever waiting for a response that will never arrive. In fact, only a call can wake up the server after it has received a shutdown command in the busy state, but this call cannot be issued by the client as long as the client does not receive the response to its previous call that the server was processing. Fortunately, this unwanted interference can be avoided by means of suitable modifications.

Firstly, we recognize that the client should implement a timeout mechanism, so that it no longer deadlocks. This complicates not only the client but also the server, as they now must be able to discard old packets due to useless retransmissions. On the other hand, the timeout mechanism allows the client to cope with a more realistic radio channel that can lose packets.

Secondly, we recognize that the DPM should not shut down the server while it is busy, which is achieved by making the server inform the DPM about its state changes via the busy and idle triggers as shown in Fig. 7.10. Therefore, the DPM activities are now divided into two classes. In the first class we have the only DPM activity that modifies the state of the power-manageable device, i.e., send_shutdown, while the activities of the second class are those used to collect information about the state of the power-manageable device, termed receive_idle_notice and receive_busy_notice. When the DPM can modify the state of the power-manageable device, i.e., send_shutdown can be executed, we say that the DPM is enabled. On the contrary, when the state-modifying activity of the DPM cannot be performed, we say that the DPM is disabled.

The revised version of the architectural type RPC_DPM includes two additional parameters:

```
const rate    client_timeout := 0.5,
const weight packet_loss     := 0.02
```

The former is the average client timeout, which corresponds to 2 ms, while the latter is the packet loss probability. The revised version of the AETs is illustrated in Tables 7.10, 7.11, 7.12, and 7.13, while the revised version of the architectural topology section includes the following additional attachments, which do not alter the abstract enriched flow graph of the system:

```
FROM S.notify_busy TO DPM.receive_busy_notice;
FROM S.notify_idle TO DPM.receive_idle_notice
```

In order to apply the noninterference check to the revised version of the system, we assume that the set *Low* is the same as before, while the set *High* changes as follows. The only state-modifying activity of the AEI DPM, i.e., send_shutdown, belongs to *High*, while the other information-collecting activities of the AEI DPM can be ignored, because they do not contribute to alter the behavior of the power-manageable device.

Table 7.10 Power-manageable system model: revised version of the client AET

```
ARCHI_ELEM_TYPE Client_Type(const rate client_proc,
                            const rate client_timeout)

BEHAVIOR
 Requesting_Client(void; void) =
  choice
  {
   <send_rpc_packet, inf(1, 1)> . Waiting_Client(),
   <receive_result_packet, _(1, 1)> .
    <ignore_result_packet, _(1, 1)> . Requesting_Client()
  };
 Waiting_Client(void; void) =
  choice
  {
   <receive_result_packet, _(1, 1)> . Processing_Client(),
   <expire_timeout, exp(client_timeout)> . Resending_Client()
  };
 Processing_Client(void; void) =
  choice
  {
   <process_result_packet, exp(client_proc)> .
    Requesting_Client(),
   <receive_result_packet, _(1, 1)> .
    <ignore_result_packet, _(1, 1)> . Processing_Client()
  };
 Resending_Client(void; void) =
  choice
  {
   <send_rpc_packet, inf(1, 1)> . Waiting_Client(),
   <receive_result_packet, _(1, 1)> . Processing_Client()
  }

 INPUT_INTERACTIONS   SYNC UNI receive_result_packet
 OUTPUT_INTERACTIONS  SYNC UNI send_rpc_packet
```

The revised version of the system meets nondeterministic noninterference. This means that the introduction of the DPM in the more realistic scenario is transparent from the functional viewpoint, i.e., it does not alter the behavior of the system as perceived by the client. In order to formally verify whether such a transparency is perceived also from the quantitative viewpoint, it is necessary to apply a stochastic noninterference check, so as to capture possible timed covert channels.

The result of the application of the stochastic noninterference check is negative. Hence, the two system views under comparison do not behave the same with respect to a performance-aware notion of behavioral equivalence. The intuitive reason is that the time needed to process a client request changes depending on the activation/deactivation of the DPM. Therefore, the metrics related to this behavior, as well as any other metric related to quality of service, have to be analyzed in the second phase of DEPPERF.

Table 7.11 Power-manageable system model: revised version of the radio channel AET

```
ARCHI_ELEM_TYPE Radio_Channel_Type(const rate    packet_prop,
                                    const weight packet_loss)


  BEHAVIOR
   Radio_Channel(void; void) =
    <get_packet, _(1, 1)> .
     <propagate_packet, exp(packet_prop)> .
      choice
      {
       <keep_packet, inf(1, 1 - packet_loss)> .
        <deliver_packet, inf(1, 1)> . Radio_Channel(),
        <lose_packet, inf(1, packet_loss)> . Radio_Channel()
      }

  INPUT_INTERACTIONS  SYNC UNI get_packet
  OUTPUT_INTERACTIONS SYNC UNI deliver_packet
```

7.6.4 Performance Evaluation

We then apply the second phase of DEPPERF to the revised ÆMILIA description of
the power-manageable system for RPC. In particular, we estimate the DPM impact
on the quality of service delivered by the system. For this purpose, we concentrate
on three metrics that are critical for the power-manageable system. The first two
are system throughput and the percentage of time spent by the client waiting for
the result, whose choice is a direct consequence of the analysis of the feedback
provided by the stochastic noninterference check. The third one is the energy that
is consumed by the server, which measures the success of the DPM strategy. Such
measures are evaluated for several typical values of the DPM shutdown rate, in order
to get insight in the trend of both the power consumption and the overall system
efficiency.

These performance indices can be expressed through the measure definition
mechanism in MSL. The system throughput is described as follows:

```
MEASURE system_throughput(C.process_result_packet)
     IS throughput(C.process_result_packet)
```

The percentage of time spent by the client waiting for the result is given by the
probability of being in the Waiting_Client behavior of the AEI C. The probability of being in a specific behavior B of an individual component K of the system
represents a class of performance measures described through the basic MSL measure behavior_prob. This formula is parameterized with respect to the behavior
K.B of interest, while its body establishes that each system state including K.B as
local state gains an additional unit contribution to the rate at which the reward is
accumulated while staying there. This basic MSL measure is employed as follows:

```
MEASURE client_waiting_time(Waiting_Client)
     IS behavior_prob(Waiting_Client)
```

Table 7.12 Power-manageable system model: revised version of the server AET

```
ARCHI_ELEM_TYPE Server_Type(const rate server_proc,
                            const rate server_awaking)

BEHAVIOR
 Idle_Server(void; void) =
  choice
  {
   <receive_rpc_packet, _(1, 1)> .
    <notify_busy, inf(1, 1)> . Busy_Server(),
   <receive_shutdown, _(0, 1)> . Sleeping_Server()
  };
 Busy_Server(void; void) =
  choice
  {
   <prepare_result_packet, exp(server_proc)> .
    Responding_Server(),
   <receive_rpc_packet, _(1, 1)> .
    <ignore_rpc_packet, inf(1, 1)> . Busy_Server()
  };
 Responding_Server(void; void) =
  choice
  {
   <send_result_packet, inf(1, 1)> .
    <notify_idle, inf(1, 1)> . Idle_Server(),
   <receive_rpc_packet, _(1, 1)> .
    <ignore_rpc_packet, inf(1, 1)> . Busy_Server()
  };
 Sleeping_Server(void; void) =
  <receive_rpc_packet, _(1, 1)> . Awaking_Server();
 Awaking_Server(void; void) =
  choice
  {
   <awake, exp(server_awaking)> . Busy_Server(),
   <receive_rpc_packet, _(1, 1)> .
    <ignore_rpc_packet, inf(1, 1)> . Busy_Server()
  }

INPUT_INTERACTIONS   SYNC UNI receive_rpc_packet;
                              receive_shutdown
OUTPUT_INTERACTIONS  SYNC UNI send_result_packet;
                              notify_busy;
                              notify_idle
```

As far as the energy consumed by the server is concerned, we observe that the power consumption depends on the probabilities of being in the various server states. Hence, we employ a generalization of the basic measure behavior_prob in which the parameter K.B of the metric identifier is equipped with a real number l denoting the value of the power consumption associated with K.B. This value replaces the unit reward used in the body of the measure behavior_prob.

Table 7.13 Power-manageable system model: revised version of the DPM AET

```
ARCHI_ELEM_TYPE DPM_Type(const rate dpm_shutdown)

 BEHAVIOR
  Enabled_DPM(void; void) =
   choice
   {
    <send_shutdown, exp(dpm_shutdown)> . Disabled_DPM(),
    <receive_busy_notice, _(1, 1)> . Disabled_DPM()
   };
  Disabled_DPM(void; void) =
   <receive_idle_notice, _(1, 1)> . Enabled_DPM()

 INPUT_INTERACTIONS   SYNC UNI receive_busy_notice;
                               receive_idle_notice
 OUTPUT_INTERACTIONS  SYNC UNI send_shutdown
```

The obtained metric, called state_power_consumption, is then used to define
the following derived measure expressing the overall power consumption of the
server:

```
MEASURE  power_consumption(K.Idle(l_i), K.Busy(l_b),
                           K.Responding(l_r),
                           K.Sleeping(l_s), K.Awaking(l_a))
     IS  state_power_consumption(K.Idle(l_i)) +
         state_power_consumption(K.Busy(l_b)) +
         state_power_consumption(K.Responding(l_r)) +
         state_power_consumption(K.Sleeping(l_s)) +
         state_power_consumption(K.Awaking(l_a))
```

Based on the assumption that the energy consumed in the busy state is 50% more
than the energy consumed in the idle and awaking state, while of course no energy
is consumed in the sleeping state, the overall energy consumption can be easily
evaluated through the following measure invocation:

```
power_consumption(S.Idle_Server(2),
                  S.Busy_Server(3),
                  S.Responding_Server(3),
                  S.Sleeping_Server(0),
                  S.Awaking_Server(2))
```

The results of the performance analysis conducted with and without the DPM
are reported in Fig. 7.12, for values of the DPM shutdown timeout between 0 and
25 ms. Dot-dashed lines refer to the system with the AEI DPM disabled, while solid
lines refer to the system with the AEI DPM enabled. Throughput, average waiting
time, and energy per request are plotted as a function of the timeout used by the
DPM to issue shutdown commands. The energy per request is obtained as the ratio
of the energy to the throughput.

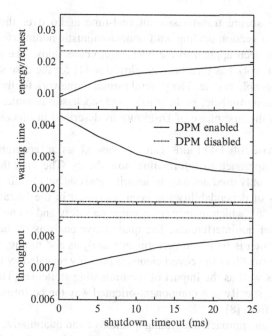

Fig. 7.12 Performance results with and without the DPM component

As expected, the shorter the DPM timeout, the larger the impact of the DPM. The limiting situations are represented by a DPM that issues a shutdown command as soon as the server goes idle (timeout = 0) and by a DPM that never issues shutdown commands (timeout = ∞). In the former case the impact of the DPM is maximum, while in the latter case the DPM has no effect.

In general, from the analysis of the figure we derive that the DPM is never counterproductive in terms of energy, meaning that the additional energy required to wake up the server from the sleeping state is compensated, on average, by the energy saved while sleeping. On the other hand, it is worth noting that energy savings are always paid in terms of performance penalties – reduced throughput and increased waiting time – so that the DPM is not transparent in terms of quality of service perceived by the client. In conclusion, depending on the specific scenario – expressed in terms of the number of clients and of the characteristics of the communication channels and of the server – the designer can decide whether tuning the DPM configuration parameters is enough to ensure a balanced tradeoff.

7.7 Comparisons

The basic ideas behind the considered predictive methodology for integrating dependability and performance come from [14], where a version based on probabilistic noninterference [11] and discrete time [55] has been applied to an adaptive protocol for the secure transmission of real-time audio over the Internet, and from [9], where a version dealing with nondeterministic noninterference and continuous time has been applied to the NRL pump case study. The same approach used in the latter work has then been employed in [4] for the case study related to the power-manageable system. The general formal framework for the definition and analysis of nondeterministic, probabilistic, and stochastic noninterference, which is at the base of the first phase of DEPPERF as described in this chapter, is taken from [10].

The first phase of DEPPERF can be viewed as a generalization of the noninterference approach to information flow theory. The idea that noninterference can be profitably used not only in security analysis but also for the assessment of other aspects of dependability has been addressed in the literature in specific cases [185, 189, 86], which mainly concentrate on safety and do not employ quantitative notions of noninterference. The quantitative analysis of the second phase of DEPPERF, which is based on performance analysis and tuning, is necessary to estimate the bandwidth of the covert channels possibly revealed by the noninterference analysis, as well as the impact of the mitigating strategies. The notation that has been used to specify in a component-oriented way the performance metrics of interest is taken from [8].

The need for an approach integrating qualitative and quantitative analysis of the dependences among components stems from the fact that real-world systems suffer from information flows that affect both dependability and performance. For instance, applications based on real-time communications typically require both critical performance constraints and privacy guarantees. Applications such as these often offer customized security (choice of the authentication and privacy methods, tolerance to replay attacks, use of caching and prefetching strategies) to achieve a customized tradeoff between security and performance (see, e.g., [197, 15]). As another example, fault- and intrusion-tolerant architectures employing mobile platforms usually need safety-critical functions that may be under the control of faulty system components, so that it is important to verify to which extent the system is tolerant against accidental rather than deliberate faults (see, e.g., [26]).

In the literature, several existing approaches tackle the problem of combining dependability analysis and performance evaluation. Some of them employ different modeling techniques to achieve a balanced tradeoff, like, e.g., in [110], where architecture-workload models and failure-repair models are combined to ensure the analysis of fault-tolerant parallel computer systems. In other cases, a single formal framework is employed to build dependability models that can be quantitatively evaluated. For instance, a unifying framework for dependability and performance is offered by Markovian models, see, e.g., [23, 108, 143]. While [108, 143] deal with efficiency issues in the analysis of such models, [23] concentrates on the formal, structured specification of metrics. In particular, a logic-based specification technique is introduced that facilitates the definition of performance, dependability, and performability measures. However, these works consider neither component-oriented analysis nor methodologies for the analysis of the tradeoff between dependability and performance.

Recently, several efforts have been done to translate high-level design languages like UML into enriched models that augment UML-based design tools with mathematical analysis techniques. For instance, in [51] a transformation from structural UML diagrams to timed Petri nets is described for the quantitative evaluation of availability and reliability. The work closest to that presented in this chapter in aim and techniques is [107], which uses the formal paradigm of stochastic activity networks – a high-level language for capturing the stochastic behavior of systems – to model and evaluate several different intrusion-tolerant server architectures. The analysis is then conducted by defining a series of relevant metrics characterizing both dependability aspects, such as service availability, and performance indices, such as throughput. However, this work does not illustrate a unifying methodology for singling out the interrelations among dependability and performance through a formal theory like noninterference.

References

1. G.D. Abowd, R. Allen, and D. Garlan, *Formalizing Style to Understand Descriptions of Software Architecture*, ACM Transactions on Software Engineering and Methodology 4:319–364, 1995.
2. S. Abramsky, *Observational Equivalence as a Testing Equivalence*, Theoretical Computer Science 53:225–241, 1987.
3. L. Aceto and D. Murphy, *Timing and Causality in Process Algebra*, Acta Informatica 33:317–350, 1996.
4. A. Acquaviva, A. Aldini, M. Bernardo, A. Bogliolo, E. Bontà, and E. Lattanzi, *A Methodology Based on Formal Methods for Predicting the Impact of Dynamic Power Management*, in *Formal Methods for Mobile Computing*, Springer, LNCS 3465:155–189, Berlin (Germany), 2005.
5. M. Ajmone Marsan, G. Balbo, G. Conte, S. Donatelli, and G. Franceschinis, *Modelling with Generalized Stochastic Petri Nets*, Wiley, New York (NY), 1995.
6. A. Aldini, *Classification of Security Properties in a Linda-Like Process Algebra*, Science of Computer Programming 63:16–38, 2006.
7. A. Aldini and M. Bernardo, *On the Usability of Process Algebra: An Architectural View*, Theoretical Computer Science 335:281–329, 2005.
8. A. Aldini and M. Bernardo, *Mixing Logics and Rewards for the Component-Oriented Specification of Performance Measures*, Theoretical Computer Science 382:3–23, 2007.
9. A. Aldini and M. Bernardo, *A Formal Approach to the Integrated Analysis of Security and QoS*, Reliability Engineering & System Safety 92:1503–1520, 2007.
10. A. Aldini and M. Bernardo, *A General Framework for Nondeterministic, Probabilistic, and Stochastic Noninterference*, in Proc. of the *1st Joint Workshop on Automated Reasoning for Security Protocol Analysis and Issues in the Theory of Security (ARSPA/WITS 2009)*, Springer, LNCS 5511:18–33, York (UK), 2009.
11. A. Aldini, M. Bravetti, and R. Gorrieri, *A Process-Algebraic Approach for the Analysis of Probabilistic Noninterference*, Journal of Computer Security 12:191–245, 2004.
12. A. Aldini and A. Di Pierro, *Estimating the Maximum Information Leakage*, Journal of Information Security 7:219–242, 2008.
13. A. Aldini and R. Gorrieri, *Security Analysis of a Probabilistic Non-Repudiation Protocol*, in Proc. of the *2nd Joint Int. Workshop on Process Algebra and Performance Modelling and Probabilistic Methods in Verification (PAPM/PROBMIV 2002)*, Springer, LNCS 2399:17–36, Copenhagen (Denmark), 2002.
14. A. Aldini and R. Gorrieri, *A Study About Trade-Off Between Performance and Security in an Internet Audio Mechanism*, in *Global Computing: Programming Environments, Languages, Security and Analysis of Systems*, Springer, LNCS 2874:203–228, Berlin (Germany), 2003.

15. A. Aldini, M. Roccetti, and R. Gorrieri, *On Securing Real Time Speech Transmission over the Internet: An Experimental Study*, EURASIP Journal on Applied Signal Processing 2003(10):1027–1042, 2003.

16. J. Aldrich, C. Chambers, and D. Notkin, *ArchJava: Connecting Software Architecture to Implementation*, in Proc. of the *24th Int. Conf. on Software Engineering (ICSE 2002)*, ACM Press, pp. 187–197, Orlando (FL), 2002.

17. R. Allen, R. Douence, and D. Garlan, *Specifying and Analyzing Dynamic Software Architectures*, in Proc. of the *1st Int. Conf. on Fundamental Approaches to Software Engineering (FASE 1998)*, Springer, LNCS 1382:21–37, Lisbon (Portugal), 1998.

18. R. Allen and D. Garlan, *A Formal Basis for Architectural Connection*, ACM Transactions on Software Engineering and Methodology 6:213–249, 1997.

19. F. Aquilani, S. Balsamo, and P. Inverardi, *Performance Analysis at the Software Architectural Design Level*, Performance Evaluation 45:205–221, 2001.

20. J.C.M. Baeten and J.A. Bergstra, *Real Time Process Algebra*, Formal Aspects of Computing 3:142–188, 1991.

21. J.C.M. Baeten, J.A. Bergstra, and J.W. Klop, *Ready-Trace Semantics for Concrete Process Algebra with the Priority Operator*, Computer Journal 30:498–506, 1987.

22. J.C.M. Baeten and W.P. Weijland, *Process Algebra*, Cambridge University Press, Cambridge (UK), 1990.

23. C. Baier, B. Haverkort, H. Hermanns, and J.-P. Katoen, *Automated Performance and Dependability Evaluation Using Model Checking*, in *Performance Evaluation of Complex Systems: Techniques and Tools*, Springer, LNCS 2459:261–289, Berlin (Germany), 2002.

24. C. Baier, J.-P. Katoen, H. Hermanns, and V. Wolf, *Comparative Branching-Time Semantics for Markov Chains*, Information and Computation 200:149–214, 2005.

25. S. Balsamo, M. Bernardo, and M. Simeoni, *Performance Evaluation at the Software Architecture Level*, in *Formal Methods for Software Architectures*, Springer, LNCS 2804:207–258, Heidelberg (Germany), 2003.

26. C. Basile, *Intrusion and Fault Tolerance: For Wireline and Wireless Networks*, Ph.D. Thesis, University of Illinois at Urbana-Champaign (IL), 2005.

27. F. Baskett, K.M. Chandy, R.R. Muntz, and G. Palacios, *Open, Closed, and Mixed Networks of Queues with Different Classes of Customers*, Journal of the ACM 22:248–260, 1975.

28. H. Bekic, *Towards a Mathematical Theory of Processes*, Technical Report TR 25.125, IBM Laboratory Vienna (Austria), 1971 (published in *Programming Languages and Their Definition*, Springer, LNCS 177:168–206, New York (NY), 1984).

29. L. Benini, A. Bogliolo, and G. De Micheli, *A Survey of Design Techniques for System-Level Dynamic Power Management*, IEEE Transactions on VLSI Systems 8:299–316, 2000.

30. J.A. Bergstra, A. Ponse, and S.A. Smolka (eds.), *Handbook of Process Algebra*, Elsevier, Amsterdam (The Netherlands), 2001.

31. M. Bernardo, *Non-Bisimulation-Based Markovian Behavioral Equivalences*, Journal of Logic and Algebraic Programming 72:3–49, 2007.

32. M. Bernardo, *Towards State Space Reduction Based on T-Lumpability-Consistent Relations*, in Proc. of the *5th European Performance Engineering Workshop (EPEW 2008)*, Springer, LNCS 5261:64–78, Palma de Mallorca (Spain), 2008.

33. M. Bernardo, *Uniform Logical Characterizations of Testing Equivalences for Nondeterministic, Probabilistic and Markovian Processes*, in Proc. of the *7th Int. Workshop on Quantitative Aspects of Programming Languages (QAPL 2009)*, Elsevier, ENTCS, York (UK), 2009 in press.

34. M. Bernardo, *Markovian Testing Equivalence and Exponentially Timed Internal Actions*, in Proc. of the *1st Int. Workshop on Quantitative Formal Methods (QFM 2009)*, EPTCS, Eindhoven (The Netherlands), 2009 in press.

35. M. Bernardo and A. Aldini, *Weak Markovian Bisimilarity: Abstracting from Prioritized/Weighted Internal Immediate Actions*, in Proc. of the *10th Italian Conf. on Theoretical Computer Science (ICTCS 2007)*, World Scientific, pp. 39–56, Rome (Italy), 2007.

36. M. Bernardo and E. Bontà, *Generating Well-Synchronized Multithreaded Programs from Software Architecture Descriptions*, in Proc. of the *4th Working IEEE/IFIP Conf. on Software Architecture (WICSA 2004)*, IEEE-CS Press, pp. 167–176, Oslo (Norway), 2004.

37. M. Bernardo and E. Bontà, *Preserving Architectural Properties in Multithreaded Code Generation*, in Proc. of the *7th Int. Conf. on Coordination Models and Languages (COORDINATION 2005)*, Springer, LNCS 3454:188–203, Namur (Belgium), 2005.

38. M. Bernardo, E. Bontà, and A. Aldini, *Handling Communications in Process Algebraic Architectural Description Languages: Modeling, Verification, and Implementation*, Journal of Systems and Software, 2010 in press.

39. M. Bernardo and S. Botta, *A Survey of Modal Logics Characterizing Behavioral Equivalences for Nondeterministic and Stochastic Systems*, Mathematical Structures in Computer Science 18:29–55, 2008.

40. M. Bernardo and M. Bravetti, *Performance Measure Sensitive Congruences for Markovian Process Algebras*, Theoretical Computer Science 290:117–160, 2003.

41. M. Bernardo, P. Ciancarini, and L. Donatiello, *Architecting Families of Software Systems with Process Algebras*, ACM Transactions on Software Engineering and Methodology 11:386–426, 2002.

42. M. Bernardo and R. Cleaveland, *A Theory of Testing for Markovian Processes*, in Proc. of the *11th Int. Conf. on Concurrency Theory (CONCUR 2000)*, Springer, LNCS 1877:305–319, State College (PA), 2000.

43. M. Bernardo, L. Donatiello, and P. Ciancarini, *Stochastic Process Algebra: From an Algebraic Formalism to an Architectural Description Language*, in *Performance Evaluation of Complex Systems: Techniques and Tools*, Springer, LNCS 2459:236–260, Berlin (Germany), 2002.

44. M. Bernardo and R. Gorrieri, *A Tutorial on EMPA: A Theory of Concurrent Processes with Nondeterminism, Priorities, Probabilities and Time*, Theoretical Computer Science 202:1–54, 1998.

45. M. Bernardo and P. Inverardi (eds.), *Formal Methods for Software Architectures*, Springer, LNCS 2804, Heidelberg (Germany), 2003.

46. A. Bertolino, F. Corradini, P. Inverardi, and H. Muccini, *Deriving Test Plans from Architectural Descriptions*, in Proc. of the *22nd Int. Conf. on Software Engineering (ICSE 2000)*, ACM Press, pp. 220–229, Limerick (Ireland), 2000.

47. A. Bertolino, P. Inverardi, and H. Muccini, *An Explorative Journey from Architectural Tests Definition downto Code Tests Execution*, in Proc. of the *23rd Int. Conf. on Software Engineering (ICSE 2001)*, ACM Press, pp. 211–220, Toronto (Canada), 2001.

48. B. Bloom, S. Istrail, and A.R. Meyer, *Bisimulation Can't Be Traced*, Journal of the ACM 42:232–268, 1995.

49. T. Bolognesi and E. Brinksma, *Introduction to the ISO Specification Language LOTOS*, Computer Networks and ISDN Systems 14:25–59, 1987.

50. T. Bolognesi and F. Lucidi, *LOTOS-Like Process Algebras with Urgent or Timed Interactions*, in Proc. of the *4th Int. Conf. on Formal Description Techniques for Distributed Systems and Communication Protocols (FORTE 1991)*, IFIP Trans. C-2:249–264, Sidney (Australia), 1991.

51. A. Bondavalli, I. Majzik, and A. Pataricza, *Stochastic Dependability Analysis of System Architecture Based on UML Designs*, in *Architecting Dependable Systems*, Springer, LNCS 2677:219–244, Berlin (Germany), 2003.

52. E. Bontà, M. Bernardo, J. Magee, and J. Kramer, *Synthesizing Concurrency Control Components from Process Algebraic Specifications*, in Proc. of the *8th Int. Conf. on Coordination Models and Languages (COORDINATION 2006)*, Springer, LNCS 4038:28–43, Bologna (Italy), 2006.

53. A. Bracciali, A. Brogi, and C. Canal, *A Formal Approach to Component Adaptation*, Journal of Systems and Software 74:45–54, 2005.

54. M. Bravetti, *Specification and Analysis of Stochastic Real-Time Systems*, Ph.D. Thesis, University of Bologna (Italy), 2002.

55. M. Bravetti and A. Aldini, *Discrete Time Generative-Reactive Probabilistic Processes with Different Advancing Speeds*, Theoretical Computer Science 290:355–406, 2003.

56. M. Bravetti, M. Bernardo, and R. Gorrieri, *A Note on the Congruence Proof for Recursion in Markovian Bisimulation Equivalence*, in Proc. of the *6th Int. Workshop on Process Algebra and Performance Modelling (PAPM 1998)*, pp. 153–164, Nice (France), 1998.

57. S.D. Brookes, C.A.R. Hoare, and A.W. Roscoe, *A Theory of Communicating Sequential Processes*, Journal of the ACM 31:560–599, 1984.

58. P. Buchholz, *Exact and Ordinary Lumpability in Finite Markov Chains*, Journal of Applied Probability 31:59–75, 1994.

59. P. Buchholz, *Markovian Process Algebra: Composition and Equivalence*, in Proc. of the *2nd Int. Workshop on Process Algebra and Performance Modelling (PAPM 1994)*, Technical Report 27-4, pp. 11–30, Erlangen (Germany), 1994.

60. J.P. Buzen, *Computational Algorithms for Closed Queueing Networks with Exponential Servers*, Communications of the ACM 16:527–531, 1973.

61. C. Canal, E. Pimentel, and J.M. Troya, *Specification and Refinement of Dynamic Software Architectures*, in Proc. of the *1st Working IFIP Conf. on Software Architecture (WICSA 1999)*, Kluwer, pp. 107–126, San Antonio (TX), 1999.

62. C. Canal, E. Pimentel, and J.M. Troya, *Compatibility and Inheritance in Software Architectures*, Science of Computer Programming 41:105–138, 2001.

63. K.M. Chandy and C.H. Sauer, *Computational Algorithms for Product Form Queueing Networks*, Communications of the ACM 23:573–583, 1980.

64. I. Christoff, *Testing Equivalences and Fully Abstract Models for Probabilistic Processes*, in Proc. of the *1st Int. Conf. on Concurrency Theory (CONCUR 1990)*, Springer, LNCS 458:126–140, Amsterdam (The Netherlands), 1990.

65. G. Clark, S. Gilmore, and J. Hillston, *Specifying Performance Measures for PEPA*, in Proc. of the *5th AMAST Int. Workshop on Formal Methods for Real Time and Probabilistic Systems (ARTS 1999)*, Springer, LNCS 1601:211–227, Bamberg (Germany), 1999.

66. G. Clark, S. Gilmore, J. Hillston, and M. Ribaudo, *Exploiting Modal Logic to Express Performance Measures*, in Proc. of the *11th Int. Conf. on Modeling Techniques and Tools for Computer Performance Evaluation (PERFORMANCE TOOLS 2000)*, Springer, LNCS 1786: 247–261, Schaumburg (IL), 2000.

67. E.M. Clarke, O. Grumberg, and D.A. Peled, *Model Checking*, MIT Press, Cambridge (MA), 1999.

68. R. Cleaveland, Z. Dayar, S.A. Smolka, and S. Yuen, *Testing Preorders for Probabilistic Processes*, Information and Computation 154:93–148, 1999.

69. R. Cleaveland and M. Hennessy, *Testing Equivalence as a Bisimulation Equivalence*, Formal Aspects of Computing 5:1–20, 1993.

70. R. Cleaveland, J. Parrow, and B. Steffen, *The Concurrency Workbench: A Semantics-Based Tool for the Verification of Concurrent Systems*, ACM Transactions on Programming Languages and Systems 15:36–72, 1993.

71. R. Cleaveland and O. Sokolsky, *Equivalence and Preorder Checking for Finite-State Systems*, in *Handbook of Process Algebra*, Elsevier, pp. 391–424, Amsterdam (The Netherlands), 2001.

72. A.E. Conway and N.D. Georganas, *RECAL – A New Efficient Algorithm for the Exact Analysis of Multiple-Chain Closed Queueing Networks*, Journal of the ACM 33:786–791, 1986.

73. F. Corradini, *On Performance Congruences for Process Algebras*, Information and Computation 145:191–230, 1998.

74. F. Corradini, *Absolute Versus Relative Time in Process Algebras*, Information and Computation 156:122–172, 2000.

75. F. Corradini and D. Di Cola, *The Expressive Power of Urgent, Lazy and Busy-Waiting Actions in Timed Processes*, Mathematical Structures in Computer Science 13:619–656, 2003.

76. F. Corradini and M. Pistore, *Specification and Verification of Timed Lazy Systems*, in Proc. of the *21st Int. Symp. on Mathematical Foundations of Computer Science (MFCS 1996)*, Springer, LNCS 1113:279–290, Cracow (Poland), 1996.

77. F. Corradini and M. Pistore, *'Closed Interval Process Algebra Versus Interval Process Algebra*, Acta Informatica 37:467–509, 2001.
78. F. Corradini, W. Vogler, and L. Jenner, *Comparing the Worst-Case Efficiency of Asynchronous Systems with PAFAS*, Acta Informatica 38:735–792, 2002.
79. T.M. Cover and J.A. Thomas, *Elements of Information Theory*, Wiley, New York (NY), 1991.
80. P. D'Argenio, *Algebras and Automata for Timed and Stochastic Systems*, Ph.D. Thesis, University of Twente (The Netherlands), 1999.
81. T.R. Dean and J.R. Cordy, *A Syntactic Theory of Software Architecture*, IEEE Transactions on Software Engineering 21:302–313, 1995.
82. R. De Nicola and M. Hennessy, *Testing Equivalences for Processes*, Theoretical Computer Science 34:83–133, 1984.
83. F. De Remer and H.H. Kron, *Programming-in-the-Large Versus Programming-in-the-Small*, IEEE Transactions on Software Engineering 2:80–86, 1976.
84. S. Derisavi, H. Hermanns, and W.H. Sanders, *Optimal State-Space Lumping in Markov Chains*, Information Processing Letters 87:309–315, 2003.
85. A. Di Pierro and H. Wiklicky, *Quantifying Timing Leaks and Cost Optimisation*, in Proc. of the *10th Int. Conf. on Information and Communications Security (ICICS 2008)*, Springer, LNCS 5308:81–96, Birmingham (UK), 2008.
86. B.L. Di Vito, *A Model of Cooperative Noninterference for Integrated Modular Avionics*, in Proc. of the *7th IFIP Int. Working Conf. on Dependable Computing for Critical Applications (DCCA-7)*, IEEE-CS Press, pp. 269–286, San Jose (CA), 1999.
87. N. Evans and S. Schneider, *Analysing Time Dependent Security Properties in CSP Using PVS*, in Proc. of the *5th European Symp. on Research in Computer Security (ESORICS 2000)*, Springer, LNCS 1895:222–237, Toulouse (France), 2000.
88. D. Ferrari, *Considerations on the Insularity of Performance Evaluation*, IEEE Transactions on Software Engineering 12:678–683, 1986.
89. R. Focardi and R. Gorrieri, *A Classification of Security Properties*, Journal of Computer Security 3:5–33, 1995.
90. R. Focardi and R. Gorrieri, *Classification of Security Properties (Part I: Information Flow)*, in *Foundations of Security Analysis and Design*, Springer, LNCS 2171:331–396, Berlin (Germany), 2001.
91. R. Focardi, F. Martinelli, and R. Gorrieri, *Information Flow Analysis in a Discrete-Time Process Algebra*, in Proc. of the *13th IEEE Computer Security Foundations Workshop (CSFW 2000)*, IEEE-CS Press, pp. 170–184, Cambridge (UK), 2000.
92. S.N. Foley, *A Taxonomy for Information Flow Policies and Models*, in Proc. of the *12th IEEE Symp. on Security and Privacy (SSP 1991)*, IEEE-CS Press, pp. 98–108, Oakland (CA), 1991.
93. H. Garavel, R. Mateescu, F. Lang, and W. Serwe, *CADP 2006: A Toolbox for the Construction and Analysis of Distributed Processes*, in Proc. of the *19th Int. Conf. on Computer Aided Verification (CAV 2007)*, Springer, LNCS 4590:158–163, Berlin (Germany), 2007.
94. H. Garavel and M. Sighireanu, *A Graphical Parallel Composition Operator for Process Algebras*, in Proc. of the *IFIP Joint Int. Conf. on Formal Description Techniques for Distributed Systems and Communication Protocols and Protocol Specification, Testing and Verification (FORTE/PSTV 1999)*, Kluwer, pp. 185–202, Beijing (China), 1999.
95. D. Garlan, R. Allen, and J. Ockerbloom, *Exploiting Style in Architectural Design Environments*, in Proc. of the *2nd ACM Int. Symp. on the Foundations of Software Engineering (FSE-2)*, ACM Press, pp. 175–188, New Orleans (LA), 1994.
96. D. Garlan, R. Allen, and J. Ockerbloom, *Architectural Mismatch: Why Reuse Is So Hard*, IEEE Software 12(6):17–26, 1995.
97. D. Garlan, R.T. Monroe, and D. Wile, *Acme: Architectural Description of Component-Based Systems*, in *Foundations of Component-Based Systems*, Cambridge University Press, pp. 47–68, Cambridge (UK), 2000.
98. R.J. van Glabbeek, *The Linear Time – Branching Time Spectrum I*, in *Handbook of Process Algebra*, Elsevier, pp. 3–99, Amsterdam (The Netherlands), 2001.
99. R.J. van Glabbeek, S.A. Smolka, and B. Steffen, *Reactive, Generative and Stratified Models of Probabilistic Processes*, Information and Computation 121:59–80, 1995.

100. R.J. van Glabbeek and W.P. Weijland, *Branching Time and Abstraction in Bisimulation Semantics*, Journal of the ACM 43:555–600, 1996.

101. J.A. Goguen and J. Meseguer, *Security Policy and Security Models*, in Proc. of the *3rd IEEE Symp. on Security and Privacy (SSP 1982)*, IEEE-CS Press, pp. 11–20, Oakland (CA), 1982.

102. R. Gorrieri, M. Roccetti, and E. Stancampiano, *A Theory of Processes with Durational Actions*, Theoretical Computer Science 140:73–94, 1995.

103. G. Gössler and J. Sifakis, *Composition for Component-Based Modeling*, in Proc. of the *1st Int. Symp. on Formal Methods for Components and Objects (FMCO 2002)*, Springer, LNCS 2852:443–466, Leiden (The Netherlands), 2002.

104. N. Götz, U. Herzog, and M. Rettelbach, *Multiprocessor and Distributed System Design: The Integration of Functional Specification and Performance Analysis Using Stochastic Process Algebras*, in Proc. of the *16th Int. Symp. on Computer Performance Modelling, Measurement and Evaluation (PERFORMANCE 1993)*, Springer, LNCS 729:121–146, Rome (Italy), 1993.

105. S. Graf, B. Steffen, and G. Lüttgen, *Compositional Minimization of Finite State Systems Using Interface Specifications*, Formal Aspects of Computing 8:607–616, 1996.

106. J.W. Gray III and P.F. Syverson, *A Logical Approach to Multilevel Security of Probabilistic Systems*, in Proc. of the *13th IEEE Symp. on Security and Privacy*, IEEE-CS Press, pp. 164–176, Oakland (CA), 1992.

107. V. Gupta, V. Lam, H.V. Ramasamy, W.H. Sanders, and S. Singh, *Dependability and Performance Evaluation of Intrusion-Tolerant Server Architectures*, in Proc. of the *1st Latin-American Symp. on Dependable Computing (LADC 2003)*, Springer, LNCS 2847:81–101, Sao Paulo (Brazil), 2003.

108. B.R. Haverkort, *Markovian Models for Performance and Dependability Evaluation*, in *Trends in Computer Science*, Springer, LNCS 2090:38–83, Berlin (Germany), 2001.

109. B.R. Haverkort and K.S. Trivedi, *Specification Techniques for Markov Reward Models*, Discrete Event Dynamic Systems: Theory and Applications 3:219–247, 1993.

110. A. Hein and M. Dal Cin, *Performance and Dependability Evaluation of Scalable Massively Parallel Computer Systems with Conjoint Simulation*, ACM Transactions on Modeling and Computer Simulation 8:333–373, 1998.

111. M. Hennessy, *Acceptance Trees*, Journal of the ACM 32:896–928, 1985.

112. M. Hennessy, *Algebraic Theory of Processes*, MIT Press, Cambridge (MA), 1988.

113. M. Hennessy and R. Milner, *Algebraic Laws for Nondeterminism and Concurrency*, Journal of the ACM 32:137–162, 1985.

114. M. Hennessy and T. Regan, *A Process Algebra for Timed Systems*, Information and Computation 117:221–239, 1995.

115. H. Hermanns, *Interactive Markov Chains*, Springer, LNCS 2428, Berlin (Germany), 2002.

116. H. Hermanns and M. Rettelbach, *Syntax, Semantics, Equivalences, and Axioms for MTIPP*, in Proc. of the *2nd Int. Workshop on Process Algebra and Performance Modelling (PAPM 1994)*, Technical Report 27-4, pp. 71–87, Erlangen (Germany), 1994.

117. J. Hillston, *The Nature of Synchronisation*, in Proc. of the *2nd Int. Workshop on Process Algebra and Performance Modelling (PAPM 1994)*, Technical Report 27-4, pp. 51–70, Erlangen (Germany), 1994.

118. J. Hillston, *A Compositional Approach to Performance Modelling*, Cambridge University Press, Cambridge (UK), 1996.

119. C.A.R. Hoare, *Communicating Sequential Processes*, Prentice-Hall, Englewood Cliffs (NJ), 1985.

120. R.A. Howard, *Dynamic Probabilistic Systems*, Wiley, New York (NY), 1971.

121. D.T. Huynh and L. Tian, *On Some Equivalence Relations for Probabilistic Processes*, Fundamenta Informaticae 17:211–234, 1992.

122. P. Inverardi and S. Uchitel, *Proving Deadlock Freedom in Component-Based Programming*, in Proc. of the *4th Int. Conf. on Fundamental Approaches to Software Engineering (FASE 2001)*, Springer, LNCS 2029:60–75, Genoa (Italy), 2001.

123. P. Inverardi and A.L. Wolf, *Formal Specification and Analysis of Software Architectures Using the Chemical Abstract Machine Model*, IEEE Transactions on Software Engineering 21:373–386, 1995.

124. P. Inverardi, A.L. Wolf, and D. Yankelevich, *Static Checking of System Behaviors Using Derived Component Assumptions*, ACM Transactions on Software Engineering and Methodology 9:239–272, 2000.

125. F. Javier Thayer, J.C. Herzog, and J.D. Guttman, *Strand Spaces: Why Is a Security Protocol Correct?*, in Proc. of the *19th IEEE Symp. on Security and Privacy (SSP 1998)*, IEEE-CS Press, pp. 160–171, Oakland (CA), 1998.

126. B. Jonsson and K.G. Larsen, *Specification and Refinement of Probabilistic Processes*, in Proc. of the *6th IEEE Symp. on Logic in Computer Science (LICS 1991)*, IEEE-CS Press, pp. 266–277, Amsterdam (The Netherlands), 1991.

127. C.-C. Jou and S.A. Smolka, *Equivalences, Congruences, and Complete Axiomatizations for Probabilistic Processes*, in Proc. of the *1st Int. Conf. on Concurrency Theory (CONCUR 1990)*, Springer, LNCS 458:367–383, Amsterdam (The Netherlands), 1990.

128. P.C. Kanellakis and S.A. Smolka, *CCS Expressions, Finite State Processes, and Three Problems of Equivalence*, Information and Computation 86:43–68, 1990.

129. M.H. Kang, A.P. Moore, and I.S. Moskowitz, *Design and Assurance Strategy for the NRL Pump*, IEEE Computer Magazine 31:56–64, 1998.

130. L. Kleinrock, *Queueing Systems*, Wiley, New York (NY), 1975.

131. J. Kramer and J. Magee, *Exposing the Skeleton in the Coordination Closet*, in Proc. of the *2nd Int. Conf. on Coordination Models and Languages (COORDINATION 1997)*, Springer, LNCS 1282:18–31, Berlin (Germany), 1997.

132. M.Z. Kwiatkowska and G.J. Norman, *A Testing Equivalence for Reactive Probabilistic Processes*, in Proc. of the *2nd Int. Workshop on Expressiveness in Concurrency (EXPRESS 1998)*, Elsevier, ENTCS 16(2):114–132, Nice (France), 1998.

133. R. Lanotte, A. Maggiolo-Schettini, S. Tini, A. Troina, and E. Tronci, *Automatic Analysis of the NRL Pump*, in *Formal Methods for Security and Time*, Elsevier, ENTCS 99:245–266, Amsterdam (The Netherlands), 2004.

134. R. Lanotte, A. Maggiolo-Schettini, and A. Troina, *A Classification of Time and/or Probability Dependent Security Properties*, in Proc. of the *3rd Int. Workshop on Quantitative Aspects of Programming Languages (QAPL 2005)*, Elsevier, ENTCS 153(2):177–193, Edinburgh (UK), 2005.

135. J.C. Laprie (ed.), *Dependability: Basic Concepts and Terminology*, Springer, Berlin (Germany), 1992.

136. K.G. Larsen and A. Skou, *Bisimulation through Probabilistic Testing*, Information and Computation 94:1–28, 1991.

137. E.D. Lazowska, J. Zahorjan, G. Scott Graham, and K.C. Sevcik, *Quantitative System Performance: Computer System Analysis Using Queueing Network Models*, Prentice-Hall, Englewood Cliffs (NJ), 1984.

138. D. Le Metayer, *Describing Software Architecture Styles Using Graph Grammars*, IEEE Transactions on Software Engineering 24:521–533, 1998.

139. G. Lowe, *Casper: A Compiler for the Analysis of Security Protocols*, in Proc. of the *10th IEEE Computer Security Foundations Workshop (CSFW 1997)*, IEEE-CS Press, pp. 18–30, Rockport (MA), 1997.

140. D.C. Luckham, J.J. Kenney, L.M. Augustin, J. Vera, D. Bryan, and W. Mann, *Specification and Analysis of System Architecture Using Rapide*, IEEE Transactions on Software Engineering 21:336–355, 1995.

141. J. Magee, N. Dulay, S. Eisenbach, and J. Kramer, *Specifying Distributed Software Architectures*, in Proc. of the *5th European Software Engineering Conf. (ESEC 1995)*, Springer, LNCS 989:137–153, Barcelona (Spain), 1995.

142. J. Magee and J. Kramer, *Concurrency: State Models & Java Programs*, Wiley, New York (NY), 1999.

143. S. Mahevas and G. Rubino, *Bound Computation of Dependability and Performance Measures*, IEEE Transactions on Computers 50:399–413, 2001.

144. H. Mantel, *Possibilistic Definitions of Security – An Assembly Kit*, in Proc. of the *13th IEEE Computer Security Foundations Workshop (CSFW 2000)*, IEEE-CS Press, pp. 185–199, Cambridge (UK), 2000.

145. H. Mantel and H. Sudbrock, *Comparing Countermeasures Against Interrupt-Related Covert Channels in an Information-Theoretic Framework*, in Proc. of the *20th IEEE Computer Security Foundations Symposium (CSFW 2007)*, IEEE-CS Press, pp. 326–340, Venice (Italy), 2007.

146. J. McLean, *Security Models and Information Flow*, in Proc. of the *11th IEEE Symp. on Security and Privacy (SSP 1990)*, IEEE-CS Press, pp. 180–187, Oakland (CA), 1990.

147. C. Meadows, *What Makes a Cryptographic Protocol Secure? The Evolution of Requirements Specification in Formal Cryptographic Protocol Analysis*, in Proc. of the *12th European Symp. on Programming Languages and Systems (ESOP 2003)*, Springer, LNCS 2618:10–21, Warsaw (Poland), 2003.

148. N. Medvidovic, P. Oreizy, J.E. Robbins, and R.N. Taylor, *Using Object-Oriented Typing to Support Architectural Design in the C2 Style*, in Proc. of the *4th ACM Int. Symp. on the Foundations of Software Engineering (FSE-4)*, ACM Press, pp. 24–32, San Francisco (CA), 1996.

149. N. Medvidovic, D.S. Rosenblum, D.F. Redmiles, and J.E. Robbins, *Modeling Software Architectures in the Unified Modeling Language*, ACM Transactions on Software Engineering and Methodology 11:2–57, 2002.

150. N. Medvidovic and R.N. Taylor, *A Classification and Comparison Framework for Software Architecture Description Languages*, IEEE Transactions on Software Engineering 26:70–93, 2000.

151. J.F. Meyer, *Performability: A Retrospective and Some Pointers to the Future*, Performance Evaluation 14:139–156, 1992.

152. L. Michotte, R.B. France, and F. Fleurey, *Modeling and Integrating Aspects into Component Architectures*, in Proc. of the *10th IEEE Int. Enterprise Distributed Object Computing Conference (EDOC 2006)*, IEEE-CS Press, pp. 181–190, Hong Kong, 2006.

153. R. Milner, *A Calculus of Communicating Systems*, Springer, LNCS 92, Berlin (Germany), 1980.

154. R. Milner, *Communication and Concurrency*, Prentice-Hall, Englewood Cliffs (NJ), 1989.

155. R. Milner, *Communicating and Mobile Systems: The π-Calculus*, Cambridge University Press, Cambridge (UK), 1999.

156. R. Milner, J. Parrow, and D. Walker, *A Calculus of Mobile Processes*, Information and Computation 100:1–77, 1992.

157. F. Moller and C. Tofts, *A Temporal Calculus of Communicating Systems*, in Proc. of the *1st Int. Conf. on Concurrency Theory (CONCUR 1990)*, Springer, LNCS 458:401–415, Amsterdam (The Netherlands), 1990.

158. F. Moller and C. Tofts, *Relating Processes with Respect to Speed*, in Proc. of the *2nd Int. Conf. on Concurrency Theory (CONCUR 1991)*, Springer, LNCS 527:424–438, Amsterdam (The Netherlands), 1991.

159. M. Moriconi, X. Qian, and R.A. Riemenschneider, *Correct Architecture Refinement*, IEEE Transactions on Software Engineering 21:356–372, 1995.

160. I.S. Moskowitz and M.H. Kang, *Covert Channels – Here to Stay?*, in Proc. of the *9th Conf. on Computer Assurance (COMPASS 1994)*, NIST, pp. 235–244, Gaithersburg (MD), 1994.

161. M.F. Neuts, *Matrix-Geometric Solutions in Stochastic Models – An Algorithmic Approach*, John Hopkins University Press, Baltimore (MD), 1981.

162. X. Nicollin and J. Sifakis, *An Overview and Synthesis on Timed Process Algebras*, in Proc. of the *REX Workshop on Real Time: Theory in Practice*, Springer, LNCS 600:526–548, Mook (The Netherlands), 1991.

163. X. Nicollin and J. Sifakis, *The Algebra of Timed Processes ATP: Theory and Application*, Information and Computation 114:131–178, 1994.

164. E.-R. Olderog and C.A.R. Hoare, *Specification-Oriented Semantics for Communicating Processes*, Acta Informatica 23:9–66, 1986.

165. G. On, J. Schmitt, and R. Steinmetz, *On Availability QoS for Replicated Multimedia Service and Content*, in Proc. of the *Joint Int. Workshops on Interactive Distributed Multimedia Systems and Protocols for Multimedia Systems (IDMS/PROMS 2002)*, Springer, LNCS 2515:313–326, Coimbra (Portugal), 2002.

166. F. Oquendo, *π-ADL: An Architecture Description Language Based on the Higher-Order Typed π-Calculus for Specifying Dynamic and Mobile Software Architectures*, ACM SIG-SOFT Software Engineering Notes 29:1–14, 2004.

167. R. Paige and R.E. Tarjan, *Three Partition Refinement Algorithms*, SIAM Journal on Computing 16:973–989, 1987.

168. D. Park, *Concurrency and Automata on Infinite Sequences*, in Proc. of the *5th GI Conf. on Theoretical Computer Science*, Springer, LNCS 104:167–183, Karlsruhe (Germany), 1981.

169. D.E. Perry and A.L. Wolf, *Foundations for the Study of Software Architecture*, ACM SIG-SOFT Software Engineering Notes 17:40–52, 1992.

170. C.A. Petri, *Kommunikation mit Automaten*, Ph.D. Thesis, Technical University of Darmstadt (Germany), 1962.

171. G.D. Plotkin, *A Structural Approach to Operational Semantics*, Technical Report DAIMI-FN-19, Aarhus University (Denmark), 1981 (published in Journal of Logic and Algebraic Programming 60/61:17–139, 2004).

172. C. Priami, *Stochastic π-Calculus*, Computer Journal 38:578–589, 1995.

173. J. Quemada, D. de Frutos, and A. Azcorra, *TIC: A Timed Calculus*, Formal Aspects of Computing 5:224–252, 1993.

174. G.M. Reed and A.W. Roscoe, *A Timed Model for Communicating Sequential Processes*, Theoretical Computer Science 58:249–261, 1988.

175. M. Reiser and S.S. Lavenberg, *Mean-Value Analysis of Closed Multichain Queueing Networks*, Journal of the ACM 27:313–322, 1980.

176. M. Rettelbach, *Probabilistic Branching in Markovian Process Algebras*, Computer Journal 38:590–599, 1995.

177. P.Y.A. Ryan, J. McLean, J. Millen, and V. Gligor, *Non-interference: Who Needs It?*, in Proc. of the *14th IEEE Computer Security Foundations Workshop (CSFW 2001)*, IEEE-CS Press, pp. 237–238, Cape Breton (Canada), 2001.

178. P.Y.A. Ryan and S. Schneider, *Process Algebra and Noninterference*, in Proc. of the *12th IEEE Computer Security Foundations Workshop (CSFW 1999)*, IEEE-CS Press, pp. 214–227, Mordano (Italy), 1999.

179. A. Sabelfeld and D. Sands, *Probabilistic Noninterference for Multi-Threaded Programs*, in Proc. of the *13th IEEE Computer Security Foundations Workshop (CSFW 2000)*, IEEE-CS Press, pp. 200–214, Cambridge (UK), 2000.

180. W.H. Sanders and J.F. Meyer, *A Unified Approach for Specifying Measures of Performance, Dependability, and Performability*, Dependable Computing and Fault Tolerant Systems 4:215–237, 1991.

181. D. Sangiorgi and D. Walker, *The π-Calculus: A Theory of Mobile Processes*, Cambridge University Press, Cambridge (UK), 2001.

182. D.S. Scott, *Data Types as Lattices*, SIAM Journal on Computing 5:522–587, 1976.

183. M. Shaw, R. De Line, D.V. Klein, T.L. Ross, D.M. Young, and G. Zelesnik, *Abstractions for Software Architecture and Tools to Support Them*, IEEE Transactions on Software Engineering 21:314–335, 1995.

184. M. Shaw and D. Garlan, *Software Architecture: Perspectives on an Emerging Discipline*, Prentice-Hall, Englewood Cliffs (NJ), 1996.

185. A. Simpson, J. Woodcock, and J. Davies, *Safety Through Security*, in Proc. of the *9th IEEE Workshop on Software Specification and Design (IWSSD-9)*, IEEE-CS Press, pp. 18–24, Ise-Shima (Japan), 1998.

186. C. Smith, *Performance Engineering of Software Systems*, Addison-Wesley, Reading (MA), 1990.

187. E.W. Stark, R. Cleaveland, and S.A. Smolka, *A Process-Algebraic Language for Probabilistic I/O Automata*, in Proc. of the *14th Int. Conf. on Concurrency Theory (CONCUR 2003)*, Springer, LNCS 2761:189–203, Marseille (France), 2003.

188. W.J. Stewart, *Introduction to the Numerical Solution of Markov Chains*, Princeton University Press, Princeton (NJ), 1994.

189. V. Stravridou and B. Dutertre, *From Security to Safety and Back*, in Proc. of the *IEEE Workshop on Computer Security, Dependability, and Assurance: From Needs to Solutions (CSDA 1998)*, IEEE-CS Press, pp. 182–195, Williamsburg (VA), 1998.

190. M. Tivoli and P. Inverardi, *Failure-Free Coordinators Synthesis for Component-Based Architectures*, Science of Computer Programming 71:181–212, 2008.

191. W.-G. Tzeng, *A Polynomial-Time Algorithm for the Equivalence of Probabilistic Automata*, SIAM Journal on Computing 21:216–227, 1992.

192. G. Winskel, *Events in Computation*, Ph.D. Thesis, University of Edinburgh (UK), 1980.

193. J.T. Wittbold and D.M. Johnson, *Information Flow in Nondeterministic Systems*, in Proc. of the *11th IEEE Symp. on Security and Privacy (SSP 1990)*, IEEE-CS Press, pp. 144–161, Oakland (CA), 1990.

194. V. Wolf, C. Baier, and M. Majster-Cederbaum, *Trace Machines for Observing Continuous-Time Markov Chains*, in Proc. of the *3rd Int. Workshop on Quantitative Aspects of Programming Languages (QAPL 2005)*, Elsevier, ENTCS 153(2):259–277, Edinburgh (UK), 2005.

195. C.M. Woodside, J.E. Neilson, D.C. Petriu, and S. Majumdar, *The Stochastic Rendezvous Network Model for Performance of Synchronous Client-Server-Like Distributed Software*, IEEE Transactions on Computers 44:20–34, 1995.

196. F. Wu, H. Johnson, and A. Nilsson, *SOLA: Lightweight Security for Access Control in IEEE 802.11*, IT Professional 6:10–16, 2004.

197. S. Yau, M. Yan, and D. Huang, *Design of Service-Based Systems with Adaptive Tradeoff Between Security and Service Delay*, in Proc. of the *4th Int. Conf. on Autonomic and Trusted Computing (ATC 2007)*, Springer, LNCS 4610:103–113, Hong Kong, 2007.

198. D.M. Yellin and R.E. Strom, *Protocol Specifications and Component Adaptors*, ACM Transactions on Programming Languages and Systems 19:292–333, 1997.

199. W. Yi, *CCS + Time = An Interleaving Model for Real Time Systems*, in Proc. of the *18th Int. Coll. on Automata, Languages and Programming (ICALP 1991)*, Springer, LNCS 510:217–228, Madrid (Spain), 1991.

Index